Reflections of The Way It Was

Volume I

AN ENDURING LOVE STORY

D1566653

Dr. Peter J. Cirigliano

This book was published in the USA.

ISBN-13: 979-8579548047

Library of Congress Control Number:

*"Life isn't measured by the number of breaths we take,
but by the moments that take our breath away"*

CONTENTS

PROLOGUE

My purpose in writing this manuscript was to describe various stages of my life, beginning with the Best of Times - memories of growing up in Brooklyn and Monroe NY during a wonderful era seemingly frozen in time. Fortunately, at the young age of 70, I'm still blessed with a good long-term memory. As for the short term, well, that's another story!

I found that, for some reason, my recollections were most vivid during the Theta phase of sleep, just before awakening, which presented a real sharing problem. Early on, I would often awaken with a sudden *burst of clarity*, followed by a sense of urgency to hopefully capture the essence of an entire paragraph in a single sentence - good luck! Rather than ruminating all night, however, I resorted to a bedside notepad. But at 3 am, the glare from my gooseneck lamp was a frequent source of consternation for my dear wife.

Unfortunately, these memories are mostly stored in the deep recesses of my mind, and as the floodgates suddenly opened, I faced the daunting task of trying to paint a *descriptive picture* of the marvelous times, places, and feelings experienced during a unique time period. A time when kids could walk to school and play in *their streets* without fear of abduction or molestation - always feeling safe under the watchful eye of *their neighborhood* - what more could a family ask for.

In retrospect, my recollections of the *early years* were mixed. My childhood years were wonderful, whereas my adolescent years were often less blissful. To paraphrase Charles Dickens, I sub-titled Part I of my manuscript, *The Best and the Worst of Times*. However, what to include and conversely, what to exclude, presented a real dilemma, and therein lies the rub. Initially, rather than a free-flowing narrative, I recalled the relevant events chronologically. My *writing style* often vacillated between a memoir and an autobiography - best described as an *Autobiographical Memoir*. Also, sometimes the narrative resembles the ramblings of a personal Diary, and the detailed descriptions were perhaps only important to me.

I also tried to find humor amid adversity, sprinkling the detailed narratives with humorous vignettes. Realizing, however, that perception is reality, rather than inventing the truth, I attempted to describe events to the best of my recollection, or how I choose to remember them as seen through the filtered lens of my mind's eye. Admittedly, some of my recollections may be at variance with those of my siblings, in which case I suggest that perhaps they should write their own memoir. But the factual details seemed far less relevant than the associated feelings!

While Growing up in a large Italian family, eating and storytelling went together. The joy of unbridled laughter was contagious, especially if you added a little Vino. Similarly, in our own household, I would occasionally regale some of our dinner guests by recalling some humorous stories of growing up in Brooklyn and Monroe NY. Likewise, such storytelling is always enhanced when told in the presence of someone who also shared similar stories. In mid-September 2015, it was on such an occasion when a dear friend, Helene, shared similar memories of growing up in an Italian family in Brooklyn and suggested, "You should consider writing a book!"

It's said that Tony Bennett rarely, if ever, sings a song the same way. Likewise, it's entertaining to witness when, after whispering a secret to guests sitting around a table, the outcome is often different. So, too, with storytelling. The sole purpose of occasional embellishment is to add revelry to an old story. However, upon hearing my latest rendition of an old story, if I deviated from the *script* or omitted some minor detail, my wife would occasionally feel compelled to correct me, failing to realize that the essence of the story remained unchanged. While writing my memoirs, although all the accounts are accurate to the best of my recollection, much to my wife's chagrin, I chose to call occasional embellishments, *Literary license!*

Coincidentally, Helene had recently taken an introductory *book writing* course and offered to share some pointers. I explained that I lacked the required talent and interest to be a *Writer* and that I had no interest in writing a book - I just wanted to share my life story for Posterity.

Then, one day she came over to our house with an inexpensive, but very meaningful, spiral notebook and said, "I've listened to you and you're a natural storyteller. So, just start writing and tell your story ". Although I've been toying with the idea of writing a memoir, it was Helene's encouragement and the inspiration of my loving wife, who shared much of my early life, that was the nudge I needed. Now it was just a question of where and when to start. The *Where* was easy, Bay Ridge Brooklyn and Monroe NY and the *When* is - Carpe Diem! (seize the day)

PREFACE

I wish to thank my loving wife for her unwavering support while enduring this seemingly endless journey. At one point, sensing that her patience was running thin, she quipped, "By now, you must be on your second life!" Thankfully, she was always willing to fill in the gaps, sometimes offering, "It wasn't Tuesday, it was on Wednesday!" She was and still is the sustaining *Wind Beneath My Wings,* and I would be nothing without her. I also wish to thank my darling sister, Maria, who I dubbed, *The Family Historian*. I often relied on her to refresh my memory of the long-forgotten names and relationships of our deceased family relatives.

LA FAMILIA

It's only fitting to begin at the beginning with a very abbreviated family tree. Both of my parents, Caesar and Alice were born in New York City of Italian immigrants from the Basilicata Region, southeast of Naples. Each time when I asked my father, "What town did we come from?" His initial response was, "We came from Naples". However, upon subsequent questioning, he said that it was Potenza. Then finally, despite the fact that there is a very small town called, Cirigliano (elevation, 7000'), he insisted that his parents, Rocco, and Mary Martocci came from a small mountain town southeast of Potenza called, Laurenzana, (elevation, 4000').

Likewise, when I would ask my mother where her family came from, she said matter of factly, "Oh, we're Neapolitan". However, her parents, Nicola Tronalone and Mary Silvestri came from the small town of San Feli, just north of Laurenzana. In hindsight, however, I realized that, as with most immigrant families, it was the port of exit that determined their designated place of origin. Hence, we were said to be, "Neapolitan!".

My Father's Cirigliano- Martocci lineage

My Paternal Great Grandfather (Peter?) Cesare Anthony Cirigliano married Maria Angela Martocci. They had 7 children: Frank, Rocco (my Grandfather), Mary, Dominic, Michael, Salvatore, and Joseph - all of whom eventually emigrated to New York City. Upon entering the mouth of the New York harbor, formed by Staten Island and Bay Ridge, Brooklyn, I'm sure they were in awe at the sight of the enormous Statue of Liberty. After disembarking on Ellis Island, they were screened and processed as new immigrants eventually settling on Spring St.in NYC.

7

My Paternal Great Grands
Frank, Rocco, Mary, Dominic, Michael, Salvatore, Joseph

Incidentally, the lone sister, Mary had 7 children and her brother Frank also had 7 surviving children: Joseph, Dominic (Pep), Matilda, Adele, Lucy, Salvatore (Whitey), and Frank (Irish). Except for Uncle Joe, who lived in Bay Ridge, the others resided in the Bronx and were only known to us as the Bronx Ciriglianos. In the future, however, during times of our greatest need, their help would prove to be invaluable!

While sifting through the tangled web of my family ancestry, I found it fascinating to note the origin of familiar family names on both sides and that, especially on the Cirigliano side, having seven children wasn't unusual.

The fourth oldest sibling, Dominic was ordained as a Jesuit priest and eventually became a prominent figure in the NY Archdiocese and a trusted family confidant. He was initially assigned to the old St Joseph's church in Philadelphia. Then, he was assigned to the Nativity Parish in NYC. He was not only greatly admired and revered as the Pastor but was also involved with initiating the Parish's *Youth Relief Program* at the Gonzaga Retreat in Monroe NY. As the Headmaster of the sprawling Jesuit seminary, St Andrews on the Hudson, now occupied by the

Culinary Institute, he was noted to be somewhat lenient with curfews and affectionately dubbed the *Black Pope*. Although he died before I was born, it was evident that he played an especially important role in the family and as my father's mentor.

Father Dominic, SJ

My other Paternal Great Grandfather, Peter Martocci married Rose Falottico and they had four daughters, Mary Agnes (my Grandmother), Mildred (Mille), Emelia (Molly) and Teresa (Tessie) and they lived on Mott St. in NYC.

Incidentally, according to my sister Maria, although Mary Angela Martocci and Peter Martocci both came from Laurenzana, they were not related. However, Rose Falottico's nephew, Rocco Falottico (the shoemaker) married his second cousin aunt Molly Martocci - Very confusing!

My Paternal Grandfather, Rocco eventually married his sweetheart, Mary Agnes Martocci and they raised their three children: Mary (Mae), Caesar Anthony (my father), and his younger brother, Peter in a simple house on Spring St. in NYC.

My Paternal Grandparents
Rocco Ciri & Mary Martocci

My Paternal grandmother, Mary Agnes Martocci, had three sisters and was apparently from a prominent family in Laurenzana. After recently visiting the towns of Cirigliano and Laurenzana, more than likely Rocco moved from tiny Cirigliano to the larger, Laurenzana, in order to court Mary Martocci. In any event, it was evident to me that my grandfather married up! (more about that later).

My Paternal Grandparents   Rocco Ciri and Mary Agnes Martocci, better known as Papa and Grandma Ciri, were said to be mild mannered, generous and very devoted to each other. Unfortunately, shortly before I was born, both tragically died within one day of each other. It was said that, after his beloved wife succumbed to stomach cancer, within 24 hours, Papa Ciri, simply died of a "broken heart" (Takotsubo cardiomyopathy).

Although they both spoke with a thick Italian accent, Grandma Ciri at least attended grade school, but Papa Ciri was illiterate. However, he was very proud of the fact that he initially rented and eventually owned a shoeshine concession stand in a prime location, directly outside a busy New York City subway station. He furthered his business enterprise by eventually selling shoe polish to other concession stands, and thus was able to adequately support his wife and three children

My father, in turn, took great pride in demonstrating how to correctly *spit-shine* shoes using two brushes and buffing cloth. One year he bought me a shoeshine box and encouraged me to ring the neighborhood doorbells offering the salutation, "Excuse me, sir may I have the privilege of shining your shoes". Later, my brother Caesar took advantage of my *training* by bribing me with a stick of Beechnut gum to shine his shoes before going on dates - sometimes springing as much as 5 cents for two pairs of shoes.

My father was very dedicated and respectful of his older sister, Mae, and she adored him. Mae took formal piano lessons and consequently, played beautifully. Likewise, unlike my father, who mostly played chords, my uncle Pete became a talented club pianist, entertaining patrons at various upscale bars in Scarsdale NJ and Daytona Beach Fl. He eventually married an attractive young lady, Lee Cavallo and they had a son named, Peter. Being that we were roughly the same age, he was nicknamed Peterkins.

Uncle Pete   While serving in China during World War II, my namesake, Uncle Pete, developed hepatitis and became very ill. Ironically, during his protracted recovery, he received a *Dear Pete letter* from his wife, informing him of their child's birth, and that she had fallen in love with someone else and wanted a divorce. Two years later, upon returning from the war, he tried desperately to see his son for the first time. However, by this time, Lee was living with this man who was purportedly connected to a local mob in Bensonhurst Brooklyn. Despite this, when my uncle attempted to visit Lee, he was beaten up and left in the gutter with the warning to never attempt to visit his wife or his son again!

Consequently, my uncle respectfully kept his distance and left the immediate area, resorting to play seasonally at local piano bars in

Scarsdale and Daytona Beach. I remember him paying a rare visit from Florida. He was well tanned and had an unusual *Donald Duck* laugh! I remember while sitting with him at our kitchen table, my eyes bulged when he pulled out a wad of cash from his pocket - a rare commodity in our house and the likes of which I'd never seen before.

After a while, he eventually fell in love with a woman in Daytona only known to us as Kiki. They were to take a well -deserved cruise together, and for whatever reason, prior to the cruise he had a complete physical and was reported to be in good health. However, shortly afterward we were notified that tragically, he suffered a fatal heart attack at the young age of 48. I remember my father being deeply affected by the sudden loss of his only brother. He sat quietly in the darkened Living room by himself for long periods of time, apparently choosing to deal with his grief alone. Interestingly, I never witnessed or heard any crying or sobbing. I vaguely remember attending my uncle's wake and standing in the back of the funeral parlor, too frightened to even approach the casket.

My Mother's Tronalone- Silvestri lineage

My Maternal Great Grandfather, Vito Tronalone married Lucia Barno and they had a son named Nicola.

My other Maternal Great Grandfather, Leonardo Silvestri married Maria Ferraro and they had five children: Anthony, Frank, Victor, Maria Angela (Titsy) and Mary Antonia (my grandmother)

My Maternal Grandparents   Nicola Tronalone married Mary Antonia Silvestri and they lived in a small house on Baxter St. in NYC. They eventually had four children: Lee, Lucia Clorinda (my mother), Victor and Mildred. My grandmother had three brothers, Anthony, Victor, and Frank, and one sister, Molly. Unfortunately, her life was marred by tragedy and health issues. At a very young age, her husband, Nicola suffered a serious injury to his leg following a fall from a trolley car in NYC. He eventually developed gangrene and despite a partial leg amputation, he died in his mid-twenties from an overwhelming infection.

My Maternal Grandparents
Nicola Tronalone & Mary Silvestri

My grandmother remained widowed for five years, struggling to support her four young children. Tragedy struck again when Mildred and Victor both died during infancy. Victor's death resulted from a fall down a flight of stairs, possibly while being cared for by one of his older sisters. Following these tragedies, my grandmother eventually married a Truant officer named, Anthony Datre (aka Papa Datre) and they, in turn, had a set of twin boys, Biagio (Bass) and Leonard as well as a daughter, Olga - a total of 7 children including a pair of twins. I knew that my grandmother suffered from type I (Insulin) diabetes as did her son Biagio, and in retrospect, I suspect my maternal grandfather may have also had diabetes.

Although my mother's first name was Lucia Clorinda, for some reason, her elementary school teacher arbitrarily changed her first name to Alice. She completed elementary school and thereafter, by exaggerating her age, she entered the workforce at the age of 13. She became an accomplished seamstress and a telephone switchboard operator. They continued living on Baxter Street, and although she never complained, it must have been an extremely difficult adolescence which is a testimony to her true grit. By assuming the responsibilities of a wage earner at such a young age, she demonstrated the courage, determination, and resourcefulness of an adult.

My parents first met at the Raven club on Coney Island. According to my mother, there was supposed to be an arranged meeting between my mother's sister, Lee, and some handsome young man named, Caesar Cirigliano. Fortunately, however, my father demurred, preferring instead the company of my mother. My mother was very reserved about their early courtship never expounding in any detail and my father said even less. The most she ever offered was that my father was tall, trim, and muscular, the result of swimming between the jetties at Coney Island, and that he frequently recited poetry, sang while playing the ukulele or playing chords on the piano - what a catch!.

My father would often tease my mother, referring to her as "the girl from Baxter Street" and imitating her refined elocution while delivering a phonetic salutation, "Haddow," as a telephone switchboard operator. From what I could gather, their courtship lasted about three or four years and was mostly uneventful. Then in August of 1931, shortly after my father graduated from Fordham Law school, they were married in Nativity church officiated by Father Dominic. This marvelous union fortunately set in motion the beginning of the next generation.

My parents wedding

PART I

The Early Years

The Best and the Worst of Times

THE BEST OF TIMES

CH - 1
BROOKLYN N.Y.

A h, Brooklyn, New York, the eighth wonder of the world, and Ebbets Field, the home of the Dodgers! Prior to my grand arrival, my parents rented the first floor of a three-family house at 1128 45th Street Brooklyn, which was owned by my uncle and future godfather, Joe Trento. In time, the small apartment became very cramped with five children, all of whom slept in one bedroom, and a newborn, Nicholas!

My father's fledgling law practice gradually gravitated towards criminal law. He was frequently called upon to deliver speeches on the street corners of Brooklyn for various Democratic candidates. However, no one ever knew which party he privately endorsed or voted for. As his practice steadily grew, so did his family, and eventually he could afford more spacious accommodations for his burgeoning family. So, in 1943, my parents and their six children moved *Uptown,* to Colonial Road in Bay Ridge, Brooklyn.

8311 Colonial Road Prior to my late arrival, besides their six children, my mother had two miscarriages, one after Caesar and another after Nicholas. Considering the deaths of my other two siblings, this must have been very disheartening for my mother. Perhaps a sign of the times, however, these tragic losses were never mentioned or commemorated by either of my parents! From my perspective, these miscarriages represent either two sibling-Souls or two prior attempts to finally make my grand debut on the morning of November 20th, 1944.

My earliest recollections are of growing up as the youngest of seven children in a large loving Italian family in Bay Ridge, Brooklyn. We lived at 8311 Colonial Road, between 83rd and 84th Streets. Bay Ridge and, in particular, Colonial Road was considered a prime location.

Compared to many of the monstrous homes in the neighborhood, however, our house was relatively modest, which seemed comparatively large to me. Our house was directly across the street from Fort Hamilton Park, known as *The Park*. The huge public park provided just about every conceivable sporting activity which was also shared with Ft. Hamilton High School. Brooklyn is large and densely populated. However, *my* Bay Ridge comprised Colonial Road, The Park, 83rd Street. and St. Anselm's -our local grammar school three city blocks from our house. *However, when I googled Bay Ridge, I realized how little I knew about the rest of Bay Ridge!*

At such a young age, even 84th Street. was considered a different neighborhood and off-limits. In retrospect, my entire world revolved around this relatively small community, comprising neighborhood friends, sports activities in the park, and our local parish school - a truly small area, but then again, I too was small. When I came of age, however, a foreign excursion was venturing down 83rd Street for three city blocks to Shore Road and the *Narrows*.

Neighbors   Compared to 1148 45th Street, the move to Colonial Road was a quantum leap - considered an affluent area and out of our league. 8311 was typical of the other homes on Colonial Road, squished between the corner homes which were considerably larger and statelier, both in size and property dimensions.

Our immediate neighbors on the left were Ben and Abby Leibowitz, and their son, Stevie, was one of my earliest friends. To the right, I vaguely remember a pretty redhead, Maureen Brennan, around Anita's age, who was living with her two aunts. The aunts eventually sold the house to Dr. and Mrs. Hubbard. A Syrian family, the Awamys. owned the large brick corner home on the left. Their son Joseph was a classmate of mine in St Anselm. The equally large brick home on the right corner was only known as Leelete's house, which was later purchased by Dr. Basso.

Our House The front of our house was relatively narrow, with pretty front window boxes and a narrow steep lawn which was extremely difficult to cut, especially with our push reel mower with blades that were never sharpened. I remember poor Jimmy McManus, having a terrible crush on my sister Anita, and in her own inimitable way, she persuaded him to cut our lawn during the hot summer while we were in cool Monroe - what a nice fool.

8311 with siblings on the front stoop

Steep narrow driveways, flanked by cement steps and flat stoops, separated the houses. Although the driveways extended back to a one-car garage, the narrowness made it difficult to navigate a large car. Our garage had a single large spring assisted door and was used solely for storage

Directly behind the house and between the respective garages was a small grassed yard bordered in the rear by a tall lattice fence separating it from the property directly behind our house. The backyard was always well kept with pretty flower beds and a central birdbath, but I don't remember it being large enough to play in.

The cement entry steps on the left side led to the side door, and the one on the right led to the front door. There was a tiny coat closet in the front Vestibule which led to a wide hallway. The Vestibule was where you would meet and greet guests and conversely, say goodnight to that someone special. During the Christmas season, we would usually hang mistletoe over the hallway entrance. As my sisters would say goodnight to their boyfriends, if my father thought it was going on too long, he was known to throw a roll of unwrapped toilet paper bouncing down the stairs, unraveling further with each step. This sent an unmistakable message–enough BS!

Facing forward from the hallway, a stately staircase ascended to a landing adorned with a large stained-glass window. The big round banister was highly polished, providing a rapid descent, hopefully stopping just short of the newel post. To the right of the staircase and below the landing was a narrow corridor leading to the Kitchen. The hallway also provided direct access to a formal dining room on the right and glass-paneled French doors on the left, which led to a formal Living room beyond which was the front Sunroom, overlooking the Park. The Living Room was accented by a closed fireplace on the right and my father's desk to the left. Incidentally, this was the only room that could accommodate our enormous Christmas trees!

The Sunroom had windows on three sides overlooking the Park and Ft. Hamilton High School. It also had permanent tall bookcases lining the back wall, comprising my father's library. During my preschool years, I would often entertain myself by using the books to build fortresses and my mother's sewing buttons as soldiers while substituting my shoes for trucks, etc. In addition, for family entertainment, this room had a vintage 13" black and white Admiral TV. Incidentally, the first time I saw a color TV was while peering through our side window into Hubbard's Sunroom, and noticed the large multi-colored NBC Peacock.

The Dining room was accented by formal green drapes and meticulously polished Mediterranean furniture. This was where we had Sunday dinners, the table extending long enough to accommodate our entire family plus several guests. There was a matching sideboard and china cabinet, the upper half of which served as a liquor cabinet. A formal swinging door on the left led to the most important room in the house, a large Kitchen, with built-in benches on three sides of a large rectangular table and a long moveable bench on the fourth side. The benches were built at my mother's request by Nick Santella, my father's childhood friend, and my mother's reliable handyman.

My father always sat at the head of the table next to the bathroom. During the winter, the prime seat was on the opposite end of the table which was against an enclosed radiator. Directly to the rear of the kitchen was a small bathroom with a tub, which I don't believe contained a shower. To the right of the bathroom was a small room with a tiny closet and dresser that served as my mother's ironing and Sewing room. I remember when my mother's uncle, Frank, would occasionally visit us, he always brought gifts of assorted socks and underwear which Mom would hide in her sewing room dresser, eventually crediting Uncle Frank as the silent benefactor.

Nick Santella   My father first met Nick during his childhood summers at Gonzaga. Nick was a mature teenager supervising the adolescent youths of Manhattan's Nativity parish. My earliest recollection of Nick was during my preschool years in Brooklyn. He commuted by bus from his modest basement apartment in Coney Island, arriving at our house carrying his handmade wooden toolbox, prepared to tackle my mother's next household renovation.

Although he was a jack of all trades, he was a superb craftsman. I remember his huge muscular forearms and his familiar, pleasant *wood smell*. He usually tucked a short pencil over his left ear and wore the same blue denim work-shirt and overalls, with shoulder straps and side thigh pockets for small tools. Interestingly, I don't think he ever perspired because, other than the ever-present scent of wood, I never noticed the pungent odor of perspiration!

I remember sneaking into his private *sanctuary*, a tiny room tucked under the basement stairs, with handmade wooden shelves on which he kept an assortment of used screws and straightened nails in glass jars. He economized space by cleverly hanging the jars after fastening the metal caps to the undersurface of the shelves.

The side door served as the primary entry portal and to retrieve milk and mail deliveries. From a tiny landing, a curved staircase led up to the kitchen and a straight staircase leading down to the Basement, the focal point of which was a large Party room. The flooring consisted of green and maroon Kentile tiles which always appeared polished, and in the center of which was a decorative circular design. The dropped ceiling had sound dampening panels and recessed fluorescent lights - very cool! I remember sitting on the stairs watching my older siblings and their friends dancing to the old 78 records.

To the left of the Party room was a Laundry room with two large slop sinks, scrub boards and a clothes wringer in which the rollers occasionally caught my fingers. To the left of the Laundry room was the Furnace room. After hanging the damp clothes in front of the furnace, my mother used a knee operated machine for pressing clothes. To the right of the furnace room was a small room where my mother stored canned goods along with my father's legal files, which were always considered off-limits.

To the right of the Party room was a step up room that contained a large plywood table built by Nick Santella that extended along the entire back wall, and on top of which we erected an elaborate electric train set - hence it was called the Train room. In addition to traditional tracks, we also had a set of tracks that didn't require connections. Apparently, my father represented someone from the Lionel model train company, because each Christmas we might be surprised by an additional Lionel car. Beneath the plywood train platform, we stored our *hand-me-down* winter boots, gloves, and sports equipment, including roller and ice skates, hockey sticks, baseball bats, several mitts - all of which were well *broken-in!*

Boxing   To the right of the Train room was a very small room that had a boxing speed bag mounted to the ceiling. I occasionally watched my father rhythmically punching the speed bag, using alternating hands and ending with a rapid circular motion. Although I would occasionally try to imitate his motion and rhythm, because it was easily heard upstairs, it was only a matter of time before I heard, "that's enough!"

I believe there was also a light-heavy bag hanging from the ceiling. According to my mother, in his youth, my father would train on both the speed and heavy bags, occasionally sparring in a small boxing gym. Initially, we only had lightweight gloves for the speed bag, but one Christmas we received *authentic* Joe Louis gloves.

Friday Night Fights   My father loved watching professional boxing and wrestling matches on the small Admiral TV in the Sunroom. At the time, his idols were the current wrestling champion, Antonino Rocca, and of course, the Brown Bomber, Joe Louis. I remember reading Dad's copy of Joe Louis's," Fundamentals of shadow boxing".

After reigning as the world heavyweight champion for 12 years, he was now in the waning years of his illustrious boxing career. In 1951 his remarkable career, with a 68-3 54 KO record ended when he was defeated by Rocky Marciano, who eventually retired undefeated with a perfect, 49-0 43K0 record. Personally, however, I felt that pound for pound, the best boxer was the light heavyweight champion, Sugar Ray Robinson, and my sentimental favorite was heavyweight champion, Floyd Patterson.

At some point, intent on teaching us some of what my father might have taught him, my brother Caesar decided to set up a makeshift *boxing ring* in the Party room in order to teach Nick and me the *Basics of Survival*! So, after lacing up our Joe Louis gloves, he turned us loose - what a mistake! As Nick was pummeling me, Caesar kept telling me to duck and block his punches with my elbows. Each three-minute round seemed like an eternity, and my legs were weary from constantly circling the ring in order to evade Nick's merciless punches. All I can say is, while my body provided Nick with a constant moving punching bag, he learned how to box at my expense!

Comically, whenever Dad turned on the Gillette Cavalcade of Sports channel, there would be a silent mutiny as, one by one, viewers quietly exited the Sunroom room, eventually leaving my father all by his lonesome.

However, judgment being the better part of valor, Dad purchased an even smaller, 12" TV for the little Sewing room off the kitchen. Ironically, this would eventually prove to be a form of indoctrination or test of endurance as my future brother in laws would dutifully accompany my father in the tiny room, hoping to win his approval by pretending to enjoy watching a boring boxing match - sort of a rite of passage! Meanwhile, during intermission breaks in the Sunroom, we would amuse ourselves by peering into the crowded Sewing room.

Another of my father's idols was, the preeminent bodybuilder, and forerunner of Jack LaLanne, Charles Atlas! I still remember his standard musclebound pose on the inside cover of numerous magazines, flexing his massive, but well proportioned, biceps while wearing a skimpy leopard-skin bathing suit. I think it was his, non-grotesque, well-proportioned body that caught my father's attention and admiration. I surmised that he was a St Anselm parishioner because I remember seeing his shiny yellow Cadillac convertible in the parking lot with his initials, C A, embossed on the driver's side door.

After ascending from the landing, straight ahead was a small private bedroom with a single bed and a tiny closet. It was appropriately dubbed the *Special Bedroom.* To the best of my recollection, the lucky inhabitants of the bedroom were my sister, Anita, followed by my brother, Caesar, and then yours truly, *Petesy.* There were four other bedrooms and one bathroom off the upstairs hallway. In addition to a conventional tub, the bathroom featured a very unique large tiled shower. In addition to the overhead shower, it also had shower heads on three of the side walls.

To the right of the Special bedroom was a large Front bedroom, which overlooked the Park. Considering its prime location and having two large closets with full-length mirrors, it was surely considered the Master Bedroom. However, having older twin sisters, I suspect my parents forfeited the room for them. Or perhaps it was when I was born. Incidentally, the twins were both gifted with superior intellects.

My mother proudly kept their report cards from elementary school, and upon glancing at them, I was surprised to see that Virginia had higher grades. In time, however, it became self-evident that I clearly wasn't a beneficiary of their genetic brain pool!

In any event, they each had separate beds and, due to the scarcity of beds, I slept in a *Crib* until the age of seven! Fortunately, they eventually lowered the side rail so I could more easily climb out. While lying in my crib, I remember enjoying the lightheaded sensation of rocking my head back and forth. My brothers would encourage me to rock faster and faster until I eventually became so dizzy, I vomited in my crib which infuriated my mother.

I remember one morning being startled by the sight of the *Blessed Mother* at the foot of my bed! The apparition lasted for several minutes and I remember, while looking down at me she had a faint smile but remained speechless. Then, without saying a word, her image slowly faded away. Skeptics would probably opine that it was the result of too much head rocking, but to this day I firmly believe that her presence was real, and to this day, in times of trouble, I resort to the Memorare.

To the left of the Special bedroom and across from the bathroom was my Parent's bedroom. It was relatively small with a double bed and a single small closet. Further down the hallway was a large Back bedroom overlooking the backyard. It had a Double bed and a Single bed, which accommodated my three older brothers. Caesar and Nick slept in the Double bed and Rocco in the Single bed. It had a large walk-in cedar closet, half of which contained my father's suits and ceiling panel which opened to the attic.

Fast-forwarding to February 1954, my sister Maria was the first one to leave the fold, accepting a marriage proposal from a handsome young man, John (Jack)Weiser. Being a Regis graduate, during their early courtship Jack would often arrive at our house with his Latin book in hand, and we soon understood their mutual attraction.

They were both in their early twenties when they were married. The church ceremony was in Manhattan followed by a reception at the St George Hotel. I recently looked at their wedding pictures and took note of my father's expression. To me, it was one of sadness or perhaps of weighty financial concerns?

Maria's Wedding 1954 St. George Hotel

Incidentally, Jack's father, Arthur Weiser MD, who was Hungarian by birth and a Vienna trained urologist, was the epitome of a caring physician and would greatly influence my future career in medicine.

Thankfully, with Maria's early departure, a series of musical bedroom exchanges ensued. Begrudgingly, Anita moved into the Front room with Virginia, Caesar moved into the hallowed Special bedroom and I was finally liberated from my crib, only to be tortured while sharing the double bed with Nick in the back bedroom.

CH - 2
SLEEPING WITH NICK

Sleeping with Nick was a necessity which, at times was fun and at other times, pure torture. We both slept in the Double bed and when my brother Rocco was home from college, he slept in the Single bed.

Night Prayers   Before going to bed, I would routinely say my night prayers, sometimes even a full decade of the rosary. For whatever reason, Nick saw this as an opportunity to tantalize me which forced me to overcome his incessant teasing by saying my prayers out loud. When he wouldn't stop, I would yell "Mom, Nick is making fun of my prayers again!" This was quickly followed by the sound of my mother's bounding footsteps. However, Nick would often pretend to be fast asleep which made me look like an absolute lunatic!

Bed Secrets   Nick would always manage to successfully lure me by asking, "Do you want to hear a secret?" Of course, I would take the bait, at which point he would say, "I don't want Mom to hear, so I'll tell you the secret under the covers". Trusting my older brother and expecting him to do the same when I put my head under the covers, he would hold my head and proceed to Fart in my face. Although muffled by the covers, when I would start yelling, my mother would come running into the bedroom and, while trying to explain what Nick did to me, he would disarm her by maintaining a saintly expression.

With a very contrite and reassuring tone, I trusted my older brother when he promised that he wouldn't do that again. Then he lured me again saying, "This time, I'm willing to share a very important secret!"

Again, trusting my older brother, I fell for it, and when I finally resurfaced from under the covers I yelled, "Mom he did it again!" But this time, when she came storming into the room, Nick had his palms fervently pressed together as if in prayer.

Imaginary Line   My brother devised a new method of torture. After drawing an imaginary line on the bedsheet with his finger he said, "Now don't cross that line!" I didn't understand why, and I knew it was futile to ask. Then, shortly before falling asleep, *Bam*! He suddenly punched me in the shoulder. When I screamed, "What was that for?" he said, "You crossed the line!" Then he redrew the mysterious line again, of course, advancing it in his favor. Ten minutes later, "Bam!" he punched me in the shoulder, claiming that I crossed the line again! Despite my protestations, however, he repeated the same scenario two more times until I ended up with about a foot of bed space.

Sucker Punch   Another sucker scenario was when he suggested a variation of the *punch for punch* contest. Normally, the two contestants take turns punching each other in the shoulder (deltoid muscle) until one contestant finally yields. It's an asinine contest that, as a teenager, I regrettably engaged in one too many times. In any event, he began by saying, "Let's see who can punch the hardest, you go first. Naturally, after punching me much harder, he claimed victory. When I objected, he said, "Okay, let's see who can punch the lightest, you go first." Abiding by the rules, I delivered a feathery love tap, barely touching his arm. But then, *Bam*! - he let me have it and said, "Ok you win." Either way, I couldn't win!

Whenever Rocco came home from college, he joined Nick and me in the back bedroom by sleeping in the Single bed. Knowing that he would soon be coming up to bed, we would either short-sheet his bed or place items such as marbles or hangers under his sheets, down towards the foot of the bed. There was only one problem. Shortly after he came into the bedroom, we had all to do to muffle our snickering, even under the covers.

The first two times were successful, but thereafter, the snickering was a dead giveaway and the ruse was short-lived.

The Gladwell Mansion   An unusually large Mansion on the corner of Colonial Rd. and 83rd St. was owned by the Gladwell's Their two children, Billy, was Nick's age and Bobby was my age. In addition to their parents, Mr. Gladwell's sister-in-law, Aunt Nancy, also lived in the Main house. She was considerably younger than Mr. Gladwell and rather good looking which made me suspicious. However, she appeared tomboyish and acted very gruff. In fact, one afternoon I remember her punching my friend Chris in the stomach for presumably, *mouthing off.*

The estate occupied the entire length of Colonial Rd between 82nd and 83rd streets, approximately an acre in size. The property included a three-story Main house, a three-car detached garage, a small guesthouse, tennis court, and a large covered sandbox. The Main house was won in a card game by Bobby's grandfather and the winning hand was framed in a glass enclosure and proudly displayed on their living room wall. I would often play in Bobby's mansion for hours and never even be seen or heard.

Nick, Stevie & Me, with the Gladwell Mansion in the background

The Perfect Tree Hunt   Holidays were always special in our household, but most especially Christmas. Aside from the festive meals, each year we hunted for the *Perfect Christmas Tree!* Being that he grew up on Spring Street and his office was on Broadway, my father was very familiar with lower Manhattan. Consequently, each year we would drive down to the Bowery section in the evening under the elevated West Side highway, roaming from one tree stand to another, in search of the *Perfect* Christmas Tree.

I remember one such evening when, In his own inimitable way, my father had the skinny 5' 4" attendant convinced that he owned the marketplace, and despite the frigid weather, the little attendant was more than happy to accommodate *the Boss* by pulling out one 10' tree after another from the racks. After cutting the heavy twine to allow the branches to unfold, the little attendant was swallowed while balancing and slowly turning the monstrous tree to ensure its fullness and symmetry.

After tipping the little attendant handsomely, the finale was watching my father artfully negotiate the price with the unsuspecting vendor. Once we got the enormous tree home, it occupied a third of the Living room and it took at least three days to decorate, especially when applying one strand of tinsel at a time.

I suspect, as with most households, the anticipatory excitement of Christmas morning was particularly special. I can still remember all of us sitting on the top of the stairs waiting for my mother's signal to come down and open the presents. It brought back such fond memories that It was something I tried to replicate with our own children. Everyone's stockings were carefully hung from the fireplace mantle, and although at the time, I didn't know that the flue was permanently sealed, I didn't dare risk the consequence of peeking for fear that Santa Clause would suddenly bolt up the chimney. In fact, I remained a firm believer until my father eventually broke the devastating news by delicately saying. "Son, don't expect much for Christmas this year, Santa Clause was shot in the back pocket!"

Holiday Dinners Celebrating Easter Sunday was second only to Christmas followed closely by the seemingly endless feast of Thanksgiving. These festive meals, served in the beautifully decorated Dining room, usually lasted more than three hours. They began with either a generous fruit cup or warm grapefruit garnished with a cherry, followed by a lavish assortment of antipasto platters. This was followed by a pasta dish - either homemade ravioli, manicotti, or lasagna. After a brief respite, this would be followed by a meat dish of either ham, turkey, or roast beef accompanied by a large bowl of tossed salad. After another respite, was followed by an assortment of homemade Italian pastries, sliced fruits, nuts, and coffee.

Invariably, the invited guests included one or two Jesuit Priests who were old friends of my father and former seminarians under Fr. Dominic. Dad wasn't necessarily a wine drinker, preferring instead an occasional cold beer or a shot of Haig & Haig Pinch. The Priests, on the other hand, enjoyed their wine, and although they customarily brought him some holy water, they invariably left with a bottle of my father's *holy water*. Considering that they must have intended to say a lot of masses, I guess it was an even trade!

Palm Sundays were also particularly memorable because, even with priests in attendance, my father would dip the blessed palm in holy water, and sprinkling us would say, "There's no greater blessing than that of a Father for his children". To this day, I believe he meant this both personally and metaphorically as in," The Father of us All!"

Indeed, we were truly fortunate to live in such a prime area as Bay Ridge. And if we ever complained about what we didn't have, my father would nod and shake his head like Jackie Gleason, and with a sardonic smile say, "Why you ungrateful son of a bitch!" Not very poetic, but the message was unmistakable. My Father never lost sight of his meager roots, and if he sensed we were getting too presumptuous or cocky, he would take Nick and me to his childhood neighborhood on Spring St. saying, "Let me show you where it all began!"

Bowery Offerings   We always had plenty of fruit in the house, certainly enough to share. I remember one occasion when, for whatever reason, my father decided to drive Nick and me down to the Bowery where many of the homeless and alcoholics commonly slept on the sidewalks. Upon seeing them, he would pull the car over to the curb and after rolling down the window he had us say, "Excuse me sir, may I offer you some fruit?". I don't ever remember the offer being refused. On the contrary, there was an expression of gratitude. Perhaps, it had less to do with benevolence and more to do with a life lesson - be grateful for what you have!

CH - 3
THE PARK AND THE PARKEYS

F ort Hamilton Park (The Park) was always well supervised by three uniformed Park Attendants (aka *Parkeys*), Edie, Ray, and Artie. Their green uniforms, always neatly pressed, included a matching cap, a shiny badge, and, of course, a brass whistle. Being that the Park was directly across the street from our house, it provided for virtually every sport any kid could want. The width of the park extended from 83rd St.to 85th St, and the depth extended all the way back to Ft Hamilton High School on Shore Road. *Incidentally, one of my twin sisters, Virginia, and my oldest brother, Rocco, attended Ft Hamilton H.S.*

While attending Ft Hamilton, Rocco had already achieved swimming fame as a National record holder. At some point, he told me that the school had a swimming pool on the 5th floor, which I readily shared with all my friends. However, when I mentioned it to several of the students that my brother swims in the pool on the 5th floor, I was utterly embarrassed when they laughed, saying, "The school only has 4 floors!" Thereafter my credibility was in the toilet.

Central Park In the center of the Park's upper level was a very large rectangular concrete foundation, enclosed by a tall wrought iron fence. The unique sunken interior had a 2-foot high perimeter wall with eight powerful spray fountains. The central drain could be closed allowing for flooding of the sunken interior. while the fountain's spray during the summer and ice skating during the winter.

During the hot season, the fountain's powerful spray provided cooling and the flooded basin provided the perfect place to play Murderball or

33

Dodge ball. Of course, Nick would invariably throw the ball as hard as he could in my direction and naturally, I was usually *Out* early in the game.

Likewise, during the winter the frozen basin would provide an ice-skating rink. One of the Parkeys would designate two of the better skaters to periodically clean the ice with special large shovels, and with the sound of his whistle, everyone would promptly clear the ice without question.

Stroller Abuse   I remember one cold winter day my sister Anita took me in a stroller to the park, presumably for fresh air. While watching the ice skaters, however, she would invariably strike up a very lengthy conversation with some boyfriend. Meanwhile, despite being covered with a wool blanket, I'm freezing to death with a frozen upper lip from a constant runny nose. I still remember how the combination of the frozen snot and the wool blanket would chafe my upper lip and chin. And the awful burning sensation every time I turned my head.

Likewise, the same scenario would occur behind the handball courts. When she finished her flirtatious conversation and finally brought me home, my mother took one look at me and yelled, "What the hell did you do to this poor child? His chin is all red and his nose and hands are blue!" Then she instinctively took my frozen hands and put them between her ample breasts for warmth. Sadly, that was perhaps the only physical sign of affection that I can remember!

We were never avid picture takers, but at some point, I believe we had a Brownie camera. However, having film was another matter! Consequently, other than four or five black-and-white photos, I have very few pictures with which to refresh my memory. While writing this memoir, I'm looking at a rare black and white photo of a snow scene of me and Dad with the park in the background. I suspect I'm about four years old, wearing a hat with ear flaps, a long white scarf, leggings, and high snow boots. My father is dressed in his usual Homburg hat and long black wool coat, smiling while squatting behind me.

Me and Dad Park Snow scene

The Park House The Park House was a solid brick building with men and women's bathrooms on opposite sides of the building. I always felt welcome inside and, especially on cold winter days, the comforting warmth and distinctive smell of fresh coffee was a welcome relief. And if I stared long enough, they might offer me a chocolate-covered marshmallow. so, I tended to stare a lot.

If you didn't have a basketball, you could *check one out* in the Park House and promptly return it at the sound of the whistle just before closing. There was never any doubt who was in charge. Being rather tall and large-boned, Edie's intimidating size guaranteed that no one ever messed with her, and at the sound of her whistle, everyone froze!

To the far left of the Park house, and beyond the full-size basketball court, was a high stone wall with four handball courts on both sides - the front side also used for playing stickball.

To the right of the Park House were both large and small swing sets, seesaws, monkey bars, and a fenced sandbox beyond which was another full-size basketball court. On the lower level of the Park, was a professional Baseball diamond encircled by a one-mile red clay track, and to the right were four tennis courts. We had access to all the above when not in use by the Ft Hamilton high school students.

The Parkeys were fair but firm and took the responsibility of their job very seriously. Consequently, we always felt protected and safe, and living just across the street, they knew us by name, which wasn't always a good thing, but certainly a comfort to my mother. Needless to say, the Park and the Parkeys made an indelible impression on my early years.

Sports Equipment When it came to playing sports that required *equipment* such as basketballs, baseballs, footballs, bats, gloves, etc. it was a necessary evil to always include the kid who had the necessary equipment, even if he was lousy at the sport. Then the next issue was, which team was going to get saddled with him? Likewise, whoever had a *skate key* was king.

Being the youngest of seven, I mostly dealt with very used skates, both roller and ice skates. Even though large shell clamps existed, our roller skates only had the small ones that clamped onto the edges of your shoe sole. When the sole eventually tore from the shoe, you simply repaired it with tape. Try playing street hockey with those babies. You just manage enough speed to shoot and guess what comes off - either the clamp or worse, your sole!

My ice skates were always two sizes too big. So, I wore two pairs of socks and stuffed the tip with paper - which inevitably caused me to lose feeling in my toes! Many of the kids had rubber blade covers In order to cross the street or enter and exit the ice rink. However, being that my blades were never sharpened, I figured, "It didn't really matter!" Besides, regardless of how tight my brother Caesar would lace them up, I ended up skating on my inner ankles, and by the end of the day, Houdini would have trouble getting them off!

Once, after listening to my whining and out of total frustration my mother gave me $ 50 cents and told me to bring the skates to the shoemaker on fourth Avenue for sharpening. Although he had the grinding wheel, he said it would cost $ 75 cents for both blades. Knowing that I always skated counterclockwise, crossing my right foot over my left, I said, "How about if you just sharpen the right skate?" After looking at me incredulously, when I explained my predicament he said, "Just give me the $ 50 cents and I'll sharpen both".

For some reason, my sister Anita was the only one in the family who had *Special* Skates - white figure skates, with fancy front blade picks! One day, purely out of desperation, I thought that I'd wear her perfectly white Special Skates. However, after twenty minutes I couldn't tolerate the unflattering *Sissy* comments from my friends.

Our baseball equipment mostly consisted of my brother Caesar's *broken in* catcher's mitt which we regularly oiled with Crisco to soften the cracked leather. We had two baseball bats of different lengths, both with cracked handles wrapped with tape. Needless to say, I wasn't required to bring my equipment to many baseball games! Now, don't get me wrong, in all honesty, these minor inconveniences only added to the fond memories and were common to many of my friends.

Rothstein's   Speaking of footwear, my father was famous for taking us to Rothstein's clothing store to *negotiate* the purchase of several pairs of sneakers for his sons. Unfortunately, his philosophy was to buy sneakers that were two sizes larger than your feet required. Hence, for the first six months, you walked around like *Flipper* and by the time you grew into them, they inevitably required taping of the tips. Although white sneakers were in vogue, black high top Keds were on sale, so guess which ones we got! At some point, I remember complaining about my footwear at which point my father said, "you remind me of the man who complained about his tight shoes until he saw a man without any feet!" - I never complained again.

My parents never openly discussed finances, and although there were no excesses and cash always seemed to be scarce, I honestly never wanted for anything. As a matter of fact, I was the only one to ever get a bike (for Christmas), an English Racer to boot! Of course, each one of my brothers had to demonstrate how to use the gears, leaving me to be the last one to try the new bike.

CH - 4
THE NEIGHBORHOOD

When I said my world revolved around a 3 to 4 block radius, at least half of that was *around the corner* on 83rd St. between Colonial Road and Ridge Boulevard - and even that was confined to the lower third of the street. With few exceptions, just about all my neighborhood friends lived in the same general area and, as I said, even 84 Street was considered foreign territory. So, other than St Anselms school, everything else revolved around the Park and lower 83rd St.

Friends Coincidentally, most of my childhood friends in Bay Ridge and Monroe, had siblings with similar age differences as Nick and me, producing two different age group tiers. As expected, the older tier was always trying to lose the younger tier - fat chance!

Although neighborhood friendships tend to vacillate with the years and circumstances, I'd have to say that, of all my childhood Bay Ridge friends, Chris Gruening was probably my longest and closest friend. Being one year older, he was more daring and troublesome which was strangely alluring. He was also more mature, whereas I didn't pay much attention to girls he already had a mad crush on Danny Nolte. Although Chris's older brother, Frank, was about Nick's age, they rarely hung out together,

Next would probably be Peter Bergren or my next-door neighbor, Stevie Liebowitz. Speaking for Nick, I think he would say his best friends were the Salami twins, Joseph, and Albert, who, being a little older, were adored by Nick. A close second would be Bill Bergren, mostly because of his older sister, Jane, who was a real knockout. New arrivals to the neighborhood were the Brancaccios who shared a common driveway with the Bergrens. Dr. and Mrs. Brancaccio had two young children, Michael and his younger sister, Lyn, who, even at a young age, was very cute.

We'd spend hours flipping and pitching baseball cards or flicking marbles into a hole in the dirt and it didn't cost a dime. Step ball, box ball, and best of all, street stickball was the all-time favorite pastime. We used the same metal sewer covers for home plate and second base and a sidewalk tree and fire hydrant as first and third bases.

We improvised by creating a makeshift hideaway fort in the large V formed between the roofs of the Bergren and Brancaccio garages which could then be covered by a piece of cardboard or old plywood. We also had a secret clubhouse in Peter Bergen's basement.

The Lot   Much of our time was spent on a vacant lot on 83rd St. between Nolte and Germack's house. It featured a 20-foot high flagpole that never flew a flag but provided for endless climbing contests. We would play buck-buck and flyball against the side of the Germack's house which, although it was only a soft handball, drove poor Mrs.Germack nuts. Alternatively, we would play stoop ball on Danny Nolte's front steps.

One year we dug a huge hole in the center of the lot in order to burn Christmas trees until we were busted by the fire department, Then we made it an underground fort by covering the opening on top. During the winter, we camouflaged the top and used to throw snowballs at the high school students as they walked up 83rd St. Despite storing an ample supply of premade snowballs in the fort, being that they clearly had stronger arms and outnumbered us, we got killed.

JD Cards   I remember another time when Chris Gruening and I were throwing snowballs at passing cars, one happened to sail through the open window of a car driven by a plainclothes cop. He quickly backed the car up and snagged the both of us, and flashing his badge told us, "Get in the back of the car!" Then after driving us up to the 68th precinct, he parked in front and said, "Wait in the car while I go inside for a minute!"

We thought for sure we were being arrested, and the horrifying prospect that my father and Chris's parents, who were also attorneys, would have to bail us out of jail was truly terrifying. As we both sat trembling in the back seat, we briefly considered making a run for it, only to discover that the rear doors were locked! When he finally returned and threatened to bring us inside to issue *JD cards* (juvenile delinquent) - we both started crying and pleading for mercy. After a lengthy lecture and a very stern warning, he eventually drove us back home. After a long sigh of relief, I thought, "If my parents ever found out about this, I'd rather get the *JD card*! So, we both swore to never utter a word about our misadventure.

Pyromania   During the Christmas season, since no one parked their cars in the narrow garages, we thought, "What a great idea to store old Christmas trees in Peter Bergen's garage for future burning." I doubt that Peter's parents were aware of the potential of a catastrophic event. When the trees were dangerously brown, we dragged them down to the corner of 83rd St, and Colonial Rd. in front of the Park. Then we started burning them, adding more trees until the blaze was so high the overhead street wires were in danger of burning, Thankfully, some responsible person called the fire department and once again we received another *JD card* warning.

In early spring and the promise of warmer weather, came the long-awaited jingle of the Ice cream trucks. They would roam along Colonial road and the side streets, especially child laden 83rd St. Some of my friends received allowances and consequently, carried more money than I. After They bought a delicious ice cream and it would be a contest which of the bystanders was going to yell, "Licks" before the purchaser yelled, "No Licks!" And If he won, he would desperately try to avoid my constant staring.

Also, twice a week a wooden cart displaying an assortment of fresh fruits and vegetables would slowly make its way up 83rd St. drawn by an old donkey guided by a toothless man yelling something unintelligible that sounded like "watermelon!". If one of the neighbors came out to buy produce while we were about to play stickball, the fear was that, while the donkey was idle, he would deposit a very smelly mound in the street, that was neither fruit nor vegetables. So, as a precaution, while the attendant was preoccupied with customers, we would throw a tiny pebble at the donkey's back-side causing a brief, *Donkey distraction.*

The Narrows   The homes along the right side of 83rd St. Heading towards Narrows Ave. resembled a virtual showcase of elegant homes, one more beautiful than the next, especially on the corners. The house on the corner of 83rd St. and Narrows Ave. was particularly beautiful - with a unique metal turnstile at the bottom of the driveway which automatically turned to enable the car to exit the driveway. Continuing further on 83rd St. towards Shore Road, the homes were even more impressive in size and quality.

We would often play hide and seek for hours among the blooming forsythia bushes lining Shore Road. Also, by crossing an overpass over the Belt Parkway you could easily access a very romantic walkway along the Narrows River. The ferry that ran between 69th St. and Staten Island only cost five cents, which was considered a very romantic cheap date, especially if you hopped over the railing in Staten Island and came back for free!

The Great Bridge   I remember the Verrazano Bridge being built from 1959 to 64. At the time, it was the world's longest suspension bridge, connecting Bay Ridge to Staten Island. Although its construction changed some of the landscape on 6th Ave. between 86th and 95th streets, it didn't affect our area of Bay Ridge. Walking along the Narrows provided a spectacular view of the two monumental towers, and the connecting cables formed a graceful convex curve simulating the curve of the earth into the sky. Of critical concern was that it was high enough to provide passage for the elegant Queen Mary II.

In the evenings, it was particularly beautiful when the giant cables were illuminated, further highlighting the beauty of the Goliath structure. And best of all, it only cost $.50 to cross the majestic structure. Even today it is still considered America's longest suspension bridge! I remember walking to the 96th St. Park which had a very tall flagpole and a huge black Canon perched on a large circular granite terrace with strategically placed semicircular granite benches for gazing at the Great Bridge.

Walking along Shore Rd, at 85 th street, was a very unusual residential compound protected by a very high wrought iron fence with long pointed tips curved inward, presumably designed to keep someone or something contained inside. In the center of the compound was a large stone Mansion, to the right of which was a large wrought iron cage with very thick bars, resembling those seen in a zoo. Inside the cage was a large Gorilla that was said to be, "Mighty Joe Young!"

The Avenues Third avenue was mostly commercial with two local grocery stores and a barbershop between 83rd and 84th streets. There was a much larger food store around 78th St. Bohacks. However, we rarely used it, relying mostly on the smaller, more personal, local stores. It was common for the smaller grocery stores to extend credit and the preferred store, Ralston's, was on Third Avenue between 82nd and 83rd St. A couple of times a week, before leaving for school, my mother would give me a grocery list including meats, eggs, canned goods etc. and I would drop off the list on my way to school.

The proprietor would prepare the order and most often have it delivered by a special *Delivery Bicycle* that had a large front basket and relatively small tires with special gears for navigating the steep streets. There were similar bikes for carrying folded newspapers. With almost laser-like accuracy, the *Paperboy* would fling the folded newspaper to within a foot of the front door, without even breaking stride - truly incredible.

There was another small grocery store, Nick's, on Third Avenue between 83rd and 84th streets. It was owned by the father of one of my St Anselm classmates. The inside of the local grocery stores always had a distinctive wholesome smell. In addition to the wood counters and old creaking wood floors, the contents of the high shelves were retrieved by using a long pole on the end of which was a hand-operated clasp. I hardly ever remember the exchange of money, except when my mother gave me an envelope to settle a bill.

The local Dry Cleaner was on the corner of Fourth Avenue and 86 Street. My mother and I would often bring my father's shirts and suits to be dry cleaned. I remember that the woman behind the counter always had chocolate mints hidden below the counter. If I stared long enough, she would eventually offer me one and I would usually take two.

Fourth and Fifth Avenues were more residential. Needicks was on the corner of 86 Street and Fourth Avenue. Periodically, they offered a *Lunch Special* - two hot dogs and a Needicks orange drink for $ 25 cents. If I pleaded long enough, as a special treat, Mom would occasionally allow me to go to Needicks instead of walking home for lunch. Halfway up 86 Street, between Fourth and Fifth avenues, was the famous Ebinger's bakery. After accompanying my mother a couple of times, she would send me up with a list which always included their delicious, one-of-a-kind, Crumb cake or Coconut Custard pie!

The Alice Curse   One year, for Mother's Day, I decided to ride my English racer up to 4th Ave and 86th street in order to buy my mother a present at Woolworths. I was just about to leave when my mother noticed that I was wearing a new pair of pants that I received for Easter. Before leaving for my secret mission my mother said, "Mark my words, (prelude to the Alice Curse) you better change your pants before you ruin them!" (the Curse!) Well, I figured I was on a good mission and besides, nothing could happen, I'll be riding my English racer!

So, off I went wearing my good pants. I knew my mother enjoyed a cup of afternoon tea and I found a relatively inexpensive tea set that included a small teapot and four small cups and saucers. Feeling that my mother would surely be impressed with my selection, I proudly and happily left for home with the tea set in a shopping bag firmly secured to my handlebars. While biking down 84th St. my front tire hit a rock and I lost control of the bike as well as the shopping bag.

Needless to say, I was totally distraught that, not only was the tea set in pieces but worst of all, my good pants were torn over the right knee. When I arrived home with the shopping bag in hand, my mother asked me where I'd been. When I explained what had happened, she said, "But I already have a tea set. What made you think I needed another one!"

Although I was totally crushed, I was just thankful that she didn't notice my torn pants. With that, I quickly went upstairs, changed my pants, and waited till evening to repair the damage. I found her sewing box and proceeded to stitch the tear as best I could and hung the pants on my bedpost. The next day, my mother saw my botched sewing job, and after her fury subsided, she was able to patch and re-stitch the tear from the inside. The moral of the story – beware of the Alice curse!

Alice Feet Similar to the Alice Curse, was the infamous, *Alice Feet* measurements. One year my mother was ordering a new couch for the living room. She paced the desired length stepping heel to toe in her size six shoes. When she told the man in the furniture store that she needed a 12-foot couch he looked at her inquisitively and said, "Madam, that's an unusually long couch. You must have an exceptionally large living room!" When she said it was of average size, he asked, "Did you use a tape measure?" And she responded, "No, I used my feet!" Upon looking down at her tiny feet, the mystery was solved!

Although biking was a common means of transportation among my friends, before receiving my English racer, our family only had one bike - a cumbersome foldable *Paratrooper* bike. It was given to us by my uncle Pete, who served as a paratrooper in World War II. Despite its antiquity, venturing to the *outer world*, such as the RKO theater on 86 Street between fourth and fifth avenues, was still considered a worthwhile hike. After all, where else could you see two feature movies and 23 cartoons for 50 cents? And the theater stage also hosted the regional yo-yo contests! However, by the time you got to a dance in a neighboring parish, it was almost over.

Barber Shops   Upon exiting the subway on 4th Ave. and 85th St, there was a barbershop which Rocco frequented, having befriended the elderly owner, Caesar. In those days, a routine haircut costs about $ 3. Caesar had an assistant barber, Joe, who was much younger and far more friendly than the old grumpy owner. There was a row of chairs against the far wall and I would patiently watch the flow of customers, praying to get Joe.

When Caesar would ask, "Who's next?", I would slither down in my chair and pretend not to hear him - hoping that some other victim would occupy his butcher chair! Occasionally this strategy worked, but unfortunately, if there were no takers, embarrassed by the long lull, I would fall on the sword and allow Caesar to butcher my hair. Thankfully, Joe eventually moved to a location on 3rd Ave. between 83rd and 84th St. which solved any future butchery dilemmas.

Dental Torture   Prior to my arrival and before the *other family* moved from 45th street to Colonial Rd. in 1942, their dentist was Dr. Weiland, who had an office on 48th St. In any event, our family continued using his services and as a 9 yr. old, I would take the elevated subway to 48th St. Fortunately, Colonial Road was located within short walking distance to a bus stop, located on the corner of Colonial Road and 86th Street which provided service to the BMT subway located on the corner of 86th St. and 5th Avenue. My mother would prepare a tag for my jacket or shirt with Dr. Weiland's office address and she would tell me to just find the subway conductor and ask him to let you know when to get off the train. Ironically, In keeping with the times, I don't remember being fearful whatsoever.

My mother would hand me an envelope containing a partial payment to give to Dr. Weiland's wife and assistant. His office was on the second floor, and the elevated portion of the subway curved so close to his corner office that, while sitting in the dental chair, as the thunderous train cars passed by the whole building, and especially my body would vibrate. I remember one year my father went ballistic when Dr. Weiland said, I had a total of 8 cavities!

This was before the days of painless dentistry or anesthetic injections. However, Dr Weiland assured me that I wouldn't have much pain because he had a new revolutionary device that sprayed cold water on the hot drill bit. All I remember is squeezing the arms of that damn chair while the miracle machine sprayed copious amounts of seemingly warm water with little or no suctioning, which resulted in soaking the front of my entire shirt.

Also, for some reason, my upper front incisor tooth was growing inwardly. After discussing the options with my father, the option of costly braces was out of the question. So, as an alternative, Dr.Weiland instructed me to use a popsicle stick on a daily basis to push my upper tooth forward by using my lower teeth as a fulcrum. To this day, I still have the same recessed sabertooth. During my vulnerable adolescent years, I remained very self-conscious while smiling, which still exists to a lesser degree to this day - thanks, Dad!

Coney Island   Coney Island was apparently very sentimental for my father. Perhaps it was because this was where he first met my mother or where, according to my mother, he swam between the jetties. In any event, on Sunday mornings, it would be a real treat when Dad would drive Nick and me to Coney Island. My father would always take the same route, hugging the Narrows shoreline on the winding Gowanus Parkway.

From afar, the first telltale sign of the magical Island was seeing the top of the giant Ferris Wheel, followed by the towering Parachute Jump. I knew we were almost there when we passed a creepy, fortune-telling gypsy mannequin with a colorful turban, viewable through a four-sided glass structure. Upon inserting 5 cents, her head would move, and her mouth would open to deliver a message. When we finally arrived at the long wooden Boardwalk, we looked in awe at the gigantic wooden structure of the legendary, Steeplechase Cyclone.

Admittedly, Dad had an ulterior motive. While we walked along the beach and the old wooden Boardwalk, he would rent a reclining chair in a designated tanning area using a tri-fold aluminum reflector to ensure an even facial tan. Believing that perception is either an illusion or reality, this produced the appearance of one who was healthy and well-rested - obviously, the result of a well-deserved, Caribbean vacation. However only we knew that it was from the neck up. Likewise, every two years he would purchase a large new sedan - surely the sign of a successful professional. All smoke and mirrors!

Before embarking on our customary stroll on the Boardwalk, he would instruct us on the importance of proper breathing, especially of the therapeutic salt air. He would briefly demonstrate how to breathe in through the nose using the diaphragm and slowly exhale through pursed lips. However, since we usually went during the late Fall or early Winter seasons, invariably, our noses would start running. Just picture trying to breathe in through your runny nose while it's starting to freeze on your upper lip. But we would faithfully endure knowing that the best was yet to come!

After we finished our abbreviated breathing exercises and he finished his artificial tanning, he would take us to Nathan's for a hot dog and then to the electric Bumper Cars. Of course, since we were often the only customers, he would negotiate a special Sunday rate. I remember Dad patiently waiting and laughing as we drove like maniacs, smashing into each other for three or four sessions, and with each session, we implored the lowly operator to extend the clock longer - what a blast!

Head Injury   Now as wonderful as Bay Ridge was, it also held some dark memories. One late fall afternoon Nick and I, along with my friend, Stevie, were standing on the corner of 85th street and Colonial Rd. For some reason, Stevie and I decided to race across the street. Halfway across, however, while in full stride, my left shoe came off. Despite this obvious handicap, not to be beaten, I finished running across with only one shoe.

After catching my breath, I figured I would run back and retrieve my other shoe. To the best of my recollection, It was dusk and when Stevie and I started running back to retrieve my shoe, Nick apparently saw an oncoming car but was only able to grab Stevie in time. While bending over to pick up my shoe, the last thing I heard was Nick yelling, but apparently too late. The car hit me in the forehead rendering me unconscious and bleeding from a large gash.

I presume I was unconscious because I only remember bits and pieces. I remember feeling a terrible burning sensation on my right forehead. and I heard someone yell to notify my mother, and at some point, I felt a rough wool blanket on me. I only have a fragmented recollection of being brought by ambulance to the local Bay Ridge Hospital. Then, while lying in bed the next morning, several of my friends visited me and brought me a present of cowboy and Indian figures.

Apparently, even though it was dusk, the car didn't have any lights on, making it difficult to see me. In any event, just to tease my brother, I always told the story a little differently. I suggested that Nick chose to hold Stevie back instead of me! I know it seems really cruel or perhaps, simply payback for torturing me in our bed!

First Train Trip I remember Rocco accompanying Virginia and me to Grand Central Station. I was about seven or eight years old and terribly frightened that, much like our Lionel trains, when rounding a sharp turn, the car might go flying off the tracks! He calmed my fears explaining how the wheel and track design stabilizes the train cars, especially around turns.

believe we were headed to either Connecticut or Boston, perhaps to visit Maria. But the most memorable part of our journey was visiting the fancy Dining car for lunch. All the tables were covered with white tablecloths and napkins with tall wine glasses and a center flower vase. The unfamiliar luxury of *Table Service* was over the top!

CH - 5
ST. ANSELMS

Our elementary parochial school was St. Anselms. The school was a four-story brick building on the corner of 84th St. and 4th Avenue, three city blocks from our house. It had two side entrances on 83rd St. that allowed for entry into the adjoining Parish Church. The teaching staff consisted of the Sisters of Notre Dame as well as lay teachers.

Our parish extended from Shore Road to the Gowanus Parkway between 78th St. and 87th St. The students were required to wear uniforms and by the time I attended the school, I mostly wore uniforms previously worn by my older brother, Nick. This usually meant a collar size one or two sizes larger than I needed, and in addition to turning my cuffs inside out, I would often wear rubber bands above my elbows, so my sleeves didn't cover my fingers.

Parishes In Brooklyn it was customary to designate your general geographic area by your respective parish. However, the only time I can remember venturing into other parishes such as Our Lady of Angels (*OLA* 73rd st and 4th Ave), Our Lady of Perpetual Help (*OLPH* 59th st and 5th Ave) or St Patrick's(95th st and4th Ave) was on Holy Thursday when it was customary to walk to other parishes to view their interior flower arrangements. The only other exception was when I would attend a church Bazaar in St. Bernadette's Parish, in Bensonhurst, Brooklyn.

Castanets The old Parish Church was attached to the school and accessed by the students through the front and rear side entrances, while a large front entrance provided entry for the local parishioners. While in church the Nuns carried special *Clickers* that would prompt all eight classes when

50

we should sit, stand, and kneel. To make matters worse, the lower grades would sit in the main church while the upper grades sat in the upper gallery or choir area. So, if the clickers were not in sync, which was quite often, the clickers sounded like discordant *Castanets*

First Confession   Having finally achieved the "age of reason", I remember preparing for the Sacrament of Reconciliation (Confession), which was a prerequisite for the all-important, First Communion! Unfortunately, we learned all about venial and mortal sins and the *Near occasions of sin* - all of which could doom you to burn in the eternal fires of Hell!

My 3rd-grade teacher, Sister Ermingale, constantly stressed the importance of confessing "All of your sins and the number of times you committed each sin," especially misbehaving and lying! And when someone mentioned "Impure thoughts," I didn't have a clue what they were talking about! In any event, despite being shown the inside of the mysterious confessional booth beforehand, when it was my turn to enter the confines of the dark booth and kneel on the hard wooden board, rather than reviewing my sins, my mind went completely blank!

Upon hearing the tiny screen panel slide open, when I began my rehearsed line, "Bless me, Father, for I have sinned", I couldn't remember my sins, let alone their number. So, I just made them up, and at a loss, after mentioning 30 "impure thoughts", I was sentenced to say an entire rosary. Needless to say, I was embarrassed to be the last one still kneeling at the altar saying my penance.

First Communion   My first communion was celebrated in the Old Church, and I remember processing up to the altar rail and being surprised how bland and dry the Host was. I remember while walking back to my seat having great difficulty dislodging the host from the roof of my mouth. Since It was considered taboo to chew the host, the only permissible maneuver was using your tongue. So, I tried in vain contorting my tongue in all directions, trying to dislodge the stubborn host. I thought, "Maybe they added some sort of glue in the unleavened bread!".

In any event, I only have a small black and white photo of me dressed in my spiffy white suit against the back of our house with my Mother standing behind me. I don't remember any kind of party or celebration which wasn't unusual in our family.

My First Communion

The Lollipop Dilemma   Ever since my first communion, I was always steadfast about fasting the night before receiving communion for fear of going to hell. However, one particular Sunday morning, I forgot and sucked on a lollipop three times. Realizing what I had done, I immediately threw it away and after saying a fervent prayer, I went to receive communion anyway. Ironically, this lollipop catastrophe occurred shortly before Maria's wedding ceremony! This, of course, would require going to mass and receive holy communion!

Faced with this conundrum, I felt I had to go to church as soon as possible in order to confess my sacramental indiscretion. So, my brother Rocco and my future brother-in-law, Bob Hartman, took me to a Franciscan church in lower Manhattan, which heard confessions of the *worst of the worst* twenty-four hours a day! It was an extremely hot Saturday, and despite the oppressive heat, my confessional booth's Friar was still wearing his stifling brown wool robes which prompted him to leave the door partially open in order to extend his large sandaled feet.

When I entered the confessional, I knelt down, and making the sign of the cross I said, "Bless me, Father, for I have sinned. Before receiving communion, I sucked a lollipop three times!" I thought he must have been hard of hearing because the Fryer seemed aghast and screamed, "You sucked what three times! How old are you?" This further confirmed that I was surely going to hell. When I responded, "I'm seven years old Father," I thought for sure he must be hard of hearing because now he was yelling about losing my immortal soul!

Since the confessional door was open, I was sure that everyone in the church could hear that I was a sinner about to lose my immortal soul. He obviously must have assumed the worst because my penance was to say an entire rosary and promise to never conduct myself like that again. Utterly embarrassed, I walked up to the large altar rail and said my penance which took about twenty minutes. Needless to say, Rocco and Bob were infuriated with having to wait so long. But hell, my immortal soul was at stake!

Slay Riding St Anselms was within easy walking distance from our house. We would walk up 83rd St.to Ridge Boulevard, continuing up a very steep street, the first half of which was lined with cobblestones, unlike any other street. During the winter, since the plows had difficulty clearing the snow off the cobblestones, it was very difficult for cars to climb. This made it ideal for slay riding, but potentially dangerous. Consequently, we positioned someone at the bottom of the hill to signal if any cars were approaching the intersection of Ridge Boulevard and 83rd St.

Mr. Leibowitz Speaking of the cobblestone street reminds me of one particularly cold morning, when our neighbor, Mr. Leibowitz, took pity on Nick and me by offering to drive us up to school. He even had the car running and warm. My friend Stevie sat in the front passenger seat and Nick and I sat in the backseat. Shortly after leaving home we noticed that Mr. Leibowitz had a bad cold with a deep cough and an obvious postnasal drip.

While driving up the cobblestone street, after several aborted attempts, Mr. Leibowitz finally managed to bring up a copious amount of phlegm from down around his toes. Then he turned his head in order to spit the phlegm out his side window. In his haste, however, he failed to open the window, at which point Nick and I looked at each other and could hardly contain ourselves. With sleight of hand, Mr. Leibowitz made several vain attempts to mask the unsightly glob, I guess, expecting that it would somehow mysteriously disappear! In desperation he rolled the window up and down several times which only made matters worse! Thank God we arrived at our school before we peed our pants!

Green Peas   Under normal circumstances, we usually walked home for lunch, which took about 15 minutes each way - allowing 30 minutes to eat. One afternoon, in addition to a half sandwich, my mother also cooked green peas which I hated. I readily ate my sandwich but dispersed the peas on my plate. Noticing this clever maneuver, my mother merely took a fork and re-gathered all the peas into one pile and said, "Now finish your peas!"

Realizing that I was running out of time, I said, "I have to go to the bathroom!" When she wasn't looking, I quickly shoved the peas into my mouth and ran into the kitchen bathroom, spitting the peas into the toilet bowl. Not to be outdone, however, when Mom saw my clean plate she simply said, "I told you you'd like them!" Then after putting another heaping spoonful on my plate she said, "Next time I'll make you more!"

Collection Baskets   We had special Sunday envelopes for the collection baskets. One Sunday I didn't have any money for my envelope, so I asked my father for some change. He told me to check in the small inner change pocket of his suit jacket. However, Dad also carried various vitamins, especially Vitamin C tablets, in this small change pocket. Being that I was in a hurry and at a loss for a solution to this dilemma, I took the vitamin C tablets and stuffed them in the collection envelope. During Mass, when it was time to pass the collection basket, Sister Ermingale seemed very impressed with the weightiness of my envelope, and naturally assumed it was a very generous offering. That is until she opened the envelope and found the vitamins, which took a lot of explaining.

Altar Boys   It was common for the sixth and seventh graders to be selected as altar boys, which required memorizing the Confiteor Dei. Much to my surprise and dismay, I was somehow selected. During one particular practice session, however, not having memorized the required text, while kneeling reverently on the altar, I tried to imitate my fellow altar server. I noticed that, at some point, he bent all the way forward at the waist and began swaying from side to side while mumbling something totally foreign to me. So, while doing my best to imitate him, at some point, Sr Ermingale bent over trying to listen to what I was saying, which was truly pure *gibberish*.

Utterly bewildered, she asked me to repeat *my version* of the Confiteor. When I repeated a slightly different version of *gibberish*, she rudely interrupted me and informed me that my altar services were no longer needed. When I came home earlier than expected, my mother asked, "Does your uniform have to be pressed?" I said, "Oh, I don't think that it'll be necessary" Then she asked, "Well. did you bring them home?" And I responded *somewhat* truthfully, "Since they had enough altar boys, Sister said, 'my services wouldn't be needed'"

Crossing Guards   After climbing the steep cobblestone portion of 83rd St, the remainder of the street was relatively flat to the light on the corner of 3rd Ave. After crossing the wide intersection, halfway down the block, our school was located on the corner of 83rd St and 4th Ave. The 3rd and 4th avenue intersections were quite busy and some of the more *responsible* eighth graders were chosen to be official *Crossing Guards, wearing bright yellow vests*. For some strange reason, however, I was never chosen to be a crossing guard.

Bay Ridge Mansions   As with much of Bay Ridge, the corner homes in this particular intersection was immense. Each home occupied one half of Ridge Boulevard. The one on the left was always immaculately landscaped, with a huge pink magnolia tree and a partially underground garage housing a chauffeured limousine. The one on the right was a large beige three-story stucco Mansion well hidden behind a 15' high wall. The interior courtyard was accessed through tall heavy wooden doors that were always closed. This mysterious compound was rumored to be owned by someone in the Mafia.

The other 8311   The house on the corner of Ridge Boulevard and 82nd st was an exceptionally large wood frame white Mansion, with a large two-story portico supported by four enormous round pillars. Being perched high on a hill, it was highly visible and accessed by a series of granite stairways. It also had an underground garage on 82nd St. which also housed a chauffeured limousine. Ironically, the house number of the Mansion was also 8311, which was the only similarity to our house.

Fr Ilardi   Once my father invited an old childhood Gonzaga friend, Fr Ilardi SJ, to our house for dinner. However, not being familiar with the area, he drove around for a while in search of our house. Finally, upon seeing 8311 on the granite steps, he assumed it must be our house. As he was climbing the granite stairway, he thought to himself, "God bless you, Caesar, you've come a long way!"

Then, while standing under the gracious portico, when he rang the doorbell chimes and was greeted by a butler, he was taken aback! At a loss, when he explained the purpose for his visit, the butler politely informed him of the *other* 8311. When he finally arrived at our house, he apologized for being late and simply laughed saying, "Now this is more like the Caesar I knew!" It wasn't until during dinner that he explained the embarrassing reason for his delay.

CH - 6
SISTER ERMINGALE

The class sizes were typically in the mid-50s. For the first two years, I mostly attended split *A & B Sessions* - with the A session in the morning and B sessions in the afternoon. Strict discipline, especially by the Nuns, was the norm, never to be questioned and readily enforced by a lightning swat with a wooden ruler.

Remedial Reading   Unfortunately, I was cursed with Sr. Ermingale from the 3rd through 5th grades. I was never a strong student. As a matter of fact, In the 5th grade, I was considered so stupid that, Sister Ermingale arranged for the equivalent of, *Remedial Reading* sessions, which required me to sit in the last row of the 3rd-grade classroom. Just think of the humiliation of a fifth-grade body trying to fit into a third-grade bench seat. At the time, I don't know if Dyslexia was even in the dictionary, but while attempting to read, I was aware of constantly scanning sentences from right to left.

The Coat Room   In the back of each classroom was a *Coat Room* which had two entrances- enter on the right and exit on the left. In addition to being cracked with a ruler or having your hair pulled, a common punishment for misbehaving would be to sit in a back corner of the Coatroom. I remember spending a lot of time out of sight in the coatroom! To humiliate me further, once Sister Ermingale told me to stand in the back of the room facing the window, - which actually wasn't so bad, because I would daydream while gazing out the window. When she got wise to this, however, she had me sit on a high stool facing the corner of the room while wearing a pointed "Dunce Hat"

Air Raid Drills   Speaking of the Coat Rooms, during the Korean war, I still remember the Air Raid routines. There were two different procedures. Considering that the coat rooms were way too small to accommodate all 52 students, we were initially told to hide under our desks. Later on, however, we were directed to exit our classrooms in a silent orderly fashion into the hallway corridors and instructed to sit against the walls with our heads down.

At the time I didn't understand the true gravity of the situation, but nonetheless, it was still very frightening. Years later, facing the constant threat of the atomic age, I remember the frenzy of preparing for the worst. This included stockpiling very sophisticated atomic bomb shelter stocked with the bare essentials to sustain a prolonged period under ground.

Nasal Ritual   I always watched with amusement and wondered if the nuns had taken a course in the Convent on how to efficiently blow and clean their nostrils in public, because they all did it exactly the same way. First, retrieve the handkerchief hidden in their pendulous habit sleeve. Next, the initial delicate blow, then inserting one finger in each nostril followed by a simultaneous bimanual circular rotation in opposite directions!

It was on such an occasion when sister Ermingale had the courtesy of turning around before going through this interesting maneuver. However, while her back was turned away from us, she inadvertently and unwittingly caught her upper lip under her upper dentures. After completing the mission at hand, and turning around to face the class, those of us sitting in front, began snickering upon seeing her unfortunate mishap.

Realizing there was a problem, Sister quickly turned around in order to rectify the situation. Ironically, because she considered me *learning disabled*, Sister assigned me to sit in the first row with the *smart kids*. So, just in case those in the back didn't see the show, while she was turned around, I simulated her unfortunate mishap by tucking my upper lip inwardly above my gum line and then turned around for the rest of the class to see. This, of course, caused the snickering resume!

Upon turning around, she was obviously befuddled by the persistent snickering, and immediately turned around again to recheck her upper lip. I thought, "Sister, that's what you get for sending me for remedial reading!" Incidentally, my wife, who was also taught by nuns, cleans her nose with the same circular motion as Sr. Ermingale, producing hair raising flashbacks!

Perhaps purely coincidental, but following this incident, Sister Ermingale had the audacity to phone our house asking to speak with my mother. Since I was the one who answered the phone, I decided to listen-in on the conversation. Sister proceeded to give my mother a lecture on child-rearing and appropriate discipline, repeatedly saying, "Now my dear, when it comes to discipline, don't spare the rod". My mother politely explained, "Trust me, Sister, after raising seven children, I don't use the rod, I use a wooden spoon!" After which sister Ermingale just gasped!

Report Cards   Obviously, my grades were borderline horrible. Although it was required to have a parent sign your monthly report card, by the fourth grade I had mastered the signatures of both my parents. My philosophy was, "If they didn't ask, I didn't show them," and simply handed them in beautifully signed. This *might have been* one of the reasons sister Ermingale asked to see both my parents and me in the convent house. I was amazed when my parents consented, and thus we all stood in a small crowded room facing the 5-foot witch.

The two issues at hand were my conduct and my grades. The first was known, but the issue of poor grades was a mystery. Thankfully, neither of them acknowledged not having seen my report cards. As Sister lectured both my parents, my father pretended to appear mesmerized by the little sister. However, when he began his Jackie Gleason ocular bulge and gyrations, I couldn't help but start laughing. This further infuriated the good Sister saying, "Young man, do you think this is funny?"

The Middle Finger I also blame sister Ermingale for a permanent deformity of my right middle finger. She was notorious for assigning ridiculous non-instructive punishments. I remember one particular infraction when my classmate, Joseph Awamy and I were caught talking in class. True to form, we were each assigned the punishment of writing, "I should not talk in class," 5000 times. Being very ingenious we decided to use five sheets of paper separated by three sheets of carbon paper!

This, of course, required us to press extremely hard in order to penetrate the last page. As a result of pressing down hard for several hours, I gradually developed severe pain and swelling of the distal (farthest joint) of my right middle finger. It took about four weeks for the pain to subside, but the swelling persisted much longer, and my finger remained permanently curved. To this day, when I raise my middle finger and look at the tip, I think of sister Ermingale!

Faulty Habit   I continued to view poor little, Sr. Ermingale as my perpetual nemesis which, I suspect, was mutual. She would often walk up and down the narrow classroom aisles carrying her wooden ruler with her black habit trailing far behind her short stature. She would peer over the shoulder of each student to assess their work while tapping her menacing weapon in her left hand.

When she finally got to my desk however, she stopped for an inordinate amount of time, scrutinizing my work. Then, after several disapproving grunts, she thankfully started to slowly walk away. Still, in striking distance and wondering what her hair looks like, under that silly habit, my shoe *accidentally* stepped on the back of her trailing habit, pulling the front portion of her habit partially exposing a bald head. Needless to say, despite my lame apology, she was apoplectic with justifiable rage.

First Love   By the end of the fifth grade, I eventually turned the corner and actually enjoyed Mrs. Barrett's sixth grade class. The highlight was traveling by train to the New York Planetarium. Also, the fact that I finally noticed that there were girls in my class, might have had something to do with it. In fact, there was one particular girl who caught my eye, Bernadette Maglino. I thought she was the young equivalent of the Italian bombshell, Gina Lollobrgida. At some point we were told that, in the seventh grade we would be rotating our seats, and I religiously prayed that somehow I would get to sit next to the love of my life, "Gina" Maglino

Sundays   While in Brooklyn, I don't remember my father ever attending Sunday mass or any other day for that matter. However, he always enforced our attendance. My mother, on the other hand, had a nightly ritual of saying the rosary and a special novena, followed by two Anacin tablets before going to sleep. She would also walk up to church each morning in order to attend the 6 am mass and be back home in time to make breakfast for everyone. I remember one morning, her telling us that, while walking home from church a plainclothes cop drove by and concerned for her safety, he pulled over and offered to drive her home - would never happen today!

Now, that's not to say that my father was less of a Catholic or Christian than my mother, it was perhaps, just less visible. He seemed less concerned with how we were dressed for church, saying, "God looks at your soul, not what you're wearing". Considering my oversized school uniform, I thought that gave me a pass. However, my mother didn't share his sentiments, and insisted that we look presentable and suitably dressed for the occasion.

Some things you never forget! I still remember coming home from church on Sunday mornings and upon opening the door, being greeted with the familiar aroma of simmering tomato sauce (not gravy). This was quickly followed by the irresistible urge to begin the ritual of dipping the warm semolina bread into the sauce and inhaling one or two freshly cooked meatballs smothered with grated Locatelli cheese. Sometimes, if my mother pre-baked the meatballs before putting them in the sauce, I would have a choice of eating either the pre-baked meatballs or smothering them in the hot sauce. Either way, it was absolutely delicious and just a prelude of the larger meal to come.

CH - 7
THE JOURNEY

The journey from Bay Ridge to Monroe (the country), began on the Gowanus Expressway to the Brooklyn Battery Tunnel. On the approach to the tunnel, to the left was a highly visible, five-story industrial building, on the top of which was a large red sign, E J Trum. In fact, the large red" R "is still standing and is considered a Red Hook historic landmark.

The BB Tunnel The toll booths for the Brooklyn Battery (BB) tunnel were manned by uniformed police officers whose names were displayed just below the collection window. Knowing this, as my father pulled up to the window, he would invariably ask the officer, "Good morning Sgt. Jones. How's business today?" after which the attendant would usually say, "Pretty good sir", leaving us to assume, "Dad must be one of the owners of the tunnel!" - an assumption he never bothered to dispel.

Occasionally, while waiting on the long toll line, Dad would purposely tap the rear bumper of the car in front of us lightly, of course, pretending that it was a mistake. Seeing how easy this was, we would often encourage him to do it again! On one such occasion, the other driver got out of his car and quickly approached us with a very menacing demeanor.

Then, upon seeing my two gorilla brothers in the front seat, he simply waved, as if to say, "Everything's ok" and without turning around, he walked slowly back to his car. Also, while driving through the tunnel, if the traffic was particularly slow in our lane, despite the double lines, Dad could easily be convinced to switch lanes. Upon exiting the tunnel, we would gradually make our way onto the elevated portion of the Henry Hudson Parkway which led to the George Washington bridge.

Riley's Market My father's office was at 291 Broadway, in lower Manhattan. Before leaving for Monroe, we would invariably stop at Riley's fruit market located in the Bowery section, under the elevated portion of the Henry Hudson Parkway. Dad was a particularly good, long-standing customer, usually placing a large order for the weekend.

At times, when he felt that the service was too slow, if he spotted some homeless men walking on the other side of the street, he would get Riley's attention by yelling, "Hey there, Riley is giving away free fruit!" Upon seeing the men crossing the street, Riley would yell to the nearest worker, "Take care of the counselor right away!". Consequently, on the way up to Monroe, the trunk would be filled with fruit, and on the way down, it was filled with the weekend garbage!

Henry Hudson Parkway (HHP) My father always drove a large sedan which meant that as many as nine passengers would be crammed into a hot car with wool seats for 2 to 3 hours. I would often lie on the large shelf ledge below the rear window and my mother would always ride in the back with a brown paper bag handy. The hot summer traffic on the HHP was always predictably slow, and the stop and go motion would invariably cause someone to yell, "Dad pull over!" - and out came the handy brown paper bag. And if we were acting up, Dad would yell, "Don't make me pull the car over!" However, considering that we were usually on congested highways, we soon learned that it was a vale threat.

One brutally hot summer evening and all the windows down, as the car next to us crept past, the driver looked at my father, sweating in his white guinea tee shirt, squished in the crowded sedan, and just shook his head sympathetically. Upon seeing the driver's sympathetic expression, Dad said, "Yea, and there's four more at home!"

After crossing the George Washington Bridge, we would travel northward on Rt 17 for about 90 minutes to Monroe NY. At the time, Rt 17 was a simple two-lane highway with a wide grassed center median. I distinctly remember noticing the stark contrast once we entered Fort Lee

NJ. - the pleasant cooling effect of the evening dew, and the distinctive smell of freshly cut grass on the median. If my father and I were traveling alone, this would be the time when I would tap his knee, which was our signal to allow me to press on the gas pedal for most of the way to Monroe.

At a young age, he taught me how to regulate the car speed in order to provide a smooth journey. He usually had a cup holder on the dashboard held firmly in place by a sand-filled bag on the bottom. After filling the cup with water to within an inch of the top, he would tell me to try and *smoothly* adjust the car speed without spilling the water. To this day I think about that lesson and find that, along with poor eyesight and slow reflexes, it moderates my driving speed considerably.

Before completion of the New York State Thruway, the last portion of the long journey entailed, driving slowly through all the small towns and villages on the narrow two-lane highway. Once we passed the roadside landmark, Red Apple Rest, we knew it was only another twenty minutes before we would arrive in the small village of Monroe.

The Red Apple Rest   En route to Monroe was a famous bus stop restaurant called the Red Apple Rest. It featured a long outdoor counter with a huge metal grill filled with the most delicious long hot dogs. The counters had large silver containers filled with either horseradish, mustard, or sauerkraut. It was very similar to Nathan's large counter on Coney Island, and being that Dad loved them as much as we did, it didn't take much to coax him to pull over - of course, subject to his artful negotiation for a volume discount. Despite the lengthy journey, once we smelled the familiar fragrance of the country, the long trip was always worth it!

Grand Opening   This brings to mind a similar fast food restaurant in Ramsey NJ. While driving south on Rt 17, my father noticed a large outdoor banner advertising a Grand Opening! Never one to pass up a golden opportunity, with seven of us in the car, my father pulled over to try it out. While the others waited in the car, the excited proprietor greeted my father and me warmly, explaining that he was celebrating his first week of business and welcomed our patronage.

Dad proceeded to place an order for the seven of us, but upon hearing the total price, began to negotiate with the owner. The man emphasized that the hot dogs and hamburgers came with *all the Fixings*, including, catsup, mustard, relish, pickles, sauerkraut, etc. and that he really couldn't discount the price - even considering the large order.

Apparently, Dad noticed that, despite the paucity of customers, the service seemed to be awfully slow. When he suggested that, as a business inducement, perhaps the man should consider offering a *money back guarantee* if not satisfied with the service. The man quickly replied, "Yea, then I'd probably have to buy a second cash register, one to take the money, and the other, to give it back!"

Sensing the apparent impasse, after placing an order for seven hot dogs, and confirming that all the fixings were unlimited, Dad asked the man for seven paper cups. When the man asked, "What kind of sodas would you like?" Dad replied, "None thank you", and told me to start filling the cups with the various *Fixings*. Upon seeing this, the poor dumbfounded man reconsidered a discount.

CH - 8
MONROE NY

While growing up we were truly blessed with the Best *of both worlds*, Bay Ridge and Monroe NY. Monroe was our home away from home, located in the foothills of the beautiful Catskill mountains in Orange County NY. This little *Slice of heaven was* commonly referred to as, *The Country* or *Upstate.*

During the summer we lived in Cottage 10, a lovely white clapboard house in a private lakeside community known as Idle Hour Park (IHP). The Cottage was purchased by my parents in 1940, approximately two years before moving from 45th St to Colonial Rd.

Incidentally, Monroe was not entirely unfamiliar to my father. As an adolescent, he spent several weeks during the summer at a Jesuit Retreat House known as Gonzaga. This "Get *the kids out of the City*" initiative was co-sponsored by Fr Dominic and Fr. Walsh, to enable kids from Manhattan's Nativity parish to experience the health and beauty of *The Country*

My father originally rented a house owned by Frank Grande, which was on the far-right corner, three houses from cottage 10. As the story goes, although my siblings enjoyed getting out of the city, the Grande house had snakes under the front porch. Consequently, after one or two seasons, Fr. Dominic encouraged my father to purchase Cottage 10.

The entrance to the private Park was accessed through two majestic fieldstone pillars which supported an arched wrought iron sign, *Idle Hour Park*. The narrow interior roadway had three major sharp turns - the first was a steep ascending hairpin turn directly in front of the Trum's house. The second equally steep turn descended sharply in front of Silverstein's house and the third descending turn wrapped around the far corner of the Clark estate.

The Trums   As I mentioned previously, the Trums owned a third generation, five-story folding box factory, in the Red Hook section of Brooklyn. They were known to be affluent, having several horse stalls and paddocks on their Park property. Walter Trum was an accomplished equestrian, having had a riding academy at an early age while living on his parent's 100-acre gentleman's farm in Monroe.

They signaled their summer arrival with telltale horse manure on the roadway leading to their house. Walter and Virginia also had 7 children, some of whom were roughly the same age as some of my siblings. The oldest, Patricia (Pat), was close in age to Caesar, Kip was close to Nick and George was a year older and Mary Margaret (MM) 2 years younger than me. MM's sister, Roberta, her brother, Dennis, and another sister, Susie, were all younger than me. Both Walter and Virginia were unusually tall, Walter being 6'2" with a deep intimidating gruff voice and, Virginia, an intelligent elegant woman being, 5'11".

The standoff   As I mentioned, the roadways within the Park were extremely narrow, accommodating only one car in one direction. Being that the first and most difficult turn was directly in front of the Trum's house, despite the posted one-way signs, Mr. Trum (Walter) would occasionally decide to take a shorter route by going down the steep turn rather than up and around the hill. I remember one particular occasion when my father and I encountered Walter coming down the wrong way. This led to a prolonged and uncomfortable *Standoff*, each of them refusing to back down. After a lengthy period of staring at each other, Walter eventually decided to back up and go the right way.

The Silversteins   The second turn was in front of Silverstein's house where Judith and Freddie lived. This was a particularly beautiful, unique fieldstone house, one of only three homes in the park, constructed of stone - the other two were McCarthy and Vaccaro's brick homes. The interior of Silverstein's house featured a heavy log beam construction and a side staircase leading to a balcony overlooking the living room highlighted by a beautiful fieldstone fireplace. Whereas virtually all the other homes in the park were considered wood frame *Cottages,* Silverstein's house was initially inhabited by somebody particularly important.

Each year Dr. and Mrs. Silverstein would host and choreograph a Broadway play in their living room. The cast consisted of the kids in the Park and well attended by the proud parents. To the left of their house was a vacant lot with an overgrown pathway providing convenient access to an adjacent private park, Lake View Estates, where our good friends, Howie and Philip Umansky lived.

The Monte Carlo   Occupying a prime six-acre parcel in the center of the park was, the Monte Carlo, a stately four-story, 250 room Greek Hotel. It was considered the premier Greek hotel on the east coast, featuring elaborate dining, private gambling and the top Greek entertainers providing festive Greek dancing.

Prior to becoming a hotel, however, the large white wood framed structure was a private school and most of the surrounding Cottages were uninsulated clapboard homes for the teachers. Being perched high atop the highest hill in the Park, the massive structure had a commanding view of Walton Lake down below. It had a striking red asphalt roof that had an impressive four- story Dutch colonial extension over the main entrance. Beneath the extension was a long highly polished front porch lined with Adirondack chairs, providing a cool relaxing view two acres of manicured lawn and the pristine lake below

Monte Carlo Hotel

Mr. Panos   The proprietor of the hotel, Mr. Panos, was a tall handsome man sporting a thin finely trimmed mustache. He was always dressed immaculately, often wearing a colorful jacket with light tan pants and two-tone spectator shoes. The front lawn had small clusters of umbrellas and chaise lounges scattered around the tennis courts and a fence enclosed, 60 x 24-foot swimming pool.

I Remember both Rocco and Caesar working as lifeguards at the pool which eventually paved the way for my father to transition his swimming lessons from the Idle Hour dock to the hotel's pool which would prove to be a more convenient setting for early morning lessons.

Greek Talk   In addition to the Monte Carlo, there was another, infinitely smaller, Greek hotel known as Castelles. It was nicely secluded on a five-acre parcel in the rear corner of Idle Hour Park. Given its small size, it mostly depended on overflow guests from Monte Carlo. At dusk, the hotel guests, especially the ladies, would often stroll the roadway between the two hotels, dressed to the nines and wreaking perfume.

While driving around the Park, if my father spotted them walking, he would invariably pull the car up slowly beside them to ostensibly, ask for directions to the Hotel in unintelligible Greek saying, "chelevecous on de Vue, Hotel Monte Carlo?". Upon hearing the magic words, Monte Carlo, they would gleefully respond in unintelligible Greek while pointing in the right direction. His ruse accomplished, Dad would smile, nod his head, and simply say, "thank you" and drive off. I don't know why we always encouraged him to do it, but he would always oblige us.

On weekends, especially during the evenings, the hotel guests always managed to park their cars at least halfway in the roadside ditches. Then, come morning, my friends and I would offer to help push their cars out of the ditch. It was an opportunity to make some easy money, and the more we grunted and groaned, the higher the price!

The Baccis   The left side of the Monte Carlo's lawn was lined with beautiful large weeping willow trees which provided additional privacy. Diagonally across the road on the right and perched high on a hill, was a beautiful white house with a wraparound porch providing spectacular views of the lake. The house was owned by the Baccis, dear friends of my parents and home to my childhood friends, Bridget, and Roy.

The Bacci brothers and their brother-in-law, Jess Tempone, were lifelong friends of my parents. I believe Tony Bacci was my father's best man at my parent's wedding. Jess' occupation was as the front bartender at several of the finest New York hotels. I remember his impressive size and stature. He wore a large pinky ring and a gold neck chain, and being a heavy smoker, he had a deep, gravelly voice and a distinctive laugh. Later on, they would play an important role related to the Castelle Greek Hotel.

The Mirendas   The Mirenda brothers, Freddie and Rusty, lived in the same general area as the Baccis. I was particularly fond of Rusty, who, aside from being handsome, was also a talented musician who readily entertained everyone by singing while playing his guitar. One of Nick's distant friends, Vinny Bellela, also lived in the same general area.

CH - 9
COTTAGE 10

Cottage 10 was a well-proportioned two-story white clapboard summer home, with stately round white columns resting on the edge of a porch that extended on three sides of the house - the front and both sides. It was a pretty house, with nice simple lines and solid bones. I usually reserve the adjective, pretty, for a lady, and on reflection, a *Pretty Lady* aptly describes Cottage 10.

Cottage 10

The front entrance was marked by two large umbrella trees on either side of a long walkway paved with large turquoise patio blocks leading to wide porch steps and the front door. The left side porch welcomed the radiant early morning sun, and in addition to a small coffee table and two chairs, a canvas hammock hung from the left corner pillar to the house. Lacking a railing added to its open dimension, and my father would often bask in the morning sun, sipping coffee while reading a newspaper.

On the right side, a screen door opened to an enclosed screen porch, which provided for many memorable *alfresco* dinners during the hot summer evenings. To the right of the house, two very tall evergreen trees marked the entrance to the driveway which extended back to a large wood framed garage with double front doors and a perpetually sagging roof.

The front door opened to a nice sized living room with a large fieldstone fireplace atop of which was mounted an eight-point Buck deer head. While staring at the lowly fixture, I would crack up when my father would occasionally start singing the song, "I ain't got nobody!" Standing upright against the far-right wall was a, mostly out of tune, white piano. I remember my brothers eventually carrying the piano across the road and disposing of it deep in the woods. To the left was a staircase with an initial three-step landing, in the corner of which stood a tall grandfather clock. The stairs ascended to a second landing which, upon turning right led to the center of the house.

There were separate passageways on both sides of the living room fireplace. The one on the left led to a moderately sized kitchen, and the one on the right led to a large dining room with three bay windows, and a doorway that led to an enclosed *Porch bedroom* occupied by Rocco and Caesar. This bedroom also served as a passageway to a second, screened in *al fresco* Dining area.

As with most households, the kitchen was the *Hub,* and the internal circle was completed by a large passageway to the dining room, thereby connecting all three essential rooms. But the kitchen also had three additional doorways. A back-entry door, one on the left leading to a small single bedroom and a third opening to a winding staircase with a tiny landing for the hot water heater and ultimately leading down to the basement.

Our Basement was very unique, in that it constantly had 2 feet of crystal clear, ice cold spring water supplied by an underground stream that crossed our lawn on the left side. This unique happenstance, however, also provided constant coolness of the first floor, especially in the kitchen - passive air conditioning way before it's time! It was cold enough to refrigerate an oversupply of milk or other beverages or to fill the toilet tank if the Park's water pump failed. The only downside was that, in addition to the audible "ribbit" *sound* of the frogs, the rocks and dirt floor made it otherwise unusable.

Although this was not the original layout of the Cottage, it's the one that I recall. I was told, however, that with Nick Santella's enduring patience and superb carpentry skills, it was mostly the result of my mother's fertile imagination and assertive ingenuity. Nick was truly a Godsend, with a seemingly unlimited skill set including, carpentry, electrical, plumbing, and mechanical expertise. The weekday demolition projects were usually initiated by my mother's familiar prefix, *Just* (Just do this or that), which was eventually adopted by my sister Anita. I've been told that, on Wednesday evenings, when my father would arrive from the city, the impromptu renovations weren't always a *welcome home surprise*. In fact, It took him several days of re-orientation!

I believe it was my mother's penchant for spontaneous demolition and renovation that would inevitably become a common hallmark for all of us - sometimes just for the sake of tackling a challenge, often bordering on reckless abandon! However, I also noticed from personal experience that this sudden surge of creativity seemed to occur more often during times of boredom or emotional stress - a means of mindless coping.

The Second-floor landing had three bedrooms and one small bathroom with a claw foot tub. Considering that we swam in the lake every day and used the outdoor shower on the left rear corner of the garage, I doubt it was ever used. To the right of the bathroom was a very large bedroom that spanned the entire front of the house with two double beds and one single bed. To the left were two bedrooms. My parent's bedroom in the left corner overlooked a large garden behind the house and another bedroom on the right corner had a single double bed.

The Park's hilltop plateau of quarter-acre parcels always appeared well cared for, with manicured lawns devoid of visible barriers. And if there was a barrier, it was no more than a low well-trimmed hedge line. When viewing this swath of green from the back of cottage 10, it always evoked a pleasing sense of pastoral openness.

Our Lawnmower   Speaking of manicured lawns we had a fairly large lawn and a *special,* pull start, gas-powered reel mower, with separate controls for the throttle and wheel speed. From our limited perspective, this was considered *state of the art.*

At a very young age, I was into building saltbox racers, using large carriage wheels and axles, with a round wooden barrel front and rope rigging for a steering wheel and back hand brake. This, of course, required either a steep hill or someone to push. I remember imagining how neat it would be if the lawnmower engine could somehow be used to power my racer! So, while cutting the lawn, I would race that mower at full throttle, causing the wheels to spin on the grass or gravel, envisioning it as propelling my racer. My delusional revelry ended abruptly when I heard, "Peter, what the hell are you doing!"

Neighbors   Our neighbors on the right were Joe and Ann Persichetti and their three children, Bobby, his younger brother, Richie, and their youngest Anna. Bobby and I were so inseparable that we even tried to connect our bedrooms, by using a long string with a tin can on both ends in order to talk to each other, but it never worked. Other than sleeping at night, we spent the rest of the day outdoors in the sun, either swimming in the lake or building forts in the woods, which invariably resulted in a seasonal variety of poison ivy, oak, or sumac. By mid-summer, our constant sun exposure produced very dark tans which presently keeps my dermatologist very busy!

Ironically, since Ann's maiden surname was Bergio, she was more often referred to as Ann Bergio. She was considerably taller than her husband, Joe Persichetti, who worked for the US Postal Service, and was a gifted baseball and softball player. I remember when Ann would kiss each of her kids. It was apparently with so much suction that the distinctive sound was clearly heard from next door.

Blueberries   Very early in the morning, after donning special overalls, Ann and my mother would go trekking in the woods to pick blueberries and arriving back home just in time for breakfast. This weekly mission ended abruptly, however, when my mother reached into a bush loaded with berries and noticed a coiled black snake sunning itself on one of the branches! That was the end of the fresh blueberry treats.

Sal Bergio   Ann had two brothers, Charles, and Salvatore (aka Sal) Bergio. Sal was blessed with a 6' 3" muscular frame, exhibiting brute strength and graced with Rock Hudson's looks! And he fit the part perfectly, always driving a flashy Cadillac convertible matched with a magnetic smile that attracted just about any female he desired.

Considering that Sal was older and more worldly, it was understandable that he became Rocco's idol and role model. Likewise, Sal was very fond of his young protege. I remember, regardless of the hour, as soon as Sal arrived next door to visit his sister, I would hear him yelling across the lawn for Rocco to get out of bed. In the future, Sal's genuine friendship and silent allegiance remained steadfast and his timely assistance in times of need was very much appreciated.

The Grandes   To the right of the Persichettis was Luke Sr. (aka Old Man) Grande's house which occupied the right lower corner, and his son, Frank, occupied the house in the right upper corner. While tending to his small grape vineyard, the old man would often carry a long stick fashioned with a fork at one end used as a deterrent for occasional snakes sunning themselves on the vines, and he encouraged us to do the same! I remember my mother often consulting with his wife, Ma Grandy, for her sage advice, especially regarding old household and medicinal remedies.

Frank's son, Luke, was a physician as was Frank's brother, John Grande, who had a home office in the Park Slope section of Brooklyn. He served as our family physician, and as a personal favor, he occasionally made house calls to 8311. I remember that he had a thick mustache and a peculiar nervous tick which triggered a sudden salvo of uncontrollable blinking. I barely remember a third brother, Victor. He only visited occasionally, always appearing well dressed, wearing brown and white spectator shoes, and sporting a well-trimmed thin mustache.

On the corner directly behind the Persichetti's and across from, Frank Grandy were the Chiaramontes. Lou was a masonry contractor who helped lay a cement patio behind cottage 10.

Directly behind our house were the Bilardy brothers, Jim, and Joe. Although Jimmy was a painter by profession, he was also a jack of all trades, and despite the fact that his house always appeared in total disarray with several unfinished projects, he was always willing to lend a helping hand to others.

Their property had a round fieldstone pond on their back lawn which I was told, was used by the prior owner, Jerry Ray, as a small swimming pond. I have a vague recollection of Jerry, as being very flamboyant and very wealthy. Apparently, he did extremely well in the stock market, and he employed several black servants.

The Kowals   The Kowals lived to the left of our house. Jack Kowal was an executive in the shoe merchandising business, and his wife, Rhoda, smoked like a chimney. They had four children. Two sons, a very tall Physician, Jerry and a Rabbi, Martin. As well as two daughters, Ronnie, and Diane. Ronnie was a beautiful shapely young lady close in age to Rocco, and Diane was my age. Very early on, I often played *pick-up-sticks* with Diane on her front porch. They had a miniature house in the left rear corner of their property, known as the *Dollhouse*.

They also owned a quarter-acre parcel of barren field directly in front of their house, and on which, the local fathers and their teenage sons would occasionally play softball. Although I was only a spectator, I remember cutting the tall grass prior to the games, outlining the bases. To the left of the Kowels, were the Burks. They had twins, Bruce, and his sister Robin, who were around my age and with whom I also played.

The Poggies   The Poggies lived directly behind the Kowals and diagonally behind our house. The front of their house always had a colorful awning which provided welcome shade for the front porch. Mary Poggie had a garden the size of which rivaled my father's. Being roughly the same age as my father, she adored him, and he would seize every opportunity to tease her in a playful, albeit somewhat flirtatious, manner. Mary was married to a very mild-mannered quiet Dentist, and I think my father added a certain zest to her otherwise boring life.

Mrs. Poggie was always immaculately dressed, often wearing expensive jewelry. While gardening, she would often wear colorful print dresses with very revealing necklines. Considering the close proximity of our respective gardens, and being very well endowed, while bending over to pick her tomatoes she would inevitably expose her endowments even further. Upon seeing this, my father would yell, "Mary, cover up before you get sunburn!" to which she would just laugh exclaiming, "Oh Caesar, I didn't see you there!" which he knew wasn't true. Likewise, if she was bending over in the opposite direction, he would start singing, "When the moon comes over the mountain" loud enough for her to hear!

The Vaccaros   To the left of the Poggies was a handsome brick home owned by the Vaccaros. They had two children, Joel, and Claudia. Joel was Nick's age, and he and Kip Trum, were undoubtedly two of Nick's best Monroe friends. Claudia was a tall attractive slender girl who, unfortunately, was a year older than me. Once while on a picnic with several friends, I took particular note of her. But given our age difference and her elegant stature, she was clearly way out of my league.

Further down the road, and adjacent to the Monte Carlo's parking lot, were the DeSchrievers. Betty and Paul DeSchriever had two sons, Richie, and Pauly (aka"Bullets"). Directly across the road from the DeSchrievers, was a dull grey three-story vacant house, known only as, *The Haunted House*. It was situated at the rear of a large overgrown field, and I only remember walking through the scary house when in the company of several friends.

The property was eventually purchased and refurbished by a Greek family, the Skaletes. Eventually I befriended their son, Jimmy, who was a year older than me, and I remember him teaching me to play Monopoly on his screened side porch. He was a real pro and the games would last for hours.

On The Fence   One late Sunday afternoon in early September, I was trying to tag along with Nick, Joel Vaccaro, and Kip Trum, and they were trying their best to lose me by hopping over a barbed wire fence along the rear of the Galetti property. When they each made it over the fence unscathed, they quickly ran away. However, when I climbed over the fence and attempted to jump off, my right elbow got caught on the barbed wire! I could see them running away far in the distance, apparently unable to hear my screams. I remember feeling helpless, debating how to free myself. Exhausted, I finally decided to just jump, and I could feel the tear of flesh! When I noticed the deep 6"gash over my inner elbow, I started running up the road toward home.

Fortunately, the Persichettis happened to be driving by on their way home to Brooklyn when they spotted me running up the hill holding my bleeding elbow. After wrapping my elbow with a towel, they drove me back to cottage 10. Upon seeing the copious bleeding, my mother started to rinse the deep wound in the sink. At that point, when my father walked into the kitchen and glanced at the bloody gash, he immediately turned ashen, and the fragile man made a dash for the kitchen door.

My mother wrapped my arm tightly in a towel, and they drove me to Dr. Heusin's office in the village, above Palen's drugstore. He commented that I was lucky to have missed the (Brachial) artery. Then I became frantic when I realized that I was about to be stitched up! But he calmed my fear by gently saying, "Trust me, you won't feel any pain!"

He explained that, as a former naval doctor, he learned a *Secret* for painless suturing. He simply squirted a generous amount of Novocain into the wound, and patiently waited for about 5 to 10 minutes, after which he sutured the deep wound with absolutely no pain. I always remembered that painless experience. Many years later I came to realize that the *Secret* was threefold: the power of suggestion, use of a topical anesthetic and a modicum of patience - a *Secret* that I would eventually repeat many times over as a practicing physician.

The McCarthys   Mack and Mary McCarthy lived in a brick house set behind a well-trimmed hedge directly across the road from Cottage 10. They always had a well-manicured half acre lawn to the left of their house. Mr. McCarthy (aka, Mr. Mack) had the first riding lawnmower in the Park which, being mechanically inclined, he was always fixing in his immaculate driveway. He was also frequently called upon, or volunteered, to help with the Park's periodic water pump and pressure problems. Consequently, he was considered the resident *Pump Master.* He always drove the latest model Chrysler Imperial or Cadillac, and ironically, having posted 15 mph speed limit signs throughout the Park, he had the only car capable of navigating the steep hills while adhering to the self- imposed speed limit.

Buddy   The McCarthys had an only child, Buddy, who, unfortunately, suffered from juvenile diabetes resulting in total blindness. In spite of this, however, he was gifted with an uncanny spatial awareness and dexterity. I remember watching in amazement as he rewired an old lamp fixture while sitting at our kitchen table. However, his brittle diabetes was slowly taking its toll, and at some point, desperate for a miracle, Mrs. McCarthy had a beautiful statue of the Blessed Mother mounted on their lawn surrounded by a pretty flower bed. Buddy eventually succumbed to the ravages of his disease at a relatively young age.

Being that the stretch of road from the Kowels to the Persichetti's was originally dirt, we would periodically spray the dirt road with water in order to limit the dust from the passing cars. However, Mr. Mac would also bring up 50 -gallon barrels of smelly oil to spread on the dirt road. Consequently, shortly after its application, although it limited the dust, it gave off a strong noxious odor that lingered for several days, exacerbated by the heat and humidity.

Park Meetings   Being that the McCartney's lawn provided spaciousness and shade, they often hosted the Park's monthly homeowner meetings. I remember the large circle of chairs under the shade of a large maple tree, attended by mostly male homeowners. At times, the tenor of the meetings became very contentious. Inevitably, my father would become embroiled in an argument with Walter Trum. As a result of his Parkinson's disease, he developed a very deep voice and his 6' 2" stature made for an imposing figure which he often exploited.

Although he was very generous, Walter was also quite demanding, and although his bark was often worse than his bite, it wasn't readily tolerated by my father. Never intimidated by anyone, I believe Dad understood the difference between one who demands respect and one who commands respect. Their differences, however, were usually short-lived, and they eventually developed a close personal friendship based on mutual respect. Little did I know then that Walter would become an integral part of my future life.

The Orchard & Vineyard   Although my father was very proud of his fruit trees and Concord grapes, to call them an Orchard or Vineyard was a gross overstatement! Behind the house, the *Orchard* consisted of a single row of two peach and two cherry trees and a lowly green apple tree. Beyond the orchard, on a narrow swath of lawn was Dad's *Vineyard, which* consisted of a single row of Concorde grapes supported by two rows of wire fencing. The perimeter of Cottage 10 was lined with vibrant orange daylilies, and the lawns encompassed mostly the front and left side of the property extending just beyond the vineyard.

Unfortunately, the cherry trees always attracted bees, the cherries were mostly eaten by the birds and the apples were very tart. Similarly, the Vineyards' grape leaves attracted Japanese beetles! I was assigned the tedious job of manually removing those damn Beatles before they devoured the poor leaves. Consequently, the combined harvest was very scarce. However, what I remember most was the idyllic setting of a large picnic table set under the fruit trees and the outstretched arms of an immense oak tree providing shade for afternoon lunches or early dinners. During these hot summer days, my father enjoyed a sangria mix with fresh sliced peaches, pitted cherries, and his precious Concord grapes, crushed, and marinated in Ruffino Chianti.

Numerous attempts to deter the birds by spraying the cherry trees with an old-fashioned hand pump was not only ineffective, but I think the birds were actually emboldened by the challenge! One summer, being inundated with the damn Japanese beetles, I decided to also spray the grape leaves, which appeared to be surprisingly effective. Proud of my ingenuity, when my father filled his glass and took a swig of the delicious Sangria, with considerable drama, he immediately spit it out exclaiming, "Peter, what the hell did you do?" - so much for ingenuity!

Dad's Orchard

The Garden   To the right of the Vineyard and extending behind the garage was a large L shaped Garden. We knew it was time to plant the garden when, upon arriving late at night from the city, we were greeted by the pungent aroma of cow manure. Invariably, we always planted more tomato plants than we needed, yielding far more tomatoes than we could possibly consume. Consequently, at the end of the season, even after my mother Jared as many tomatoes as possible, we always had bushels left over.

Dad's Garden

My father assured me that, if I carted them around the hill in a wagon, the neighbors would surely appreciate them. And if I made a sign, "Garden fresh Tomatoes" they might even buy some! I can assure you that, despite his assertions, after dragging that damn wagon around the hill, that was never the case!

The Corn Field   One year, having negotiated a great deal, my father decided to grow delicious summer Corn. After patiently waiting for the corn stalks to sprout and gradually mature, they finally appeared ready for harvest. After excitedly husking the prized corn however, we were disappointed to find that most of the kernels were like nothing we've ever seen before and tasted even worse. We eventually learned that the reason my father got such a great deal was that he had unwittingly purchased feed corn.

I have very few pictures of my childhood or my parents, but as I sit here writing this memoir, I'm looking at two black-and-white photos that were recently given to me. They're of each of my parents standing separately in the famous Cornfield. My father is dressed in his customary gardening attire - good dress slacks and shoes, a white guinea T-shirt holding a hoe. He's smiling, apparently admiring the corn stalks. My mother is in a sundress with her hair pinned up and smiling adoringly while holding a stalk of the prized feed corn.

Dad and Mom in the infamous cornfield

The mighty Oak   As I mentioned, when in full bloom, the mighty Oak Tree's expansive limbs provided a welcome relief from the blazing sun. Its mere girth told you it was ancient. Sadly, however, over the course of two years, it began to show signs of withering, with its leaves gradually losing their vibrant color, followed by early shedding. My father called upon the services of Mr. Brower, an old farmer who was also a horticulturist. Despite trying a series of *Nutrient Injections*, for reasons unknown, the aging giant continued to decline signaling that nature had its own plan. Posing a potential destructive calamity, a decision was made to end its long life.

Fortunately, Ann Persichetti's two brothers, Sal, and Charles Bergio, were visiting their sister, and being older and more experienced than my brothers, they offered to assist with the monumental undertaking. Sal certainly had the superior strength, but Charles demonstrated fearless climbing agility, and appeared to know what he was doing. With only a couple of bow saws, branch by branch, they began to slowly dismantle the giant tree. Even with everyone's coordinated efforts, I think it took the entire weekend to complete the task.

Theirs was truly an act of selfless generosity and genuine friendship that I still remember to this day. I don't remember how they managed to saw through the immense trunk, but I remember trying to estimate the giant's age by counting the concentric rings. As a fitting repose, the remains of the giant's prominent base were surrounded by a flower garden, encircled by large rocks.

The Fragile Man   I believe my father's predilection for a large garden was rooted in his past. Unlike my mother, despite his youthful accomplishments, he was emotionally fragile. Shortly after the birth of my twin sisters, my father suffered a *nervous breakdown* of sorts, and Father Dominic arranged for him to stay at a *Retreat Facility* for approximately three months. Meanwhile, during this stressful time, despite her stoicism, my mother was grateful for the love and support of her own mother and her in-laws, Papa and Mama Ciri.

While at this treatment facility, part of his daily *therapy* was communing with nature through gardening, which played a vital role in his eventual recovery. Initially, his daily routine was to simply plant and care for several tomato plants each day. Over time, although the number of plants gradually increased, the importance of maintaining the same meticulous care was never to be compromised - in essence, a *baby step* approach to recovery.

Consequently, he would demonstrate the same method of gardening, emphasizing the importance of planting only five seedlings a day, and always repeating the same process - weeding followed by making a furrow around each seedling. Then adding fertilizer in the furrow through the hole in the bottom of a clay pot filled with Vigoro, and lastly, watering the furrows in the morning and evening.

Zia Carmela My father's elderly aunt, Zia Carmela, was a frequent house guest at Cottage 10. She was a heavy-set woman with a thick Italian accent. I don't know how, or even if, she was truly related, but Dad always treated her with respect, and by example, he expected us to do the same. For some reason, she was deathly afraid of lightning, and whenever an electrical storm occurred, she would go through the house pulling down all the shades and stand in the middle of the living room saying the rosary in Italian. I wasn't afraid of lightning until I spent such an evening with Zia Carmela!

She would also leave our house with far more than she came with - a large brown paper bag filled with fresh garden vegetables, especially zucchini (squash). While everyone was still asleep, she would routinely pick the vegetables very early in the morning, and squirrel them in her room concealed in the brown bag. However, her comical routine was well known by my father, as well as the rest of us. Although he would have gladly given her two bags full, I guess he just enjoyed watching the charade.

In any event, my parent's bedroom overlooked the garden, and on the evening before Carmella's covert operation, my father placed a watermelon in the Squash patch. Then early in the morning, he watched from his bedroom window as Carmella walked quietly through the garden selecting an assortment of vegetables until she eventually came upon the huge *Squash!* He laughed when she suddenly stopped in her tracks, and blessing herself exclaimed, "Gesù, Giuseppe e Maria"! (Jesus, Joseph, and Mary).

Jack Dubinsky Another memorable visitor to Cottage 10 was, Jack Dubinsky, a long- time friend of my father's. I remember him as being a charismatic pseudo successful sales executive for the Hormel company who, unfortunately, also suffered from a bipolar disorder.

He would often *just appear* unannounced, and If we weren't home, we would occasionally find a long salami or pepperoni hanging from the back-porch light- a telltale sign that he had paid a surprise visit! My father often said, "When Jack was on his game, he could sell the

Brooklyn Bridge!" However, when he was off, he was mostly destitute, often requiring hospitalization. Although he adored my father, I suspect that their relationship was mostly of a professional nature, with Jack often needing urgent legal advice.

The Garage   Our garage had a bowed roof and two double doors, presumably meant to accommodate two cars. However, to my knowledge, other than for repairs, we never stored or drove a car into the sagging garage, As I may have mentioned, there was a simple outdoor shower on the left rear corner of the garage with wooden slats resembling a palate on top of a bed of fieldstones for drainage. Since we never used the upstairs bathtub, we either washed in the lake or under the open shower. I doubt if it supplied hot water because I remember Nick and I often showering together in haste!

Incidentally, this memory prompted me to bid at an auction for a watercolor painting entitled Water Babies depicting two young boys showering outdoors while standing on wooden slats - which I still proudly display in my home,

Pre- Summer Season   The Pre-summer Season consisted of weekend visits to the *Country* from Memorial Day to the last week of June, after which the official *Summer Season* began, until the start of school around September 7th. Depending on the weather, this was followed by weekend visits for six to eight weeks. Although we had a propane gas heater, as with most of the homes in the Park, Cottage 10 wasn't winterized.

I clearly remember our first arrival at cottage 10 after the long cold winter. Upon opening the back door, the initial smell of camphor permeated the entire house, and was particularly prevalent when slithering into the ice-cold bed sheets. After such a long spell, the experience of once again seeing the brilliant bright stars unmarred by ambient light, and the unfamiliar sound of crickets, was truly unforgettable. Likewise, smelling the early morning dew on lush grass was such a stark contrast to City living - even in Bay Ridge!

CH - 10
THE MAGICAL PARK

It doesn't seem possible, but as much as I loved Bay Ridge, Monroe seemed even more magical, especially Idle Hour Park (IHP). Perhaps it was the anticipation of seeing friends I hadn't seen in nine months. Or the prospect of playing nine hours a day, swimming in the lake and building forts in the woods - without the distractions of school and homework. It was quite remarkable that the respective age group tiers that Nick and I had in Bay Ridge, we also had in Monroe. Interestingly, particularly in Idle Hour Park, this wasn't unique to us. It was also experienced by our older siblings! More importantly, the overall surroundings and sense of communal supervision were remarkably the same. Peer group safeguards meant- we each looked out for one another!

According to my older siblings, they and their friends had a somewhat different form of entertainment, such as simply walking around the Park at night or sitting on someone's front porch singing and harmonizing. And although I'm sure there was a fair amount of heartthrob, there wasn't much talk about love entanglements. In short, with perhaps my wife being a notable exception, just about everyone I know who experienced the magic of Idle Hour Park and Walton Lake has never forgotten it. And we all experience the same sense of revelry when recalling and sharing fond memories.

Somehow, the summers always seemed hotter, drier, and longer. Interestingly, the beginning of the summer season always seemed to move slowly, but by mid-August, the inevitable *Countdown* to Sept 7th would suddenly take hold. Although the start of a new school year elicited a sense of sadness, it was mitigated somewhat by the seemingly abrupt changes of the seasons, and the anticipation of once again seeing my neighborhood and school friends. The transition was also tempered by the likely prospect of frequent weekend visits to the *Country* through early November.

At some point, Rocco had a 1937 Plymouth sedan parked in Cottage 10's driveway for several months - with most of the engine removed and random parts strewn all over the lawn. I remember being content to just sit in the back on the tan wool seats admiring the side window shades and a clock that didn't work. At the time, it seemed very spacious and elegant! Perhaps it was my fertile imagination, but I believe, after it was re-assembled, it actually started, and I vaguely remember being driven around the Park while sitting in the *luxurious* back seat.

The Blue Beetle   I don't recall what became of his antique treasure, but he eventually redeemed himself with the *Blue Beetle*. It was a light blue,1950 Mercury coupe, resembling the one driven by James Dean in the movie, "Rebel Without a Cause"! This was truly a dynamite car, procured from Jerry Wright, who, at the time, was dating my sister, Virginia. Jerry worked at the Ford Motor assembly plant in Mahwah NJ, and the Blue Beetle was obviously his personal project - a true labor of love. He re-fitted the Beast with dual Hollywood mufflers and a larger high-performance engine. In short, the Blue Beetle would play a significant role in my young life, and at the ripe old age of 13, I learned how to drive a clutch car with a column shift.

The living was easy   I remember the early morning milk deliveries on the back porch - usually six large glass bottles in a metal container, cooled by a block of ice covered with a thick piece of burlap. The milk bottles were always topped with a thick layer of cream, the prize going to whoever opened the bottle first. Fresh eggs were often purchased at Ace farm. I would often accompany my father because, in addition to eggs, the barn also had a large horizontal freezer which contained an assortment of ice cream. I remember Dad holding my legs while I bent over the edge with my head down into the freezer in search of my favorite ice cream bar.

Every other day, the Dugan truck would drive around the park offering an assortment of bread, cupcakes, pies, etc. Our mailbox was out front, and I remember the postage being $.03 for postcards and five cents for a letter. We would simply raise the red flag for a pickup, and If you didn't have the correct postage stamp, simply scotch tape the coins on the envelope or leave the appropriate amount in the mailbox. In reality, however, being that we rarely had anyone's correct address, we had mostly incoming mail.

We had a rotary telephone, which was on a *Party line* serviced by a live operator. This meant if you picked up the receiver you might be listening to someone else's conversation. In the event that someone was tying up the line by gabbing on the phone, it wasn't unusual to politely ask the person to end the call as soon as possible, and if it was urgent, you could ask the operator to cut in on the conversation, in order to place your call. As you can imagine, this wasn't always well received.

Poison Ivy   One of my favorite adventures was building forts in the woods. This, however, was also fraught with inherent dangers such as snakes, and worst of all, poison ivy. Bobby Persichetti and I would spend hours in the woods, and invariably, within days of our excursion, we would be dealing with agonizing poison ivy, oak, or sumac.

Despite a popular misconception, most poison ivy eruptions result from direct contact with the plant's oil, which is then easily transferred (spread) by touching other body parts. Unfortunately, I rarely heeded my mother's sage advice of washing with brown soap as soon as possible after exposure. Consequently, I would invariably develop poison ivy on a very delicate part of my anatomy, referred to phonetically as my, *"Chi-Chi"*.

On one memorable occasion, while complaining of the intense itching, and seeing the extensive blisters on all my extremities, Dr. Luke Grandy told me to apply dilute Clorox to all the blisters. Well, the itching certainly subsided because, not only were my extremities burning like hell, but I developed a brawny discoloration which lasted for weeks! Thank God I didn't put it on my Chi-Chi!

Incidentally, my mother's favorite household remedies for the three most common ailments were an enema for abdominal pain, mustard plaster for a chest cold, and bathing whatever's swollen in Epsom salt, Regarding my chi-chi dilemma, being that Clorox was out of the question, I wisely chose to dilute Epsom salts instead.

Impending Heart Attack   I remember one morning, while lying in bed with my ear resting on my pillow, I suddenly became aware of my heartbeat. I noticed that the more I listened, the louder and faster my heartbeat, which of course, increased my anxiety creating a vicious cycle! I thought, surely this was a sign of an impending heart attack! Fearing the worst, I quickly sprung out of bed and went downstairs to notify anybody who would listen to me.

I remember it being a nice sunny morning, and my sister Maria sat quietly beside me on the front porch for at least 30 minutes, patiently trying to calm me down, reassuring me that having a heart attack at seven years of age was highly unlikely. However, considering that I currently have four stents, I was obviously clairvoyant at a very young age!

Smoking Experiment   when I was eight or nine, I experimented with smoking cigarettes upstairs in the front bedroom of Cottage 10. Unbeknownst to me, my father was sitting downstairs on the front porch talking with some friends. Upon smelling the spoke, Dad called for me to come downstairs. I quickly put out the cigarette, and when I went downstairs my father asked, "Were you smoking upstairs?" Of course, I adamantly denied the allegation. Knowing that I was right-handed, however, he took my hand, and after smelling my right index and middle fingers ,he again asked, "Are you sure you weren't smoking?" Although I shamefully denied it again, we both knew the truth.

Incidentally, up until then, my father would jokingly recite my name as," Pedro, Gonzalez, Della Torres, Poncho, Giuseppe, Dirty Draws, Cirigliano. However, thereafter he added, Liar, Cirigliano!

CH - 11
WALTON LAKE

W hen talking about memories of Idle Hour Park (IHP) or simply, *The Park,* it naturally included Walton Lake. Although it's often said that a picture paints a 1000 words, Unfortunately, I have none, and if I did, they couldn't possibly capture its essence. The crystal-clear lake was actually a reservoir, and as such, was fed by cold springs and underground streams. It was extremely deep, and the legend was that it was a *bottomless* Glacial Lake. We would often dive down 10 or 15 feet and after taking a big gulp, quickly resurface to swallow the ice-cold refreshing water. Lakes Rd was a narrow two-lane roadway which hugged the northwestern shore of the tranquil lake. During the summer, however, due to the number of cars parked along the roadside, it was often reduced to a single lane.

Idle Hour Dock (IHD) We would usually get up early in the morning, eat breakfast, complete any garden or household chores, and then, with a towel in hand, Nick and I would walk barefoot (before Zories) down to Idle Hour Park's private dock to meet our friends. The Dock's complex included an elevated stone patio on the left with a corrugated opaque covering supported by metal poles which provided shade from the blazing sun.

I remember my sister's boyfriends demonstrating their masculine prowess by performing *flagpole feats* on the metal poles (flag poling). Impressed by this feat, this would eventually become our *rite of passage.* The elevated patio overlooked a small shallow swimming area for the younger kids. To the right of the patio were steps leading to a 20 x 20' rectangular wood plank dock, supported on large boulders. The Dock was solely for the use of the Park's homeowners who were also solely responsible for the daily upkeep and maintenance.

The winter ice always played havoc with the boulders supporting the Dock, and I remember the two Miranda brothers, Rusty and Freddie, volunteering to help Caesar reset the dock on its stone foundation. This required lifting each side of the dock while Caesar lifted and repositioned the heavy boulders. The Miranda brothers were having such great difficulty lifting each side of the dock that they eventually resorted to the use of a car jack. At some point, Caesar became frustrated with how long they were taking, and after waving them off, he merely walked waist high to the front of the dock, and single-handedly lifted the entire front while they quickly realigned the supporting stones.

In addition to a small floating dock anchored 50' feet offshore, for several seasons, we also had use of a large cork Life Raft, also anchored offshore. It had a heavy woven rope interior basket, and we would try in vain to tip the large raft over. I remember spending virtually the whole day just swimming around the dock and rafts, relying on each other for safety without any fear of abduction. On particularly hot summer afternoons my mother and occasionally my father would come down to swim in the lake or just bask in the cool lake breeze.

Dad and Mom on Idle Hour Dock

The lake provided a virtual oasis of vibrant activity all summer long, and especially on weekends, there was a carnival-like atmosphere. The narrow roadway which hugged at least half of the lake's western shore was appropriately called Lakes Road. It coursed gently between the lake and a scattering of precious lake-view homes perched on the opposite hillside - several of which also had private lakefront docks.

In stark contrast, however, the eastern shoreline was known to be sparsely inhabited with a small cluster of rustic cabins embedded in the thick woods. Strangely, the other side always appeared dark, and it was considered foreign territory. Although we occasionally swam or boated along that shoreline, I don't ever remember setting foot on the foreign shore.

Besides, given that Nick Santella floated the romantic notion that the other side was possibly inhabited by Indians, I never dared to venture into *Indian territory* for fear of running into a band of Iroquois. Eventually, however, I learned that the entrance to Osseo Park led to an access pathway through the dark forest to these remote homesites.

To the left of the Idle Hour dock was Mrs. Clark's Gazebo, and to the right was Galette's private lakefront dock. At some point, my father estimated that the lake was a quarter mile across and two miles around. Also, directly across from the Idle Hour dock was a prominent white Boat House, which served as a landmark for a shorter triangle course. Both of these facts would prove to be important for long distance training.

Rocco on the dock with a view of the cork raft

On the corner of Lakes Rd and Cromwell Hill Road, was a popular Bar which changed hands several times. My earliest recollection of the bar was called Casablanca. This was followed by Johnny's and eventually Hennessy's. The interior was rustic with a long bar, and the live rock bands always drew large weekend crowds - even from distant, Greenwood Lake,

Schaeffers   There were three lakeside Concession Stands selling hamburgers, hotdogs, ice cream and candy. The closest stand to our Dock was called *Ma Schaeffer's* which was approximately 500' away. It was owned and operated by Ma's daughter, Agnes. The stand was a small white wood frame building that was partially dug into the hillside which provided ample counter space. Directly across Lake Road, there was enough parking space for approximately 8 cars. They offered ice cream, shakes, malts, hamburgers, hot dogs and candy, a novelty being frozen milky ways. As with the other competing stands, they also offered an assortment of small and large boats some of which were designated as fishing boats, having a special center seat compartment that allowed lake water to enter in order to store the freshly caught fish.

The large lakeside complex consisted of two stationary docks, separated by a small cordoned off area of shallow water for the smaller kids. Attached to the left side of the main dock was a very unique large rectangular swimming *Crib*. It had wood flooring slots intended to provide relatively safe swimming, even for toddlers. The only downside was that the wooden slats often became very slippery, and occasionally your toes would get caught between the slats. To the right of the main dock was a second smaller dock separated by 25' of relatively shallow water which was cordoned off for young kids.

Schaeffer's Dock Crib

In addition, there was a floating dock anchored about 50' from the stationary docks. In addition to a diving board, it featured an aluminum water slide with two humps in the middle, and a hand operated water pump to provide a slippery surface on the hot aluminum slide. In the common event that the pump didn't work, the alternative was to follow right behind someone with a wet bathing suit otherwise, you burned your ass. It also had a 20' high tower with a small platform for high diving. I remember once hesitating to jump from the top of the tower and falling on the dock below with only one foot landing on the edge. This resulted in a painfully jammed hip which lasted for about a month, but which could have been much worse!

Diving Tower on the floating dock

Although Schaeffer's was only 15 minutes away, we usually brought a simple PB&J sandwich and a piece of fruit for lunch. Occasionally, however, my mother would surprise us by walking down to the dock with a far better lunch. Sometimes, as a special treat, she would give Nick and me enough money to buy ice cream cones for the three of us. This, however, always presented a melting dilemma. Of course, while Nick licked his cone, I was the designated carrier, and as fast as I walked, the cones were melting faster. Between my cone melting down my forearm and me licking my mother's cone, when we finally arrived, she could barely see the top of the scoop.

Bulls   Approximately 800' further down the road was a second, somewhat fancier, lakeside concession stand called Bulls which was owned by the

Gordons. It was a shingled wood frame lakefront building that provided interior seating, and offered a somewhat larger selection of grilled food, French fries, ice cream and fresh bait. In addition, they stocked containers of milk, eggs, and blocks of ice for the homes across the lake. I distinctly remember how appetizing the greasy grill smelled, and the French fries were intoxicating! The real attraction, however, was the pinball machines. They were truly addictive, providing endless entertainment for the nominal cost of five cents. Unlike Shaeffer's, in addition to a large assortment of rowboats, they also offered an elevated Sandy Beach.

As I mentioned, directly across the lake, was a row of 3 or 4 barely visible rustic cabins tucked deep in the woods along the eastern shore which were apparently passed down for several generations. Some had covered front porches, and small docks for fishing and mooring their boats. The cabins had very limited appliances and bathroom facilities were serviced by outhouses. The only means of access was either, taking a long footpath through the woods from the Osseo Park entrance or rowing across the lake from Bulls. Being that the twenty-minute boat excursions were the preferred method, they usually rented their boats for the entire summer.

Donna   One of my dearest and oldest friends, Donna, lived in one of those cabins. My first recollection of her was while swimming along their shore and noticing this seven years old girl wearing dungarees and a plaid shirt, fishing from her dock. Ever since that fateful day, our lives have remained closely intertwined to the present. Although those of us living on the *civilized* western shore might have considered living on the *wilderness* side as austere, she often described it as a serene *wonderland*. In addition to Bulls, however, they were also able to purchase the bare essentials at the only convenience store on the western shore which had to be transported across the lake by boat - obviously essential, but very inconvenient!

Heetons   There was a third, much smaller, lakeside concession stand approximately 1000' further down the road from Bulls. It was a small wood frame structure owned by the Heeton family and situated across the road from the 488 American Legion club. Directly across the lake was the Rose Marin summer camp. I remember trying to catch a glimpse of the young camp counselors from afar or while swimming around the lake and breathing only on my left side, Either way, it was always a very pleasant distraction. Between Bulls and Heaton's was a private elevated rectangular sandy beach area for the residents of Lake View Estates - a private community adjacent to Idle Hour Park

The Clark Estate   Usually around 5 pm, we would begin walking back up the hill to our respective homes. However by this late hour, as a result of the hot sun beating down on the black macadam, it was often a challenge to avoid scorching your bare feet on the hot bubbles, let alone contending with the gravel along the steep inclines.

At the onset of our long trek up the hill, we would frequently stop to raid Mrs. Clark's pear tree laden with hard but deliciously ripened brown pears. The Clark estate was always well maintained and beautifully manicured, occupying the lower left corner of the Park's entryway and encircled by the third sharp turn.

The estate had its own waterfront gazebo, and the white three-story wood framed mini mansion was graced with covered porches on the second and third floors supported by beautiful round columns. It had a winding red pebbled driveway leading to the front of the house and ultimately to a garage under the left porch which housed a chauffeur-driven limousine.

Mrs. Clark was known to be a very wealthy woman, presumably an heiress of the Coats and Clark Company. Although she was somewhat reclusive, she was often seen wearing a large brimmed straw hat while kneeling on a foam knee pad using small hand trowels to tend to her exquisite flower beds scattered throughout the property. Despite our obvious pear tree raids, she never forbid our intrusions.

My sister Anita recalls when Mrs. Clark offered to host a dance at her house and furnished refreshments for the Park's teenagers. Anita recalled that the interior was exquisite with highly polished woodwork and parquet floors throughout. She commented that their hostess was very cordial, gracious, and surprisingly unpretentious, making all her teenage *guests* feel very welcomed.

The Coves   The northern and southern ends of the lake contained coves which had an abundance of lily pads which, during the summer, were quite colorful. The one which was closest to the Park, gradually narrowed forming a very deep cove. We would occasionally take a small rowboat into the cove, and among the lily pads we would find an abundance of frogs and small turtles with colorful bottoms.

Speaking of turtles, there was the legendary, *Big Turtle* which had to be at least 2 feet in diameter, and when his huge head surfaced for air it became readily visible from afar, creating a mixture of hysteria and awe. Later in life, while swimming around the lake, just the thought of the *Big Turtle* would propel me through the water!

Caesar's Boat   Incidentally, none of us actually owned a boat. However, after big storms, small boats would occasionally break loose, and ultimately find their way into the small cove. This would initiate clandestine search and salvage missions.

I remember one such occasion when Caesar found a partially submerged boat in the cove, and after manually dragging it to the Dock, it became known as *Caesar's Wreck.* He worked on that boat for weeks, repairing and caulking the bottom, and after procuring a set of oars, it was finally launch time! Unfortunately, despite all his hard work, the damn boat still leaked like a sieve. But, as long as there were two in the boat, one to bail and another to row, it still remained afloat for short runs!

The Floating dock   After a hurricane in 1954 or 55, the Park's floating dock broke loose and ended up in the cove. But using Caesar's porous boat was out of the question. So, as Rocco tells the story, Caesar swam down to the cove to retrieve the raft, and single-handedly, began pushing the dock while walking shoulder high in the water along the shoreline towards the Park's Dock.

While passing Johnny's Bar & Grill, which was relatively close to the shoreline, the owner came out and started yelling at Caesar, "Get that damn raft away from my beachfront!". Initially, Caesar ignored the man, and continued pushing the dock slowly along the shoreline. Seeing this, the man became irate, and in a threatening manner, he started walking towards the shoreline to confront my brother while brandishing a big stick!

Upon seeing this, Caesar immediately changed course, and he began pushing the dock closer to the shoreline. Naturally, the closer he got, the more he emerged from the water, and as a result of pushing the heavy dock through the water for an hour, his muscles were visibly pumped. By the time Caesar was waist high, upon seeing his size, the man's tone softened somewhat. When he was mid-thigh, the man said, "Listen, it's okay. You can temporarily anchor the dock out there!" By knee height, however, the man dropped the stick and offered, "Listen, no problem, I'll help you push the dock to where it belongs!"

Parking   In addition to swimming and fishing, especially on weekends, the activity surrounding the concession stands was carnival- like. Lakes Road was often jammed with cars parked single file along the hillside, which was lined with a deep drainage ditch, making parallel parking a nightmare. To make matters worse, the cars often got stuck in the ditch which was another opportunity for a small token of appreciation for pushing them out! Consequently, traffic along Lakes Road moved at a snail's pace which allowed pedestrians to walk along the roadway with moderate safety. Needless to say, while the lake provided endless swimming activity, it also provided the nidus for our family to eventually become known as, *The Swimming Family*.

CH - 12
THE SWIMMING FAMILY

Although my mother would often say, "Your father was an excellent swimmer," she was referring to when he would swim between the jetties at Coney Island. Ironically, however, despite his unquestionable fervor, I never saw him actually in the water. Recently I was shocked to see a photo of him standing on the Idle Hour Dock wearing a dark blue wool bathing suit while donning my mother's terry cloth bathrobe draped over his shoulders. As in the garden, however, he would usually stand on the dock wearing his dress pants and shoes while wearing a white guinea tee-shirt.

The Twins   My twin sisters each set a very high bar for the rest of us. They were both very intelligent and talented, readily entertaining adults with their harmonizing and dancing routine. Interestingly, my mother kept their elementary report cards which she occasionally shared with the rest of us. They were very humiliating - nothing less than A or A+, with Virginia often edging out her younger twin, Maria. Apparently, their intellectual gene pool wasn't passed on to the rest of us. In fact, I suspect there was a gradual diminution, and I'm living testimony of that supposition which, I'm sure, Sr Ermingale would readily attest to. During their later adolescent years, they were also the ones to set the bar for competitive swimming.

Virginia   Virginia was really the impetus for my father's renewed interest in swimming. From what I was told, at the age of seven, while at camp, she was struck in the back of the head by a swing. Afterward, she developed progressive weakness of her right extremities followed by recurrent seizures that began during puberty. At the time, It was presumed that this was the result of a traumatic head injury.

My father was a personal friend of Dr. Salvatore Cutolo MD, the Chief of staff of Bellevue Hospital and author of the book, "Bellvue is my Home". Consequently, Virginia was examined by several specialists, one of whom was a highly regarded neurosurgeon. Although he recommended a relatively new surgical procedure, after weighing all the potential risks, my father chose not to proceed with the delicate operation.

Thereafter, my father focused on the therapeutic benefits of hydrotherapy, in particular swimming, as a practical means of physical rehabilitation. Consequently, the natural benefits of swimming were strongly encouraged and gradually embraced by all of my siblings. Thus, the beginning of The *Swimming Family*.

Siblings on Idle Hour Dock

Incidentally, much later in life, upon questioning Virginia regarding the onset of her symptoms, I felt strongly that she had suffered a ruptured Berry aneurysm while straining on the toilet - probably unrelated to her head contusion.

My father would save and cherish the newspaper articles regarding all of their respective swimming accomplishments - most often written by Jimmy Murphy, a sports columnist for the Brooklyn Daily Eagle. I remember many Saturday mornings, all of us sitting on the stairs while my father proudly read aloud the results of Friday evening's swimming races. During the winters, my older siblings swam at various YMCA pools in Brooklyn, and during the summers, they swam long distances in Walton Lake.

During their high school years, the twins became very accomplished club swimmers. They each attended local high schools, Maria attending Bishop McDonnell HS after which she graduated summa cum laude from Fordham University. However, due to her recurrent seizures, Virginia was forced to attend Ft Hamilton HS, after which she entered the workplace.

Despite having a very smooth powerful stroke, Anita was also very strong-minded, and she frustrated my father by preferring tennis and the company of boys, rather than competitive swimming. Unlike the rest of us, she was always conscious of her appearance, ultimately becoming a fashion statement, as evidenced by her *special* white ice skates. My father would often shake his head saying, "She has one boy coming in the front door while another is going out the back door!". She attended Bay Ridge High followed by St John's University where she met her future husband Robert Hartmann.

Among my brothers, at a very young age, Caesar was the first one out of the gate, and as such, he was considered the *Golden Boy*. At the ripe age of nine, my father would prompt him to demonstrate his ability to do 150 push-ups at a clip. Although Caesar initially swam faster, Rocco eventually caught up and surpassed him by the age of 18. They both swam for the New York Athletic Club (NYAC), achieving national recognition as long distance record holders, and both competed in the same events during the 1952 Olympic trials in Flushing Meadows NY.

While Rocco was attending Ft, Hamilton HS, I remember as a six-year-old, sitting on his feet while he did endless sit-ups and other calisthenics on the Party Room floor. Afterward, he traveled by train to the NYAC in order to work-out with their team. In the future, this association would prove to be very beneficial, eventually becoming the de facto coach of the NYAC swimming team.

He was awarded a full swimming scholarship to Ohio State University, ultimately making the coveted, All American swim team. He eventually set his sights on the 1958 Olympic trials. In preparation for the event, he attended a summer training session at Yale University under Bob Kiphuth, a progressive coach well known for incorporating land exercises, calisthenics, and light weight training. I remember my father expressing concern that Kiphuth would attempt to change or modify Rocco's stroke -which my father felt had served him very well thus far.

At the time, Ohio State was a virtual powerhouse of international swimmers, including Ford Kono, a world record holder who would prove to be Rocco's idol and nemesis. Both of them were long-distance swimmers, and despite the fact that Rocco would most often place second to Kono, he was already doing the required times to qualify for the Olympic trials in Detroit MI.

From what I was told, however, a misguided strategy ensued involving his teammate, Dick Cleveland, who had already qualified for the 100m freestyle. Although Rocco's event was the 200m freestyle, his coach entered Dick in the same heat in order to pace Rocco. However, this proved to be a tragic mistake. Dick went out much faster than expected, and while trying to keep pace with him, Rocco burned out far too soon and missed the cut off by 1/10th of a second.

Understandably, the loss was devastating for Rocco, and I believe my father was upset and terribly disappointed for Rocco's sake. Not because of his time, but because he had it within his grasp, but lacked the confidence to swim his own race. I believe that, had he swam his own race but missed the mark, somehow the loss would have been less traumatic. Never conceding total failure however, my father would often say, "Rocco is the half-world champion!" Of course, I would proudly tell all my friends, but was at a loss when they'd ask, "Which half!"

I remember Ford Kono visiting our home in Bay Ridge. Considering the size of my brothers and knowing that Kono was a swimming icon, I naturally expected an imposing figure of equal stature. Instead, in walked a relatively small, 5" 9" guy of slight frame, and I thought, "Go figure, I guess the water really is the great equalizer!"

Meanwhile, Caesar was awarded a full four-year swimming scholarship to St. John's Prep. While at the Prep, he was the undisputed superstar, breaking all sorts of high school and metropolitan swimming records. I remember once, while he was competing at the NYAC, several of his classmates were seated in the bleachers, and unfamiliar with the protocol of silence, when his name was announced to mount the starting block, they all stood up in unison and yelled, "Hail Caesar!".

During his later years at the Prep, much to my father's chagrin, he signed up to also play baseball and football, thereby earning varsity letters in all three sports. During his senior year, he was persuaded to run for school President. When four of his closest Italian friends gathered for a strategy session in the downstairs Party Room, I remember helping them make signs for an upcoming school rally. Unfortunately, despite a valiant effort, he suffered a painful defeat to a nice Irishman, and he graciously accepted the role as Vice President,

I remember as an eighth grader, thumbing through his senior yearbook, and noting that, having played three major sports, practically the entire sports section was dedicated to him. There was a spectacular one-page photo of him diving from the edge of the Prep's pool directly into the camera. My father was very concerned however, that he might suffer a serious football injury to his knee or shoulder, thereby jeopardizing the likelihood of a swimming scholarship to college. Fortunately, this never happened, and he was subsequently offered a four-year swimming scholarship to Fordham University.

Meanwhile, while I was still struggling with sister Ermingale, Nick earned a full four-year swimming scholarship to St. Francis Prep. Sadly, this set in motion a gradual drifting apart from our former close relationship. Although as a freshman, Nick was considered to be exceptional, he would eventually have to compete against Caesar, now a Senior at St John's Prep.

Following their dual meets, I remember Nick coming home demoralized and humiliated after being decimated by his own brother! Ironically however, in four short years, I would experience the same humiliation! By his Junior year, Nick became known as, *The Machine* in Monroe and *The Fish* in St Francis Prep. He regularly set new school and national records, eventually establishing himself as the new NCCA long-distance champion who would eventually humiliate and decimate his own brother -confirming that, "What goes around comes around"!

The Elusive Catch   In time, Nick demonstrated that he was perhaps the most *gifted* member of the swimming family, propelled by a natural *catch*. Much later on, while swimming next to Nick at various pools, and purposely studying his stroke underwater, I asked him, "Where is the *catch* in your stroke?" While standing at the poolside, he slowly went through the motions of his hand entry and sweep saying, "I think it's somewhere between here" - which still remained elusive for me!

Rocco & Caesar   As a result of their constant training, Rocco and Caesar had well proportioned, muscular physiques which were almost legendary. Even as teenagers, they had already achieved national recognition as long distance record holders - the family benchmark being, the 4-mile Nationals. In my family, this event was considered a *rite of passage*, the critical hallmark distinguishing a *Swimmer* from one who swims.

Rocco, Nick, and Caesar

While training in Walton Lake for the heralded event, they would swim daily and sometimes twice daily, in preparation for the grueling 4-mile race. Anyone living on or around the lake would see them swimming either 16 times across or twice around the lake - the equivalent of 4 miles. My father would strategically position himself in the middle of the lake or while I rowed alongside, Dad would sit in the back carefully observing and critiquing their swimming technique.

incidentally, Dad's remedy for painful hands and preventing blisters, was to dip them in the cold lake water. However, despite his ingenuity, I don't know why he never thought of gloves!

Oftentimes, I would row alongside my brothers alone in one of the smaller boats, paying close attention to their stroke and breathing rhythm. In particular, I took note of their relaxed hand entry and smooth glide followed by a visible propulsion (catch) with each stroke. I often found myself mesmerized by the cadence of their controlled, mantra-like, breathing, varying between four and six strokes.

Woody I remember being awakened at dawn by the rumble of a motorcycle pulling into Cottage 10's driveway, driven by Rocco's friend,

Woody Prokosh. He was much older than Rocco, and I recall that he had an injury related deformity of his left hand and forearm. I also remember his wife having some form of turrets syndrome or Petit Mal seizures, wherein she would suddenly start moving her hand back and forth in front of her eyes for about 30 seconds and then recover.

For whatever reason, Woody drove all the way from Newburgh N.Y. just to swim with Rocco in Walton Lake. I don't know if it was intended for Rocco's benefit or his. but I never got the impression that it was for the purpose of competition. Shortly after his arrival, they would both straddle the cycle and rumble out of the driveway on their way to begin their early morning swim around the lake.

Caesar's Wager   I remember my brother, Caesar, having a wager with several Greeks who challenged him to swim across the lake from the dock without stopping, which my brother readily accepted. However, one of the Greeks said he would double the wager if he was able to swim across with his legs tied, which my brother also accepted. Raising the ante, a third Greek said he would triple the wager if he was able to swim across with his feet and hands tied. After dolphin kicking across the lake on his back, the Greeks lost a lot of money. Too bad they didn't quadruple the wager for a round trip!

The Coach   While in Monroe, it was common for my father to invite any of the Park kids to take advantage of free weekend swimming lessons at the Park's Dock, provided they were willing to follow his instructions. In no- time, Dad became known as the de facto, *Coach of Walton Lake*, preferring instead to be called, Mr.C.

In Retrospect, My father's philosophy and training methods were way ahead of their time. Just as he emphasized the importance of proper abdominal or diaphragmatic breathing while walking on Coney Island's boardwalk, he emphasized the same breathing and relaxation while swimming. He would attend as many swimming events as possible, observing more seasoned swimmers and alternate coaching techniques.

This was especially true from the left poolside bleachers at the NYAC. And as his constant companion and faithful sidekick, I would observe him observing others.

Considering his appreciation for educational and professional pursuits, aside from the obvious health benefits of swimming, and with such a large family, I think he also viewed swimming as a necessary means to an essential end -namely, athletic scholarships. As a result of his incessant reading and studying, he came to appreciate and embrace the inherent benefits of proper nutrition, vitamin supplements and exercise, especially swimming.

Although initially intended for the benefit of my sister, Virginia, he eventually espoused this philosophy to all of us, and for that matter, anyone else who would listen and had a willingness to learn. In many respects, he embraced many of the present-day tenants of Alternative or Complementary Medicine. Unfortunately, however, my Dad also adhered to the adage, "Do as I say, not as I do"

His appreciation for relaxation and controlled breathing techniques were manifest in his training methods, always stressing the importance of a relaxed stroke, described metaphorically as a *Rag Doll* hand entry and recovery. He also emphasized yoga-like controlled breathing, slowly exhaling underwater through pursed lips, and improving breath control by breathing every four or six strokes with a mantra-like rhythm.

In those days, since weight training was virtually nonexistent, instead he relied on push-ups and sit-ups, and increasing shoulder strength by pulling with your ankles tied together or wearing cotton gloves. He intentionally increased drag by occasionally swimming with a tee shirt or a heavy cloth bathing suit, and kicking mostly underwater, preferably without a kickboard.

He also concentrated on various methods of self-improvement such as the importance of a mind-body connection, and the influence of one's *mind over matter*. For the most part, he was a teacher, often demonstrating the art of *Persuasion* and the power of *Suggestion*. He often reinforced one's *Confidence* by saying, "I have the Secret" - suggesting that, if you did as he said, you would feel better or swim faster! Even at a young age, I took note and studied him.

You are what you Eat   Growing up, we never had soda in the house, only milk or freshly squeezed citrus juices. Nor did we have white sugar or white bread, only brown sugar and whole-wheat or Italian semolina bread. Hot oatmeal was a staple, and breakfast cereals were always garnished with sliced fruit smothered with Wheat Germ. The primary source of sweets were fresh fruits, and on special occasions, homemade pastries.

Stuck like glue   Most of my friends were allowed to buy one cent baseball cards, which came with a flat card size piece of delicious bubble gum - what a deal! However, regardless of the deal, I was never allowed to buy gum. But being resourceful, it wasn't unusual to find pieces of gum stuck under our school desks. After carefully scraping a piece off, I'd save it for future use. One day, while walking home from school, I got the bright idea of using an ice cream stick to scrape gum off the sidewalks. Aside from the fact that it was hard and mostly tasteless, despite repeated attempts to clean the nasty gum, it still contained residual grains of sand.

After harvesting a fair amount, by the time I arrived home I was chewing a huge wad of recycled bubble gum. When my mother saw this, infuriated, she asked, "Who gave you the gum?" Perplexed, I said, "Nobody." "Then, where'd you get the money to buy it?" she asked. With an air of righteous indignation, I exclaimed, "I didn't buy it!" However, she pressed further, and when I finally explained how I came to procure such a windfall, she went absolutely berserk. I would have been better off claiming that I stole it!

Vitamin supplements were plentiful and readily consumed by the handful, especially, Brewer's yeast and desiccated liver tablets. Milk was often spiked with copious amounts of Black Strap molasses or special concoctions recommended by nutritionists such as Carlton Fredericks and

Gayelord Hauser. In fact, my father was even invited to attend a Saturday morning breakfast forum with Carlton Fredericks. Being concerned about my weight, my father asked Dr. Fredricks to recommend a *tonic* to improve my appetite. I still remember the God awful brown concoction that was kept in the refrigerator. Every morning, I would pinch my nose, just to get the horrid tasting syrup down and then immediately follow it with juice.

In particular, Brewer's yeast tablets, especially in large quantities, were notorious for producing indigestion and acid reflux followed by flatulence (gas). I remember one morning while sitting at the breakfast table, my father patiently waited for Rocco to finish taking his boatload of Brewer's Yeast tablets. Growing increasingly more impatient, Dad chided my brother, "Why don't you just take a handful and swallow them?" Surprisingly, my brother challenged my father to demonstrate the proper method of consumption. Not to be outdone and with ample drama, Dad gainfully took a handful of Brewer's Yeast tablets, and slugged them down with a mouthful of coffee. Within seconds, he suddenly belched, and proceeded to vomit the undigested contents on the kitchen table!.

Despite the initial embarrassment and universal snickering, Dad took it in stride, and he actually laughed when my mother weighed in saying, "Caesar, you damn fool!" Incidentally, in High school, believing that I would surely swim faster if I took all my vitamins, the only thing I experienced was, incessant belching of foul tasting yeast and liver - which I would have readily accepted, had I swam faster!

Butch the Dog   In fact, vitamins were so pervasive, that my father even fed vitamins under the kitchen table to our dog, Butch. As a result, although Butch developed a huge chest and leg muscles, he wasn't spared the untoward side effects of the Brewers yeast tablets - excessive foul smelling gas. Butch would often join us by lying on the floor in either the dining room or the front sunroom while we watched TV. Sooner or later, the fully fermented yeast tablets would reveal themselves by the release of a silent but deadly aroma. Once detected, almost in unison, we would tell Butch to get up and leave the room. However, before exiting, he would invariably pause, turn his head around and look at us, as if to say, "So what's the problem?"

This also occurred on more than one occasion while watching a late night TV show in the company of a young lady. Now, how long would Ann Landers suggest that you pretend to ignore the pungent aroma before telling Butch to leave the room - assuming. of course, that he was the culprit! I often wondered how often he was falsely accused, and, upon leaving the room, turned around and whined, "Hey, it wasn't me!"

Swimming Lessons (1953-54) In rather quick succession, my father's initial intent of offering free weekend swimming lessons at the Dock gradually increased in both number and frequency. Concerned that if Rocco was the instructor of record, it might jeopardize his amateur status, Dad designated Maria, a former N.Y. Metropolitan swimming champion, as the head instructor.

Incidentally, I recently came across a copy of several newspaper articles written by the sports columnist, Paul Gould, featuring both Virginia and Maria as members of coach, Al Johnson's, illustrious Dragon club team. Another featured five young female members of the Dragon team posing on the edge of the St George Hotel's pool. They were hailed to be future Olympians - one of whom was Maria.

Monte Carlo Pool (1955-56) In 1954, both Rocco and Caesar were employed as lifeguards at the Monte Carlo pool. This eventually provided a golden opportunity to move the swimming lessons to a more convenient pool location, thereby transitioning from purely swimming lessons, to an actual swim Team. In fact, following a Newburg News swimming meet at which we won 10 blue ribbons, I have a newspaper article featuring my father as the heralded, "Coach of the Cirigliano Family". I also have a small black and white photo of Richie and Bobby Persichetti, Jimmy' Skeletes and me, taken at the Monte Carlo pool, wherein we all have our shoulders thrust back while expanding our massive chests, closely resembling four Ethiopians after the famine!

THE CIRIGLIANO FAMILY — ALL FINE SWIMMERS

Monte Carlo Pool Richie and Bobby Persichetti, Jimmy Skaletes, and me

Synchronized Swimming   I remember one summer, my three sisters and several of their girlfriends decided to entertain the Monte Carlo Hotel guests by putting on a synchronized swimming exhibition. Although their only frame of reference was watching newsreels of Esther Williams, they diligently practiced in the evenings until they were ready for their grand debut. With artificial flower corsages strapped to their wrists, they dazzled their spectators who, fortunately, knew even less about synchronized swimming than they did!

Hudson NY Swim Meet   Traveling to Hudson NY was an unforgettable adventure. I remember my father scurrying at the last minute to satisfy the requirements for registering the *Idle Hour swim club* in order to compete in a small lake in Hudson, N.Y. Our team consisted solely of the local neighborhood kids who were taking lessons from my father et al.

I was about 8 years old, and I remember Rocco leading a convoy of three station wagons, one graciously provided by the Trums. Following the long 3 hr. drive, we stayed briefly in an armory or school auditorium, stretching, and resting on the wood floor. I have a small black and white photo of Howard and Philip Umansky, Barry Rosinsky, Freddie Silverstein, Joel Vaccaro, Nick, and me, sitting on the front steps.

Hudson NY Swim meet Freddie Silverstein, Nick, Kip Trum and
Billy Hegarty

Although I barely remember the wooden starting dock and even less of the various swimming events, I clearly remember the long ride home. While driving ho in the pitch black darkness of night, with only dim headlights to guide us, Rocco devised an ingenious method of entertaining us, by asking us to vote on which way we anticipated the dimly lit road would turn, left, right or straight, and before we knew it, we were back home.

Paladin Club   I remember another hastily organized team, composed of Walton Lake and Idle Hour Park kids, to compete against a well-groomed Paladin Club team in Newburgh N.Y. When we arrived, the Paladin swimmers were all handsomely dressed in colorful sweat suits, embossed with the Paladin Club Crest on their jackets. In stark contrast, however, we had a wide variety of faded bathing trunks, and an assortment of colorful beach towels. Initially, the race was close, but with Nick's help, we eventually beat them handily. The motto being, "It's not how you look. It's how you perform!

Sunset Park   In our family, an early swimming milestone was the 1500 m (60 laps) event. So, at the ripe age of 9, following in my brothers' footsteps, I trained for and swam the grueling race in Brooklyn's Sunset Pool. Not surprisingly, however, unlike each of my brothers who handily won the event, I came in next to last, totally exhausted but feeling victorious that, at least I beat my elder, Freddie Silverstein. *Incidentally, as of that date, at the age of 11, I believe Caesar was the youngest swimmer to compete in the coveted event but he sure as hell didn't come in next to last!*

Turning Point   At each of the concession stands it was common for my father to reward (*bribe)* his swimmers by offering them either an ice cream cone or a milkshake for their extra efforts. I remember when I was 11 years old, my father offered me a milkshake if I would *Just* attempt to swim butterfly across the lake. He obviously had more faith in me than I had in myself. In any event, while rowing a small boat, he sat facing me, and keeping the back of the boat just beyond my grasp, he kept repeating, "Come on, you can do it, just a little bit further!" And as I got closer to the other shore he yelled, "Keep going, you're almost there!" - I can still hear his voice! Sure enough, I made it to the other side, and thank God he didn't ask me to butterfly back!

Just to be acknowledged by my father was an unforgettable milestone and a turning point in my life. From that point forward I told him that he didn't have to *bribe* me to swim, that I wanted to do it out of choice. He turned and looked at me for a seemingly long time, and without saying a word, just smiled and shook my hand - much more memorable than two milkshakes!

Incidentally, many years later, while swimming in the Masters and competing in the 200 yd butterfly, I was always motivated by the vision and echo of my father's voice prompting me to Just reach beyond my grasp!

CH - 13
TOWN

The center of the town of Monroe was roughly five miles away from the Park. After exiting left, there were two roads leading to town, Cromwell Hill Rd and Lakes Rd. which meandered along the northern perimeter of Walton Lake. Shortly after passing the entrance to Osseo Park on the right, the southern shoreline of Round Lake comes into view. In the center of the lake was a picturesque island forested by mostly evergreen trees. There were no dwellings or visible campsites on the island, and stroking my fertile imagination again, Nick Santella said, it was likely inhabited by Indians.

Unlike Walton Lake, however, Round Lake only had one public bathing area with an elevated sandy beach and a small concession stand. Continuing north on Lakes Road eventually led to the center of the town which was flanked by two beautiful ponds connected by an active stream. The pond on the right, Mill Pond, was frequently inhabited by white ducks and geese, and it fed a thunderous waterfall that powered a large water wheel. The left pond had a small island in the middle, studded with beautiful evergreen trees.

Main Street   Although Main Street was narrow and relatively short in length, it provided just about everything one needed. We were fortunate to have two pharmacies, Thrifts and Palens. Each one had almost identical ice cream parlors featuring old-fashioned soda fountain counters with tall mirrors behind, and a long row of red vinyl swivel seats in front. Upon entering the parlors, the sweet smell of ice cream and chocolate syrup provided the irresistible ingredients for delicious sundaes or shakes.

Main street was also lined by a Dayton's five and dime store, a barber shop, and a small Grand Union. During the summer, considering that my mother didn't drive, and my father was only in Monroe on weekends and Wednesday evenings, the only opportunity for food shopping was on Saturdays or asking for a ride with a neighbor.

It also featured a small quaint inexpensive Movie Theater owned by the Strauss family. In time, however, they eventually closed it and opened a much larger theater on Goose Pond Rd. The Smith and Streible hardware store provided one-stop shopping for just about every conceivable piece of hardware, including guns and household appliances. I still remember the old fashion wooden counters and walking on the creaking wood floors. In the rear of the building was the Carpenter and Smith company which provided deliveries of oil and propane gas.

Most of the local businesses and shop owners lining Main street were known by name. Down the street from the hardware store was a small lumber yard owned by Mr. Ross, the Monroe Bank was owned by Mr. Todd, the Jewelry Store was owned by Charlie Lescher and Kitty Korners small boutique owned by Mr.Jewels. Just around the corner was an old Italian Shoemaker, similar to the one in Bay Ridge.

While walking along Main St, there was a well enforced, mandatory Dress Code. Although children and adolescents were allowed to wear shorts, adults were required to wear slacks and collared dress shirts. Perhaps befitting the times, there was a sense of general acceptance and a willingness to conform to the dress code.

Public commuting to Monroe was provided by the Erie railroad and the Shortline bus service. The quaint Train Station was conveniently located in the center of town, and the Bus Station was strategically located opposite Phillips liquor store.

The Sheriff On Sundays, traffic was directed at the main intersection in the center of town by the lone sheriff, known only as Tex. His unconventional uniform included a white cowboy hat and boots, white gloves and an ivory-handled western six shooter, holstered loosely at his mid-thigh. It was always amusing to watch him directing four way traffic on Sunday mornings. Much like an orchestra conductor, he would stand in the middle of the busy intersection, rapidly pointing and gesturing with his white-gloved hands in all directions, rarely blowing the whistle clenched between his teeth. To top it off, he drove a vintage, highly polished red Pontiac convertible with bull horns attached to the front hood, and while wearing his trademark hat, he would often announce his presence with a 5 note musical horn.

Sacred Heart Church   Sacred Heart was our parish church located in the center of town. It was a small quaint white frame structure with a pretty bell tower. The narrow center aisle was flanked by a row of twenty pews facing a simple, pretty white altar. Church services always seemed well attended, but the seating was limited to approximately 200 parishioners, with the overflow choosing or forced to stand in the back or along the narrow side aisles.

My father would faithfully drive us to church, and after dropping us off, he would claim that he was going to park the car. However when the church service was over, we would Invariably find him sitting in the car reading a newspaper. It never occurred to us, "At what point did he get the newspaper?"

25th Anniversary   I'm looking at a black and white photograph taken in 1956, of my parent's 25th wedding anniversary party, held on the back lawn of Cottage 10. It was a surprise party given by all of their immediate Park friends and neighbors. I was about 10 yrs. old and apparently fighting to stay awake in order to take it all in - but fading fast. From what I remember, it was a very festive mild summer evening with lots of dancing on the lawn. I have a rare photo of my parents dancing together, and of Nick dancing with Judy Umansky and Joel Vacarro dancing with another girl. In particular, I remember Anita dancing the lindy with Jimmy Bilardi, who was a surprisingly good dancer.

Thankfully, the cake cutting ceremony was captured on film for posterity. The pose was of both my parents cutting a large sheet cake, with my Dad holding the knife, and Mom pointing at the large cake. Dad appears to be dressed, true to form, in a white terry cloth shirt (someone must have hidden his guinea tee-shirt) with his eyebrows arched above his prominent eyes and a faint smile. Mom is wearing a very pretty white dress, white earrings, a lightweight white sweater covering her shoulders, and smiling with pursed lips. They both appear young, and Mom's stunning appearance made for a very attractive couple. With this in mind, who would have predicted that, in just two short years, everything would change!

My parent's 25th Wedding Anniversary

CH - 14
THE HOTEL

On September 12th, 1956, my father somehow managed to purchase the smaller Greek hotel known as Castelles for $17,000. Perhaps, it was common knowledge among the others, but it was a total surprise to Nick and me - after all, who buys a Hotel! At the time I was 11, and I remember Nick and me spending endless hours imagining what it would be like to spend the winter weekends in Monroe. Although we rarely saw Walton lake frozen, certainly not thick enough to walk on, now we were envisioning skating on the magical Lake.

We couldn't wait to see the Hotel, and our first attempt was during the dead of winter. Although Rocco was driving the Big M, without snow chains, it was virtually impossible to navigate the steep roadways. The next attempt was in early Spring. I recently saw a small black and white photo of Dad, Caesar, Nick, and me standing in deep snow on the front lawn, with the Hotel in the background.

Nick Dad, and me Winter Scene

Hotel Spring Scene

The Hotel was a circa 1900 three-story wood-frame structure with a large open front porch and a screened side porch on the right. It was well secluded in the middle of a 5-acre parcel situated between the private summer communities of, Idle Hour Park and Lakeview Estates. The property featured expansive lawns on the front and the left side, bordered by dense woodlands. Facing the front Lawn, there was a concrete semicircle in the center of which was a large flower garden. The Hotel's perimeter was surrounded by mature lilac bushes which, in the spring, produced magnificent deep purple blooms.

The approach from Idle Hour Park was via a private, well crowned, winding dirt road, lined with mature spruce trees. After passing a regulation-sized, red clay Tennis court on the right, the road split to the left past the front of the Hotel and continued through a vacant quarter-acre lot providing "Ingress and Egress" to Lake View Estates. At some point, I believe, this became a legal bone of contention which was eventually resolved in our favor.

The split to the right passed a small four-room Cottage presumably for the help and continuing further provided access to the rear of the Hotel for deliveries to the kitchen and the basement. Directly behind the Hotel was a much larger rectangular wood-framed Cottage with eight bedrooms. Beyond the Cottage and deep in the woods, was a fieldstone Pump House for the well, accessed by a narrow footpath.

The wide front steps to the expansive front porch provided entry to a spacious Living Room. It featured four equally spaced, 18' square columns adorned with leaded glass brass fixtures. There was a floor to ceiling fieldstone Fireplace on the right, with a 5'x6' open-hearth above which was a massive wood mantle.

The left rear corner was graced with a beautiful Grand Staircase leading to the second and third-floor bedrooms. A small reception counter lined the center back wall, to the left of which was a swinging doorway leading to a large commercial kitchen. To the far right, were a pair of French doors which opened to the long screened -in side porch, which was a seasonal Dining Room. Rolled maroon canvases served as protect ion from the elements, which were eventually replaced by jalousie windows.

Directly behind the Living room, was a commercial-sized Kitchen with a large walk-in freezer and direct access to the back of the seasonal Dining room. There was a small common hallway behind the staircase which led to men and women's bathrooms as well as to a small Bar.

The quaint Bar was approximately 20' x 50' featuring a well-seasoned counter with four bar stools and a handsome back bar mirror. There was an upright piano on the right and French doors on the left leading to a small terraced patio area.

The Grand Staircase amply complimented the beauty of the large columned living room and massive fieldstone fireplace. The craftsmanship of its thick banister and railings were clearly of a bygone era. The first three broad steps led to a spacious lower landing which, turning right, ascended to an equally spacious second landing which, turning right again, led to the second-floor hallway.

I believe the second floor had five standard-sized bedrooms and one exceptionally large front bedroom. The staircase continued in a similar fashion to the third floor which had basically the same configuration of bedrooms. Each floor had a single communal bathroom, and each bedroom had double beds, a dresser, and a sink with hot and cold running water. There was a fire escape from the rear of the third-floor hallway along the back of the Hotel.

The balance of the property to the rear of the hotel was mostly wooded which became denser as the terrain gradually elevated to a summit, followed by a steep decline. I particularly remember the steep terrain because I spent many hours in search of the perfect spot to build a secluded fort.

My father intended the Hotel property to be used solely as a private Family Compound. I think he considered it to be a worthwhile investment for the future, certainly large enough to accommodate all of his children and their extended families. I believe his intentions were truly benevolent and accordingly, he structured ownership consisting of seven equal shares, one for each of his children. He, nor we, knew anything about running a Hotel, and to my knowledge, the notion of a commercial venture was never discussed. But, from my personal perspective, his dream or desired legacy was contagious!

He occasionally entertained some of his closest friends and clients, serving them with the finest cheeses, meats, fruits, and wine. I remember when particular clients came to visit, to ensure absolute privacy, Dad would tell me to set up two red metal chairs in the far-right corner of the front lawn.

By the spring of 1957, we slowly became acquainted with the size and scope of the undertaking. We gradually rummaged through each room, taking inventory, and trying to sort out what to keep and what to discard. This was apparently an "as-Is purchase", including all the contents and equipment necessary to operate a Hotel. It was as though, on Sept 12th, 1956, the Castelles just left everything frozen in time. However, it was agreed that the elderly Castelles would be permitted to occupy a room in the back Cottage for the following summer, which proved to be mutually beneficial. However, fearful that the ghost of Castelle might be wandering the hallways, none of us wanted to sleep in the old Hotel. So, we used Cottage 10 as our base for eating and sleeping.

The responsibilities at Cottage 10 seemed minuscule compared to those at the Hotel. Admittedly, being 12, my initial contribution was mostly a Gofer, riding my English racer between both locations -oftentimes watching more than doing. In time, however, unlike at Cottage 10, working at the Hotel was somehow different, it was strangely fulfilling. As I was gradually entrusted with more responsibility, the resulting tiredness offered its own reward. I can only describe it as satisfying or gratifying Tiredness, especially if I was pleased with the completed task. Perhaps it was also seeking acknowledgment for a job well done - that I had finally "Come of Age!" Ironically, this was itself an incentive to continually raise the bar!

Considering the extensive lawns, the first major investment was to purchase a used L Model Gravely from a dealership in Allendale, New Jersey. Considering that our only exposure to lawn mowers was the push reel mower in Brooklyn and the gas-powered reel mower at Cottage 10, both having the same 12-inch diameter.

By comparison, the Gravely had a 36" rotary blade with both forward and reverse gears as well as slow and fast wheel and rotary blade speeds, powered by a powerful 5hp engine. It was so powerful that if you weren't astute, it could easily drag you across the lawn or worse, pin you against a tree or a wall. Consequently, considering my relatively small frame, I was very respectful of the Gravely, often referring to it as the" Beast. " In time, however, because of the extensive tall grass and low brush, we eventually purchased sickle blades and circular saw attachments.

Nick quickly got the hang of handling the Beast, and eventually, under his supervision, I gradually became more confident, but always wary of its awesome power. Initially, however, I was mostly restricted to cutting the lawns, leaving the sickle and circular blade operations to Nick. As he gradually cut and cleared more areas with the sickle, it naturally meant I would eventually be cutting more lawns!

During early spring, it was endless walking, often requiring two weekly cuttings. Thank God, after enough moaning, Rocco relented and purchased a Sulky and a dirt Plow attachment which proved to be invaluable. The powerful Beast easily moved dirt and gravel as well as pulling stumps, logs, and boulders.

At some point, Rocco was determined to transform the overgrown surface of the clay Tennis court to one that would be the envy of the Park! I was assigned the mindless job of using the Beast to drag two old bed springs for hours in endless circles around the court in order to provide a smooth surface that was hardly ever used!

As the first Hotel season ended, it was time to return to Bay Ridge, and with light-hearted excitement, prepare for eighth grade, which was looking very promising! For one thing, given that the dreaded specter of sister Ermingale was no longer haunting me, I was anxious to see who my next teacher would be. I was fearful that it could be Sr.Ermingale's equivalent, Sr. Malicia - just her name should be a clue! I was greatly relieved, however, to learn that, in stark contrast, it would be the young lovable, Sr. Barbara. More importantly, as hope springs eternal, I was also looking forward to seeing what changes the summer might have bestowed on lovely Bernadette!

We continued to visit Cottage 10 and the Hotel on weekends, but foremost was the challenge of doing well academically in order to hopefully gain admission to a High School of my choice. Thankfully, as the school year progressed, Eighth grade was proving to be a better year, both academically and socially. But, the more imminent obstacles were the midterm exams, followed by the dreaded Regents finals and the tedious High School application process. Also, considering that my three brothers had all received Athletic Scholarships, it was time to take swimming more seriously.

SJP Audition   (Oct 1957) As I may have mentioned, to date, my only *Claim to Fame* was swimming the 1500m at the ripe age of 11. Although during the summer I had a decent swimming season, thereafter, access to a pool was extremely limited. With the help of Jimmy Murphy's article in the Daily Brooklyn Eagle, in October 1957, I was invited to audition for a swimming scholarship at St. John's Prep.

Sister Barbara Unlike Sister Ermingale, my eighth- grade teacher, Sister Barbara, was young, pretty, and very cool. I often mused, "How could they possibly be in the same order?" She would occasionally allow us to move our desks to the side of the room and encourage us to dance in the middle of the classroom, alternating *Boys and Girl's choice*- a great mixer!

However, once again, the dark cloud of fate descended when our class received a transfer student by the name of Victor, who was two years older, and one foot taller than any of the other boys in the class! He wasn't necessarily handsome, but he certainly appeared more mature, sporting signs of a faint mustache. Much to my chagrin, as I patiently waited on the sidelines for Boy's *choice*, when I finally got up enough courage to stealthily make my move, Bernadette was already taken by that big dufus, Victor. Upon seeing this, Sister Barbara came over beside me and whispered, "You're gonna have to move a little faster than that, Sport!"

Then, in the second half of the year, Sister announced on Friday that, come Monday our seats would be rotated, and either by design or pure luck, I would finally be seated next to "Gina" Maglino. I couldn't believe that my prayers had finally been answered, and I thought, "God truly is merciful!" I was in ecstasy, and school took on a whole new dimension, but the long weekend was also absolute torture.

On Monday morning, with my hair neatly combed, much to my dismay, when I walked into our classroom, I noticed that Gina's seat was empty! Then my heart sank further when Sister informed the class of the tragic news. Over the weekend, Bernadette was diagnosed with rheumatic fever, and she would probably be out of school for several months! I was absolutely devastated, and I mumbled to myself, "How could God be so cruel! He giveth with the right hand and snatcheth with the left!"

Dance Parties It always baffled me how, during the short summer vacation, seventh-grade girls suddenly matured and *developed!* Consequently, I found 8th grade increasingly more exciting, especially towards the end of the year. Also, the girls were surprisingly eager to teach the boys how to dance, and I was more than eager to learn. During the last few weeks, the girls seemed to host the majority of the basement parties. And for some reason, one girl, in particular, Joyce D'Amico, appeared to take pity on me.

Being that Joyce was very well developed, learning to dance the Lindy, the Cha-Cha and especially, the slow box step became far more interesting!

In some measure, this helped prepare me for our Friday night Confraternity dances. Truthfully, however, I often sought the comradery and safety of the more timid boys like me, who cowered in a remote corner of the room, watching the cooler guys dancing with the girl of their dreams.

I remember one afternoon when my sister Virginia took pity on me and tried teaching me a more sophisticated lindy, one with rhythm and aggressive twirls. I soon learned, however, that it was extremely important to not let go of the girl, especially when spinning her around and out - a sudden retrieval is very embarrassing!

I also remember, Anita, coming to one of my Confraternity dances, and telling me, "Now, in the very beginning, just pick out a girl and ask her to dance!" So, heeding her sage advice, when I spotted my rather tall classmate, Judith De Menthe, sitting on the sidelines, I casually sauntered over and with a suave high pitched voice asked, Would you like to dance?" Much to my surprise, she accepted, but when she stood up, she was at least six inches taller than me, and I realized that she was wearing heels. I just turned and gave my sister a look that said it all.

The New Church   The long-overdue construction of a new Parish church began in the early fifties on the corner of 4th Ave and 84th St. and was completed in 1954. By comparison, It was an enormous modern edifice with light pinkish marble floors and walls and gorgeous stained-glass windows. I remember the strange "echo" with even the slightest whisper, and certainly way too loud for the clicking *Castanets*. Realizing that we still relied on the clickers like a flock of mindless sheep rely on dogs, we were still relegated to the Old Church until our Confirmation.

Uncle Joe's Wake   Recalling the echoing in the New Church reminds me of a particular incident Rocco and I experienced. My father's dear cousin, Joe Cirigliano, lived in an apartment in Carol Court on Third Ave and 81stt St. He and his wife, Lena, would occasionally walk down to our house with his trademark, cigar tightly clenched between his teeth. He would always greet me by pretending to shadow box with me. When he eventually died at a very respectable old age, my mother delegated Rocco and me to represent the family at his wake.

It was in the early evening, and for some reason, we decided to stop in the New church to say a prayer prior to the wake. Given the hour, the church was sparsely attended and extremely quiet. Due to the extensive amount of marble, you could literally hear a pin drop. As we both marched up the center aisle in search of a remote pew, I noticed that one of Rocco's shiny Cordovan shoes emitted a very loud *Squeak*. So, with every other step, there was this annoying *squeak* that sounded thunderous in the church's cavernous echo-chamber.

When we finally occupied a pew and knelt down, I could still hear the sound of that rhythmic squeak in my head and immediately started laughing, causing the kneeler to start bouncing up and down. Feeling this, and sensing what I was laughing about, Rocco also started laughing, and in no time, we were both hysterical, bouncing up and down on the kneeler, like two idiots. The crescendo of uncontrollable laughter and bouncing was so obvious, that we had to quickly exit the pew in disgrace, walking down the aisle disturbing everyone with the same annoying squeak.

Now it was time to attend the Wake which was in an upstairs Funeral Parlor. I clearly remember, upon entering the small room, there was a sudden *hush,* and typical of most Italian wakes, all the elderly ladies were completely dressed in black, with black lace covering their head and face. They were all sitting quietly along both sides of the room gazing at the open casket in the far end of the room. Above the hush, however, we could clearly hear, "That's the Cirigliano boys!". Trying to be respectful of the somber occasion, as we slowly approached the open casket, once again, the annoying *squeak* became very audible.

While we both knelt on the narrow kneeler in front of the casket, I could feel the kneeler starting to bounce up and down. Within seconds, we were both bouncing up and down uncontrollably. Seeing this, the elders naturally assumed that we were both grief-stricken and crying, prompting them to bring us tissues to dry our eyes. That only made matters worse, and just when we thought we had it under control, it would start all over again. After fifteen long minutes of bouncing, we gradually regained a modicum of composure, and after offering our sincere condolences, we exited the parlor room as quickly as possible in order to minimize the annoying squeak. I doubt that there will ever be redemption for either of us.

Confirmation   The day before our Confirmation ceremony, we had a rehearsal in the New Church in preparation for the main event. Of course, I had to choose a confirmation name and when I asked my mother for a suggestion, after a very brief pause, she said, "Joseph". When I reminded her of my middle name, she said, "Well, now it's Joseph Joseph!" I believe that my brothers also had Joseph as their middle name.

I remember getting dressed in our red gowns and processing up the shiny marble center aisle. When I knelt in front of the elderly Bishop, he was handed an index card and then asked me, "Peter Joseph, what name do you take for confirmation?" when I answered, Joseph, he seemed momentarily perplexed and after a long pause said, "Well, that's easy to remember" - then I realized my mother's logic! After the traditional light slap on the side of my face, he gave me his blessing. I don't recall if anyone came to the ceremony and we certainly didn't have any celebration.

Gonzaga   Gonzaga and the Mountain House retreat center was a monastery of sorts, intended for not only elderly Jesuit priests, but also a refuge for those Jesuits who had either sobriety or a variety of other recovery issues. The compound was also the first Jesuit retreat in the United States, intended for *Inner-city youths.*

At the time, Fr. Dominic was the pastor of Nativity Parish, located in lower Manhattan. Many of the local kids from his parish were the beneficiaries of this unique, "get the kids out of the city," summer camp program. The goal was to send young underprivileged boys from the parish to experience several weeks in the beautiful Catskill mountains surrounding the Gonzaga retreat center.

Nick Santella   Nick Santella was about 10 years older than the other boys at Gonzaga ,and In addition to his daily chores as a manual laborer, he also functioned as a mentor, supervising the younger boys. Apparently, he and my father forged a close lifelong friendship. As a gifted craftsman, he continued to provide valuable services for our family, doing just about any job required, especially carpentry. The bonds of love and respect were mutual, and he eventually became one of the family, playing a very important role in our future.

Dad with Gonzaga Boys

Gonzaga was located on an expansive piece of property on Skunymonk mountain range in Monroe N.Y. Entry to the Retreat House was by way of Seven Springs Mountain Rd, a winding dirt road which gradually climbed to the summit of the mountain, thereby providing a commanding view of the surrounding countryside. The main entrance was marked by two large fieldstone pillars, flanked by impressive fieldstone walls. Immediately to the left of the entrance was a life-sized statue depicting the crucifixion on Mount Calvary, and directly across from the entrance was a large spring fed pond with an old wooden diving board.

After passing through the pillars, the interior property consisted of the main stone Castle building on the left. Incidentally, In the sub-basement of the Castle was a tiny *Grotto Chapel* which contained a beautiful stained glass window dedicated to my father and two other Gonzaga benefactors.

To the right was a 3 story wood frame building known as the *Mountain House*, with a tiny first- floor Chapel. This chapel was particularly memorable because, on weekends during the fall, my parents and I would attend eight o'clock Sunday masses in the intimate chapel with a very simple altar and a narrow center aisle flanked by four wooden pews.

What I remember most was the deafening silence and close proximity to the altar which added to the sense of reverence. Also, in contrast to Sacred Heart, where dad would attend mass by reading the newspaper in his car, I was shocked when, prior to the consecration, he would actually offer to assist the priest as a server on the altar! Bewildered, when I looked at my mother she whispered, "You know, your father was an altar boy!"

Between these two buildings was a very unusual octagonal stone **Chapel in the Round**. The interior was unusually ornate with a beautiful center altar, but only able to accommodate relatively small groups to attend mass. I only recall one such occasion when, during an annual Picnic Reunion, all the men and boys crowded into the chapel for the quickest mass I've ever seen. To the left of the chapel entrance, was a life-size bronze statue of The Boy Jesus.

Gonzaga Jesuit Retreat Center

The Stations   Beyond the chapel, there was a path that meandered through the dense woodlands and along which were life-size statues depicting the Stations of the Cross. During one annual picnic, I clearly remember that, at precisely 3 pm, all the men and their families walked reverently along the winding path, stopping at each Station to recite the rosary. The procession eventually came full circle ending in front of the Hill Chapel. I remember this small chapel as being perched high on a hill, strangely resembling a desolate mausoleum, and In front of which, were several Jesuit gravestones. One being, Fr Walsh, a revered contemporary of Fr. Dominic.

I can only surmise that Fr. Walsh was possibly the originator of the camp program or the one in charge of the boys during their stay at Gonzaga. I remember while standing in front of the chapel being surprised when it was my father's turn to recite a decade of the rosary. I was shocked that he not only knew how to say the rosary, but actually knew the name of the decade!

Picnic Reunions   I clearly remember the annual picnics as being very festive, and Nick and I going from table to table smelling and sampling the various foods, especially grilled sausage, and peppers. I enjoyed meeting some of these men and witnessing their laughter as they regaled each other with fond memories, retelling stories of their youthful past. Most of all, I enjoyed watching Dad's pride and joy when introducing Nick and me to these old friends. It allowed us a brief glimpse of how Gonzaga obviously provided a reprieve from the crowded city streets of their beloved Nativity parish. It was also an opportunity to meet many of Dad's cousins, known as the Bronx Ciriglianos, who would play a vital role in our future.

The Ice Pool   Veering off the Station path was another path traversing deep in the woods. It led to a large rectangular fieldstone structure with 10' high walls covered with Ivy, enclosing a large strange rectangular pool. There were a series of 4' high pipes running across the entire length of the pool which, I suspect, was a showering system. In addition to a rust tint, I remember the water temperature being extremely cold. Dad always came prepared for any opportunity to demonstrate our swimming ability. So, without hesitation, he told Nick and me to suit-up behind one of the stone walls!

Then, with a small audience of well-wishers, we both dipped our toes into the ice-cold pool, and looking at each other with the same startled expression, we simultaneously muttered "He must be kidding!" Needless to say, he wasn't. After the initial entry shock, I raced to the other end and quickly jumped out before he had a chance to say, "Just, do another lap". Talk about shrinkage, it's a wonder I ever had children!

Nativity Reunion   My father, along with 50 or 60 other men who were also beneficiaries of this unique youth program, congregated each year for a Gonzaga benefactor Reunion. I recently saw a picture taken in 1955 of these men assembled in front of the Castle building. They were all proudly smiling, having shared such a marvelous youth program.

Gonzaga Reunion 1955

Sadly, many years later, I discovered that the entire Gonzaga property was up for sale, and I contacted the remaining Jesuit in charge of overseeing the orderly transfer of the property. After telling him my tale of woe, he allowed me to retrieve the commemorative stained glass window from the Grotto Chapel which I proudly displayed in our Goshen home.

He also allowed me to remove the statue of the Boy Jesus which I eventually donated to St John's parochial school where it currently resides. Ironically, although the Boy Jesus was appropriately holding a staff in his right hand, I subsequently learned that Fr. Muldoon SJ removed the staff claiming, "The boy Jesus never carried a staff!" Incensed, I reasoned that the staff was symbolic. Besides, how the hell would he know what Jesus carried!.

CH 15
MY PARENTS

Dad Caesar Anthony Cirigliano 8/22/04 - 8/06/58
Mom Lucia (Alice) Clorinda Tronalone 10/17/05- 5/10/85

*D**ad*** My father attended Xavier high school, and as part of his curriculum, he became a member of the debate team and elocution club for which he received a distinguished award. He also received the Edgar Allan Poe award for his recitation of the Raven.

Dad's Xavier HS Poe Award

After graduation, he attended Columbia University for either six months or a year and was *persuaded* by Father Dominic to switch to Fordham University. Being that he was the first of his generation to graduate from a University, it was considered quite an achievement. Subsequently, he was accepted to and graduated from Fordham Law school.

Dad's graduation from Fordham Law School

While doing my homework, when confronted with grammar or math questions, my mother would often defer to my father saying, "you know, your father was a grammar and math teacher!" However, I never really knew if that was just to get rid of me. The bookcases in the front Sunroom contained numerous texts such as, Famous Shakespearean Quotations and Toastmaster Stories and Jokes which made him an ideal candidate as a *Master of Ceremonies.*

I remember one morning, before leaving for school I was in a total panic because I was supposed to present a humorous story in front of the entire class. Almost instantly he came up with a short story entitled, "The Scotsman and his wife" which was very funny, and saved me from a lifetime of embarrassment, especially in front of Bernadette.

As mentioned previously, during Dad's three-month *Retreat* following the birth of the twin's, my mother carried the burden of parenting and managing the household. As part of his recovery, he focused on self-improvement measures, embracing the mind-body connection, eventually realizing that true recovery was a question of, Mind over Matter.

His relaxation and breathing techniques were mostly the result of paying close attention to the diaphragmatic breathing of most opera singers. In the future, perhaps recalling his past, he would demonstrate empathy for and a willingness to teach others based on his own life experiences. For the most part, if you paid attention, he often shared lifelong messages or lessons, and I would come to regard him as a far better Teacher than I would ever be. He would often say, "I'd rather teach someone with limited gifts and the desire to learn and improve than one who takes their gifts for granted!"

Once he regained stability, the most pressing issue was to provide for his family by concentrating on his fledgling law practice. Early on he began honing his craft, calling upon his earlier debating, elocution, and public speaking skills. He gradually developed an impressive vocabulary by memorizing 10 new dictionary words every night. His penchant for elocution extended even to the rest of us by frequently asking us to recite with perfect diction, "How now brown cow, sitting in the green green grass." He embraced the nuances of effective drama, often quoting Shakespeare for theatrical emphasis, especially during his court summations.

Let's Take a Ride   His mastery of the Socratic method, combined with his courtroom logic, eloquence and drama projected the image of an old world Barrister - often referred to as a *Mouthpiece*. In time, however, representing high profile criminal defendants was taking its toll, and at some point, he wanted to transition to pure Negligence and personal Injury cases.

However he was being pressured to take one more high profile case. As an inducement, one evening when he arrived home from work, a black limousine was waiting across the street from our Bay Ridge home. He was *offered* to take a ride along the Palisades, and according to my mother, when he returned home, his complexion was ashen. Needless to say, he accepted the case!

I remember hearing the story of when my father was representing a real Dead- Beat Wise- guy who owed my father a considerable amount of money. Just before the judge asked how the defendant intended to plead, my further turned to his client and said, "Now, about your outstanding balance. Do you want me to merely represent you or present a vigorous Defense?" The dead beat got the message and assured my father of prompt payment!

Professionally, he was always well dressed, wearing mostly brown or gray, single, or double-breasted suits, accented with a lapel carnation and a breast pocket-handkerchief. He would often invite us to, "Come and watch me do battle in the courtroom arena!" Unfortunately, to my knowledge, none of us seized the opportunity, relying instead on his stellar reputation.

He very much wanted one of his sons to eventually join him in the practice of law. While my brother Caesar was attending Fordham University, which was across the street from his office, Caesar would occasionally visit my father. More often, however, my father would request to see him. Invariably, when he arrived at the office, although he wore the required jacket, he refused to comply with the tie, and he always wore the same tan khakis, which always disappointed Dad. Being his namesake, however, despite his apparent nonconformity, I think Dad had great expectations that, one day, Caesar would likely follow in his footsteps.

Since Bay Ridge was adjacent to the notorious Bensonhurst section of Brooklyn, Dad was always concerned about the possibility of Guilt by Association- whether it be the neighborhood or the private school system. He considered such an association as potentially jeopardizing one's approval by the Bar Association's character committee.

Uncle Sil Eventually, my father's law partner, Sylvester Cosentino, (Uncle Sil), handled the majority of the high profile criminal cases, especially in the federal court system. They shared a large 10th-floor office suite at 291 Broadway, each with their own large corner office and private secretaries in the front reception room. There was also a smaller third office occupied by the partner's Private Investigator, who my father said was invaluable. Uncle Sil and his wife, Aunt Kitty, would often join us for various holiday dinner celebrations. Dad respected his partner's legal talent and expertise, but from a personal perspective, I'm not so sure he completely trusted his ethics.

As the story goes, uncle Sil kept large sums of cash in his office safe. One Saturday morning I remember my father receiving a frantic phone call from uncle Sil ,claiming that his safe had been burglarized! Although he considered it an inside job, considering the unusual circumstances, he was reluctant to report the theft to the police.

Dad called his close friend, John Dondero, who lived on 85th St in Bay Ridge. As a chemist, John developed new methods to detect fingerprint and gunpowder residue. Accordingly, in addition to working for the Treasury Department, he was also a contractor for the FBI. Dad met John at the office in order to dust for fingerprints matching any of the employees, but I never knew the outcome. Incidentally, being that John worked in the Treasury Department, I remember one Christmas he brought over an uncut sheet of $1.00 bills which I thought was the coolest gift I'd ever seen.

Uncle Julie   Julius Siegel was an attorney who occupied an office on the same floor as my father and for whom he had a great deal of professional respect. Uncle Julie suffered from a very evident nervous tic, which apparently didn't hamper his notable success in the courtroom. I remember one morning, driving with my father to his office and stopping for a red light on the corner of Broadway. Dad happened to notice Uncle Julie patiently waiting for the light to turn green. He was carrying a well-worn brown leather briefcase, presumably on his way to court which was diagonally across the street.

As the light turned green, my father said, "Now watch this!" As Uncle Julie began walking in the crosswalk, my father waited until he was directly in front of our car and blasted the horn! Poor Uncle Julie, immediately jumped, dropping his briefcase, and his nervous tic became so pronounced, he looked as though he just got zapped with a 12-volt battery. I thought for sure poor uncle Julie was about to have a seizure. Incidentally, to this day,

I think of Uncle Julie every time my unsuspecting wife crosses in front of our car and jumps when I blast the horn!

Despite my father's sick sense of humor, he had great respect for Uncle Julie's professionalism and integrity. In fact, I remember him saying, "If ever we had to call upon one of the Uncles for guidance, choose Julie"- which, in the future, would prove to be very sage advice.

Mom   I don't ever remember my father cooking. In fact, I doubt if he even knew how to boil an egg! But without question, I firmly believe that his lifelong goal was to hone his professional craft and to selflessly provide for his family. My mother, on the other hand, was a virtual workhorse exhibiting unyielding strength, courage, and endurance, while quietly tending to all the household needs. She was boldly imaginative and decisive, especially when, with the help of Nick Santella, it came to making executive decisions regarding physical changes in each of our homes. As a matter of fact, my father at one point quipped that he was wary of coming home from work at night fearing that she had rearranged their bedroom!

By now, It should be readily apparent that I held my father on a high pedestal, and from my perspective, he left a lasting impression of one who cast a very big shadow. Although it might have appeared that my mother was subservient to my father - allowing him to take center stage while she waited patiently in the wings. In truth, it was her courage, strength and determination that provided the sustaining *Wind beneath the Wings* of the fragile man.

No doubt, she greatly admired his accomplishments, and he adored her. Although he was certainly acknowledged and more visible in his world, she remained the steadfast Worker Bee, providing the Family Glue. He may have been the Bricks, but she was the Mortar. True, my father managed the big picture, but on a daily basis, my mother managed the household, the meals, and the daily needs of seven kids on $20 a day - which he would leave on the kitchen counter each morning before leaving for work.

Special Mornings   As I mentioned earlier, because of the large number of students attending St. Anselm's, grades one through three were split into A and B sessions. Session A was from 8 am to 12 noon, and the B sessions were from 1 pm to 5 pm - switching every 18 weeks during the school year. Although the split sessions had academic drawbacks, after the others left for school and before my father left for work, the B session allowed for a unique opportunity to spend precious time with both my parents.

Without the distraction of others, It was particularly special being the proverbial fly on the wall, allowing me to see the unfiltered interaction between my parents. At the time I was extremely thin, and despite a special foul tasting brown liquid formula provided by Carlton Fredericks, my father was worried enough that he would bribe me by offering five cents for eating each slice of wheat toast!

Affection & Emotion   Both my parents were very reserved with their outward signs of love and affection, especially towards each other. This was often dampened by my mother's quip, "Oh Caesar, don't be so demonstrative!". Although I never doubted their love, I don't remember either of my parents giving a warm embrace or saying, "I love you." Unfortunately, family photographs are very limited, and I don't recall seeing either of my parents having direct physical contact - such as an arm around the shoulder or a clasp of hands, let alone an embrace!. The most direct physical contact I recall is my mother holding my frozen hands in her bosom, or my father combing my hair with water-soaked metal brushes or shaking my hand vigorously while saying, "Put it there my best friend!"

Likewise, although humor and laughter were readily encouraged, outward signs of emotion, such as crying, were considered a sign of weakness and never to be exhibited publicly.

I thought perhaps it was a generational thing or it just wasn't their style. I know that, at some point, they each must have experienced great sadness in their lives. In particular, shortly before I was born, both of my father's parents died within one day of each other. And shortly after, the death of his guardian and mentor, Father Dominic. I often wondered, when and how did the fragile man deal with this sadness? Did he grieve silently alone, or did he share it with my mother?

Love   Later in life I would often muse, I know they loved each other, but because it was never demonstrative, I wondered, were they still in love with each other? Did they even say it to each other privately? Or was it as self-evident as it was to Goldie when responding to Tevye's repeated query, "But do you love me?" (Fiddler on the Roof). Now, with the benefit of hindsight, without question their love and sacrifice for Family and each other was self-evident. Perhaps, as with the mere, "look of love" in one's eyes, the need for affirmation somewhat diminishes the luster of that which is self-evident.

Humor   During these brief private mornings, I was privileged to witness my father's self-effacing sense of humor and amorous playfulness toward my mother. He loved watching The Honeymooners, and In many respects, he had a phenotype similar to Jackie Gleason - a large abdominal girth and round facial features with large bulging eyes. Consequently, he would readily seize any opportunity to imitate him.

Laughter   Early in the morning, my mother tuned the radio station to William B Williams, who played most of the current tunes. One morning, when my father came down to the kitchen, Perry Como was singing his hit tune, "Papa loves Mambo" on the radio. I didn't recall seeing my parents ever dance with each other, but upon hearing the catchy tune, my father attempted his version of the mambo with exaggerated "to and fro" hip gyrations, resembling Jackie Gleason. While trying to lure my mother to dance with bulging circular eye gyrations, my mother started laughing saying, "Caesar, stop it, you're going to hurt yourself!"

During the Christmas holidays, Dad would often entertain everyone at breakfast, but mostly himself, by singing, "All I want for Christmas is my two front teeth". This was particularly funny because my father had recently undergone dental extractions of his front teeth leaving him with a gaping space hidden by poorly fitting dentures. He would purposely remove the dentures in order to exaggerate the *whistle sound* made by the young child while singing the song with the loss of his front teeth.

One morning he came strolling into the kitchen in his boxer underwear, wearing a round vaudeville straw hat, a bamboo cane with the handle draped over his left forearm, and singing while strumming a ukulele. My mother just looked at him incredulously, and with controlled laughter said, "Caesar, go put your pants on before you catch a cold!"

One morning, when Dad failed to leave $20 on the counter before leaving for work, my mother said, "Caesar, you forgot to leave the money!" In typical dramatic fashion, imitating his role model, Jackie Gleason, he exclaimed, "Here Alice, take all my money!" After slamming the $20 on the counter, as a prelude to his grand exit he purposely pulled all his empty pants pockets inside-out and strutted out of the kitchen.

The Movie Theater   I never knew my parents to go to the movies, however, this was the exception. I don't remember what the occasion was, but one late afternoon my parents, and I went to the new Monroe movie theater. Perhaps it was for a brief respite from the summer heat. Upon entering the cool air-conditioned theater, I was stunned when Dad bought some popcorn. Mom was wearing a lovely low cut sundress, and naturally I sat between them in the privacy of the darkened theater. I don't remember what the movie was about, and I doubt that my father did either. He was preoccupied with throwing popcorn kernels down my mother's dress and then offering to retrieve them, which I thought was absolutely hilarious.

My mother would no sooner retrieve the kernel, and he would lob another one in. She would quietly protest, "Caesar, stop making a fool of yourself!" But that was all the encouragement he needed. Despite her protests, however, this went on for quite a while, and when there was a brief pause, it didn't take much coaxing for him to do it again. At times, my mother seemed amused, but she kept trying to subdue her silent laughter.

Although the time was brief, they were precious moments which provided many lasting memories. More importantly, from my limited perspective I came to know and appreciate each of my parents, not only as loving caregivers, but also in the fullness of their individual qualities. Undoubtedly, my recollection of our parents, and in particular of my father, may be at variance with those of my siblings for obvious reasons. Our relative ages, circumstances and consequent relationships were understandably quite different. I was fortunate to have a more exclusive relationship, as a companion, appendage, or sidekick before any adolescent or teenage rebelliousness.

Profanity   I never heard either of my parents use blatant profanity, and it wasn't permitted by guests or anyone else in our household. Dad's occasional refrains, "Why you ungrateful sonofabitch" or "Why you horse's ass" were usually for just cause. The only other memorable one was, "Well, you can kiss my ass in Macy's window'!" Just the absurd visual provoked silent laughter!

As you might expect, along with a healthy diet, vitamins, and exercise, smoking in the house was out of the question. However, I know my aunt Olga smoked, and it was inferred that, in her younger years, Mom may have also smoked. I remember once teasing my mother and prodded her to light a cigarette and smoke it in the kitchen. I was absolutely stunned when she lit one of my Aunt's cigarettes, and she nonchalantly smoked half the cigarette maintaining a cavalier demeanor.

Sports   My father enjoyed playing pinochle in the house with Papa Datre and Uncle Tony. Although I doubt he ever smoked cigarettes, I suspect he may have occasionally smoked a cigar, especially while playing pinochle at the local social (political) club. He was either a manager or a sponsor for the local, Victoria baseball team. I recently saw a small black and white photo of him standing with the entire team, and I suspect he enjoyed sharing a few beers with them after practice or a game. He also enjoyed an occasional shot of scotch, his favorite being Haig & Haig Pinch.

Other than swimming and boxing, he offered very little in terms of sports. On occasion, he would emphasize the importance of keeping your eye on the ball and a level swing while at-bat. When it came to basketball, he loved to watch the Globetrotters. In those days, foul shots were most often delivered underhand from between the knees. But when it came to shooting from the outside, he would emphasize to shoot from above your head rather than your chest in order to avoid even a brief interruption of visual focus.

Meals   Mom could make delicious weekday meals from scratch or disguising leftovers with additional vegetables, beans, or potatoes. The meals were always very nourishing and healthy. They mostly consisted of a bean or vegetable base, such as lentil soup with without pasta, escarole with or without meatballs, pasta Fagioli, spinach with eggs, or potatoes. For dessert, homemade custards, and various puddings - bread, rice, and my favorite, chocolate pudding. Each morning our handful of vitamins were washed down with freshly squeezed orange or grapefruit juice. Of course, on Thursdays and Sundays, we would have pasta and freshly made meatballs complemented with fresh semolina Italian bread and a tossed salad.

Discipline   When it came to discipline, Dad could kill you with just his eyes and whip you with his tongue. I don't remember him ever really hitting Nick or me. There was, however, one notable exception when he slapped me in the face for imitating Virginia's boyfriend, Art Fowler, who was afflicted with a stuttering disorder.

My father usually arrived home from the office around 6 pm. If you didn't come home on time, especially if you ignored being called for dinner when you finally arrived at the front door, Dad would greet you by standing in the vestibule saying, "Come on in, I'm not going to hit you" However, that didn't mean that, upon passing by him in the vestibule he wasn't going to pull your sideburns, causing you to walk on your tiptoes!

Alternatively, being very quick with his hands, he might intentionally skin the back of your head with his hand which was far better than the sideburn pull. Shortly afterward, while still smarting, he would occasionally say, "Now, kiss my hand because someday you're going to thank me!" I can assure you, that never came to pass.

Mom, on the other hand, would run after me saying, "Don't let me catch you because I'm going to give you a licking you'll never forget!". Although that threat never made sense to me, I ran like hell anyway! Perhaps as a deterrent or fair warning, when you heard her loudly opening the kitchen drawer that meant, "The dreaded wooden spoon was coming out!" And that was serious!

Once, Caesar was cornered in the front Sunroom by Mom's 5'2" frame, wielding the lethal wooden spoon in her hand. When she went to hit him he reflexively blocked it with his forearm, shattering mom's lethal weapon. Thereafter, she resorted to the more durable, metal spoon!

Grandma Datre　Unfortunately, I only had the privilege of knowing one set of grandparents, and except under special situations, I rarely heard my parents speaking to each other in cryptic Italian. However, when Grandma Datre was visiting my mother, I would often overhear them speaking to each other in, what I presumed was, Italian.

Ironically, my grandmother would occasionally refer to my mother by her given name, Lucia. On one such occasion, due to Grandma's dentures, I observed that she was chewing her food with a scissoring motion. Seeing this, I brazenly commented, "Gee Grandma, you chew like a cow!" Hearing this she exclaimed, "Lucia, did you hear what he said to me!".

On another occasion, I was lying with my head resting on Grandma's lap while watching TV in the Sunroom. Suddenly, I heard continuous rumbling and loud gurgling coming from her soft belly. Hearing this I said, "Gee grandma, you have a lot of gas!" Once again she exclaimed, "Lucia, did you hear what this little fresh boy just said to me!" Sadly, unless specifically asked, my parents rarely discussed their Italian heritage. Even then, considering that the prevalent emphasis was on Americanization, the responses were usually generic and cursory, as though it was no longer important or relevant.

Monroe Visits   During the fall, my parents and I would frequently drive to Monroe on weekends - which was a golden opportunity for me to press on the gas pedal for the second half of the long trip. Considering the lack of heat and frigid beds, If it was particularly cold, I would often sleep between my parents in order to keep warm. Much to my dismay, they would mumble something to each other in Italian and just start laughing. Being about seven or eight years of age, what did I know? But then again, sister Ermingale always said, I wasn't too smart!

Arguments   I don't recall my parents having arguments, and if they did, they must have been in private. However there was apparently one that must have been a real doozy! My mother suddenly left home to visit her sister, Lee, for several days. Being a gutsy lady, I suspect that she packed a bag and took a train to Aunt Lee's home in Connecticut.

I don't know if it was due to an argument or perhaps she just felt unappreciated. I remember the fragile man being absolutely devastated and paralyzed. As I said, he had difficulty boiling water, let alone making coffee or frying an egg. I think her extended absence reminded all of us of how dependent we were on her guiding presence. She was truly the essential cog in the family wheel.

I remember my father calling her daily from his desk phone in the living room, trying to persuade her to return home. I assume he was eventually successful, and he drove to Connecticut in order to bring her back home. Upon her return, he appeared unusually contrite and overly attentive, demonstrating a renewed sense of appreciation - suggesting that he was the likely culprit!

Vacations   I don't recall my parents ever taking a vacation. Perhaps, given that we were privileged to spend the hot summers in a beautiful cool country setting, it was equivalent to a long Vacation. However that

Vacation only applied to us because, during the weekdays Dad drove from 8311 to his Manhattan Office and Mom continued with the daily household chores at Cottage 10. This was truly a personal Sacrifice for the sake and well-being of their Family!

Incidentally, I become physically weakened when considering that they shared a brief 25 years together as selfless parents, without the benefit of even a brief respite alone. Perhaps, it was the weightiness of my father's financial burdens of supporting and educating seven children while providing upscale living in two ideal locations that ultimately led to his early demise - or was it just how their generation handled their family obligations?

Respect Everything revolved around La Familia (the Family). Their generation seemed to show far more respect, bordering on reverence, for their Anziani (Elders) - including, not only grandparents, but also aunts, uncles, and cousins. It wasn't just respect for their age and council, but also for their storytelling.

My father would bring us regularly to visit his sister, Aunt Mae (Mary) and to Grandma Ciri's sister, Aunt Millie. I remember visiting her second floor apartment and being greeted with the same predictable salutation, "Vieni qui" (come here). And then, with arms outstretched, she would exclaim, "Ma come sei Bella" (how beautiful you are) while grabbing both my cheeks and twisting them, causing me to stand on my tiptoes and my eyes to tear!

Then I remember walking down a long dark corridor to an empty back bedroom which was particularly cold and dark. All the windows were covered with brown paper, and a single dull light bulb hung from the ceiling, emitting just enough light to see the Provolone, Soppressata,(salami) and Pepperoni hanging from the rafters.

Aunt Millie was married to my godfather, Uncle Joe Trento, who became very wealthy as a result of inventing or perfecting the dying agents for the colorful feathers commonly worn on various Fedora hats. He eventually trained his nephew, Anthony (aka LaLa), who likewise became very successful. He was a handsome young man who always appeared well-groomed, wearing very classy clothes.

Cush   Living in the same household was another frequent guest, known only as "Cush with the glass eye." The peculiar thing about Cush's eye was that the lid covering the glass eye didn't close, giving the impression that he was always looking at you -even when he was presumably asleep! So, as the story goes, when Cush eventually died, the mortician's solution for the eyelid conundrum was to place a coin over the affected lid long enough to ensure permanent closure. At some point during the wake, however, while kneeling respectfully before the casket, several of the visitors were understandably startled to suddenly see Cush staring back at them!

Dad's Office   I enjoyed going with my father to his Manhattan office at 291 Broadway. I remember being in awe of the elevator's polished floor bank, interior brass railings and shiny brass accordion gate, operated by a very polite uniformed black attendant with whom my father was very fond.

Dad's waiting room reminded me of a Perry Mason courtroom. The sitting area was separated from the two separate secretarial desks by a highly polished broad railing with thick spindles and two swinging entry railings. Dad's secretary, Evelyn, was on the left, and his partner, Sylvester Cosentino's secretary was on the right. Evelyn would often entertain me by allowing me to use her typewriter.

Schraffts   Dad would occasionally take Nick and me for lunch at his favorite restaurant, Schraffts, which was just down the street from his office. Before leaving, however, he would always make sure that I looked presentable by combing my hair, which was never a quick process. First, he would start by drenching my hair with water. Then, using a stiff metal comb and two metal brushes soaked with more water, he would comb my hair straight back with a part in the middle resembling Alfalfa.

With my entire head and face dripping, and without drying my hair, he'd say, "Ok, let's go!" During the warm weather, while walking the two city blocks it looked like I was sweating profusely. However during the winter, my hair eventually formed ice sickles and my head resembled an unusual ice cap

The Hygienic Pearl   Dad had another peculiar ritual - a Hygienic Pearl - the equivalent of a European bidet! When using the toilet, he said I should remain on the toilet seat while flushing, not just once, but twice, allowing the water's spray to provide hygienic cleansing. This is Interesting, considering that my parents never took a vacation, and neither of them had ever traveled outside the tri-state area! I must admit, however, that the gentle spray of cold water was initially refreshing, and the invigorating second flush ensured a very memorable, wet pearl. At the time I thought, "Gee, Dad is really onto something here!"

However, now being thoroughly soaked, just imagine the next adventure - trying to effectively use the toilet paper! Despite the wet challenge, by using ample amounts of toilet paper, I eventually achieved semi-dryness. However when I flushed the toilet, I saw a mound of white paper slowly rising. I quickly hopped off the seat just in time to watch in horror as it nearly overflowed the rim. That's when I decided, the hell with the European Bidet, I'll stick with the American toilet. In order to not disappoint my father, upon exiting the bathroom I loudly exclaimed, "Boy, now I feel totally refreshed!

Golden Chocolates   Being that Fordham University was relatively close to Schrafft's, if Dad noticed a couple of priests or nuns in the restaurant, it wasn't unusual for him to anonymously pay for their meals. One afternoon Dad took Nick and me to the fancy restaurant, and after finishing our lunch, he shocked us by buying a Golden box of Schrafft's famous chocolates - which we couldn't wait to open!

Then, for some reason, he took us to a private second story pool where we met with a woman who was obviously in charge. I remember Dad trying to persuade her to allow us to swim In the pool, and as an added inducement, we were both stunned when he offered her "our" golden box of chocolates! Despite plying her with chocolates Dad was dismayed when she failed to offer a concession. To boot, even though our eyes were glued to the golden box, she didn't even have the courtesy or mercy to offer us a sample! I could sense an air of dejection, and I think this was perhaps one of Dad's rare personal defeats. Meanwhile, Nick and I just looked at each bewildered as if to say, "What the hell just happened?"

Clay Pottery   At home, I have a unique two-liter clay pottery vessel which gradually narrows towards the top with a peculiar nipple spout. At some point, Dad felt that Nick and I should become more cultured by experiencing the various exotic flavors of international foods. So, instead of Schrafft's, he decided to take us to eat in some mid-eastern restaurant in order to, "savor their exotic cuisine!".

Although we rarely ate lamb at home, it was apparently just enough to know that I couldn't even stand the smell, and this restaurant reeked of lamb! Being that we couldn't even read the menu, Dad asked the waiter for some assistance. As the waiter rambled on we didn't understand a word he said. Needless to say, nothing that was even remotely familiar to either of us, and I'm not so sure about my father. Truthfully, I would have given anything for a simple peanut butter and jelly sandwich.

While scanning the room, I noticed a shelf along the perimeter of the walls, just below the molding. It was lined with a variety of oddly shaped clay pottery vessels, obviously from some mid-eastern region. My father asked the owner if he would demonstrate how one particular vessel was used. The man filled the vessel with water, and while standing beside our table, he raised the vessel high above his head. Then while gently tilting it, he poured the water through the nipple spout directly into his mouth, without spilling a drop.

My father was so impressed with his performance that, when the check came, I was embarrassed when he asked if the clay vessel was included in the bill. I honestly don't know if he ever paid for the pottery, but somehow we ended up bringing it home - which is still displayed in my home.

Impromptu Swim Meet   Dad would go to any swim meet at the drop of a hat. When I was 12, I took the subway to his office expecting that we would then drive up to Monroe. Shortly after I arrived, however, while sitting in front of his desk, he picked up the phone and called someone to register me in a swimming race! Not having a bathing suit was no problem, he simply pulled one out of his bottom desk drawer. Rather than the traditional lightweight nylon suits, this was a much heavier cloth boxer suit, the kind he preferred for providing more *Drag*. Just what I needed, a heavy cloth bathing suit that was two sizes too big, adding to my natural Drag!

When we arrived at the meet, he told me that the only available entry was for the 500 yd. (20 laps) Freestyle, at which point I choked. He said, "Just pretend you're working out!". At the time, although Caesar was a senior at Fordham, he was still considered one of the best in the Metropolitan area, and Nick, the *Fish*, was already a superstar at St Francis Prep. So, naturally, considering that my last name was Cirigliano, I must surely be the next wonder boy!

Somehow, I was inappropriately assigned to the center lane, which is usually reserved for the fastest swimmer. After taking my position behind the starting block, I couldn't help but notice that all the other swimmers towered over me. Then I realized that dad had entered me in the 17 and older age group!

To make matters worse, either the officials had great expectations, or Dad had grossly exaggerated my times! In any event, after my name was announced, and I mounted the starting block, it further highlighted the contrast in our heights. Then I was shocked when the swimmers on either side of me offered to shake my hand - clearly a sign that they were expecting an adolescent prodigy in their midst.

As often happens with heavy cloth bathing suits when they're wet they tend to stretch. So, after the first turn, I felt the back of my suit slipping down toward the crack between my buttocks! Instinctively, when I went to pull up my suit, my rhythm was so disrupted that I decided a less embarrassing option would be to push off the wall with less effort. However, with each subsequent turn, as my drag suit dragged lower exposing more of my crack. So, naturally I pushed off the wall with even less effort. Aside from being emotionally exhausted, I dreaded every agonizing lap!

Aside from twenty embarrassing laps, and being the last one out of the pool, in an effort to preserve my dignity, I briefly thought of feigning an injury. After all, I did sustain a mortal wound to my ego!. As I walked off the deck, the bewildered stares of the judges were offset by the broad smile on my father's face!

Compromising Situations   My father had a penchant for intentionally finding himself in compromising situations, and then reveling in the *Challenge* of extricating himself from the self-imposed embarrassing circumstances - usually with a humorous conclusion!

Syracuse University   Rocco often told the story of an intercollegiate swimming championship at Syracuse University. My parents drove four hours to watch the two day event ,and my mother was ecstatic that it would be their first time staying overnight in a Motel. As the story goes, being an extremely well-attended championship, anyone would be hard-pressed to gain admittance, let alone a seat, without a prior ticket. Anticipating such a formidable *Challenge*, my father purposely wore his homburg hat and black overcoat for the occasion.

As he approached the ticket booth, he buttoned the top of his white shirt, and turned up his coat collar revealing only his face. When the attendant asked where he was to be seated, my father shrugged saying, "Someplace close to the poolside of course!". Perplexed, the attendant asked to see his admission ticket, which would clearly indicate his assigned seat number.

When Dad explained that his secretary was supposed to take care of those arrangements, the attendant said, "I'm sorry Sir, but the stadium is packed, and I'm not supposed to admit anyone in without a valid ticket!". Then Dad rattled the poor man by asking, "Don't you recognize the President of the University?" Embarrassed, the poor man said, "Of course I do!" Then he immediately left his ticket booth to escort the "President" into the Aquatic Center.

Rocco watched in utter amazement as the unwitting attendant proudly escorted the "President of the University" down the stadium steps to one of the few remaining front row seats. It would have been really interesting if the *other* President also showed up for the meet!

The Big M Adventure   In 1955 my father transitioned from the stodgy Hudson Hornet to a sleek new orange and white Mercury known as, *The Big M*. It was always a big event when Dad bought a new car because he rarely took anyone with him before purchasing it. However for some reason, he took me with him to check out a novel new Ford, Edsall. It featured an unusual push-button gear selector mounted in the center of the steering wheel.

Being that it was prior to airbags, Dad reasoned that, in the event of an accident, upon impact, the driver's chest would likely hit and damage the center console of the steering wheel ! So, he chose to buy the Big M instead. When we arrived home, everyone flew outside to inspect the new car ,and Dad was easily convinced to take it out for a spin. He loved the power of this high-performance car, and he was willing to demonstrate its acceleration and cruising speed.

I remember when Nick and I accompanied Dad driving the Big M up to Monroe. As we approached the yellow traffic light in Ramsey N.J, Dad said, "You want to see how fast this car can go?" Then without waiting for a response, he quickly accelerated and zoomed down the highway, blazing through the light, just as it turned red. As we continued at a very fast clip, Dad noticed flashing lights in his rearview mirror of a rapidly approaching cop car. He guesstimated that the New Jersey-New York border was fast approaching, and he seriously considered trying to outrun the cop car across the border.

As the gap closed further, being that good judgment is often the better part of valor, Dad eventually pulled over, just short of the border. Then he told Nick to climb into the backseat saying, "When I give the signal by taking off my hat, just hold your belly and start moaning!" As soon as the cop approached the driver side window, Dad took off his hat and Nick played his part, holding his belly and moaning loudly - quite an impressive performance! Dad explained to the cop that he feared his son might be suffering from acute appendicitis, and he was trying to get him to the nearest hospital. I'm sure he had absolutely no idea where the nearest hospital was, but it sounded good!

Being that this was before the days of radar, my father asked, "Officer, at what point did you "clock" me?" The cop responded, "I *paced* you from the light" - implying that Dad had stopped at the light. Rather than accepting a summons, Dad requested to appear before a judge. The cop replied, "Well then, you'll have to follow me back to Fort Lee, N.J." which surprisingly, Dad, agreed to - so much for the trip to Monroe!

While following the cop car from a very respectable distance, at the Rt 17 and Rt 4 intersection, rather than exiting the roundabout for eastbound Rt 4, Dad kept driving south on Rt 17. Suddenly realizing that he lost my father's car in his rearview mirror, the cop immediately made a U-turn and sped south on Rt 17.

When he finally caught up, he pulled Dad over again. This time, with his right hand on his pistol, the cop glared at Dad saying, "Are you resisting arrest?" Dad responded, "Officer, I wasn't aware that I was under arrest, but you were driving so fast, I couldn't keep up with you! Besides, you're a young man with a gun at your side, and I'm an old man with two children. Do you really think I would resist you?"

Infuriated, the cop said, "Well you're in my custody now, and you better follow me without any more detours!" Dad obliged the cop, by following him to the courthouse in Fort Lee, N.J. We weren't privy to what transpired in the courtroom, but somehow my father had the case moved to New York. As the story goes, given that the cop indicated that he had *paced* my father from the light, Dad had his private investigator measure the distance from the light to where he was pulled over, demonstrating that, given that distance. our car could not have possibly accelerated to the speed indicated by the cop. During a sidebar, the judge said, "Caesar, I can't let you walk out of here without, at least a fine!" I believe my father received a token fine of five dollars.

Chaminade Game   I remember one Saturday morning Nick being very upset that he missed St. Francis' school bus providing transportation to the annual, St. Francis vs Chaminade football game. Knowing this, I accompanied Dad as he drove Nick out to Mineola, L I. for the exciting game. When we finally arrived in the Big M, Nick felt terrible that he only had one ticket for himself. Dad said, "Don't worry, we'll go park the car, and see if we can buy two tickets at the gate." Nick explained that the game was sold out, and it would be impossible to buy tickets. Nevertheless, Dad dropped Nick off at the gate, and we went to park the car.

Shortly after, while wearing his hallmark Homburg hat and long dark blue topcoat, he told me, "Just stay behind me and don't say a word!". While approaching the entry gate, he buttoned the top of his white shirt and turned up the color of his topcoat. After introducing himself, he politely asked the attendant for his tickets. When the attendant delivered the unfortunate news saying, "Sorry Sir, but the game is sold out" Dad replied, "Don't you recognize me?"

Fortunately, the attendant took the bait saying, "No sir, should I?" to which Dad quickly responded, "You don't recognize the President of the school? I'm Fr. Dominic and this is my nephew!" Fortunately, the attendant never asked which school! Obviously befuddled, the attendant ushered us through the gate. Nick was sitting up in the stands with his friends, and he was astounded to see us being escorted in by the attendant. Although we didn't have seats, we stood on the sidelines up against the fence enjoying most of the game while eating hot dogs.

Sibling Relationships   During these early years, my relationship with my sisters was, for the most part, steady and constant. However given the four-year spread between each of my brothers, those relationships were far more dynamic, expanding and contracting corresponding to changes in our respective circumstances.

Although during the early years he occasionally tortured me, despite our age difference, Nick and I were very close, sharing many wonderful memories. However, when he entered High School, and he discovered girls, things gradually changed. Even at an early age, he demonstrated a natural talent for swimming, and unlike the comparatively equal talents of Rocco and Caesar, the progressive talent disparity between Nick and me created even more distance, he being the Swimmer, and me, being the Observer. Although I accepted that this was inevitable, I was saddened to lose the companionship of my best friend. Ironically, however, this left me as my parents' sole companion, and, in particular, my Father's "Best Friend" and faithful Sidekick!

Nick   Ironically, it seems particularly cruel that, being the one with whom I shared the most, is now the one with whom I'm least able to share these common memories, for he currently suffers from advanced Parkinson's disease which, unfortunately, greatly affects his ability to communicate. At times I think, or I want to believe, that he understands, and when I preface a story by saying, "Nick, do you remember when....?" I'm somewhat encouraged when his masked face musters a faint smile, or his muted voice whispers, "Sure" ,but without any further elaboration.

The Turnpike Cruiser   For some reason, my father would purchase a new car every two years and this year was no exception. He purchased a luxurious white Mercury Turnpike Cruiser. This spacious four-door sedan had air conditioning and pushbutton windows, including a unique slanted rear window. I think he figured that when people saw him driving a shiny new sedan with a suntanned face, it would certainly be the sign of a successful professional.

In any event, he would seize every opportunity to drive his new Cruiser, and being that it was a mild winter, he was excited to drive Anita, and her fiancé, Bob Hartmann, up to see the new Hotel. Considering that the Mahwah extension of the New York State Thruway was recently completed, his new car was appropriately named. Dad also purchased a special small license plate which allowed him to drive through the Mahwah and Harriman tolls without paying a fee. I remember my father and I were in the front seat with Bob and Anita sitting comfortably in the luxurious rear seats.

For whatever reason, Dad chose to drive up on New Year's Day. Realizing that the annual license plate had expired on December 31, he removed it from the left front bumper, but continued to display it on his dashboard. When we approached the Mahwah exit, the tollbooth officer explained that his precious plate had expired. My father took the position that it expired at midnight on January 1 as opposed to December 31. The officer now seemed perplexed, and unsure of the actual expiration date, but given that the toll was only $.20, he suggested that my father take the issue up with his superior at the Harriman exit.

We enjoyed a pleasant drive, of course exceeding the speed limit, on the brand new highway from Mahwah to Harriman. Upon approaching the Harriman toll booth, however, my father simply held up the precious plate in full view, and he simply proceeded to drive through the Tollbooth (before visual scanners). Needless to say, within seconds, he was being chased by two state trooper cars.

At this point, Bob was reaching into his pocket offering to pay the hefty sum of $ 20 cents. When he was eventually surrounded by the troopers, and feigning a mystified expression, Dad explained that the Mahwah officer seemed to think that the plate expired on January 1.

Now the Harriman officer was totally confused and said, "I'll have to check with my superior." Meanwhile, Bob again reached into his pocket pleading, "Mr.C, I'd be happy to pay the fee!" When the officer finally returned, he said, "Please sir, just renew the plate before you drive on this portion of the highway again." Pleasantly satisfied with his ruse, Dad happily drove off in his Turnpike Cruiser.

Incidentally, My wife often said that she would often cringe at the amount of insensitive and potentially hurtful teasing that occurred among my siblings around the dinner table - which was totally foreign to her. In particular, my brother-in-law, Bob Hartmann, possessed a great sense of humor with impeccable timing for hilarious one-liners. He had an uncanny knack of looking at a person or unusual situation, and spontaneously improvising a scenario highlighting their imperfections or deficiencies. This was usually hilarious unless, of course, you were the unfortunate recipient.

Such was the case, when he would indelicately comment on my obvious disproportionate adolescent facial features, especially focusing on my prominent nose which made me particularly self-conscious - especially when he compared it to, Jimmy Durante's nose. For the longest time, I had to contend with my recessed upper "Fang" tooth, and now, my prominent proboscis was added to the list of imperfections! - just what an awkward adolescent needs to boost his already fragile self-image. Consequently, for years to come, when posing for photographs, I didn't smile and always avoided profile shots.

Ironically, Anita always felt that she didn't resemble any of her siblings, and she would often say, "I must have been adopted!". After hearing this several times, I finally quipped, "That's impossible because you have a slightly larger version of Aunt Mae's prominent nose!". Apparently, this explains why she too, never wanted profile photographs taken! Being that we both share the same idiosyncrasy, we would often amuse ourselves, by humorously identifying people by their noses - I know, what goes around, comes around!

Being that Bob was a former marine, he would often punch me in the deltoid or chest areas saying, "Take it like a marine!". This continued for quite some time until I finally came of age. Once, while sparring with him in the kitchen at 8311, I held him close, in a tight bear hug, and gave him three good shots to his rib cage. After he noticeably winced and quickly released his grip, I pushed him away saying, "Ah, take it like a marine!". After that, he treated me with far more respect, and I grew to truly love him as my fourth brother.

Rocky's Beach   (1958 -1959) I believe the use of the Monte Carlo's pool ended in 1957. So, the following year my father leased the smallest of the three lakefront concession stands from the Heeton family and named it Rocky's Beach. It was directly across from the 488 American Legion club, and the location of the beach was conducive for long distance training, which would prove to be very advantageous in the future. Dad, of course, continued to offer free swimming lessons, often rewarding his swimmer's performances with ice cream cones and milkshakes.

It was our first foray into a commercial venture, about which we knew absolutely nothing. I remember our neighbor, Mr. Umansky, who owned a very successful meat and deli business, offering my brothers valuable advice. Unlike the other concession stands, our provisions were comparatively simple - assorted ice creams, shakes, candy, potato chips, and boiled hot dogs. Although I quickly adapted to servicing the local patrons and roadside customers, I often consumed more than I sold.

Sal Bergio was, among other things, a commercial truck driver. I remember when Sal visited us in Bay Ridge. It was particularly memorable because everyone was in awe when the giant spontaneously joined Nick, and me, along with some of our friends playing basketball in the Park, while waiting for my father to come home for some legal advice.

In any event, at some point, Rocco apparently mentioned to Sal, that we could use some pebbles for Rocky's beach. Unbeknownst to us, after driving in the dark for several hours, Sal arrived before dawn to dump

16 cubic yds of high-grade pebbles in precisely the right location. To my knowledge, he simply delivered the stone, and left without saying a word, the message being self-evident - a genuine expression of gratitude and friendship.

Things were certainly looking up. Thankfully, I was accepted to St. John's Prep, the High School of my choice, with the prospect of a full swimming scholarship. I found Sr. Barbara to be a refreshing youthful change, and the social experience of mixed 8th grade parties was very exciting. Considering even just the nearness of Bernadette, I anxiously awaited Graduation day and the following summer season.

As a family, we were truly blessed with the best of both worlds. A beautiful home and neighborhood in Bay Ridge, a lovely Cottage in magical, Idle Hour Park and a private Hotel! to boot, my father leased a lakeside Concession Stand on beautiful Walton Lake, and purchased a new luxurious white Turnpike Cruiser. - What more could you hope for! In retrospect, however, I don't know how my father managed it all - surely he must have been overextended!

THE WORST OF TIMES

CH - 16
PALM SUNDAY

It was the Easter season of 1958, and we were all preparing to celebrate Palm Sunday, the second most festive holiday of the year! My sister, Maria, was coming from Boston with her husband Jack and their two young children. She also invited her in-laws, Dr., and Mrs. Weiser, to join us for dinner. The only one missing was my brother, Rocco, who was in the Army, stationed in Arkansas. My mother, of course, made all the necessary food preparations two days in advance. After going to church and bringing home the blessed palms, I was surprised to see my father sitting in the living room in his large red reading chair - a recent Christmas present.

Apparently, Dad had a sleepless night, complaining of indigestion, and he decided to get up early to rest in his comfortable red chair. This wasn't the first time that he complained of indigestion, always assuming it was a familial gallbladder problem. Unlike prior attacks, however, this seemed to be lasting longer, and he looked pale and was sweating more than usual. Rather than lying in bed, he preferred sitting in the chair, claiming that he could breathe easier.

Upon the arrival of the guests, despite a gallant attempt to greet everyone, he remained in the red chair. It was at this point that Dr. Weiser made a quick, but careful assessment of my father's condition, and he suspected that he was either having, or had already suffered a recent heart attack. Being such a health fanatic, this almost seemed counterintuitive. However considering that his younger brother suffered a sudden fatal heart attack at the age of 48, it was a likely diagnosis.

To complicate matters, my father had neither a life insurance policy nor health insurance which precluded admission to a hospital. Furthermore, given that both his parents died in hospitals within one day of each other, he was of the mindset that, "Patients go to the hospital to die!" In light of these unfortunate circumstances, he accepted the only alternative - to be treated at home. Considering that, in the late '50s, other than bed rest, oxygen, morphine, aspirin, nitroglycerin, digitalis and a diuretic, this wasn't an unreasonable option, So, in accord with his wishes, Dr. Weiser arranged for a cardiologist, Dr. Stark, to visit him on Monday morning.

While Dad remained sitting overnight in his comfortable red chair, I remember not wanting to fall asleep, for fear that I might not see him alive in the morning. I'm not sure where, or if my mother slept that evening. The following morning, Dr. Stark arrived carrying a small portable EKG machine in a wooden box, and after completing his exam he confirmed what we all feared, that Dad had suffered a serious heart attack! Rocco was notified of the diagnosis, and he immediately began the process of requesting a hardship discharge.

The sobering reality of a serious heart attack was difficult for me to fathom. It seemed almost incomprehensible that someone who consumed copious amounts of vitamins, adhered to various healthy diets recommended by famous nutritionists, and embraced the mind-body connection of relaxation, would end up with a heart attack! But, in retrospect, he seemed to constantly struggle with his weight and never exercised. I remember him suffering from occasional nosebleeds, and occasional bouts of indigestion which, being similar to his sister, he attributed to a chronic gallbladder problem. And other than extensive dental extractions, I don't believe he ever consulted with a physician regarding any health issues.

Incidentally, It wasn't until much later in life, as the father of an equally large family, that I came to appreciate my father's stress level of being financially overextended!

During this critical time, I would often muse, did my mother reflect upon the fact that, only two years prior, they were happily celebrating their 25th wedding anniversary?" I don't know if she ever expressed or shared her fears, and if so, with whom? Or, perhaps, knowing that her expression of fear might be contagious, she dealt with it stoically, in private!

In time, Dad was eventually moved from his red chair to a convertible sofa bed in the front Sunroom. During the first week, Dr. Stark visited each morning, repeating the EKG tracing. I believe my father stayed on the sofa bed for about 10 days, after which he was allowed to get up and walk to his red chair. When Dr. Stark was satisfied, he was allowed to walk on the ground floor, joining us for meals and sitting outside in the sun on the front stoop.

At some point, Dr. Stark suggested that, in addition to his other medications, a shot of scotch was beneficial. That was music to my father's ears because he thoroughly enjoyed an occasional shot of Haig and Haig Pinch, which he kept well hidden in the dining room Liquor Cabinet.

Glass of Cold Water   During his slow recovery, I suspect that Dad was taking a diuretic because he would frequently ask me for a glass of *Cold* water, always following the simple request with the admonition, "Now, don't forget to let the water run!". Being that the tap water in Brooklyn came from the upstate reservoir system, it was actually quite good. Despite this, however, he insisted that I run the faucet for at least two minutes, which required great *patience* on my part!

Lacking this essential quality, however, I would usually give it the short version - less than thirty seconds. Upon bringing him the tepid water, he held the glass up at eye level, looking for rising bubbles - apparently, a telltale sign that I hadn't done as he asked! Then, with a whimsical expression he asked, "Did you let the water run?" Of course, I answered in the affirmative. Then, as he slowly sipped the tepid water, he suddenly made a grotesque face, and for added effect, he spit the water on the floor. Then, It dawned on me that the rising bubbles were the giveaway! Thereafter, I would run the water for several minutes until it was reasonably cold, ensuring that no residual bubbles could be seen.

Incidentally, I mention this anecdotal learning lesson because to this day, whenever I ask my wife for a glass of cold water, I always add, "Now, let the water run!" -to which she would simply roll her eyes. Then, upon returning with tepid water, and seeing the telltale rising bubbles, I would ask again, "Did you let the water run?" Disgusted, she always replies, "What do you think, of course, I did!" But, I know, it was less than two minutes!

I remember walking home from school in the afternoon, and seeing my father sitting outside in a chair on the stoop. Shortly after greeting him he would say, "Peter boy, my best friend, I think I need my medicine!" By now, I knew exactly what he meant - a shot of H&H scotch. It was somewhat comical because he always asked this softly, so that my mother wouldn't hear. Besides, I could tell that he had recently taken a dose of "medicine!" Honestly, up until then, I'd never known my father to drink more than one shot.

Compromised   In time Dad's strength gradually improved, and he was eventually allowed to freely walk upstairs, and sleep in his own bed, which was a welcome relief to everyone, especially Mom. However, I also became aware of some subtle changes in his mentation. He was somewhat slower, not as sharp as usual, and for the first time in my life, I noticed that the Great man appeared strangely Compromised - or was it the scotch?

One evening this became very evident. While attending a graduation party, my classmate's father recognized my last name, and asked if my father was Caesar, the lawyer. When I answered yes, he immediately asked me for my home phone number in order to call my father. Surmising that he had been drinking, I quickly realized that this was a regrettable mistake, and I felt fearful and protective of my father. For the first time, the invincible man, who relished verbal banter and reveled in extricating himself from compromising situations, appeared vulnerable! It was terribly unsettling to witness, and unfortunately, it was just a forerunner of things to come.

Graduation (6/58)   Time continued to tick away ever so slowly. But, after ten long agonizing weeks, much to everyone's surprise, Sister Barbara announced that Bernadette responded well to her medication and would be returning to school just in time for Graduation! The best news, however, was that Gina and I would be processing side by side up the center aisle in the new church , and I Immediately recanted, "There really is a merciful and just God!"

I patiently counted the hours until our big day finally arrived. And again, with my hair neatly combed and held firmly in place with a double dab of Brylcreem, I was once again disappointed and shocked by Gina's dramatic transformation. As a result of her steroid medication, she had gained about 30 pounds and developed facial acne. This unsightly Cushingoid appearance caused me to mumble," Once again, God changed his mind!"

I remember the boys and girls being in separate classrooms as we each donned our bright red cap and gowns. Then we joined our respective partners, and slowly processed side by side up the center aisle in the new marble Church. We all responded appropriately to the cacophony of echoing castanets, and to highlight the special occasion, I offered a brief ,but tender clasp of hands, and I was once again blissful!

I think that Nick might have driven my mother to the ceremony, but I'm certain that my father was absent. I don't recall any post-graduation celebration or pictures, but then again, that wasn't unusual. Being the last in a long line of siblings, I suspect graduations became routine and taken for granted. After all, doesn't everyone graduate!

The other memorable thing about Graduation was being invited to several parties, mostly hosted by the girls in the class - which was another opportunity for me to demonstrate my smooth, Fred Astaire, dancing moves!

Incidentally, a year later I spotted Bernadette in church, and upon seeing her remarkable re-transformation, my heart once again fluttered with the same excitement as when I first laid eyes on her. However, I realized that she was now a far more mature, Gina, - definitely out of my league.

By mid-June, my father still hadn't received clearance from Dr. Stark to drive his beloved Turnpike Cruiser. He was also steadily growing more anxious to return to his office, especially considering that now he owned two houses, a Hotel, a brand-new car, and a lakefront concession stand. To be in the prime of his career and have the money spigot suddenly turned off, must've been catastrophic! I don't think any of us truly realized the weightiness of his financial burden, which grew steadily with each passing day of "house confinement".

Also, it greatly concerned him that he now had to rely upon the *integrity* of uncle Sil to provide a just share of his pending law cases. I believe It was my father's never-ending sense of obligation to always provide for his seven children, and it was his expectation that each of them would eventually attend College.

Fortunately, due to his conviction that swimming was the ideal sport and the best form of exercise, aside from any perceived fanaticism, the fact that each of his sons obtained full swimming scholarships was a testimony to his foresight - or the necessary means to a laudable end! It's worth re-mentioning that, eventually dealing with similar circumstances, I came to a fuller appreciation of the enormity of his financial burdens.

By July Dad was permitted to travel as a passenger in the car. I remember that It was Memorial weekend, and while driving up to Monroe, Dad was resting comfortably with a pillow in the backseat of his car. At the time, his old friend, Nick Santella, was also staying at Cottage 10 in order to help with a myriad of odd jobs at the Hotel.

As a gifted craftsman, he demonstrated a limitless talent, always willing to attack any project, whether it be demolition, carpentry, electrical, plumbing, heating, or mechanical endeavors. He was also extremely neat, cleaning up after each project. He made me a makeshift toolbox, and I would follow him around doing whatever chore he asked of me. When he punched out the round nickel sized metal pieces in a junction box, he would hand them to me saying, "Save them to buy something special".

He lived in a small step down basement apartment in Coney Island, with two small windows with a view of the sidewalk. He had a simple wooden table in his tiny kitchen, covered with newspapers instead of a tablecloth. He was divorced, and although he had two sons, one being an NYC cop, I never met either of them. Ironically, similar to my father, he would often refer to me as, "My best friend", and he promised someday to take me on some of the rides on Coney Island's Boardwalk. While at Cottage 10, each morning he would make the most delicious oatmeal for breakfast, always with the same admonition, "It sticks to your bones!".

Knowing that Nick was held in such high regard by everyone in the family, I never quite knew if my father was justifiably jealous or envious of Nick's close relationship with my siblings. Or of his genuine love and respect for my mother - in the purest sense!

On Saturday morning, Mr. Gessner came to the Hotel looking for my father, seeking payment for propane deliveries. I remember being very concerned about Dad's frail condition and of the obvious scarcity of money. Being that Dad was nowhere in sight, for some reason I went looking for him in the direction of Lakeview Estates. I eventually spotted him from a distance but noticed that he seemed to be getting up from a neighbor's lawn. Then I noticed the telltale signs of grass and straw on his sweater.

As I slowly approached, he planted one knee on the ground and eventually stood upright. When I hesitantly told him that Mr. Gessner was waiting for him, he appeared very despondent. I remember walking with him back toward the Hotel and taking note of his slow, unsteady gait. Although I was fearful of my father's vulnerability, when the two men met, I knew to keep my distance. Despite my trepidation, somehow Dad was able to placate Mr. Gessner.

The Death Scene   Following this brief encounter, Dad seemed extremely tired, and decided to recline on a bare white wicker chaise lounge on the Hotel's front porch. Shortly after he called me over and asked me to stay with him. He was very pale and sweating profusely. I was terribly frightened that he might be having chest pain. I remember hearing Nick singing while cutting the front lawn with the gravely. When I implored, "let me go and call Nick!" Dad just smiled and said, "listen to him singing!" Then he whispered, "Just stay with me."

The Promise   I surmised that the pain was increasing in intensity, and as he writhed in pain, for the first time, I noticed the unmistakable expression of fear on his face - presumably of impending death. I pleaded with him, "If not Nick, then let me call someone else!" His voice was very weak, and his response was the same, "Just stay with me" At that point, he grabbed my hand and began to weep while saying, "You're the youngest, promise me you'll take care of your mother, and one day, be the caretaker of the family - promise me!" I didn't know what to say other than, "Ok, I promise". On the one hand, I was charged with an awesome responsibility befitting a man, and on the other, I was a boy of 13.

Thank God, the pain gradually subsided. However, apparently embarrassed by this awful scene, while wiping tears from his cheeks he uttered, "You saw your father cry!" It was another stark reminder that he viewed crying as a sign of weakness. Painful emotions should be handled quietly in private! When the pain completely subsided, he again reminded me of my solemn Promise, and a Vow of silence (omerta) for what had transpired was understood - one that I've kept up till now. Thereafter, I would relive the same horrifying Death Scene countless times over, always hoping for a different outcome. If I had just set aside the noble Vow of omerta and called for help, I might have been spared the haunting," What If Guilt" that still plagues me to this day.

Ironically, when my father would openly flirt with my mother, she would often rebuff him with a beguiling smile saying, "OH Caesar, don't be so demonstrative!" And yet, as non-demonstrative as their relationship appeared to be, I found it telling that, anticipating his impending demise, my father's last thoughts and concerns were of his one true love and her wellbeing!

Later that evening, I recognized that my father was still not himself - as though he was operating on only four cylinders. In retrospect, I suspect that he was probably experiencing transient episodes of cerebral ischemia (TIA) or mini-strokes. Somehow, I think that Nick Santella was also aware of Dad's frailty and subtle mental changes. I sensed a wonderful heightened sensitivity for his old friend, and despite his endearing family relationship, he always respected my father's domain.

The remainder of the holiday weekend was relatively quiet, and my father seemed to slowly regain some strength. I remember preparing for the long drive back to Bay Ridge, and Dad willingly accepting to ride in the backseat, resting his head on a soft pillow. I don't recall any other episodes of angina, and his condition gradually improved somewhat. At his request, I continued to surreptitiously provide him with his liquid *medicine*, and he would continue to ask Dr. Stark, when he could resume driving, hoping to return to his Office.

Swim Camp (1958-61) During Dad's slow convalescence, it became increasingly apparent that, over the short term, he would be unable to generate any meaningful income. Although Dad never discussed his finances, considering the tremendous overhead, he had to be financially overextended. Aside from Rocky's fledgling lakeside concession stand, we had no real business experience. Being that our only expertise was swimming, Rocco took the lead by formulating plans for a summer Swimming Camp. I remember watching him in the Party Room as he made various sketches and appropriate wording for advertisements and newspaper announcements.

Fortunately, my father's cousin, Joe Cirigliano, worked for the New York Daily News, and Rocco surreptitiously included favorable quotes ostensibly from Cousin Joe - very ballsy, but desperate times call for desperate measures! He planned to use the Hotel and the back Cottage to provide a room and board swim camp, and Rocky's beach would provide long-distance training on Walton Lake.

Incidentally, Just for clarity, unless otherwise stipulated, when I say that "we" did something, I'm referring collectively, to "the Family"

At the time, St. Francis Prep had a very formidable swimming team, and with Nick *The Fish* as their star performer, you couldn't pay for a better advertisement! He was the proverbial carrot that made for easy access to many of their best swimmers. In addition, at the time Rocco was an assistant coach at the NYAC. Consequently, after their high school practice sessions, Nick, and some of his teammates, would travel by subway to the NYAC for a second practice session under Rocco's tutelage. So, all the pieces were gradually falling into place, and the notion of a summer swimming camp not only made sense, but eventually became a reality.

CH - 17
HOTEL TRANSFORMATION

Rocco also started to think in terms of utilizing other assets of the property, such as the Hotel's 12 bedrooms, Dining room, small Bar, clay tennis court and the 3 bedroom Caretaker Cottage. This, of course, required sorely needed professional advice which was readily sought from friends in the immediate community. Someone who always made himself readily available by offering valuable advice was Mr. Umansky.

When it came time to consider operating the small Bar as a commercial venture, my father's dear friend, Jess Tempone, proved to be invaluable. His experience as the front bartender in some of Manhattan's finest restaurants provided the crash course necessary to eventually run a successful bar business. When it came to applying for a liquor license, Rocco reached out to Jerry Degan, a patron and dear friend who willingly accompanied Rocco to Albany in order to petition the ABC board for a license. Once all the necessary paperwork was completed, I remember driving up to Albany in order to hand deliver the completed documents.

When it came to painting, Jimmy Bilardi was always available to help. I remember one occasion, when we were painting all the Hotel bed springs with messy silver Rustoleum, he suggested that we stack several of them so that the drippings would fall on the springs below. When it came to jobs requiring concrete masonry or cinder block walls, Lou Chiaramonte offered his expertise, and of course, Mack McCarthy was always happy to offer advice regarding the Hotel's temperamental well pump and the old oil furnace and reservoir tank in the Hotel's basement.

Trench Warfare   I remember, after helping Rocco to surreptitiously tap into the Parks water line, with the aid of the gravely, I dug a 3' deep trench for 300' across our property into the hotel's basement. This was to be used as a backup water supply in the *likely* event that our well pump failed. However, this supply line would also prove to be an invaluable source of water for our future swimming pool and for extinguishing local fires.

The only potentially sticky issue was Rocco *forgot* to ask Mr. Skaletes for permission before tapping into the water line that happened to be on his property! Although he *rashly* accused us of being, "Thieves in the night" thankfully, nothing more came of the incursion. Aside from Mr. Skaletes, we were eternally grateful that our local community friends sensed our dire needs and rose to the occasion.

Incidentally, the saying, "What goes around, comes around" came full circle when the fire department declared that, in the case of a fire emergency, in lieu of a fire hydrant, our pool would be siphoned as a regional water supply, which included Mr. Skaletes' properties.

Poison Ivy Brigade   In late June of 1958, I was released from school early. While Caesar and I were working at the Hotel, we were sleeping at Cottage 10. There was a large overgrown wooded area to the right of the rear Cottage that Caesar declared should be cleared, and I was excited to step up and work with my older brother. He astutely assessed the situation, and decided that, in addition to cutting the trees, the most expedient way to clear the underbrush and debris was by burning them. Being that it was very hot, we naturally wore boots, work gloves and our bathing suits. Unfortunately, what he failed to recognize was that most of the trees and underbrush were laden with poison ivy and poison oak vines. With our rakes and a water hose at the ready, while masterfully tending to the blaze, we were squarely in the windward direction of the smoke.

Two days later we both woke up with swollen eyelids, puffy faces, and intense itching over most of our front torso. When my mother arrived, she could barely recognize us saying, "Why you jackasses, it just stands to reason that you were burning poison ivy and oak!" Trust me, there wasn't enough Epsom Salt in all of Monroe to reduce the swelling, and my poor little *Chi Chi* was never the same!

The novelty of a summer swimming camp, coached by two national long distance record holders, in a pristine mountain lake, attracted considerable interest. Initially, either Rocco or Caesar conducted the early morning workouts at Rocky's beach, while the other worked at either the concession stand or the Hotel.

Meanwhile, Nick and I, along with the other swimmers, would routinely work out at Rocky's beach in the mornings, and then we would mow lawns at the Hotel in the afternoon. Since Nick was mostly relegated to the powerful gravely, I was limited to the smaller push mower for trimming. Then, when I finished, I would often ride my bike back and forth between Cottage 10 and the Hotel, doing menial jobs or relieving either of my brothers at the concession stand.

Incidentally, being that I was mostly preoccupied with the Hotel and the swim camp, my best friend, Bobby Persichetti, and I gradually drifted apart. Perhaps it was only a matter of time since he now sought the company of friends in Lakeview Estates, and thereafter our paths only crossed once.

Nick The Scrapper   There was one particular swimmer at the camp by the name of Charley Whall. I remember Charley as having a well-proportioned, muscular physique without an ounce of fat. He regularly practiced throwing the discus on the Hotel's front lawn, and with his bronze tan, he resembled a young Greek God! Aside from being a decent swimmer, he was also a scholar, often reciting poetry while swimming long distances in the lake.

In any event, It just so happened that a young girl, Deborah, had a mad crush on Nick. Deborah's father, Barky, was a huge brute of a man with a shaved head and a muscular torso covered with tattoos. Befitting his intimidating figure, he drove a big ass, Harley Davidson, with a ferocious Pitbull sitting behind him in a small cage.

Somehow, Deborah's boyfriend, who was mostly toothless and also well tattooed, showed up at Rocky's Beach cursing and swearing - looking for someone named, Nick! He was obviously bolstered by the fierce courage of alcohol, yelling that he was gonna rip Nick's Goddamn head off! Hearing this, everyone scattered, including Nick, who tried to remain camouflaged among the tall weeds. Undeterred, however, after picking up a stick, the belligerent boyfriend continued his pursuit of my brother.

Sensing Nick's imminent demise, Charlie gallantly yelled, "I'm Nick!". With that, the boyfriend came charging at Charlie like a fierce rhino. Unbeknownst to us, however, Charlie was also an accomplished wrestler. After quickly disarming his assailant of the stick, Charlie easily pinned him on the ground, and while sitting on his back, he began punching his shoulders, beating him into submission. No one dared to mention Charlie's name, leaving the glorious victory to Nick, the notorious Scrapper!

At some point, however, Nick realized that Charlie would eventually be leaving, and then he shuddered at the prospect that, in addition to the crazy boyfriend, he might have to contend with the infamous Barky, or even worse, his Pitbull! Needless to say, given that his life had already been spared once, Nick kept a very low profile for the rest of the summer.

Floyd Patterson   One sunny afternoon, while manning the front counter of the concession stand, a station wagon filled with kids, many of whom were my age, parked in front of the stand, and the driver proceeded to order ice creams for everyone in the car. Due to my father's influence, I became an avid boxing fan, and I was blown away by the image of my idol, the heavyweight champion of the world, Floyd Patterson, standing in front of our Concession stand! As he stood there leaning over the counter, I was so stunned and speechless that I couldn't even muster the courage to ask him for his autograph.

I remember him as being a young, soft-spoken man, no more than 21 years of age. I knew that he trained at Greenwood Lake and supervised a small boxing camp for underprivileged kids. Subsequently, I learned that he was a deeply religious man, being a Eucharistic minister in his parish church in New Paltz New York.

As fate would have it, many years later while waiting to board a flight, I spotted a man that closely resembled my idol standing by himself near the ticket counter. With Mary's encouragement I finally got up enough courage to go over and introduce myself. He was very cordial, and while shaking his hand, I reminded him of our brief encounter some 40 yrs. earlier at a small ice cream stand on Walton Lake. He simply nodded his head and smiled, and although for me it was like yesterday, I could tell he was vainly sifting through the cobwebs of his distant memory bank.

By this time, Maria was married, and living in Boston with two small children. And both Anita and Virginia were working in the city, commuting to Monroe on weekends. Although my father was eventually given permission to drive his car, he often stayed in Bay Ridge with either of my sisters. Considering the mounting debt with each passing day, his sense of urgency to generate income must have weighed heavily on his mind. I believe he felt that he had no choice, but to make occasional forays to his Manhattan Office. I suspect that the frequency of those visits gradually increased, but at least he left the trial work to uncle Sil. I believe foremost for my father was his old world commitment of a *Never-ending Obligation* to always provide for his children in some capacity, regardless of his age or circumstances.

Sacred Heart Church   As I mentioned previously, during the summer we attended Sunday mass at Sacred Heart Church, located in the center of town. It was a small quaint wood frame structure, and given its size, virtually all the parishioners knew each other on a first name basis. It was also the church in which Caesar and my sisters, Anita and Virginia would eventually be married.

As with most churches, the front pews always seemed to have more than enough space to accommodate a few more parishioners. The Pastor was an arrogant, grumpy old man, who seemingly took great delight in embarrassing those parishioners who chose to stand in the rear of the church. Being that we were rarely on time for anything, this rebuke usually included members of my family.

He would often stop the service abruptly, telling those standing in the back to come forward and take seats in the front pews. And he would impatiently wait until they did. Rocco often threatened to accept the pastor's invitation by, ever so slowly making his way up the center aisle, dragging an obviously painful leg, and pausing to rest at strategic intervals for dramatic effect. Whether or not he ever acted on this threat is irrelevant because thereafter, when the Pastor abruptly interrupted the service, just the visual would crack me up.

This was also the church where my older brothers taught me how to circumvent the ever embarrassing *Collection Basket*. Being that spare change was always a rare commodity in our family, they proudly demonstrated that, by forcibly flicking your middle finger against the inner rim of the wicker basket, you would generate enough noise to convince even the ardent skeptic that you were a very generous parishioner!

During the month of July, my father's strength and mentation seemed to gradually improve. I distinctly remember being shocked one particular Sunday when, instead of *parking the car*, Dad actually attended mass in our small church. Being fashionably late, we both stood in the narrow left aisle next to an open stained glass window, which provided precious ventilation. Then when it came time for the Consecration, I was in absolute awe when Dad actually genuflected, and remained on one knee for the entire time, even refusing my assistance to stand up!

Other than in the small Gonzaga Retreat House chapel, this was a first! - something that I registered as being very significant, but uncertain of the meaning. Recalling the terrifying deathbed experience, I would often wonder, "was this a life message for my benefit or a prophetic sign of something more ominous? Was it a sign of repentance and resignation or gratefulness and hope? However I simply tucked it away for another day.

Random Deliberations   Over the past few weeks, I suffered the loss of three very dear friends in rather quick succession - two of whom were sudden and unexpected. At one point, I quipped to my wife, "I seem to be losing friends faster than I make them!" I believe we are all influenced by, and in some respects are a Composite of those who are dear to us. And as our loved ones depart, I feel we also lose a Piece of ourselves, and consequently, slowly diminish in size and vigor. I'm also acutely aware of the age-related frailties of my Siblings which, although unsettling, beats the inevitable alternative!

I recently visited my brother Nick in the hospital, now suffering the physical and mental ravages of advanced Parkinson's disease. As in the past, I had hoped to share some of my humorous memoir vignettes from our past. However, despite the fact that he's the one with whom I shared most of my childhood memories, once again, I came away greatly disappointed and disheartened, realizing that he's neither able to comprehend nor able to comment on them. In some respects, being robbed of the joy of *Sharing*, defeats the very purpose of writing. And the culmination of these recent events shook my *Inner Core!*

My Inner Core   My *Inner Core* consists of my immediate family, composed of my parents and siblings, depicted metaphorically as an early Rosebud. The large, vibrantly colored outermost petals are enveloping and protecting the delicate tightly compressed inner petals. Being in the center of the core feels safe, devoid of internal dissension or personality issues. In many respects, this harmonious Inner Core molded me into the person I am today.

Compression   In many respects, in addition to being informative, I find that writing one's memoirs can also be cathartic. Interestingly, during this long journey, some of our children would occasionally ask, "What did you say about me?" Or, willing to offer helpful suggestions they'd say, "Don't forget to mention such and such!" However from the outset, I decided to fast-forward through their hectic middle years which may be disturbing to some, without realizing the Why. They fail to realize that that time period should be the subject of their own memoirs, molded by their *Inner Core!*

I'm embarrassed to admit, however, that in many instances, it's because I don't remember particular incidents with the same degree of clarity. And by saying, "It was a complete blur," I run the risk of offending them or appearing insensitive. Not because they weren't important or relevant, but because of a *Compression Factor* - the result of spinning too many plates at a hectic pace. Hopefully, in time they too will come to appreciate their Inner core, and upon experiencing the same Compression, will pause to smell the roses- savoring the wonderful childhood and challenging adolescent years of their own children!

Time is relative   During my early years, time seemed to move at a much slower pace in seemingly endless fashion. And while writing about those early years, I often felt that my recollections were also in slow motion, as if watching a movie reel, one frame at a time, each frame projecting a vivid scene frozen in time. During the hectic child-rearing years, however, time seemed to pass at warp speed, as if fanning a 4" 'thick calendar spanning 30 years, the projected images being blurred by compression. Again, that in no way diminishes their importance, but are more appropriately the subject matter for their own memoirs.

During the Senior years, I naturally move slower and experience another form of Compression. Time becomes increasingly more precious. Sadly, along with forgetfulness, it's often marked by the painful loss of dear friends with whom you can no longer sing, laugh, drink, or commiserate. A benefit of the slower pace, however, is that it allows for ample time to reflect on the early years and my Inner Core.

However, reckoning with the sad realization that the outer protective petals are now long gone, and the delicate inner petals are fading and separating from each other at an alarming rate is disheartening. During my youth, this was unimaginable, and being at the center of the core, this eventuality is particularly disturbing to watch. Time being relative, however, I realize It's not the inevitability, but the rate at which it's happening that shakes my Inner Core!

Respect I was recently reminded of the importance of family and respect, especially for the older generation. We all face difficult life situations which we think are unique. Regrettably, however, we often equate advanced age with being out of touch with reality, failing to realize that they too were once your age, perhaps even facing similar difficulties. Although the times and circumstances may be somewhat different, the solutions are often the same. For those who seek the benefit of their counsel, you might find that the wisdom and experience of their sage advice might save you from many of life's needless trials and tribulations.

In many respects, my father was an enigma and a chameleon, a cast of one portraying many different characters. Even at a young age, I was aware of his many life lessons, most often teaching not by example, but rather, "Do as I say, not as I do!" I readily admit that he was a far better teacher than I was or will ever be. And If I can impart one lasting word of advice to my children it would be, "Identify those elders whose wisdom and experience you respect and seek the benefit of their counsel!" They too were once young and may have walked a similar path, possibly in the same size shoes.

CH - 18
RETURN TO THE OFFICE

During July, despite his initial subterfuge, out of necessity my father was surreptitiously going to his Office on a regular basis. He eventually resumed his weekly routine of commuting on Monday, Wednesday, and Friday, and he appeared to be tolerating the transition fairly well. By early August, the summer season was in full swing, and we were all busy with the swimming camp, the Hotel, and Concession stand. Nick and I continued sleeping at Cottage 10 with my mother and Maria, who was visiting with her two children, John, and Kathy. I remember, during a severe rainstorm, young John Arthur fell from a chair in the Hotel's Dining room and cut his eyebrow. Rocco ended up bringing him to Doctor Hoffman's office for stitches.

The Notice   On Wednesday, August 6th, I was tending the concession stand, and around 5 pm, I was surprised when Jack drove down to pick me up. It took me about 10 minutes to close up the stand, and then we drove up to Cottage 10. Unbeknownst to us, however, earlier in the day my mother received a phone call from my sister, Virginia, saying that Dad came home from the Office early complaining of some mild chest discomfort, and decided not to drive up to Monroe that evening. My mother apparently sensed a serious problem and immediately notified my brother Caesar, asking him to drive her down to Bay ridge as soon as possible.

They sped down and got there in reasonably good time. As I understand it, when my mother walked inside the house, she found my father sitting in the front Sunroom, and upon seeing her, he jokingly said, "look who they

180

sent down!" After briefly checking on him, Mom quickly walked into the kitchen to get a glass of water and his nitroglycerin tablets. Upon returning, however, she found him unconscious and unresponsive - as quick as that! My brother tried in vain to resuscitate him and ran over to Dr. Basso's home on the corner of 83rd St. pleading for him to come and save my father, but he refused!

According to Caesar, he ran up a block and a half to Dr. Blaber's home on 83rd St. between Ridge Blvd and 3rd Ave begging for his assistance, which he did, but to no avail. In the meantime, my mother also called our local family physician, Dr. Ferrioni, who was a close friend of my parents. He arrived within minutes, but it was too late. Then placing his arm around my father's shoulder, he offered tender solace by lamenting about, "His old friend".

I was totally unaware of what had already transpired, and ironically, as we drove up Cottage 10's driveway, I was struck by an abundance of beautiful flower arrangements and bouquets encircling the rear patio. I was initially shocked and bewildered, but intuitively I felt sudden nausea and a hollow sinking feeling in my chest. We eventually learned that It was purely by coincidence that Mr. Kowell had hosted a shoe convention and had all the flower displays delivered to our home.

Jack appeared equally baffled by the scene, and it was only then that we were stunned by the tragic news that my father had suffered a fatal heart attack! Naturally, hoping against hope, I thought surely this was a mistake, but not seeing my father's car was confirmation. I was too shocked to even cry, and honestly, I don't remember if I ever did. And I have no further recollections of the rest of the evening.

I believe Rocco remained at the Hotel with my sister Maria and her children. Anita says that she remembers asking Jack to drive her down to Brooklyn that same evening? However, I have no such recollection. The following morning, we must have borrowed the Trum's car, but I don't recall who could have driven, other than Nick..

The following morning, when we arrived at 8311, my mother was sitting alone on the couch in the front Sunroom. We each greeted her, but being the last, when it was my turn, I didn't know what to do or say ,and I nervously laughed. My mother glared at me saying, "You think this is funny?" I felt terribly ashamed, but thankfully, Anita came to my rescue, explaining that it was only a nervous laugh, and said, "He already had his moment" implying that I may have cried, but I have no such recollection.

Later that morning, I remember Caesar sitting at my father's desk, and using his phone to make the funeral arrangements. Dad was to be waked at the Torregrossa funeral home on Lafayette Ave in Brooklyn, followed by a funeral mass in the Nativity Church of his childhood. Much to the chagrin of my Aunt Mae and Uncle Tony, rather than Calvary cemetery, the burial was to be in St Columba's cemetery, amidst the cow pastures and black dirt farms of Chester NY. I also remember Caesar receiving condolences from a respectful acquaintance, Mr. Joseph Profaci. He made a very generous offer to use his private limousines and the private Chapel on his Long Island estate, both of which Caesar respectfully declined.

The Wake The wake lasted three grueling days, especially for my mother. Initially, my father was assigned to the largest of the three parlor rooms. At 11 am each morning we would all arrive at the funeral parlor, and my mother went into the cold room to sit quietly by my father. Eventually, she took her position in the front row, stoically waiting for the mourners to arrive, but I don't remember her ever crying. This routine was repeated for two separate viewings over the course of three days. By the second day, however, she was so emotionally drained that she required mild sedation, especially to sleep alone in their bed.

I was managing ok until the arrival of Cousin Joe, who lived in Bay Ridge, and of his three brothers, known as the Bronx Ciriglianos. I fondly remembered his brothers, Dominic (Pep), Frank (Irish) and Salvatore(Whitey) from the Gonzaga Picnics. Cousin Joe and my father were very close in more ways than one, and after paying respects to my mother, I remember him walking up to the casket and kissing my father on the forehead.

For whatever reason, I was always particularly fond of Whitey, and when he approached me, my lower lip started to quiver. Upon seeing this, he immediately grabbed my shoulders saying, "Men don't cry!" Although he hugged me, I felt that if I broke down, he probably wouldn't know what to do with me. Sensing this, I simply pulled away and quickly walked outside to the street, finding a private place to finally sob. Anita must have witnessed the exchange because shortly after, she came outside asking, "What brought it on?" I merely shrugged without uttering a word for fear of crying in public.

By the third day, they dedicated the other two rooms in order to accommodate the constant flow of attendees. It was during the infamous Gallo- Profaci wars, and on the final evening, I was aware of four nicely dressed men in dark suits and ties, followed by another man who, upon entering the viewing room, politely removed his fedora, and while leaving the other men behind, he approached my mother offering his sincere condolences.

Having been mildly sedated, towards the end of the evening my mother inquired of Caesar about the mystery man. My brother quietly told her that he was the father of his former St John's classmates, the Profaci brothers, with whom we were all well acquainted. I have no other recollections of the wake and virtually nothing of the Funeral mass, other than that it was very crowded. However, my father's dear friends, Maronis insisted on singing in the choir loft, and their discordant ranges and disharmony added a bit of comic relief.

Following the Funeral mass, I remember riding in the back seat of someone's car, perhaps Uncle Tony's, in route to St Columba's Cemetery in, Chester N.Y. Being that we were several car lengths behind the hearse and Flower car, I felt strangely disconnected from my father and the rest of my family. There was no conversation and the empty silence was deafening. Vivid recollections of, "Put it there my best friend" and the solemn *deathbed promises* were followed by fleeting, "What if" moments. I remember feeling a heaviness in my chest as I looked back through the rear car window at the endless procession of cars, all with their headlights on. While I felt grateful to witness such a remarkable tribute, I also felt profound sadness of losing, not only my father but also, my Best Friend!

When the lengthy procession finally arrived at Chester's main intersection, the lead Flower car drove directly to St. Columba's church, expecting that the cemetery would surely be close to the Church. Although we occasionally attended mass in the church, we never had reason to visit the cemetery. I remember Rocco breaking out of the procession line and headed for the Rectory to ask for directions to the cemetery. Talk about embarrassing moments - I imagined Dad yelling, "Why you horses assess!"

While driving along the narrow country roads, I remembered how my father loved the black dirt farms, and upon seeing cows grazing behind their barbed wired pastures, he would pull the car over with the windows rolled down, and tell me and Nick to yell, "Moooo!" as loud as we could, and magically, the cows would meander close to the fence. *Ironically, it was upon recalling this that we chose this particular cemetery because it overlooked the sprawling black dirt farms and the peaceful cow pastures of Chester.*

The Burial   When we arrived at the cemetery, I was amazed at the long line of cars parked along the roadside. The simple entrance was marked by two fieldstone pillars between which was a narrow dirt road leading to a relatively large interior circle. I was absolutely astounded by the number of cars that had already lined the narrow interior roadways - mostly local residents from Idle Hour Park, Walton lake and the town of Monroe.

After exiting the car, I remember being overwhelmed by the throngs of faceless people, all of whom were quiet and terribly somber. The eerie silence was devoid of all conversation, and the following events seemed to play out in slow motion. Being that we couldn't afford a headstone, I only have a hazy recollection of the actual burial service. In fact, it wasn't until two years later that we finally had a modest headstone engraved.

Ironically, however, my father often joked, "Leave my head above ground so I can see who visits!" I believe there was a casual reception at the Hotel, but I stayed at Cottage 10 with my mother. She was totally drained, and I watched as she quietly climbed the stairs to be alone in their bedroom, but I never heard any sobbing.

The remainder of the summer is a total blur. Surely, I must have been anticipating the start of my freshman year of High School, and the obligations of my swimming scholarship, but I honestly don't recall feeling dread or excitement. In addition to not swimming, while tending the Concession stand, I must have treated myself to ice cream for two people (one scoop for you and two for me) because by the time I made my grand debut at SJP, I had gained a considerable amount of weight.

Nick & Dad   I was about to enter St John's Prep and Nick was beginning his Senior year at Francis Prep, the pinnacle of his swimming career. Lacking Nick's natural talent, it was my father's unending encouragement that served as my steady beacon of hope. However, on that fateful day in August, that sustaining light suddenly dimmed, plunging my world into utter darkness and swimming seemed to lose its luster. Although Nick was fortunate to gain Rocco's attention, I often wondered, but unfortunately never had the opportunity to ask, if his world was also affected in like manner.

Incidentally, following my father's death, one of the first things to go was his beloved Turnpike Cruiser. This was replaced by a stogie, chocolate brown, station wagon with an economical, standard transmission.

St John's Prep   (SJP) The Prep was located on Lewis Ave in the Williamsburg section of Brooklyn which, at the time, left a lot to be desired. Being a private Parochial High School, students traveled from a wide geographic area, including Long Island. Although some students were fortunate enough to commute by car, most of us took public transportation.

Commuting by public transportation took about an hour and a half. Fortunately, our house was located within a short walking distance to the Bus stop on the corner of Colonial Road and 86th Street. Then direct service to the BMT subway on the corner of 86th St. And 4th Avenue. At the Dekalb Ave. station I had the option of either switching to the Lewis Ave Bus or transferring to the elevated Train line to the Bedford Stuyvesant station and walking to Lewis Avenue.

In those days, students were provided with free bus and subway passes. In the morning we would routinely take the bus to the train, but in the evenings, we would walk home from the subway station. This was within easy walking distance, except when carrying a backpack filled with books during the cold winter nights!

The Prep was five stories high and directly across the street from St. John's Teachers College. The College building also housed the Vincentian priests who taught at both the college and the Prep. Behind the College was a fenced Baseball / Football field with red dirt, but absolutely no grass. The Swimming pool, basketball courts and auditorium were in the basement, below the locker rooms. I believe the Cafeteria was one floor below the ground floor.

CH - 19
SJP FRESHMAN YEAR

I have to admit, before my destined growth spurt, I was a relatively short, chubby adolescent. As a freshman, I remember being somewhat sullen, often brooding and feeling terribly insecure. I was aware of some simmering resentment and anger for which I received my fair share of razing from my brothers. In particular, two subjects were particularly troublesome, Algebra and Latin, which was naturally reflected in my poor grades!

Ironically, I found comic relief with my Algebra teacher who reminded me of the caricature, Ichabod Crane. He was a tall gangly man who wore dark-rimmed glasses atop a long pointed nose and had a very prominent Adam's apple that traveled up and down his long pencil neck every time he swallowed. Consequently, while he was lecturing, I was mostly preoccupied watching his bobbing Adam's apple. To make matters worse, after one of my classmates snickered, "I think he's probably a boy scout leader," I naturally pictured him wearing the traditional green summer shorts and his Adam's apple bobbing whenever he blew his whistle. I know, very weird!

On the other hand, our Latin teacher, Mr. Von Stanwitz, was a small, delicate man who was apparently a former Seminarian. Although he made a valiant effort to teach Latin, he was also easily distracted. He spent much of the period chastising us for our sinfulness, warning that we were endangering our immortal souls with impure thoughts. etc.etc. I thought, "Methinks thou doth protest too much!' In truth, however, my teachers weren't the problem - I was the problem.

I just didn't apply myself, failing to grasp even the essential building blocks for those two subjects. Perhaps it was a product of aberrant adolescence, but In retrospect I would label myself as a wise guy, a smart ass with a giant chip on his shoulder, and in desperate need of an attitude adjustment!

It was pretty standard to bring lunch from home. Early in the morning, Mom would make delicious sandwiches, her specialties being either, peppers and eggs, peppers and onions, or meatball Heroes on sliced whole-wheat Italian bread. Regardless of the type of sandwich, her telltale signature was always the same. Deep finger depressions as she mashed down on the top layer of bread. In those days, we didn't have sandwich bags, so Mom would cut the bottom half of a brown shopping bag in order to wrap the moist sandwich.

While riding on the subway, I noticed that the aroma of the sandwiches, especially the peppers and onions, would permeate the entire train or bus. To some, it was scrumptious, but to others it was very offensive and impossible to disguise. Also, since the sandwiches were stored downstairs in our warm lockers, by the time we had lunch period, the sandwiches still smelled good, but were so soggy that even with two hands they were difficult to hold.

There were many times when I would easily convince someone to switch with me for a simple peanut butter and jelly sandwich. That is, until they tried to pick up my sandwich- in which case it was too late. Following lunch, I faced the chore of swallowing at least 25 to 30 vitamins, especially Desiccated liver, and Brewer's yeast tablets. This was predictably followed by a combination of regurgitation and flatulence during swimming practice - neither of which made me swim faster!.

The Tub Pool   The Prep was one of the few private High Schools blessed with their own swimming pool. It was an old four-lane pool located in the basement,50 feet from the basketball courts. During weekday practice sessions, the pool was never filled to overflow capacity. Given that it only had side gutters, when approaching either end of the pool, you would encounter insurmountable backwash- like swimming in a virtual tub! There was a 5-foot high wall separating the pool deck from a bank of showers which were shared with the basketball and football teams.

Swimming was a very lonely sport. Unlike the more socially popular sports, there were no spectator bleachers or cheerleaders. The small viewing area was from behind the 5' wall, and the only occasional student body spectators were members of the basketball or football teams while they were showering behind the wall!

Despite my academic shortcomings, I did fairly well on the freshman swimming team. Much to my father's credit, I was one of the few freshmen adept at swimming Butterfly. With every event, I would picture my father sitting in the back of the boat, cheering me on! In time, I was asked by the coach to teach the other Freshman how to do the Dolphin kick, as well as Freestyle flip turns and racing starts, especially false start strategies.

Seton Hall   The freshman swimming finals were to be held at Seton Hall College In N.J. I managed to make the finals in the 100-yard butterfly and the butterfly leg of the 200-yard medley relay. Somehow, I missed the team's school bus, and I had no idea how to get to New Jersey, let alone Seton Hall College. I remember taking public transportation on a brutally cold winter snowy evening.

When I eventually arrived at the impressive metal gates and lighted entry pillars it was snowing heavily with frequent frigid wind gusts. The long curved entry inclined gradually, and I remember slipping and sliding while trying to run up the road carrying my swimming bag. By the time I reached the top of the hill, my shoes were full of snow, and my toes and hands were frozen. Thankfully, I spotted the well-lit Aquatic center, and sprinted inside dreading that I might have already missed my events. As I raced to the spectator area, I figured that, if I was too late, I'd just leave and claim that I was sick.

Miraculously, however, while scanning the stands, my coach, Mr. Waters spotted me, and pointing to his watch, he waved for me to come down, indicating that my butterfly event was about to start. I ran downstairs, and after quickly changing into my red nylon swimsuit, I was about to thaw out under a hot shower, when he came in yelling, "Get your ass on deck!". I ran out just in time to hear my name called for the 100 yd Butterfly event. I was assigned to lane 4, and while standing on the starting block, I was still shivering.

I figured the pool must be warmer than my core body temperature, so I might as well get wet! With that, shortly after I heard the command, "Swimmers take your mark" I intentionally false-started! Although my coach went absolutely berserk, I purposely took my time swimming to the side ladder. After the start, It took 50 yards just to get warm, and somehow I managed to place second.

My next event was the Medley relay. By the end of the breaststroke leg we were two body lengths behind. I timed the touch perfectly, and It must've been pure adrenaline because I felt like I was flying on top of the water and managed to pull slightly ahead of the field. Then, John Lupi, who was built like an ox, was our best sprinter and he kept the lead to a spectacular first-place finish. The following week, Tom Farley, our only diver and editor of our school newspaper, The Red Owl, wrote a very flattering column describing the drama of both races. Unlike my brothers, however, other than Jimmy Murphy's article, they were my only swimming accolades.

The Varsity Team   Much to my surprise, I was recruited for the varsity swim team, which set in motion an opportunity to eventually receive four varsity letters, a Cirigliano benchmark. Of course, my predecessor, Caesar, not only had four varsity letters for swimming, but also for Football and Baseball. In those days it wasn't unusual to wear a varsity "Letter Sweater" both in school and for various sporting events. My aunt Mae knitted me a white sweater with my first varsity letter attached. It was also a special sign of "commitment" to allow your letter sweater or school Ring (senior year) to be worn by that special sweetheart - even if only temporarily.

The unexpected privilege of being on the varsity team, however, also meant that, as a freshman, I would eventually have to compete against Nick, "The Fish", now a senior at St Francis Prep. When I say *compete,* that's a gross overstatement, and trust me, he exhibited no mercy! As in the past, when he zoomed past me, I would almost drown in his wake as his kick purposely accelerated when his feet passed my head.

SJP vs SFP   It was customary to have two dual meets during the swimming season. Whenever we were scheduled to race SFP, my coach would routinely pump me for information in order to strategize the most effective lineup for each event. Although we had a decent team, SFP was a virtual powerhouse, mostly due to Nick, Henry Frey and the Blenke brothers. When the long-awaited contest finally arrived, It was almost comical to watch as each coach tried to outwit the other. St Francis' coach, Tom Booras, was very cunning, and played our coach, Mr. Waters, like a fiddle.

Prior to each event, Booras would watch to see who our coach was talking to, and if it was one of our better swimmers, he would go over and pretend to talk to Nick. Seeing this, our coach would immediately substitute a lesser swimmer. Anticipating this, however, Booras would intentionally keep his original entry unchanged. But Booras always had the torpedo in hand, "The Fish"! This comedy of trying to outwit each other flipped back and forth during the entire meet.

One of our best backstrokers, 6" 3", Jeff Rothke, had a very powerful stroke, and as a senior, he was considered one of the best in the league - a reliable "shoe-in" for first place. The 100 yd backstroke was the next event, and at the last minute, Booras entered Nick in the event. Seeing this, Rothke panicked, and he came running over to me asking the obvious question, "Does your brother swim Backstroke?"

I said truthfully, "He isn't known as a backstroker, and other than an individual medley, I don't recall seeing him swim the event". Furthermore, I assured him that Nick had a very unorthodox stroke, with a high bent elbow entry rather than a hand entry, but excellent flip turns, "So, nail the turns". Much to my surprise, Nick dominated the entire race and didn't even bother with flip turns. By the end of the race, aside from trying to find a place to hide, Rothke didn't talk to me for the rest of the season.

The next event was the 100 yd butterfly, and unfortunately, I was considered the best candidate. We watched as Booras was talking to one of his best Butterflyers, Tommy Blenke. Tomy had a beautiful classic stroke, gliding over the top of the water with a hand entry directly in front of his broad shoulders, and his body was propelled by a powerful undulating dolphin kick. Needless to say, I wasn't only intimidated, I was to be the sacrificial lamb!

Then, at the last minute, that bastard, Booras, substituted Nick. Unlike Blenke, however, Nick had a peculiar high, bent elbow stroke with a hand entry well beyond his shoulders, but a very efficient underwater catch and powerful dolphin kick. This is testimony to the fact that "It's more about what you do underwater!" The race, if you could even call it that, seemed interminably long. I mostly swallowed water in his wake, especially off the turns when he would purposely accelerate his kick! It's fair to say that St. Francis easily dominated this first match, and the second was pretty much a repeat of the first. When I reluctantly commiserated about my utter humiliation, he eased my bruised ego by saying, "How do you think I felt when I had to compete against Caesar, during his senior year".

Towards the end of my first semester, I was faced with a real dilemma. In my family, the benchmark or measure of the man was, "How much could you lift and how fast could you swim?" - with far less emphasis on Academia. From a Swimming perspective, It was evident that I wasn't living up to everyone's expectations, and from an Academic perspective, I was still struggling with Latin and Algebra. I knew I wasn't living up to my expectations, but considering that no one ever bothered to ask, that was only known by me.

At the end of my Freshman and Varsity seasons, Caesar would predictably ask, "Did you at least make the finals?"- quickly followed by, "What did you place?" Obviously, not satisfied with the results, he chastised me saying, "You have a moral obligation to fulfill your scholarship commitment with a better performance!". Considering that he was a living legend at the Prep, this stern admonition added more pressure to Improve.

At the time, Rocco was a substitute science teacher at a high school in Bedford Stuyvesant, which was relatively close to the Prep. Consequently, we would often take the same subway which allowed me an opportunity to finally confide in him regarding my academic dilemma.

Being a teacher, he naturally took a very hardline, demanding to see my grades on a regular basis. Although I was relieved that he was now aware of my precarious situation, he wasn't able to help me with either Latin or Algebra. Finally, In utter desperation, I even asked Nick for help with Algebra, but I felt doomed when he acknowledged that it was already a foggy distant memory.

The NYAC   Since Rocco was also an assistant coach at the NYAC under Paul Wacker, it enabled him to train Nick after he finished workouts with Tom Booras. Likewise, considering Caesar's recent admonition, I made a crucial decision to double my swimming efforts by joining Nick and the other swimmers at the NYAC.

From a coaching perspective, I quickly recognized that Rocco was a tactician whereas Caesar was, brute strength. With a sense of renewed vigor, I also embraced Caesar's advice to start doing land exercises -namely, sit-ups and pushups. In fact, I remember how upset Rocco became when Caesar agreed to come with me to Modells sports store, in order to buy a 50-pound weight bar. In fact, I think he eventually grew tired watching me slowly pulling singles out of my pockets ,and he ended up paying for them - which I still have to this day.

Ironically, however, when Rocco befriended a fellow schoolteacher who happened to be a competitive bodybuilder, it apparently influenced his perspective regarding the benefits of weight training. Consequently, I was shocked when, prior to getting in the pool, he took all of us upstairs to the weight room on the 4th- floor. This was in stark contrast to the prior routine of land exercises and drag or resistance training in the water. Thinking that an efficient powerful stroke also required strength, in addition to my nightly pushups, I spent additional hours on the horizontal pulleys. Much to my dismay, however, my training sessions at the NYAC eventually backfired.

Just when I thought I would be bringing something back to the Prep's team by way of talent or teaching, when the Prep's athletic director, Fr. McGurty found out about this extracurricular training, he threatened to rescind my athletic scholarship - go figure!. I remember Rocco trying to reason with the good Priest on the phone. But his position was that it was more about Team *Spirit* than personal performance! To make matters worse, I had unwittingly sacrificed academia for swimming - choosing brawn over brains, and ultimately coming away with neither - so much for trying!

My French Companion   The lyrics of *My Heart Stood Still* always resonated with me. It depicts the imaginary or unrequited, *Love at first sight!* - especially the phrase, "Though not a single word was spoken, I could tell you knew, that unfelt clasp of hands, told me so well you knew"

Following my dual swimming practices, I was usually totally exhausted, and walking home from the 85th St. Subway station, carrying a heavy knapsack filled with books, seemed exceptionally long and boring. In the cold darkness of winter, however, my fertile imagination would occasionally help pass the time. I suddenly noticed a very pretty young French girl, wearing a traditional plaid scarf, pleated skirt, and beret, slowly climbing the subway stairs.

She was obviously unfamiliar with her surroundings, and while trying to get her bearings, she appeared totally bewildered. Known for my spontaneous chivalry, upon gallantly offering my assistance, she greeted me with a sweet smile, and my heart stood still! Then when she thanked me by politely kissing me on both cheeks, I wondered, "What about the famous French Kiss?"

Although she knew very little English, and I knew absolutely no French, despite our language barrier, it was an enjoyable challenge trying to converse with her. Of course, I don't remember the nature of our discussions, otherwise, I would be certifiably nuts! The weight of my heavy books were surprisingly less so with my French companion close beside me. I noticed an unexpected bounce in my step, and the inviting scent of her perfume seemed to make time pass more quickly, and the seemingly long journey much shorter.

Over time, I grew increasingly more discouraged. Although I felt that I was swimming to the best of my ability, apparently I lacked a natural talent for "feeling" the elusive *Catch*. I remember a rare occasion when I was swimming in the lake, and Rocco was rowing a small boat beside me. He grew increasingly frustrated, telling me over and over, "Don't rush your stroke- leave your hand in front longer and *Feel* the water as you glide!" To me, that was like telling a blind man, "Just open your eyes to see".

It became increasingly clear that the spotlight was squarely on Nick and his Olympic potential. I loved watching him race, appearing to always swim effortlessly, and yet towards the finish, he always seemed to have something in reserve to ward off his opponent. Despite a total daily yardage of 6000 yds, he was superbly conditioned. His stroke always appeared relaxed with a natural catch, and except near the finish, his power and efficiency rarely required him to noticeably increase his hand speed. Once he said, "I know I'm pressing when I feel my rectum burn and turn inside-out!" - a sensation I never experienced.

And yet, as remarkable as he was, I never heard him brag about his swimming accomplishments - an enviable attribute which was easy for me to emulate since I had nothing to brag about! I always wished that I too would inherit his natural talent, always hoping that one day, I too would swim like him. What I failed to realize was that wishing and hoping never produced a champion. They're the product of a burning desire, unwavering dedication, and fierce determination.

Villanova & Colgate   I remember traveling with Rocco down to Villanova University to watch Nick compete in the Regional Championships where he handedly captured first place and set National records in virtually all of his events. However, not all of his races were stellar performances.

At Colgate University, he was entered in the 200 yd IM, and although he came in first, he was disqualified! We watched in utter bewilderment as he led the field in the initial Butterfly leg, and after the 50 yd turn, he began swimming Breaststroke instead of Backstroke. When he surfaced after the turn, and noticed everyone else swimming backstroke, the expression on his face was priceless! I could tell he was trying to figure out if he should turn over and start swimming backstroke ,or continue swimming breaststroke? Either way, he was going to be disqualified, and when he decided to continue with breaststroke, we all started cheering which caused him to start laughing. However, despite almost choking to death, he still managed to come in first!

At the time, Nick's only real competition was Drury Gallagher, a sophomore swimming for Fordham University as well as the NYAC. In addition to being a superb swimmer and NCAA champion, Drury was also a very classy guy, driving a small red MG convertible while wearing a colorful plaid pee cap. Ironically, both he and Nick were coached by Rocco, often swimming the same Freestyle events, and the only metropolitan swimmer to give Nick pre-race jitters.

I remember one particular event at the NYAC. I was sitting in the left side bleachers, and from this vantage point, It was almost comical to watch as Nick and Drury each tried to avoid being psyched out. They purposely avoided being on deck at the same time by taking turns in the shower, waiting to be announced before mounting their respective starting blocks.

I was surprised when Whitey Budzago came over and sat next to me. I was particularly moved when he put his arm around my shoulders and said, "This is where your Father always sat!"

Fordham Meet   I remember accompanying my brother Caesar to a swim meet at Fordham University. I was a Freshman in SJP, and he was a senior, about to culminate his swimming career by competing in a final dual meet against Colgate University. Although he was still a very prominent figure in the metropolitan area, being that it was nearing the end of his swimming career, he was mostly resting on his laurels, relying on his formidable strength and talent.

At the time, Fordham's team mostly consisted of Caesar, Drury Gallagher, and John Heyman, each of them were still considered the crème de la crème in their respective events. I remember Caesar was scheduled to swim the 200 yd Freestyle against one of Colgate's young superstars. For the first three laps, the young swimmer smartly stayed at Caesar's waist up until the final (seventh) turn. After doing a perfect flip turn, when the young swimmer pushed off the wall he caught up to Caesar which I'm sure rattled him.

As they swam head to head toward the finish with 15 yds to go, Caesar just put his head down, and without taking a breath, he sprinted to the wall barely touching out his young challenger. After briefly offering mutual congratulations, Caesar bolted from the pool and ran into the bathroom. Shortly after I heard the loud echo of him barfing, and I mused, "That's what you get for not working out!"

Ironically, although Fordham's team consisted of only three swimmers, given that they placed first in each of their respective events, prior to the final relays, they maintained a narrow lead over Colgate. Naturally, the final Medley and Freestyle relays require four swimmers, and recognizing their obvious predicament, Colgate's coach notified Fordham's coach, John Little, that unless they came up with a fourth swimmer, they would have to forfeit the meet. After much haggling, the respective coaches agreed that I would be permitted to swim on both relays.

They managed to find a suit that almost fit me, and before I knew it, I was scheduled to swim on each of the 400 yd relays. As anticipated, when Colgate assigned their fastest swimmer as the anchor, Caesar designated me as the anchor on each relay, thereby limiting me to 100 yds of Freestyle on each. The intent was to stay in the race for as long as possible, and demonstrate that after the third leg, we would have a commanding lead. So, at the ripe age of 14, I was honored to just be in the presence of such swimming legends, let alone to actually be on their team!

As expected, with each leg, I was given a commanding lead, and although I swam as hard as I could, I eventually fell on my sword, getting killed in both events. Naturally, I felt terrible, but I rationalized that, by avoiding the alternative of forfeiture, I was afforded a badge of honor which I will never forget.

CH - 20
BOLD ENDEAVORS

1959 was the year of dramatic changes and bold endeavors at the Hotel, Rocky's Beach, and the swim camp. In addition, purely out of necessity we made preparations to open the Hotel for real paying guests!

White Cat Inn   A dear friend of my father's, Mr. Casale, was the owner of an elegant restaurant, The White Cat Inn, located in Highland Mills N.Y. I only remember having dinner at the fancy restaurant with my father once, which must have been a very special occasion. Historically, the restaurant was formerly owned by, Gypsy Rose Lee, but was now closed for business. In any event, Mr. Casale, either gave us, or we presumed he gave us, tacit approval to remove some pots and pans from the former restaurant's kitchen.

So, reminiscent of Mr. Skaletes' accusation of being, "Thieves in the knight", one dark evening, Rocco and I borrowed a pickup truck and *found our way* into the kitchen. In addition to several large pots and pans, however, we also managed to remove the 12' wooden Prep table which fit very nicely in the Hotel's kitchen. Then, on another covert mission, Anita and I removed an antique wooden rocking Cradle from the attic. At a later date, the Casales came to visit our Hotel, and while giving them the grand tour, as Mr. Casale walked through the kitchen, he commented, "Gee, that prep table looks very familiar!" *Incidentally, Mr. Casale's wife and Mr. Phillips' wife, Grace, were sisters.*

Our first major investment was purchasing a commercial dishwashing station which we located just off the kitchen in the back of the Dining room. Rocco eventually hired our first chef, *Peg leg Bill*, as well as an elderly waitress named Bertha. What a dynamic duo! Bill was a decent chef when he was sober, but he had a penchant for large quantities of vanilla extract and cooked with tons of garlic. Consequently, two of our first hotel guests, the Blitzers, were eventually dubbed, "the Burping Blitzers" because they both emitted unrestrained loud belching during and after every dinner. Also, being that Bertha was challenged by carrying anything more than one pat of butter at a time, she was affectionately dubbed, "one Patty Bertha".

Thanks to the overflow from the Hotel Monte Carlo, our weekend occupancy slowly increased. The Greek guests only ate breakfast at our Hotel ,and then, later in the evening, they would dress to the Nines and walk over to the Monte Carlo for a real Dinner and enjoy live entertainment and gambling. Aside from the Burping Blitzers, being that all our other Hotel guests were Greek, poor Bertha didn't understand a word they were saying, and neither did we. But be thankful for your Blessings!

Now that business was picking up, Rocco hired a Hotel Chambermaid who, unbeknownst to us, also had a drinking problem. We eventually discovered this when one of the Greek Hotel guests found her passed out on their bed! Welcome to the Hotel business and thank God it was only a 10 week season!

Schaeffers (1959-61) In early spring of 1959, we made a strategic move from Rocky's Beach to the much larger and more visible Schaeffers Concession stand, owned and operated by Agnes Shaeffer. In sharp contrast to Rocky's, It was the liveliest of the lakeside concessions with a very large assortment of row boats. We thought It would also provide a source of entertainment for our Hotel guests as well as the camp swimmers.

In those days you could obtain a junior driver's license at the ripe old age of 16, which made it a very busy *hang out* for teenagers, with a fair share of *daredevils*. Two in particular come to mind, Skip Gaunt and Marty Leonard. They would run from the concession stand's front counter, across Lakes road and then dive headfirst over the chain-link fence, hopefully clearing a rope stretching between two docks that marked a shallow area. Other notable feats were diving from the top step of the stairs leading down to the larger dock and hoping to clear the edge. Or doing flips off the top railing of the High dive Tower. Thank God, no one was ever seriously injured.

Despite these crazy feats they were truly the salt of the earth. Being stars on the Monroe- Woodbury football team, they were both very muscular, and if someone was giving me trouble, they would often act as *enforcers!* Also, although not necessarily known for their swimming abilities, they were willingly recruited for swimming races representing the makeshift Walton Lake Swim Team.

Another special guy was Joe Mann - the only black teenager in the group. He was also an outstanding football player, and I never remember even a hint of discrimination, almost as though, neither he nor anyone else even recognized that he was black. I remember when he enlisted in the Marine Corp and was eventually deployed to Okinawa during the 1960 Cuban missile crisis. Everyone was very concerned for his safety. However, upon his return, when asked about *the Crisis,* he just said, "Hell, we were just laughing about all the hype!"

The Blue Beetle   When the older guys would leave the lakefront parking area, it was common to suddenly drop the car in gear and peel out, leaving a long trail of smoke and rubber on the pavement. And other bystanders would actually measure the distance in human feet.

Since there was no phone communication at the stand, at the age of 14, I was permitted to drive the Blue Beetle (the Beast), on errands back and forth to the Hotel - which was a blast. One day, I thought I'd seize the moment and try to imitate my heroes. So, I slowly backed the Beast out, and imitating James Dean, I caught everyone's attention by revving the awesome Hollywood mufflers. Then flooring it again, I dropped it in first and popped the clutch producing a sudden short squeal, followed by constant bucking, squealing, and jerking for about 100 ft - not at all like

James Dean! Then I heard someone yell, "He's gonna lose his license!" and someone else yelled, "What license!

Summer School   Meanwhile, the laudable hallmarks of my freshman year was that I somehow squeaked by my first year of Latin, and I made the varsity swimming finals. However, as expected, I failed Algebra, requiring me to attend summer school 3 days a week in Newburgh NY. Fortunately, I befriended a girl named Suzanne Banks, whose mother was willing to drive both of us all three days. Although this put a temporary damper on my summer training, the sheer misery and embarrassment of summer school made such a lasting impression that I swore I would never fail another subject. I guess sister Ermingale was right, I must be intellectually challenged!

Schaeffer Drunks   In mid-August, Caesar surprised everyone by announcing that he was going to join the Marine Corps. I knew that, in the past, he struggled with acquiescing to my father's wish of eventually joining him, and I believe he was struggling again with this belated decision, but felt he needed distance in order to make such an important decision.

Unlike Rocco, he didn't go away to college, so I was always comforted by his presence. From a purely selfish perspective, I was greatly saddened that he would be leaving the fold, and his absence would leave a tremendous void in my life. True to form, In preparation for his rigorous Boot camp ordeal, I remember him doing endless push-ups and sit-ups on Schaeffer's dock, honing his body into fantastic shape.

One late afternoon, all the patrons had left, and after he finished his exercise routine, he went into the men's changing room to get dressed. While cleaning the front counter, I noticed a small rowboat with three guys in their early 20s tying their boat to the floating Dock. I watched as they proceeded to climb the ladder to the high dive platform. They were obviously drunk, and when they attempted to stand on the railing, I quickly ran across the street and started yelling for them to get down. Of course, they replied with an endless litany of profanity and dropping a beer bottle which shattered on the Dock.

Caesar had just finished getting dressed, and upon hearing the commotion he walked across the road in order to assess the situation. He told them the same thing and they likewise responded the same way. Then he said, "Boys, don't make me come out there!" Seeing that he was dressed, they just laughed and delivered another litany of profane compliments. So, Caesar told me to watch them while he stormed back into the dressing room and changed into his wet bathing suit.

Of course, having just finished his exercises, he was sufficiently pumped, and while descending the stairs he repeated the same warning. Gawking at his size and realizing that he was serious, two of the three backed down the ladder, while the third hero remained on the tower mouthing off at both Caesar and his two *coward* friends. Hearing this, Caesar dove into the water and started racing toward the Dock. Seeing this, the two smarter ones quickly jumped into their small rowboat, leaving their lone comrade on the tower, still cursing at his "coward" friends. Realizing that Caesar was fast approaching, he jumped from the tower almost hitting the boat.

Caesar was now heading towards the boat, and when the moron grabbed onto the rear of the boat, his two comrades each grabbed an oar and started rowing like hell. Now, this became a virtual comedy, because they were so drunk and uncoordinated that, while dragging their friend on the back, they kept going around in large circles. They eventually managed to make enough headway that Caesar decided to swim back to the Dock.

After his six months of Boot camp, I remember being shocked when Caesar returned home. He was in fantastic shape, and the leanest that I'd ever seen him. Fortunately, the Cuban missile crisis had passed, and after his brief stint in the Marine Corps, he was able to transfer to the Coast Guard National Guard. Then, In short order, he had a brief orientation in the DEA, and with Mr. McCarthy's help, he worked as a walk-on longshoreman, while also riding shotgun in the back of an Armored truck. Then in 1960, with Tom Clancy's endorsement, he got an evening job as a lifeguard at New Utrecht high school while attending Brooklyn Law school.

Subway Follies   During my freshman year, Nick and I would regularly ride the same bus and subway route to school. As a freshman, I struggled to carry a knapsack filled with heavy books while, as a senior he carried a single flimsy notebook and never offered to lighten my load! As students, we were issued special public transportation passes for both bus and subway service. Upon entering the subway, we gained access by flashing our student passes to the attendant in the change booth, and then entered through the pedestrian turnstiles or through a large metal turnstile cage, specifically intended for students.

Shortly after descending the stairs to the underground station, I was always struck by the pungent odor emitted from the third rail's high voltage fumes combined with the smell of urine, especially around the public telephone booths. Attached to the metal pillars, were small candy dispensing machines, containing miniature boxes of two Chiclets or small Hershey bars, each costing one cent.

In those days, instead of comfortable seat cushions and air conditioning, the subway cars had, very hard, highly lacquered, tan cane seats, and seasonal ventilation was provided by four large overhead fan blades also with matching tan caning on the blade's under surface. Also, the height of the rotating blades could conceivably deliver a free haircut to tall passengers. During unusually warm conditions, additional ventilation was provided by lowering the upper pane of the side windows, permitting the familiar electrical fumes, especially through long stretches of the dark tunnels which were often accompanied by electrical blackouts in the cars.

During the early morning rush hour, pushing into the crowded subway cars was a science. First choose a door that opens directly in front of a metal pillar. Then, before the door closes, push off the pillar with one leg pressing against the passengers inside! With everyone compressed like sardines, it was always prudent to keep your hands and arms at chest level, lest someone might accuse you of Groping. This, of course, required me to routinely press my heavy knapsack against my chest, leaving just my face exposed.

One morning, when Nick and I finally wedged ourselves into the jam packed car, we found ourselves facing each other while being wedged between a young couple who were also facing each other. Consequently, all our faces were separated by mere inches -making for a very tight foursome! Nick had the same Jackie Gleason talent of enlarging and rolling his eyes, as did my father.

While the young couple was trying to have a private conversation, without moving his head, Nick glanced at me while moving his bulging eyes back and forth at the couple, occasionally nodding as if he was included in their intimate conversation. If that wasn't enough, he would periodically make a facial expression, pretending to smell something foul, as if one of them farted. Of course, when I broke out laughing, my elbows and knapsack started bouncing up and down. The problem with trying to contain laughter, is that it invariably results in a self-perpetuating crescendo of more laughter!

Naturally bewildered, when the couple turned to look at me, I knew they were wondering, "Why the hell is this idiot or pervert laughing to himself?" - which further perpetuated the vicious cycle of uncontrollable laughter! Then, addressing their stares and foolishly hoping for a brotherly life- line, when I tried to explain that I was laughing at my brother, Nick just looked away, as though he didn't even know me. Now, if he had just done this once, it would have been bad enough, but he would wait until I was able to control myself, and then repeated the same scenario for the entire trip. At one point, I thought for sure I peed in my pants!

The Subway Drunk   After evening swimming practices at the NYAC, Rocco, Nick and I would take the long subway ride back home. During the cold winter evenings, the combination of a wet head, being hungry and very tired made the warmth of the subway car and the heated seats were very conducive to napping. While I would usually try to get a jump on my homework, Nick would either rest or talk with Rocco.

More often, however, while wearing his well-worn oversized tan trench coat, Rocco would look for a quiet location and take up an entire seat by sitting diagonally and crunching his legs like a pretzel behind the seat in front. He wasn't really disturbing anyone until he started his outrageous snoring which was quickly followed by copious drooling from the corner of his mouth. If the train was crowded and we were sitting next to him, the other passengers would look at our bloodshot eyes and constant tearing (due to the chlorine) and shake their heads sympathetically, imagining our awful circumstances! And We, of course, took full advantage of their fertile imaginations, by looking at him pitifully, while wiping away our tears.

However, if other seats were readily available, the other entertaining option was to quietly move to another location and watch as new passengers came in the car. Upon seeing the *Drunk,* they either avoided him like the plague, or after hearing the horrific snoring, quickly move to another seat. We would do our best to contain our laughter while watching this charade until we finally arrived at the 86th St. Station.

Then we'd wait until just before the doors opened to call him and watch as he tried to untangle his cramped legs from behind the seat in front. Invariably, however, due to the prolonged crunching, at least one leg would fall asleep, and as *Flipper* slowly limped towards the door, we would dutifully hold the door open for the *Drunk,* reinforcing everyone's first impression - those poor kids!

CH - 21
SOPHOMORE YEAR

Thankfully, I passed Algebra with a decent grade. I began my Sophomore year with a renewed commitment to balance my academic and swimming efforts. In contrast to Algebra I found Geometry to be logical, and our teacher, Mr. Hall, was excellent. However, Latin was another story. Lacking a sound foundation, I continued to struggle with declensions, and Mr. Von Stanwitz obsession with my immortal soul.

Vicki When Nick accepted a swimming scholarship to Fordham University, commuting to school suddenly became very boring. In time, however, I was fortunate to find another traveling companion, Vicki Mattison. Being that she only lived a few houses away on 83rd St. we had a passing acquaintance. She was a year behind me in St Anselm's, and we would occasionally walk home together. At the time she was a Freshman in St Xaviers High School, and I knew her to be very intelligent. Thankfully, she never embarrassed me by flaunting it!

When she asked me what time I left for the 86th st bus, I was surprised when she offered to join me. What I didn't know, however, was that, although I had a reputation for tardiness, she was even worse! I would often find myself pleading with the Bus driver to wait for this maniacal girl running along Colonial Rd. When she finally arrived with disheveled hair and completely out of breath, she would immediately remove her eyeglasses, revealing her very pretty blue eyes, but without them, she was blind as a bat! Then came the challenge of the *Subway Squeeze,* and although, not as many laughs as with Nick, the squeezes were admittedly, far more stimulating!

As I mentioned previously, Rocco was a substitute science teacher in Bedford Stuyvesant. This naturally allowed him to interact with impoverished youths which eventually proved to be mutually beneficial. He would occasionally invite one or two students to come and work at the Hotel which provided cheap labor, and a unique opportunity for underprivileged youths to spend a weekend in the beautiful Catskill Mountains. In a way, it reminded me of my father's adolescent experience of escaping from the streets of lower Manhattan to enjoy the beauty of Gonzaga.

There were two Peruvian brothers, Hector, and Carlos, who were polite, hard-working students who appeared to thoroughly enjoy the country's environs. I quickly befriended them as equals and eventually regarded them as, Family. There was also an older student, John Lombardi, who I respected as a hard-working contemporary, eventually becoming a close companion and a trusted friend. However, not all of the students were suited for hard work. In particular, Fred had a temper and one Sunday evening decided to just vanish! After a thorough search, he was eventually found, taken home, and never returned again.

The Varsity Team   The Varsity swim season began with a change in the coaching staff. Mr. Waters, who walked with a right prosthetic leg resembling Chester on Gunsmoke, was replaced by Fr Hines, who had Alopecia Totalis (total absence of hair) resembling Mr. Clean. However, unlike Mr. Waters, Fr. Hines actually swam laps, demonstrating a very decent stroke. Although practice sessions were more structured with somewhat better supervision, being that I was precluded from swimming at the NYAC, it limited any significant improvement which continued to be very frustrating.

There was also the addition of a transfer student, Gene Volini, a butterflier who was formerly trained by the legendary coach, Henry Fear. Gene had a disproportionately large, almost grotesque, muscular upper torso. While relying mostly on his upper body, he had an awesome butterfly for the first 50 yards, but by the third turn, I would notice his body becoming more vertical, indicating a relatively weak dolphin kick.

I remember my father stressing the importance of kicking underwater, especially the dolphin kick. So, I would practice dolphin kicking underwater on my stomach and my back. Gene eventually became the designated Butterflier on the 200 yd Medley relay, while I remained dominant in the 100-yard Fly and 200 yd Individual Medley. We had two other outstanding swimmers, John Lupi, who was our best 50 yd. Freestyler and Donny Gill, who always pushed me in the 200 yd Freestyle. I mention these three particular swimmers, because I always considered them fierce competitors, fellow teammates, and good friends.

Nick was offered a full four-year swimming scholarship at Caesar's alma mater, Fordham University. And although John Little was still the coach, he readily accepted that Nick was being trained by Rocco at the NYAC. Nick continued to dominate the metropolitan area, setting new NCAA records, and I believe, at the forefront of Rocco's mind, was the upcoming Pan American games - a prelude to the 1960 Olympic trials.

Nick's Meltdown   Upon the conclusion of a very successful winter swimming season, it was expected that there would be a well-deserved break during the Easter holidays. However, at the end of our Easter dinner, Rocco *suggested* that, in preparation for the summer season. training would resume at the NYAC the very next day. I knew that Nick had been dating a girl on a regular basis, and he told Rocco that he had no intention of resuming training so soon, if at all!

Rocco was very disappointed, and became extremely upset, emphasizing that, in his opinion, it was vitally important to resume practice as soon as possible. I knew that Nick had nothing but the highest regard for Rocco, not only as his brother, but also as his coach. However, he remained uncharacteristically steadfast, essentially ending any further discussion of the matter.

Predictably, this was followed by a prolonged period of estrangement, with minimal communication. Being that Rocco was still the de facto coach at the NYAC, he resumed practice sessions with the St. Francis prep swimmers as well as Henry Clay, a very talented swimmer from West Point, who readily challenged Drury Gallagher. Being that our winter season was over, I was no longer encumbered by Fr. McGourty's edict, and therefore seized a unique opportunity to hopefully be more closely supervised by Rocco.

After a sufficient period of reflection, communication between my two brothers gradually improved with Nick eventually rejoining the practice sessions at the NYAC. It was disheartening, however, to watch as Nick initially struggled to keep pace with Clay and Gallagher while swimming several sets of 500 yd freestyle. Of course, given his natural talent and muscle memory, it didn't take long for him to eventually reclaim his superiority. Strangely however, it appeared to me that he was content with merely *keeping* pace rather than *setting* the pace - no longer finishing with his accelerating hallmark *close*! This subtle change suggested to me that perhaps, he no longer had the *Fire in his Belly!*"

CH - 22
CIRI'S LODGE

After much family discussion, in the early spring of 1960, we decided to expand, and hopefully transform the Hotel into a revenue-producing business. The next order of business was to decide on an appropriate name for our new endeavor. One consideration was, *The Seven C's*, but we finally decided on Ciri's *Lodge* (aka, The Lodge). This new venture entailed a considerable gamble, and a major financial commitment to replace the infamous clay Tennis court with an Olympic size Swimming Pool in order to augment the Swim camp and introduce a Country Club atmosphere.

We eventually chose the Ivar Martin pool company in Ramsey N.J. which specialized in Gunite pool constructions. We negotiated for a 30' x 75' six-lane pool with a 6 x 8' side kiddie pool. The ultimate goal was to offer the local community a private, Country Club Pool, the only one of its kind in the area. In addition, it would also provide for private swimming lessons, races, and short distance training for the swim camp attendees.

The enormous pool was surrounded by an expansive red and white patio block terrace and a well-trimmed grass perimeter. The western border was lined by a row of tall evergreen trees, which provided ample privacy. The 150,000-gallon pool was filtered by a huge metal tank, concealed within an attractive, Japanese style, wood-frame structure. In keeping with a similar Japanese motif, the southern and eastern roadside perimeter was enclosed with alternating white and stained fencing panels. The north entrance to the pool was 75 feet from the three-room Caretaker's Cottage, which was destined to become a Snack Bar.

The Snack Bar   In mid-June, either by divine intervention or sensing that we desperately needed help, the Bronx Ciriglianos and Carmine Zanfordino arrived like angels from heaven offering their help. I remember them bringing a delicious assortment of cooked food., and I thought perhaps they came from the annual Gonzaga picnic. Regardless, we had an unexpected feast!

I mostly worked with Frank transforming the three-room Caretaker's Cottage into a Snack Bar. Frank was obviously very familiar with framing and electrical work. When I expressed my fear of handling electricity, he reassured me by saying, "Always wear rubber sneakers, and when in doubt, stand on a wood 2 x 4"- a pearl which I never forgot. The Ciriglianos returned unsolicited for the following three weekends, always bringing delicious sandwiches along with sorely needed encouragement. With Frank's invaluable help, we finished the interior of the Snack Bar, including a full-service counter, just in time for the Grand Opening and the start of the new season!

Staffing Changes   Rocco made sweeping staffing changes by replacing "Peg leg Bill" with an experienced elderly Chef, Tony, and his wife, Maria. He fired the alcoholic Chambermaid and replaced Bertha with a younger, more experienced waitress named Helen. Thankfully, Nick Santella agreed to remain as the resident Handyman. Then, before the start of the season, I clearly remember the morning when Nick Santella came rushing into Cottage exclaiming that our new chef, Tony, had apparently suffered a heart attack!

I quickly got dressed and ran over to the Lodge to find Dr.Heussin's 1959 Corvette convertible parked in front of the back Cottage. He confirmed our worst fears, that Tony had suffered a mild heart attack, and would be transported by ambulance to the small Goshen Hospital. During his absence, Rocco filled in as the interim cook for the staff. Fortunately, after several weeks, Tony was able to return to the kitchen, but in a limited capacity.

The Grand Opening   The Lodge was finally ready for business. All the Bedrooms were thoroughly cleaned, the Dining room tables neatly set, and the Bar fully stocked with booze. Thanks to Nick's personal friend and confidant, Fr. Neelen, the pool patio was furnished with an assortment of brand-new chaise lounges, chairs, umbrellas, and tables. The Snack Bar contained several interior tables and the counter area had all the necessary appliances and equipment for serving both food and beverages. The ultimate plan was for my mother to eventually take over the snack bar which would hopefully provide her with some income. The stage was set, and It was time for the long awaited, Grand Opening!

Ciri's Lodge Pool

Hotel Winter Scene

Aside from operating the Hotel's dishwasher, giving early morning swimming lessons, a late-night kitchen man and mowing the lawns, my primary responsibility was lifeguarding and pool maintenance. In addition to the standard poolside lounges, we also offered seasonal rentals of *Reserved* chaise lounges, which I would quickly retrieve and set up at poolside.

There was one particular member who stood out, Lenny Daidone. Unfortunately, Lenny suffered from early Parkinson's disease, and although he was a top executive at the Domino Sugar company, he was unpretentious, mild-mannered, and always very gracious. In fact, he not only rented his chaise lounge for the entire season, but he actually paid in advance and tipped me each time I retrieved his lounge.

The Country Club   Considering that we were offering the only Country Club Pool in the area, the interest and response from the extended neighborhood was excellent. In addition to the pool activities, an added attraction was having a Bar with poolside service. Interestingly, aside from the Trums and their good friends, the DeSchrievers, I don't recall any other memberships from the residents of Idle Hour Park. Ironically, however, the majority of memberships were from the business community of Monroe Township, comprised of those families who were considered to be, "the cream of the crop"

Lifeguarding   Knowing that I would be the lifeguard, in order to fit the profile, I was determined to remain committed to my exercise routine of 150 pushups and 50 sit-ups every night, and three sets of twenty curls each morning with my 5o lb. weight bar. Even before the swim camp attendees arrived, I would work out in the pool in the morning and swim in the lake in the evening, tethered to an inflated plastic tube. In short, I was finally satisfied with my wait, and I started to notice appreciable muscle mass which enhanced my body definition - both of which were gratifying and more befitting the image of a real Lifeguard.

Although I was a good swimmer, I never had any formal lifeguard training or certification. So, in order to at least look like a Lifeguard, I adopted the customary lifeguard attire - dark reflective sunglasses and my SJP red nylon bathing suit - the only bathing suit I owned.

Since it was my responsibility to ensure that only Hotel guests and paid Club members and their guests, were permitted entry to the pool, I strategically positioned myself at a round umbrella table just to the right of the semicircular entry stairs. Considering that we mostly attracted a family clientele, there was a fair range of age-appropriate young ladies at poolside - Hubba Hubba!

Aside from security issues, the strategic positioning of my table also enabled me to *selectively* engage in casual conversation! Consequently, I occasionally found myself in the company of one or two female companions. Although this might have been a minor distraction, Rocco frequently complained that I was surrounded by a virtual Harem, which was a gross exaggeration. This, however, prompted him to make frequent visits to the pool, telling me that I should make myself more visible by regularly walking around the pool! However, considering that my hormones were in overdrive, I was more concerned that I might be too visible!

PART II

An Enduring Love Story

"Where do I begin to tell the story of how great a love can be, the sweet love story that is older than the sea, where do I start? With her first hello, she gave new meaning to this empty world of mine, there'll never be another love, another time, she came into my life and made the living fine, she fills my heart!"

Although Love Story's theme song is one of my all-time favorites, unlike Hollywood's thunderbolt version of "Love at first sight," our long tenuous courtship was fraught with missed opportunities and disappointing setbacks. And, if perchance, it was *love at first sight,* perhaps my inner turmoil and low self-esteem blinded me. Rather than the metaphorical *thunderbolt,* I would describe our ten-year courtship as an *enduring love journey* - initial fragile germination followed by a slowly maturing vibrant bloom that continues blossoming to this day.

CH - 23
MARY'S 60TH BIRTHDAY

In August 2006, our kids decided that Mary should have a well-deserved "Birthday Bash" to celebrate her 60th birthday. Jake and Christy graciously offered to host the gala event at their house, which provided a perfect, private backyard setting. The kids arranged for a catered event, including a large tent with a dance floor and a DJ. They also put together an endless array of memorable photos, projected continuously onto an enormous screen by a revolving carousel. The kids did everything, and all I did was gladly pay for it.

Thankfully, the weather cooperated and as expected, the party was well attended - a testimony to how much and how many people truly love her - and rightly so. The guests included neighbors, relatives, childhood friends, and the Chicago and Florida contingent of dear friends, with John and Lori arriving fashionably late in an airport limousine. The theme was, *Sixty and Sexy,* which was befitting her casual elegance in a sexy blue dress. In fact, one of my favorite pictures is of Mary and me sitting casually on an outdoor wicker couch.

Then, when she felt the time was right, I was taken aback when Mary got up to deliver a very heartfelt speech of endearment. Although she didn't need it, I joined her, placing my hand on her shoulder for moral support. But she was in her element! At one point, while standing beside her, I was surprised and very moved when she turned to me saying, I have loved you for as long as I can remember." Ironically, this brief tender statement triggered a flood of conflicting emotions because It wasn't exactly as I remembered it, and noticeably absent was the word, *only.*

Similar to the rapid-fire shutter of a camera, I visualized a fleeting sequence of flashbacks and vivid scenes projected through my mind's eye. From my perspective, I would describe our early courtship as a series of brief, almost comical, *encounters,* and the raw feelings of a young troubled teenager in love with a beautiful young girl - both of us treading a long winding rocky road on the way to an "enduring" love story.

The First Encounter   In late June 1960, I had just finished cementing a 4' high cinder block retaining wall along the northwest corner of the pool patio. It was extremely hot, and I was ready to start pouring the cement for four semicircular steps, which would serve as the main entrance to the pool complex. Being that it was unseasonably hot, Nick's good friend, Kip Trum, drove his younger sisters, Mary Margaret (MM) and Susie up to the pool. Although the pool was filled with water, since the filtration wasn't complete, the water was still very rusty. Seeing this, they decided to at least enjoy the sun by basking on the poolside lounge chairs.

I knew MM was considerably younger than me, and although our paths may have crossed a few times in the past, they apparently didn't make a lasting impression. Then, for whatever reason, while working on the cement steps, MM sent her sister over to ask me a silly question to which I responded with an equally silly answer. This continued for quite some time until she sent Susie over with a final message, that I was a *Doofus*! Not sure why I received such a *compliment*, I simply replied," Well, I try to please!"

When it came time for them to leave, having poured the wet cement into the semi-circular forms, MM said indignantly, "Now, how am I supposed to get down?" Recalling the *Doofus* comment, I said, "just jump!" She just looked at me dumbfounded and feeling sorry for little Susie, I offered my hand to help them down from the cinderblock wall. Upon leaving, she simply said, "Now do a good job!" - not even thank you!

Second Encounter   One afternoon in early August, while I was tending the snack bar, MM walked in and sat at the counter. In contrast to our first encounter, however, she was lovely and very engaging. After some

220

small talk, I asked her what grade she was in and she answered, "I'm going into my Freshman year of High School". I immediately thought, "Although she's cute, she was way too young. After all, I would soon be a Junior- an upperclassman!"

However, she went on to tell me that she had already dated a guy named, Jimmy Dugan, a Freshman at Xavier High School, and accompanied him to their Military Ball. I thought, "Hmm… she's already more socially advanced than I am!" Finally, knowing that I was attending St John's Prep, she offered that her cousin, Bill Hegarty, played basketball at the Prep.

Thereafter, other than a passing hello, I don't recall any other interactions for the remainder of the summer. However, for some strange reason, out of the blue, she called me at home on my birthday which prompted a fleeting thought, "How did she know it was my birthday?"

Incidentally, although her family often referred to her as MM, or her proper name, Mary Margaret, I felt that was a mouthful, and at least privately, I preferred calling her, Mary. So, for the sake of brevity, while writing my memoir, I will refer to her as MM, Mary or, my wife. Interestingly, however, in the future, I would always introduce her by her given name, Mary Margaret. Likewise, with our daughters, I prefer their given names.

The Spiritos (1960) Surprisingly, rather than spending the summer in their rustic cabin across the lake, Donna's family decided to rent the largest room at Ciri's Lodge. Jack and Marion Spirito and their three daughters, Donna, Carol, and Tucker occupied the front bedroom on the second floor. Donna's father, Jack, was a well-dressed charismatic, flamboyant generous spender. He thoroughly enjoyed a good party, always demonstrating a good sense of humor.

 Her mother, Marion, was a sun worshiper, always well-tanned and lubricated with copious amounts of scented suntan lotion. She had a trim, well-preserved body, and her long dark hair and dark sunglasses complemented her glamorous features. Despite her striking appearance, however, she was always readily approachable, never forgetting her simple roots. She was also very observant, and I would often confide in her, seeking her innate wisdom and counsel.

I first noticed Donna, while swimming past her family's rustic cabin on the other side of Walton Lake. She was probably no more than seven, wearing dungarees and a plaid shirt, fishing off a small dock in front of her cabin. I knew that, at some point, she took swimming lessons from my brothers at either Schaeffers or Rocky's Beach. I remember having a vague impression that she had a crush on my brother Nick. Although that was the extent of my early recollections, our lives would eventually become closely intertwined for the next five decades and I presently regard her as a trusted confidant and one of my closest and dearest friends.

All three daughters were very pretty, always polite, and well dressed, especially on Sundays. When they first arrived in late June, they immediately got into their brand-new white bathing suits and waited patiently to take a swim in the pool. However, the pool's filtration was still incomplete and consequently, the water was still very rusty. Being that it was extremely hot, however, Marion said, "At least jump in and get cooled off!"! With that, all three girls jumped in the pool, but when they came out, their sparkling white bathing suits were magically transformed into a permanent rust color.

On Sundays, the entire family would always be neatly dressed in order to attend mass at Sacred Heart church. They appeared to be the epitome of the perfect family. In fact, Jack arranged to have a local artist, Tony Frandino, paint a portrait at the Lodge, of the well-dressed family over the course of several Sundays.

In celebration of her birthday, Jack presented Marion with a sleek 1960 white Cadillac convertible. The best part about her extravagant gift was that, despite not having a driver's license, she allowed me to drive it! Marion and I, along with Donna in the backseat, would purposely take the back roads when driving to town, and shortly after turning on Cromwell Hill Road, we would switch places. The road was famous for its sudden dips and roller-coaster-like hills. I'll never forget the exhilaration when, upon approaching a steep hill, Marion would say, "Ok, floor it!" And after cresting the hill, the sudden steep decline was like jumping off the high dive at Schaeffer's.

I remember one time, she let me take the wheel while leaving the Lodge on the dirt road. Upon seeing this, Rocco yelled to me, "Don't make this a habit!" After we looked at each other, she said, "Oh, he's just jealous, floor it!" - leaving in a thick cloud of dust.

The Bar   As I said, the bar was small, quaint, and intimate with only four counter stools. The back bar had a full-length mirror flanked by dark wood paneling and wood shelves stocked with booze. There was an upright piano against the left sidewall, and other than Bob Hartman's accordion, it was the only form of entertainment. Every Friday and Saturday night the cozy 20'x50' room was jammed with mostly local friends and neighbors from Idle Hour Park. As with many nightclubs, it seemed that the more crowded it was, the better the party.

Rocco would usually tend the bar while Caesar played the piano. However, much like my father, he only knew the cords for a few songs which the crowd never seemed to grow tired of hearing. He and Bob would alternate, simulating a bass fiddle by rubbing their moistened fingertips against either the side of the piano or the adjacent wall. The crowd would go nuts when Bob would jump off a chair while playing his accordion, without missing a beat. When things really got rock' in, couples would start dancing in the middle of the crowded room which further accelerated the evening's tempo!

I remember one particular Saturday evening when, in the midst of the raucous crowd, Jack Spirito walked into the crowded bar with disheveled hair and wearing a robe yelling, "Will you guys knock it off, I'm trying to sleep!" After the boos and laughter subsided, he bought a round of drinks for everyone in the bar.

223

Meanwhile, Rocco had assigned me the job of making late-night antipasti and 12" bar pizzas in a small convection oven in the kitchen. Gratified that I was entrusted with this important job, I was piling the antipasto on a bare platter and my pizzas were loaded with mozzarella, both of which were understandably big hits!

However, the following night Rocco came into the kitchen exclaiming, "Pete, what the hell are you doing, you're killing us!" Then he explained that I should have been laying the antipasto on a generous bed of lettuce and using half the amount of mozzarella on the pizzas! Hell, what did I know about profits, I was just flattered by all the compliments from the customers!

Then, one night, while I was still in the kitchen doing my thing, Caesar came in at 2 am yelling, "You have swimming lessons in the morning, get home and go to bed!" I explained I was just doing what I was told and maybe he should settle this with Rocco - which was probably the wrong thing to say. That was the first time that I realized there was apparently a lack of leadership communication, creating potential discord between my two brothers.

This, in turn, caused a lot of inner turmoil which was both confusing and disheartening. It was like dealing with a two-headed Dragon, both of whom I idolized. By the end of the season, however, the bottom line was, we didn't make much money, but the place rocked, the patrons had a blast and we had a hell of a lot of FUN!

Pan Am Games (1959)   With Nick's return to the NYAC, Rocco was still hopeful that he would eventually show some enthusiasm for the upcoming Pan American Games. However, Nick remained mostly noncommittal. Then, as an inducement, in mid-July, the NYAC offered to send Nick to Santa Clara California in order to train with the swimming elite of the west coast. This would allow him a unique opportunity to observe the training methods and techniques of Olympic caliber swimmers and their coaches.

After a little persuasion by Whitey Budzago and Paul Wacker, Nick reluctantly accepted the invitation to train in sunny California for several weeks. It was while Nick was in Santa Clara that he first met Murray Rose, the Australian 1956 Olympic gold medalist. Ironically, Rose set world records in many of the same events that Nick swam.

Shortly after his return, Nick received phone calls from both Wacker and Budzago inquiring about his Santa Clara experience and assessing his interest in the upcoming Pan Am Games. Nick tried to diplomatically sidestep the issue, but they were persistent. He finally told them that he decided to decline their invitation, but they implored him to reconsider.

I remember talking with Nick in the Snack Bar about his California experience. He seemed in awe of the west coast swimmers in general, and in particular, of his idol and nemesis, Murray Rose. He felt it was a humbling reality check. That, as much as he respected Rocco as a coach, there was no way to compete with that level of professional coaching while training in a warm sunny climate 12 months of the year,

Rocco was very upset with Nick's *rash decision,* which I think he interpreted as Nick *psyching himself out,* thereby forfeiting a golden opportunity. I think perhaps Rocco knew firsthand how important one's psyche is, and of his own unfortunate experience during his Olympic trials. I often thought that perhaps Rocco was enjoying a vicarious thrill and hopefully a vindication of sorts, for his own personal disappointment.

When I tried in vain to reason with him, Nick simply said, "There's more to life than swimming". Then, after finally meeting the love of his life, Barbara Brenner (Babs), I understood why. I sensed earlier that he had lost the fire in his belly - because now it was in his heart! In just two short years, they would be happily married on Dec 7th, 1962,

I always sought Rocco's attention, but apparently lacking the prerequisite of raw talent, his attention was always directed elsewhere. When Nick finally decided not to compete in the Pan Am games, Rocco's coaching career seemed to come to an abrupt end. Ironically, Nick's fateful decision essentially closed two doors. The first being his illustrious swimming career and the second, of me ever attracting Rocco's coaching attention. I thought I waived and raised my hand high enough, but I guess I was just too short!

Incidentally, Rocco, and I recently had a brief conversation regarding his reaction to Nick's decision. He bristled when I suggested that, to some degree, I felt he was living vicariously through Nick, hoping to possibly share the thrill of making the Olympic team which, due to a regrettable miscalculation, had earlier denied him. Sadly, he accused me of "Psychologizing"- I didn't know such a word even existed!

MOM   After my father's death, being that my mother was still a relatively young, attractive woman, it was amusing to witness her playfully demur the unsolicited attention of other gentlemen of similar age. At some point, she assumed the responsibility of the Snack Bar, with the understanding that she would be entitled to keep all the profits! In reality, however, due to constant siphoning of the cash, she was left with nothing!

One particular gentleman comes to mind, known to us as *the Culligan Man.* He was a relatively tall, thin, pleasant man with sparse reddish hair who regularly serviced our pool supplies. After paying his *official* service call, he would often meander down to the Snack Bar, to chit chat with my mother.

Then, one hot afternoon I noticed my mother and him sitting on the edge of the pool dangling their feet in the cool pool., I was particularly taken aback when the Culligan Man popped a chilled bottle of champagne, and while sipping champagne from their flutes, they both became giddy! Initially, I was delighted to see my mother happy for a change. But, just as quickly I thought, "What the hell is going on here!"

One summer evening, shortly after his wife, Mary, died, I was shocked to see Mack McCarthy's Cadillac parked in Anita's driveway. He was here to pay my mother a surprise visit. He was uncharacteristically, well dressed with his hair slicked back with a double dose of Brylcreem, and neatly parted in the middle. His face was clean-shaven and obviously saturated with Gillette after shave lotion - its potent aroma preceding his arrival.

Ironically, my childhood recollections of, Mr. Mack, was of a large obese man wearing, oil-stained coveralls and a guinea tee-shirt while sitting on a small stool in front of his garage, tinkering with his lawn tractor. I never got the impression that my mother was the least bit interested in him, and just the thought of this immense man pursuing my mother was almost comical - which I suspect was also shared by my mother.

CH - 24
ANITA'S SHOWER

The Trums were known to be affluent and very generous. In mid-August Mrs. Trum graciously offered to host a wedding shower for Anita at their house, and I was asked to come and assist with serving hors d'oeuvres and champagne. At the time, Anita was an assistant buyer for the Corvette's Dept store, and in order to save me from embarrassment, she bought me a very fashionable, light tan cord suit, that featured a collarless jacket. I was very nervous about being a "server" among all the older women, and although this was totally foreign to me, I was doing it for my sister.

I only recall visiting MM's summer house on three prior occasions. Once, to see her newborn brother, Dennis, in a bassinet on their front porch, and noticing a small cutaneous horn on his cheek that was eventually removed. The second was when I walked her brother, George, home from his grandparent's farm after he experienced an allergic reaction following a bee sting. And the third was sitting on their back lawn, along with Nick and some other kids, watching a fireworks display by their handyman, Mickey.

I don't remember seeing MM during the shower, and I only have a faint recollection of the interior of their house. Similar to Cottage 10, the back door led to a large country kitchen to the left of which was a formal Dining room. This, in turn, led to a Living room with a large fieldstone fireplace and a wrap-around screened porch with ample white wicker furniture to easily accommodate all the guests.

I knew that MM came from an equally large family, consisting of three older and three younger siblings. Her oldest sibling, Patricia (Pat), was followed by two older brothers, Kip, and George. Her younger siblings were, Roberta (Bobbie), Dennis, and the youngest being Susie. In addition to Mickey, they also employed a full-time Panamanian nanny and housekeeper, Viola. Her mother, Virginia, was a tall slender elegant lady. Her father, Walter, was very tall in stature and his deep gravelly voice and a fixed facial expression due to Parkinson's disease, projected an imposing figure. Mostly due to his disease, he had a part-time driver, Steve.

Everyone in the Park knew where the Trums lived -on a gentle rise directly facing the first major bend of the Park's roadway. It was a pretty black and white clapboard house with a three-sided screened porch adorned with colorful awnings which added considerable dimension to the house. To the right of the driveway was a large corral paddock with several horses, including Lady, Black Beauty, two Ponies, Pinky and Chris Cringle and Chief, housed in a separate stall. At the top of the driveway was a large black and white wooden barn that contained an assortment of horse equipment and a large horse-drawn carriage and a smaller pony cart.

The pony cart was very unique. The interior had two side benches that could accommodate 3 to 4 kids on each side, easily accessed by a small rear door and pulled by either of the ponies. I remember riding in the cart a couple of times around idle hour Park and witnessing Kip and George having pony races on a straightaway past the Vaccaro's house. It was my impression that Cringle was considered Kip's Pony and Pinky was George's, and I remember George whipping the hell out of poor little Pinky, trying to keep up with Cringle.

There was a common thread connecting our two families. We each had proud, loving parents of seven closely-knit children. All of whom were practicing Catholics, influenced by a similar Jesuit presence from either Gonzaga or Brooklyn Prep. Eventually, I learned that, in addition to our shared experiences of Idle Hour Park and Walton Lake, during the winter, they lived in a relatively modest house in the Flatbush section of Brooklyn - in many respects similar to our house in Bay Ridge. However, that seemed to be the extent of our similarities.

High Society   The Trums seemed to enjoy a somewhat exclusive, social circle, both in Monroe and Flatbush. It was apparently commonplace for them to host, or be guests at, lavish cocktail and dinner parties, often attending elaborate social affairs such as the candlelight and Emerald balls - all of which was totally foreign to us. From my jaundiced perspective, *they were considered, High society and we were, No society!*

At the time, however, I only witnessed their private weekend parties in Monroe, and to my knowledge, with the possible exception of the De Schrievers, they never included anyone from the Park - or perhaps we were the only ones excluded! Somehow, it reminded me of when I would peer through a shop window, looking at things I couldn't afford - pressing my big nose uncomfortably hard against the display window in order to overcome my own reflection.

In sharp contrast, being a prominent attorney, my father's social circle was mostly composed of professionals and politicians, and his private world was within the swimming community. Being a charismatic chameleon of sorts, he readily attracted and influenced even absolute strangers. Both in Monroe and Bay Ridge, our friends and neighbors seemed to prefer privacy, never gathering socially for cocktails or dinner parties. Although our social worlds were distinctly different, there was still a sense of parity and mutual respect.

Mary's Maternal Grandparents   Mary's Maternal Grandparents were gentle, kind people of modest means. They lived in a lovely brownstone home in Brooklyn, overlooking Ebbets Field. Her Grandfather, George Beatty, was a tall successful lumber salesman and his brother, Richard, managed to earn degrees in both Law and Engineering. Likewise, her Grandmother, Margaret Cullinan, was likewise tall and quite remarkably, a graduate of Hunter College at a young age. Considering that their daughter, Virginia Beatty -Trum, was also quite tall and likewise, excelled academically at a very young age, it's no wonder that my wife obviously tapped into their genetic height and brain pool!

Mary's Paternal Grandparents   In sharp contrast, Mary's Paternal Grandparents were quite wealthy, owning a very successful carton box company headquartered in a 5 story historical building in the Red Hook section of Brooklyn. Although they lived in a large two-story apartment in the Park Slope section of Brooklyn, they also owned a 100 acre Gentleman's farm in Monroe. The farm had extensive frontage on Doug Road, overlooking a very picturesque fieldstone Main House approached by a long winding red stone driveway. The farm complex included a huge red barn, the upper portion of which stored bales of hay while the lower portion was for milking the cows.

The surrounding landscape included various buildings and sheds for small livestock including chickens, pigs, cows, and horses. Her grandparents had a black chauffeur, Dick, who, in addition to chauffeuring them in a classy black limousine, also served as a cook and butler. Early on they vacationed at their private home in Dunedin, Fl, eventually moving to a condominium in Palm Beach - all of which fostered an unfamiliar air of aristocracy or entitlement.

I remember once visiting the Farm and playing hide and seek with several other kids among the bales of hay in the red barn. At some point, George was stung by a bee and started to experience a significant reaction indicating that he was obviously allergic to bees. We applied some ice, but he became very nervous when he experienced some nausea and dizziness and wanted to walk back home. I was concerned about letting him walk alone, so we took one of the horse paths from Doug Road eventually arriving home safely. He would occasionally retell the fateful story, always emphasizing how much he appreciated the fact that I didn't abandon him. - that's because I led him to believe that *I saved his life!*

Pat Trum   I first became aware of Mary's older sister, Pat, while she was standing at Schaeffer's talking with Caesar who was behind the counter. I had just finished "distance swimming" in the lake and rested on the dock for a short time soaking up the sun. Not knowing who she was, when I walked up to the counter and stood beside her, I couldn't help but notice her shapely figure and pretty face.

Perhaps, it was upon seeing my dry suntanned back or after I commented about her long polished fingernails that she began to lightly tickle and scratch my back and I was in total ecstasy! When she paused for a moment, I pleaded, "Oh, just a little longer!" I guess, in order to get rid of me, she said, "Why don't you ask, Mary Margaret, she has long fingernails." However, being that our paths only crossed a couple of times, I wasn't about to ask a stranger!

Rush Picnics   During one particularly hot summer day, I remember when Nick and I were graciously invited to the Trum's annual picnic barbecue on the Rush property, ideally located on a remote narrow dirt road off LaRue Rd. Actually, being that Nick and Kip were best friends, I believe Nick was "invited" and I just tagged along.

The chosen picnic area was located next to a picturesque stream, protected from the heat by a canopy of lush evergreen trees and cooled by the stream's cold cascading waterfalls. I remember, wading in the active stream and holding my breath while sitting under a cold waterfall cooling my head. Then, the inviting smell of the charcoal grills signaled that lunch was ready. Ironically, while enjoying myself during the entire afternoon, I was either too young or too preoccupied to even notice the future love of my life, that Trum girl, Mary Margaret- I guess Sister Barbara was right - I was too slow at the draw!

Western Movie   At a later date, I have a very faint recollection of MM accompanying her brother, Dennis, when he brought a pony to Bobby Persichetti's house in order to rehearse for a *Western movie* that Bobby and I were producing.

In retrospect, other than Nick's good friend, Kip, I hardly ever saw any of the other Trums in the Park or at the Lake, which caused me to wonder,

"Where did they go and what did they do all summer long?" Also, while writing this memoir I stated emphatically that, no one who experienced the magic of Idle Hour Park or Walton Lake has ever forgotten the fond memories.

Incidentally, after discussing this with my wife, she and perhaps her sisters, are the only known exceptions. Apparently, either due to a scarcity of playmates, family circumstances, or other social commitments, she didn't share the same memorable experience that I described.

Anita's wedding (Sept.1960)   Anita and Bob Hartmann announced their plans to be married in early September in Sacred Heart Church, with a reception to follow at the Lodge. True to form, as a measure of her commitment to always contribute to the needs of the family, Anita forfeited an engagement ring in order to pay for awnings on the front of the Lodge. This would be our first foray as a catering facility, and what better trial experiment than my sister's wedding!

Fr. Neelan was to officiate at the wedding ceremony, and everything seemed to be going fine until they discovered that someone forgot to pick up the wedding cake from Brooklyn's Luigi Alba bakery! Realizing this, and although he was a groomsman, they immediately dispatched Nick, to drive down to pick up the cake.

Ironically, while Bob and Anita were riding in the limousine en route to the church, they passed Nick on Lakes Rd, driving frantically with the cake in the opposite direction en route to the Lodge. Despite this minor fiasco, the bride and groom still managed to arrive at the church *almost* on time - I guess it runs in the family!

Strangely, rather than his brother, Adam, Bob chose his very good friend, Bruce, as his best man. I suspected that Father Neelen hadn't officiated at a wedding in quite some time because he appeared to be extremely nervous, and despite the mild weather, he was sweating profusely. When Nick finally arrived at the church, he was somewhat embarrassed to discover that he had forgotten his bowtie and was still wearing sneakers!

The traditional wedding pictures of the bride were taken from the elegant Grand Staircase landing. The main room was beautifully decorated with a large assortment of flowers and the long dais was set in front of the large fieldstone fireplace adorned with flowers and spruce branches across the top of the massive wood mantle.

The guest tables were spread throughout the entire main room and adjoining side Dining room. A four-course, dinner was served, the entrée being, prime rib of beef. Although they had a small combo band from the Captain's Table in Monroe, I fondly remember Bob, on his accordion and his brother, Adam, on his electric guitar, playing a few sets for the guests. Drinks were served from the small bar and everyone had a spectacular time.

My 71st Birthday   Today, I'm celebrating my 71st birthday while recuperating in bed following hip surgery to reattach two gluteal muscles - literally, a real pain in the ass! It's going to be a long haul, requiring me to lie flat on my back for six weeks followed by slow progressive weight bearing for another six weeks. In order to keep my sanity, I resumed writing this damn memoir. But the one who literally bore all the weight was my darling wife, who constantly bolstered my spirits while cheerfully lugging the heavy cooling device and the "Game-boy" exercise contraption twice daily - and, unlike me, she never complained!.

At some point, I became aware that Nick had been admitted to the hospital for the third time and I felt terribly guilty not being able to see him. So, with my darling wife's assistance, we decided to venture down to the hospital for a brief visit. As in many times past, I'm always hopeful that I'll find him alert enough to respond to some simple questions.

Upon arrival at the hospital, I transferred to a wheelchair and when Mary wheeled me into his room, I was immediately disappointed that, when he saw me, his eyes didn't appear to brighten-up as they had so many times in the past. I was anxious to share with him some of our humorous vignettes from my memoir, but even they drew only blank stares. His wife, Barbara, was also in the room and recognized my profound disappointment. I was only able to muster about 20 minutes, and with a heavy heart, I kissed my brother goodbye and left the room.

While Mary was wheeling me down the corridor, Barbara came rushing out and yelled, "He just said your name!" Hearing that simple affirmation, my heartache was relieved somewhat, and I left with a modicum of inner peace. Thereafter, whenever I would complain about how uncomfortable and boring it was to be bedridden, I felt ashamed realizing that, "It's only a temporary inconvenience compared to Nick's life sentence".

CH -25
JUNIOR YEAR

This year was marked by dramatic structural changes at the Lodge, personal uncertainty, and inner turmoil. I was now an *upperclassman* and academically, other than Trigonometry, I actually enjoyed studying. Although I thoroughly enjoyed English literature, I didn't care for the teacher's sudden outbursts of theatrical rage. His antics were even more immature than we were!

Having finished all of my required science courses, and finally relieved of the bane of my existence, Latin, I took additional courses in history, philosophy, and theology. There was one priest in particular who seemed to enjoy engaging in theological banter as much as I did. In fact, I even took an additional course with him during my senior year and he signed my yearbook, "To the future theologian, I enjoyed the challenge, keep questioning!"

Although the varsity swimming season was now pretty routine, Fr. Hines was joined by a relatively young assistant coach. He was somewhat more progressive than Fr. Hines and open to suggestions. A talented freshman freestyler, John Hopkins, moved up to the varsity, and although he represented a formidable challenge in the 200-yard freestyle, he was still young and inexperienced - thank God.

Xavier- Bklyn Prep Meet   At the time, Nick was a sophomore at Fordham, and being that he forfeited his swimming scholarship, he was recruited by Xavier High School as their swimming coach. Knowing that we would eventually compete against each other, much as he did while at St. Francis

Prep, he would try to pump me regarding our swimmers. Also, recalling our *shot for a shot contest* as kids, he would try to bait me saying, "if you tell me who your best freestyler is, I'll tell you who mine is". Having learned from many painful punches in the past, I would give him a bogus lead and he, either gave no lead or gave an equally bogus lead.

Xavier was scheduled to have a dual meet against Brooklyn prep, and since we would be facing Brooklyn prep on the following Friday, our assistant coach sent me and John Lupi to observe (scout) the meet. The contest was to be held at Brooklyn prep's brand-new, *State-of-the-art,* swimming pool. Although the aquatic center had a large bleacher area, unlike football or basketball games, hardly anyone from the student body ever attended swimming meets. So, being that the bleachers were empty when we arrived we stood out like two penguins!

Upon seeing us in the bleachers, even before the meet started, Brooklyn prep's coach, Mr. Beck, came storming up demanding that we leave immediately. Despite protesting that we had every right to be there, he became irate, yelling, "Get the hell out of the pool area now!" Upon hearing the commotion, Nick surmised what the issue was, and surprisingly, for the first time, he came to my defense, concurring that we had every right to be there.

When Mr. Beck threatened that he would delay the meet until we left, Nick countered with, "We're ready to swim, and such an indefinite delay would amount to a forfeiture!" - which was fine with Nick. Mr. Beck eventually relented and although we felt vindicated and I was extremely proud of my brother's allegiance, I could feel Mr. Beck's eyes boring into my skull. After a brief period of mutual glaring, I felt it was bad karma and decided to take the high road and leave gracefully.

When we reported back to our coaches that we didn't have any meaningful information, they were upset with us and furious with Mr. Beck. However, when I explained that, given the circumstances, it was a no-win situation, and it seemed the prudent thing to do, they eventually calmed down. The following week, however, we would take our revenge, when Brooklyn prep came to swim in our *state of the century*-Tub Pool. We beat them handily, and best of all, I beat Mr. Beck's son, Bob, in the 200 yd individual medley and swimming Butterfly on the medley relay.

New Utrecht HS   Rocco had either resigned or was replaced as assistant coach of the NYAC, which meant I wouldn't benefit from his coaching expertise. Swimming finals were fast approaching, and I desperately needed additional pool time and professional coaching. Fortunately, being that Caesar had a job as the evening lifeguard at New Utrecht High School, he invited me to come and work out three evenings a week. However, since it was a public pool, it only allowed for a limited amount of dedicated lap swimming - approximately one hour each evening.

Pyramid Training   Considering this constraint, he elected to maximize the pool time by limiting the distances to 400 yds, utilizing a series of conditioning or pyramid workouts. This consisted of progressively increasing the distances to a maximum of 400 yards followed by an identical decrease in the yardage. This was followed by 400 yds of rapid 25 yd wind sprints. Given the time constraint, this routine was efficient and ideal for my intended events. He also encouraged me to focus on my upper body strength by increasing my weight bar repetitions and my push-ups twice daily.

Lifeguard Certification   He also paved the way for me to eventually succeed him as a lifeguard at New Utrecht. This, of course, required me to obtain my, long overdue, lifeguard certification. I remember studying for and taking a performance evaluation by a certified instructor at a different pool which was purposely, very deep. One of the requirements was to retrieve a drowning subject from the bottom of the pool using a cross-chest maneuver.

The middle-aged instructor descended to the bottom of the pool and when I approached him, he purposely made it difficult by simulating an agitated and resistive drowning subject. After several attempts of the cross-chest maneuver, I eventually became frustrated and grabbed him by his scalp hair bringing him willingly to the surface, after which I applied across chest carry to the side of the pool. While rubbing his painful scalp and visibly wincing with tears in his eyes, he said, "Well, I guess that's an effective alternative!"

An unforgettable Date   One brutally cold January day, I asked Vickie to go to the movies. In order to hopefully conform to the current, *peg pants* trend and knowing that my mother was an excellent seamstress, I asked her to tailor my dress pants by tapering the legs. After she finished the first trial, however, I asked her to taper them even more! At that point, she quipped, "What do you want, leotards?" Then when I tried on the finished product she said, "They look ridiculous! Mark my words, you'll feel uncomfortable and you won't have a good time!" (the Alice curse!)

Although I arrived at Vickie's house about 20 minutes late, I was warmly greeted by her father, who apologized that his daughter was still upstairs getting dressed. I knew that Vickie's father was a widower and that he was a prominent Appellate court justice who was frequently driven to work in a large black sedan. He surprised me by expressing his condolences regarding my father's passing and said, "I only knew of your father's reputation, but unfortunately, our paths never crossed". I was very taken by this spontaneous acknowledgment and noted that, despite his professional stature, he was genuinely warm, friendly, and unpretentious.

Given that Vickie was still upstairs, he suggested that we move into the living room and chat for a while. I was still wearing my only winter coat, a heavy three-quarter length, green wool overcoat, and when I went to sit down in one of the comfortable chairs, I felt my pants rip from the bottom of my zipper to my back beltline. I was surprised that he didn't hear the loud rip or perhaps, he just pretended not to! While continuing with some small talk, he apparently noticed beads of perspiration on my forehead and offered to take my overcoat. Fearing the possibility of indecent exposure, I politely declined saying, "I'm still thawing out from the frigid weather!" With that, he turned up the thermostat - just what I needed!

After a while, he looked at his watch, excused himself and he went upstairs to check on his daughter's progress. When he came back down, noticing that my forehead was drenched, he asked If I had a fever. Thankfully, I was spared further interrogation by Vickie's arrival, dressed in stylish jeans and a nice tight-fitting cashmere sweater.

When we finally left her warm house, she said she was looking forward to the brisk evening walk to the RKO theater which was seven blocks away! I was literally, "swinging in the breeze!" In addition to the frigid temperature, it was also very windy, and my three-quarter length overcoat didn't provide much protection from the sudden updrafts. I remember being repeatedly stunned by these sudden wind gusts attacking a very sensitive area, which caused real concern genuine Blue Balls or worse - Frostbite!

When we finally arrived at the theater and thawed out in the warmth of the lobby, we settled into two secluded seats in the far back of the theater. Almost immediately, she removed her overcoat, revealing her very attractive cashmere sweater, while I continued to protect my dignity by wearing my wool overcoat. At some point, she said, "Why don't you take off your overcoat?" to which I replied, "I'm still very chilly".

Frustrated, I opened the top three buttons of my overcoat and stealthily attempted to place my arm on the back of her seat but sitting on the damn overcoat made it impossible. I tried several different maneuvers, all to no avail. Sensing this, she asked, "Aren't you warm yet?". As a distraction, I offered to buy some popcorn, which at least thwarted 15 minutes of further embarrassment.

When the movie was over, I was stunned when she suggested that we walk to Poles, the farthest of the three local ice cream parlors. This meant another 20 minutes of torture. Not only was my voice higher, but there was now a noticeable "bounce" in my step. When we finally arrived at the Parlor, we occupied a booth in the far back. Then, as luck would have it, shortly after we arrived, two friends from the neighborhood walked in, one being Kenny Powers who also attended St. John's Prep.

Of course, they assumed it was ok to join us. After introducing Vicki, and adding to my humiliation, Kenny asked, "Pete, aren't you hot with that overcoat?" I didn't know which was worse, contending with Kenny's ridicule or risking testicular frostbite. We eventually left Poles and quickly made our way back to Vicki's house. When she invited me inside, fearing the likely prospect of further interrogation, I politely declined the invitation, claiming that I had early morning swimming practice - even though it was Saturday!

St Michaels   After Friday evening swimming practices, Don Gill, and I would occasionally take the subway to St. Michael's auditorium in Queens, which hosted school dances featuring "Murray *the K* and the swinging soiree"! In addition to traditional *Rock 'n Roll*, they also featured performances by several of the, up and coming, Motown groups - my all-time favorite being the Shirelles.

Then one morning, while Vicki and I were riding the subway, I happened to mention these extravaganzas and she said, "Oh, I'd love to go!" I was initially taken aback and at a loss for words. Realizing that she misinterpreted it as an invitation, I simply said, "Sure, why not!" Then I thought, "What the hell. Perhaps this would be an opportunity to reprieve me." The next question was, "what to wear?" After enduring my mother's, "I told you so" rebuke for wearing leotards, while she was repairing the damage, I asked, "Can you just let them out a snitch?".

The Back Cottage   During this same time period, Rocco decided to renovate and modernize the two front bedrooms of the Back Cottage, which was formally reserved for the swim camp attendees. He envisioned that these bedrooms would be reserved for select patrons or for personal use. I was flattered when he asked for my help and the following three or four weekends proved to be an unforgettable experience.

It was during the dead of winter and since Cottage 10 didn't have heat, we borrowed a space heater and slept in the downstairs living room. I remember taping a white bed sheet above the stairway landing in order to prevent the heat from rising. Then, early in the morning, we covered our work boots with plastic bags and trudged through the deep snow to the Lodge.

For power, we ran electric extension cords from the hotel to the Back Cottage. I seem to remember that we mostly brought sandwiches prepared by my mother, and each evening we carried cases of frozen soda bottles back to Cottage 10, hoping they would thaw for drinking. It was a rare treat to go into town for breakfast at Mel's cafe, which overlooked Millpond. It was a small cafe and my first time having delicious scrambled eggs prepared on the large greasy grill.

One evening, Rocco decided to splurge, and we drove all the way to Greenwood Lake in order to have pizza at Patty's. I remember being surprised to see Dr. Ferrioni there and listening as he reminisced about our father. Eventually, Patty came and sat at our table, and looking at me said, "You're a young handsome fella, why are you spending a Saturday evening with this old fart?" Rocco replied, "Because he doesn't like girls!" Little did he know, I felt I was reliving a scene from Jack London's, "The Call of the Wild"

While renovating the Cottage, I learned a lot about framing and sheetrocking. Due to the high snowbanks, we retrieved lumber and sheetrock deliveries from Ross Lumber at the Lake View Estates entrance. This required us to carry ½" sheetrock, two at a time, through the deep snow for 300 yards.

Rocco would casually walk past my framing work and notice the deep hammerhead depressions at the top of the 2 x 4, and upon seeing my pencil line would ask, "Pete, what side of the line did you make the cut?" likewise, when I occasionally cut the 2x4 a snitch too short, I would quickly toenail the bottom in before he came strolling by.

Although I was a big Perry Como and Sinatra fan, I was also into the current rock'n roll and Motown craze. After the first weekend, I decided to bring up a boombox. I would drive him nuts by blasting NBC's, Murray the K, and the swinging soirée. Then I'd laugh when he'd yell, "Turn off that Jungle Bunny music!" At the time, he didn't even like Elvis Presley, often pronouncing his first name, Alvis! Then, just for fun, after raising the volume a snitch, I'd yell back, "What?" And I'd get hysterical when he'd scream the same response, even louder! This went on for several repetitions until he finally caught on and temporarily pulled the plug.

I guess in keeping with the adage, "bigger is better", Rocco made a bold decision to greatly expand the footprint of the small Hotel Bar area, in order to hopefully provide for future catering events such as weddings, communion breakfasts, Rotary club meetings, etc. This costly expansion more than quadrupled the size of the original bar. It entailed removing the wall between the Lodge's main room and the small bar, replacing it with movable Japanese style wood panels and moving the piano to the side of the staircase landing.

Virginia's Wedding (June 1961)   The upper-level addition consisted of a bar of modern design, extending across the entire left wall of the room. In addition, there was an equally large lower level, consisting of a screened-in Patio Room with a patio block flooring. I remember hurrying to lay the patio blocks in preparation for our second family wedding celebration. The marriage between my sister, Virginia, and Lew Harring, was scheduled for June 10th. The wedding ceremony took place in Sacred Heart Church, officiated by a priest from the Harring family. I don't remember many particulars of the reception other than, Virginia, having her pictures taken on the beautiful Grand Staircase landing.

CH - 26
SUMMER OF '61

Being that Virginia's wedding was a smashing success, we all directed our attention to the start of the Summer season. The first seasonal Hotel guests were the Spiritos. Once again, the entire family rented the same front room on the second floor. Donna was showing signs of maturity well beyond her years, and upon taking note of her natural beauty, I found myself assuming a more protective, big brother role.

Concerning our "constant" five year age difference, with each subsequent birthday, she would often say, "I'll never catch up, you'll always be 5 yrs. older!" Despite our age difference, however, she eventually became my trusted *sidekick,* always offering to help. Although short in stature, she was exceptionally strong and willing to do just about anything I asked of her without complaint. While lifeguarding, she would often keep me company at my table, always observing and willing to learn. These attributes set the stage for her to eventually assume the position of lifeguard.

She would often accompany me in the Snack Bar, eventually feeling confident enough to tend the counter by herself. With Marion's permission, she would frequently assist me in the kitchen on weekends, preparing antipasto platters and pizzas for the bar. In the morning, she would often sit with me while having breakfast in the Dining room, asking me about the events of the previous evening.

Likewise, I would occasionally join her and her mother at their table, and cringe when Marion would reprimand Tony, the chef, for not making her pancakes the only way she liked them - raw! After Donna would leave the table, however, I'd seize the moment to confide in Marion and seek her counsel regarding my very confusing love life. I was always amazed that she was far more observant than I gave her credit, and I always benefited from her wisdom.

While working out for the 4-mile Nationals, Marion became very concerned about my loss of weight saying, "Pete, all this swimming is making you way too thin, you have to eat more!" Then she would tell Tony to make me four scrambled eggs, bacon, and toast, making sure that I finished every last bite!

The Sound System   We installed a sound system with speakers in the Dining room, the Bar, and the pool area. The pool speaker was particularly large and strategically mounted on the roof of the Japanese structure housing the pool filter. It projected sounds with absolute clarity for a considerable distance. It was so powerful that I would occasionally entertain the pool patrons by holding the interior microphone against my chest, amplifying the sound of my *beating heart* - simulating the tense drama scenes in movies such as Jaws and Psycho.

Caesar arranged for several dual swimming meets at the pool and used an outside microphone to announce the results of each event, which was pretty cool. He also moderated a *Miss Ciri's Lodge* Junior Beauty Pageant. I remember lying in bed at cottage 10 with a high fever and chills while clearly listening to the results of the Pageant - the winner being, Miss Roberta Trum.

Al Florentino   During Dinner, our music selection consisted of three Johnny Mathis, 78 music albums. The timing of the selections was so routine that our new waitress, Helen, knew which serving to bring out based on which song Johnny was singing! In addition, we had a regular weekend guest, Al Florentino, who was a very successful hairdresser in Greenwich Village, and also a very talented pianist. He was always accompanied by Lee, a very pleasant, well-preserved woman who was presumed to be his adoring, *common-law wife.*

Regardless of the occasion, Al always wore black, high top Ked sneakers. Although he couldn't read sheet music, he was able to play a seemingly endless selection of old ballads and current Popular songs - all from memory. Towards the end of dinner, when Johnny had finished his last song, Al would start playing the upright piano to the delight of everyone in the Dining room. In fact, one evening during dinner, we had a sudden power outage, and Al immediately came to the rescue, playing the piano for hours by candlelight, Liberace style!

Bartending   Although I was only 16, Caesar started teaching me how to mix drinks from behind the new bar. According to Caesar, there was a fine line - I could mix drinks but couldn't serve them. Since no one ever questioned me, I learned the bar trade at a relatively young age. On weekends, I continued my nighttime kitchen job, turning out "economized" antipasto platters on a healthy bed of lettuce, and Bar pizzas with a measured amount of mozzarella. With Donna's invaluable help, we turned out both *specialties* in record numbers until 1 am.

C Roberts Trio   On weekends, Rocco hired a four-piece band, The C Roberts Trio. At the time, Tony Bennett had a run of top hits, and Mr. Roberts was a talented singer with a voice closely resembling the great crooner. For the first several weekends, Roberts was a smashing success, but adaptability and creativity were not his strong suit. Eventually, the crowd knew his entire repertoire by heart, often singing the next song even before he did!

The Beatles   Aside from the Trios monotonous repertoire, they also seemed to be taking longer breaks. So, In order to provide continuous music during the breaks, Bob Hartman purchased an electric organ, and ironically, Rocco's friends bought him a set of Slingerland drums for his birthday. Since the drums were mostly idle, I seized the opportunity by practicing quietly on the off hours and slowly monopolizing them. I gradually improved and thought of even playing in public. I noticed that, during the Trio's breaks, Bob would play mostly Beatles songs on the organ. Although I never paid attention to the lyrics, I was certainly familiar with the tempo of the music.

So one night, I attempted to accompany Bob on the drums, and in time, I thought we started to sound pretty good - especially while playing our signature song, the Beatles hit, "Can't buy me, love". Occasionally, if he had enough to drink, Charlie Bice, could be persuaded to play his trumpet. The irony was that, as a result of frostbite during the Korean War, all his fingers were amputated, leaving only tiny stubs beyond his knuckles. Despite this obvious handicap, he always made a valiant effort and certainly didn't sound any worse than we did. More importantly, regardless of how we sounded, we had a blast!

Jazz Trio   Caesar's good friend, Dick Sanfilippo, was an accomplished musician, often performing as an orchestral trumpeter. He was serving in the Army Reserves at Ft. Dix N.J and put together a trio of jazz musicians who agreed to drive up and play nonstop jazz in the bar for the entire weekend. - their only payment being unlimited booze! The bar absolutely rocked, and piping the music to the pool speaker, drew them into the bar - even for pure curiosity.

Third Encounter (July 1961)   Reminiscent of the dramatic physical changes that the seventh-grade girls seemed to undergo over the summer, I was looking forward to seeing what changes a whole year might have bestowed on that Trum girl, Mary Margaret. Then, while cleaning the inside of the Snack Bar, I remember glancing out at the pool and seeing this tall slender girl wearing a dark blue bathing suit with an unusually low-cut back.

My immediate reaction was, "Oh My Oh My, the long cold winter has treated you very well indeed!" Then, I remember thinking, "Hmm, she's now a sophomore and I'm still a Junior, the gap has mysteriously narrowed!" - strange how my frame of reference suddenly changed! little did I know, however, that she was, and would continue to be, a far more sought after young lady than I ever imagined - and rightly so!

Swim Camp (1961)   In early July the first group of swim camp attendees arrived. Rather than sleeping at cottage 10, I decided to move in with the other swimmers, for this was to be the summer that I would tackle the

Cirigliano, "rite of passage"- the 4-mile Nationals. Normally, we limited the camp attendees to less than 10 swimmers at a time, staggering their stay in 2 to 3-week intervals. However, Charlie Finan was the lone exception. He was the first to arrive and after two months, the last one to leave. He was a somewhat homely, mild-mannered nerdy guy, in his Junior year at Regis High school. Being that Rocco was mostly preoccupied with the Lodge, Caesar assumed the role of "Coach" and would regularly eat dinner with all of us, sitting at the last table in the rear of the Dining room.

Incidentally, in the Fall of 1960, Nick was hired as Xavier's new Varsity swimming coach and ironically, I found myself rooming with a Junior from Xavier named Mike Marshall. We initially hit it off okay, especially in the evenings, when he would play his saxophone while I was exercising. However, before I knew it, while I was doing my push-ups, Mike and Mary Margaret were already an item!

Mike was obviously far more aggressive than I, but then again, recalling Sr. Barbara's admonition, that was nothing new! I can't deny that I was disappointed by the sudden turn of events, but as they say, "He who hesitates, is a loser!" And now she was obviously spoken for. Consequently, any budding interest on my part was quickly set aside. To make matters worse, for the next three weeks, every night when he returned to our room, I had to listen to his incessant bragging about the latest exploits of his conquest!

Incidentally, While writing this memoir, I asked Mary, "How did this come about right under my big nose?" she simply replied, "Because, he paid attention to me!" I thought, "Hmm, I paid attention, but I guess you just didn't notice!". Besides, unlike their mutual thunderbolt attraction, it probably wouldn't have made any difference - I was obviously no match for Mike's self-assuredness!

The Bowling Alley   One evening, several of the guys went to the bowling alley in town. In the lane next to ours, were several counselors from camp Lenni Lenape. I was attracted to one girl, in particular, a cute blonde by the name of Sue Harley. We were having a nice conversation, and I was amazed that someone as pretty as she was even paying attention to me. After all, didn't she notice my big nose and recessed sabertooth?

But my brief moment of bliss was suddenly shattered when Mike, noticing our private conversation, wasted no time coming over, intent on showing me how to handle a woman. He quickly monopolized the entire conversation, demonstrating an unabashed sense of self-confidence which I sorely lacked.

When the other girls were about to leave, Sue pulled me aside and said, "Your friend is full of himself, why did you allow him to do that?" As she was leaving, I was shocked when she kissed me, and while handing me her address said, "You were the one I wanted to talk to!" I was absolutely speechless! We corresponded for a few weeks, but without any means of transportation, my brief fantasy died a natural death.

After leaving the bowling alley, we all returned to MM's house so that Mike could make amends for spending an evening with the guys. However, as soon as he went inside to "say goodnight," after a brief embrace, they both disappeared to a white wicker couch on the sunporch. Meanwhile, I hung out with MM's former boyfriend, Jimmy Dugan, until he was eventually picked up by his cousin, Billy Kelly.

Unfortunately, I was responsible to ensure that Mike returned back to the Cottage before the 11 pm *curfew*. Given that the witching hour had long passed, and Mike wasn't responding to my calls, I was now faced with the unenviable task of interrupting them. Although they had only known each other for two weeks, unlike my impotent "smoldering fermentation" approach, from the very beginning, theirs was one of immediate mutual attraction, as if ignited by spontaneous combustion. Ultimately, I was left with the lingering memory of MM's haunting refrains, imploring him not to leave, and the painful realization that theirs was a passion which I would never experience during our early courtship.

The following evening, apparently aware of Mike's aggressiveness, I was taken aback when MM's younger sister, Bobbie, approached me on the Lodge's front porch asking, "Why don't you do something about it?" At a loss for words, I simply shrugged and said, "What can I do?"

Cocktail Waitress   In any event, we decided to aggressively market the Bar and Poolside service. Our Dining room waitress, Helen, had no interest in providing poolside service, so we advertised as such. I heard second hand that a candidate showed up for an interview. I'd never known Rocco to take such a long time with an interview, but when he finally brought her down to meet the lowly lifeguard, I understood why.

She was a mature 18-year-old girl who, knowing that it was "poolside" bar service, much to my delight, she showed up in a two-piece bathing suit scantily hidden by a white lace coverup. I couldn't believe my eyes, she was drop-dead gorgeous, and I quietly muttered to myself, "Hubba, Hubba!" Although she was worth every penny, her salary requirements were far more than we could afford.

Fourth Encounter   I don't recall the circumstances, but in late July, a week or two after Mike left the camp, for some reason I was chasing MM, on the stretch of road heading toward Monte Carlo. I remember we were both laughing while running, she in her shoes and me in my zories (flip-flops). When I finally caught up to her, while pausing to catch my breath, I said, "You sure as hell run fast for a girl, but why were you running away?" I was taken aback by her answer, "You know I like Mike!"

At the time, I thought we were just having fun, and I honestly didn't have plans of pursuing her. So, being totally perplexed, I simply said, "Sorry" and slowly walked away- once again choosing the safety of the wings rather than risking center stage. Shortly afterward, however, I replayed the same scene in my mind several times, and conflicted, I mused, "What had I done to cause her to run away, and why was I chasing her?" This left me wondering, "Why is it that we suddenly wish for that which we can't have?"

Barbara the Lizard   Following this minor setback, I don't recall seeing her for several weeks. In the meantime, I met a girl named Barbara. Although she lived in the Bronx with her family, they were renting a house for the summer, conveniently located directly across the road from the Lodge. Her family had a seasonal membership to the Pool and were frequent Bar and Dinner guests at the Lodge. They were known to be very generous spenders, hosting large Dinner parties for friends and extended family members, often partying into the wee hours of the morning.

Barbara was very well endowed, often stretching her *lucky* bathing suit to its limits. She was extremely friendly, to the point of being unabashedly flirtatious, leaving me with the impression that she was far more experienced than I - but then again, who wasn't! One evening, I was shocked when, without warning, she kissed me on the lips.

Incidentally, while watching TV at a young age, during a love scene my father would allay my germophobic concerns by saying, "Don't worry, while they're pretending to kiss, he has his thumb between their lips". In my naïveté, that subliminal image was imprinted in my mind.

Obviously disappointed, but persistent, Barbara kissed me several more times, and with each successive kiss, much like a lizard, I felt her tongue *pecking* at my lips. Despite my best efforts to keep my lips pressed close together, the persistent lizard eventually managed to insert her tongue in my mouth. Perplexed by this dilemma, I confided in my more experienced friend and coworker, John Lombardi, who said, "Pete, that's a French Kiss, you have to cooperate by opening your mouth!" Once I submitted to her kisses, however, Barbara was intent on teaching me more than I was willing to learn. Truthfully, the ease of it seemed somehow unrewarding - leading me to conclude that, "sometimes the hunt is more important than the kill".

Cathy Albano In stark contrast to the Lizard, was Cathy Albano, daughter of Vince Albano, an influential assemblyman within the City's Democratic machine. She was very pretty with long auburn hair and a very pleasant, unassuming personality. She and her twin brother, Vinny, would frequently come to the pool, and we would easily talk for hours. Occasionally, when she and her family came to the Lodge for dinner, I felt surprisingly comfortable waiting on their table.

251

Once I asked her what her father did for a living, and when she said, "OH, he's in Public Relations." At a loss, I simply replied, "Oh, that's nice!" But, I had no idea what he actually did. Although I was 16, I never applied for a Junior driver's license. However, as luck would have it, Cathy drove a very cool, white Camaro convertible. Better yet, she was willing to pick me up and drive us to the movies which strangely, made me feel like a teenage gigolo!

Four Mile Nationals   With both Rocco and Caesar preoccupied with the Lodge and the Swim Camp, and Nick preoccupied with Barbara, I was reconciled to the fact that I would have to train myself for the grueling Four Mile Nationals. If time permitted, my daily routine was to follow the early morning swimming lessons with 1500 yards or 60 laps in the pool. Then, in the early evening after lifeguarding, I would switch to the lake, initially limiting myself to one-mile or four times across the lake.

While swimming alone in the lake, for safety purposes, I would routinely drag an inflated plastic tube tethered to my bathing suit. Remembering Caesar's advice, I remained committed to my daily exercise routine of 150 pushups, 50 sit-ups, and my 50-pound bar weights. By early August, I gradually increased my lake distance to 4 miles - 16 times across or two times around the lake.

At some point, I told Caesar of my ultimate goal and lamented about the difficulty of training myself and swimming alone unchallenged. But then again, I've always said, "Swimming is a lonely sport - just you and the water!". Unfortunately, given his other commitments, Caesar could only offer much-needed encouragement. Then, apparently aware of my passing interest in rifles, I was blown away when he said, "If you train and compete in the 4-mile Nationals, I'll buy you a 22 rifle!".

One Sunday morning, spared from swimming lessons, and following my 4-mile workout, I was resting on a small cot in a tiny room adjacent to Schaffer's front counter. For some reason, Rocco came looking for me at the Concession stand, and when he saw me lying on the cot he exclaimed, "What the hell are you doing lying down, who's taking care of the Counter?"

Fortunately, Kip Trum happened to be standing in front of the counter and said, "He just finished swimming 4 miles!" Skeptical, Rocco asked, "Oh yeah, how many times did you swim back forth?" When I answered,"2 times around nonstop!" he just walked out.

The Greek Barge   Then I learned that the reason he came down was to tell me that we had several Greek guests at the Hotel who wanted to take a boat ride in the lake! He emphasized that they were big tippers, and whatever I made, I could keep. Shortly afterward, Rocco, accompanied by three overweight Greek couples arrived for their excursion. Although they said they didn't know how to swim, knowing that we didn't have any life vests, Rocco assured them that I was a lifeguard and swam like a fish. With that Rocco left me to entertain the Greeks for the next two hours.

In order to accommodate all six of them, I chose the largest fishing boat we had, with four wood benches. After carefully loading them in the boat, I noticed that the water level was almost up to the gunnel. It reminded me of the two men treading desperately in a cesspool, and one saying to the other, "We'll be fine, just don't make waves!" Hoping for the best, I asked, "What would you like to see?" and they replied, "The entire lake!" Having just finished swimming it, I can assure you it's at least 2 miles around. To make matters worse, there was non-stop chatter which "sounded Greek to me!"

Pulling on the oars was like towing a heavy barge painfully slow. And, of course, without the benefit of gloves, triggered flashbacks as a 10 yr. old, rowing a much smaller boat with my father sitting in the far back, telling me to just wet my hands in the lake to prevent blisters. Trust me, it didn't work then, and it wasn't working now! Case in point was poor Joel Vaccaro, who also rowed for my father, and despite the same advice, developed such severe blisters, that Dr. Heuson had to lance them and insert tiny drains in order to prevent infection.

Although the Greeks carried bottled water, they never offered me even a sip to quench my parched lips and mouth. So, every now and then I would gently wet my hands and scoop a little water in my mouth, taking care not to tip the boat too much. After roughly 2 hours of nonstop rowing, we finally arrived back at the dock, my mouth parched and my hands painfully raw. After helping them out of the wooden Ark, the three big Greek spenders huddled together, and after much discussion, they gave me six singles!

Nick Santella In Memoriam   At some point during the summer, I was greatly saddened to discover that, for reasons unknown to me, Nick Santella had suddenly left the Lodge to go home! I could only speculate that Rocco made the difficult decision to let Nick go. However, knowing how much Nick loved being at the Lodge and with our family, I doubt that it was due to expense issues; especially considering that he was replaced by Fred, a deaf handyman who was even more elderly and not nearly as talented as Nick Santella.

I often imagine how awful it must've been for Nick to leave the familiar Catskill mountains and the loving family that he was so devoted to and return to his basement apartment in Coney Island. I felt we all considered Nick as a vital part of our family fabric, and in many respects, he was a lasting connection to my father and of their youthful days together at Gonzaga. I knew that, over the years Rocco had learned a great deal from Nick, and I felt that surely he had the highest regard for him. But I was reluctant to challenge my brother by asking why or how this came about, or if Nick's absence affected him as it did me. Although I grieved his absence, I handled it in my usual way - by just burying it.

Shortly afterward, I was shocked further when we received a call from his son, Anthony, that his father had suffered a fatal heart attack while in his apartment, thus closing another chapter - robbed of accompanying him to his beloved Coney Island and never again to hear his familiar salutation "Hello my best friend!" According to his son, while being removed from his apartment on a gurney, his parting words were "This is a hell of a way to go!"

CH - 27

FIFTH ENCOUNTER

The Orange County Fair always occurred during the middle two weeks of August. For me, it engendered mixed emotions of being both, the festival highlight of summer, as well as portending the end of the season. By this time most of the swimmers were gone except for a few stragglers, including Charlie Finan. I don't remember the exact details, but it was Caesar's custom to take the remaining campers to the County Fair. So, one evening he drove us in a large station wagon which, considering that MM was included, it might have been borrowed from the Trums.

In any event, I found myself sitting in the far back, squeezed among three or four other passengers including, MM. To my recollection, we hadn't seen or spoken with each other since our confusing foot race. During the 40 minute drive to the Middletown Fairgrounds, I noticed her occasionally staring at me, and then quickly turning away. This happened several times, and at one point, without a single word, our eyes seemed to lock for an extended period of time, and I swore *I saw the lovelight in her green eyes!* - or perhaps it was purely wishful thinking!

This was followed by a brief sense of excitement wherein; *I felt my heart stand still!* This unfamiliar sensation reminded me of the lyrics, "*I took one look at you, that's all I meant to do, and then My Heart Stood Still. Though not a single word was spoken, I could tell you knew, that unfelt clasp of hands, told me so well you knew!*"

We found ourselves walking together throughout the fairgrounds, and when I suggested that we take a ride on the large Ferris wheel, she explained that she was deathly afraid of heights, especially at the top. I reassured her that I wouldn't rock the seat at the top and would signal to the operator to let us off if she became frightened. I thought she was doing fine until we both got off the ride, and she immediately ran to a private area and proceeded to vomit right in front of me, splattering my Zories. After that lovely experience, any prior delusions of possibly kissing her, or nurturing a budding romance, quickly evaporated!

M M's 15th Birthday   In mid-August, MM invited three of her girlfriends, Pam, Angela, and Eleanor up to Monroe to celebrate her 15th birthday. When they all arrived at the pool in their bathing suits, seeing them through my reflective sunglasses, was like manna from heaven or a kid in a candy store! - it was just too good to be true. After brief introductions, they more or less gathered around my lifeguard table making lame comments about my tan, my curly hair, my shoulders, and most noticeably, the deep depression in my chest, (funnel chest). Thankfully, however, they politely pretended to ignore my big nose and recessed sabertooth!

Mr. Leibowitz   I was certain that this sudden congregation of attractive girls would surely validate Rocco's prior assertions, and I expected him to come racing down to disperse the *Harem*. At the time, and in typical fashion, Mr. Leibowitz was paying a spontaneous surprise visit. At some point, he pulled me aside saying, "You really shouldn't be wearing your red nylon bathing suit without a jockstrap!" I thought, "I'm not a football player, I'm a swimmer!" Apparently, he must have noticed a, not so subtle, hormone surge! Luckily, Rocco didn't come down to tell me to walk around the pool and be more visible!

The next thing I knew, on August 16th, Charlie Finan and I were invited to celebrate MM's 15th birthday party at her house. When we arrived, we met Jimmy Dugan and her cousin, Dick Hegarty. Learning that Dick was about to enter St. John's Prep in the fall, fostered a brief conversation of mutual interest. He reaffirmed that his older brother, Bill, was entering his senior year and was a star basketball player at the Prep. At some point, I learned that Jimmy was now dating Pam, and he gave me a heads up that the large horse-drawn carriage in the garage was a perfect place for making out! I thought, "Yea, that's if you can get past the smell of horse manure!"

I wasn't quite sure why Charlie and I were invited, or what my intended role was. Was this purely a mixer or a paring party? The next thing I knew, the girls decided to play a game. I was to sit on the white wicker couch with my eyes closed, and one of the girls would sit on my lap and kiss me! Then I was to pick the correct one. All I remember was someone's full-bodied lips on mine - hopefully, a girl's!. When I opened my eyes I looked warily at each of the girls and chose correctly - the lips were Angela's, and I wondered, "Is that who I'm supposed to be with?"

Considering that I was easily infatuated with just about every girl I met, I was totally confused, feeling as though there was a constant shuffling of potential pairs. What was apparent, however, was that MM seemed to remain mostly out of the mix. Although it seemed as though the girls were taking advantage of poor Charlie's innocent nerdism by tantalizing and tormenting him all evening, he appeared to be having a great time. However, at the witching hour, we both said goodnight and left the party even more clueless than before.

The following morning, Dick Hegarty came up to the pool, and among other things, he said, "MM really likes you!" I responded, "Could've fooled me!" Then he elaborated a little further, and although I was initially encouraged, considering our prior encounters, I still remained guarded. Gradually, however, I recall feeling a sense of mutual attraction which, although left unspoken, seemed to flourish with each passing day, and I found myself looking forward to seeing her again.

Mike Returns   Shortly after the party, I received a call from Mike Marshall, stating that he also planned to compete in the 4-mile Nationals In Lake Placid NY. He said that he had been training under the former Xavier coach, Joe Steady and that he'd like to come up and workout with me in the lake the week before the race. In addition, he offered that his parents were willing to drive us to Lake Placid and would even pay for us to stay overnight in a hotel room. I thought, "How could I refuse such an offer!".

Given that it was only two weeks before the race, Caesar advised me to start tapering my daily 4-mile swim by swimming 2 miles twice daily and eventually decreasing to just 2 miles daily. Based on his personal experience of swimming the same event several times, he offered additional valuable advice. He warned me, after the start, don't get sucked into the frenzy of jockeying for position saying," It's not how you start the race, but how you finish" Instead, try and stay relaxed for the first quarter-mile, maintaining a comfortable rhythm, breathing every four strokes, and gradually increasing your pace so that you have a strong finish.

Most importantly he said, "Swim your own race. It doesn't matter what position you come in, just as long as you're satisfied that you did your best!" Considering that each of my brothers came in either first or second in the same grueling event, that simple statement greatly relieved the tremendous sibling pressure that I always bore.

When Mike arrived, he was anxious to immediately start working out, extolling how much he had benefited from Joe steady's excellent coaching. During the week, we swam every day, mostly sticking to my regimen. He would usually stay with me, and at times, even push me which, although unfamiliar, was good for me. I would attempt to maintain a steady rhythm, staying relaxed, and focusing on a comfortable mantra-like breathing pattern. With a half-mile to go, he would routinely try to pull away from me and I would let him expend his energy. Then, with a quarter-mile to go, I would demoralize him by blasting past him. He never altered this predictable strategy and neither did I.

Sixth Encounter   I hadn't seen MM during the entire week of training, and on the evening before we were to depart for the race, while Mike and I were having dinner, MM walked into the Dining room and joined us at the table Whether this was purely coincidental or by design, I'll never know.

After sufficient small talk, when she said that she had to return home, Mike immediately seized the moment by asking if he could walk her home for old times' sake - the proverbial, "walk down memory lane!". After a brief awkward moment of silence, without further hesitation, MM said okay and they both got up and left the table. I just sat there stunned and speechless while thinking, "You can't make this shit up!" My tattered self-esteem was once again in the toilet!

Apparently, I was under the erroneous notion that, having seen the "lovelight in her eyes" was surely the beginning of a flourishing relationship, but I guess I didn't exactly sweep her off her feet! Knowing Mike's assertive nature, I naturally presumed the worst, which incentivized me, all the more, to kick his ass in the race!

Although at the time it seemed cruel and insensitive, I remember my father's cryptic message, attempting to assuage Caesar's jealous brooding over a presumed betrayal by his long term girlfriend, Jane. Clearly, within earshot, he sang Sinatra's rendition of *"Hey jealous lover."* Being that Dad was actually very fond of Jane, I believe his intended message was, "Don't let jealousy cloud your better judgment. If you don't give her freedom, you stand to lose her forever!"

Lake Placid NY Mike's parents picked us up at the Lodge and after driving 7 hrs., we eventually arrived in Lake Placid N.Y. by 6 PM. After checking into our hotel, we decided to at least become familiar with the quarter-mile buoy markers. However, after diving into the lake, I experienced immediate excruciating pain in my facial sinuses and felt my gonads rise into my lower abdomen - and I thought the NYAC pool was cold!

The next morning all the swimmers gathered at the designated starting area, and I met several of the former camp swimmers from St. Francis Prep. I copied some of the more seasoned contestants who applied dark charcoal under their eyes to limit the sun's glare. Then before I knew it, the race was underway, and as predicted, everyone was jockeying for position. The water was just as frigid as the night before, and it took me the first quarter-mile to regain my core body temperature. I remembered Caesar's advice and tried to maintain a constant relaxed rhythm. One advantage of the quarter-mile course was that you could easily judge your relative position.

I knew I was in the back third of the field, but I tried to remain relaxed, breathing every fourth stroke while gradually increasing my pace. I slowly passed several swimmers and with 1 mile to go, I knew I was closing in on two former camp swimmers, Tommy Zinkand and Mike Marshall. After rounding the second to last buoy, I went into finish mode, increasing my kick and breathing every other stroke. I remember feeling reasonably strong and noticing their weak kicks directly in front of me. I could tell they were waning, and in the final stretch, it was truly exhilarating as I passed each of them. I don't recall what position I came in, but unlike my brothers who were celebrated winners, I was listed as "Also swam!". Regardless, I was gratified to have beaten both of my adversaries.

The Revelation   During the long drive home, always willing to share the details of his latest conquest, Mike couldn't wait to confirm my suspicions that, when he walked MM home, he had kissed her, and for special emphasis added, "Not just a goodnight kiss!" - clearly leaving me with the impression that he had *reclaimed her.* Although this didn't surprise me, I was crushed that MM was complicit by allowing it to happen, confirming that she obviously still had strong feelings for him.

Consequently, I handled this latest in a series of setbacks, in my usual fashion - by withdrawing and quietly suppressing the pain. While trying in vain to restore my dignity and self-esteem, I found myself brooding and becoming progressively more sullen. Fearing the ignominy of rejection, the mere notion of *pursuing* was frightful. I was never able to share my humiliation with anyone, not even to my closest confidant, Marion, and certainly not Mary. Consequently, during these long dark periods, unaware of what I knew, Mary would occasionally ask, "What's wrong?" to which I would usually respond, "Nothing!"

Incidentally, while writing this memoir and hoping for truthfulness, when I would occasionally ask Mary about her recollections of specific painful events, she would often claim to simply not remember the details. I never knew if this was genuine or selective amnesia, sparing me from additional pain. However, when I pressed her further about the why of this specific incident, she conceded that obviously she still had strong feelings for him and then quipped, "You were always testing me, willing to let me go!". In truth, however, I never regarded her as a possession to let go of.

After congratulating me on completing the Cirigliano milestone, without even a subtle reminder, Caesar asked, "Which type of 22 rifle do you want, bolt action or lever action?" I had no idea of prices and would have been happy with either, but my only frame of reference was Paulie DeShriever's rifle. When I said, *"Lever action"*, he said, "I was afraid you'd say that!", clearly indicating that it was more expensive.

I'll never forget while sitting on the front steps of cottage 10, Caesar drove past blowing the horn and waving my rifle out the window, on his way to the Lodge. I ran as fast as I could all the way to the Lodge, and when I arrived exhausted and breathless, I realized that everyone except me had already fired my, Marlin, lever-action 22 rifle - which I still have to this day. *Incidentally, It reminded me of when I received my English racer on Christmas morning and all my brothers rode it before I did!*

Caesar's Challenge   That summer, I knew I came of age when Caesar challenged me to swim a 200 IM in the Lodge's pool. Knowing that he was still the current record holder for the 150 IM (no breaststroke), I was both humbled and concerned. Surprisingly, however, I took the lead in the Butterfly and he tied me during the Backstroke. Anticipating that he was going to kill me in the final Freestyle leg, I expended a lot of energy to take a generous lead in the Breaststroke. I was amazed when he wasn't able to close the gap in the Freestyle. Admittedly, he was out of shape, but I wasn't quite sure if he purposely held back. In either case, however, what I admired most was that, even though he was well behind, he never quit - the hallmark of a true champion!

Caesar's Wedding (September 1961)   Having finished his first year of Law School, Caesar made the ultimate commitment by marrying his beautiful bride, Patricia Imburgia. He chose Rocco as his best man, and on September 8th, the couple were married in Sacred Heart Church, officiated by my father's old Jesuit friend, Fr. DeMaria. Once again, Ciri's Lodge would cater another family wedding reception which was considerably larger than the two prior family weddings. Although I don't remember inviting her, presumably under better circumstances, I must have extended an invitation for MM to attend the reception as my guest.

I was still disillusioned and smarting from Mike's latest revelation. Painfully aware of the proverbial elephant in the room, I foolishly remained very quiet and aloof. I remember walking outside to clear my head, and after reflecting on my father's admonition regarding the pitfalls of *control and jealousy*, I resigned myself to, at least, ask her to dance. When I returned to the reception, however, much to my chagrin, I was told that MM had apparently liberated herself by dancing the *Twist* on the top of the bar with Bob Hartmann! Despite a few *hiccups,* the wedding celebration was a smashing success, and the following morning the newlyweds drove to the beautiful coast of Maine for their honeymoon.

Seventh Encounter   Following the wedding debacle, we didn't see each other again until the Sunday after Labor Day weekend. After mass, MM approached me in Sacred Heart's parking lot, and as though nothing had happened, I was shocked when she invited me to the Cathedral Club's annual dance in mid-November. Naturally thinking, "I guess Mike wasn't available," my initial reaction was very tentative. The dance was to be held in the Starlight Room in the St. George Hotel, with a pre-dance party at the home of Mr. and Mrs.Gallagher.

I suspect we may have had some preliminary phone conversations, but I don't remember seeing her during the interim. At the time, Caesar's good friend, Gus Frischer, happened to be working in Manhattan's garment district, and he arranged for me to meet with Gus in order to pick out a suit for the special occasion. I eventually picked out a black sharkskin suit, and when I reluctantly asked about the price, Gus said, "It's already been taken care of!"

Starlight Ballroom Despite my new suit, when we arrived at the Gallagher's home, and not knowing any of the other couples, I initially felt terribly awkward. I felt more comfortable, however, after being introduced to MM's good friend, Joanne, and learning that she was also a swimmer. Being that the only Gallagher I knew was, Drury Gallagher, I naturally assumed that Joanne must somehow be related to Drury. In fact, in my naivete, several times during the evening I asked, "But how are you related?"

Card tables for four, draped with white linen cloths were set up in their spacious living room, and Joanne's youngest brother, Arthur, waited on the tables. We sat with Joanne and her date, Ronnie Marcioni, who was dressed in a Xavier, Dress Blue uniform, and I mused, "I seem to be surrounded by Xavier guys!" I noticed that he had crutches due to a recent football injury, and I was impressed that, despite the crutches, he was still going to a dance!.

The four of us shared a taxi to the St George Hotel, and I remember Ronnie giving me the "thumbs up" sign as he kissed Joanne in the taxi and I thought, "Uh Oh, the moment of truth!" I don't remember if I took his cue, but I tend to doubt it. It's just not my style! That's assuming I even had a style!

The Starlight Ballroom was truly elegant, with huge crystal chandeliers, a large parquet dance floor, and a 12 piece orchestra band. We were seated with five other couples at a large round table situated on an elevated terrace, several steps up from the dance floor - certainly, a challenge for poor Ronnie. I remembered my sister Anita's advice to start dancing immediately. In fact, I think we were one of the first couples on the dance floor, and our very first dance together was appropriately titled, "It had to be you!".

Like an "unexpected song that only we were hearing", I felt as though we were floating on the dance floor!. The evening seemed to pass very quickly, and I felt we both had such a wonderful time that the night may have ended with our first kiss? Unfortunately, neither of us can recall - that's how memorable my kisses were! I clearly remember, however, my parting thought, "At last, we might even become a couple!"

The Visit   Shortly after the dance, however, being that Mike's fatal flaw was his penchant for bragging, I was crushed when Nick told me that Mike traveled from his home in Mt Kisco to visit MM in Flatbush. True to form, while taking an evening walk together, he seized the moment by making a series of advances -which Mary later acknowledged. I presumed this occurred before the dance and that their meeting was either by design or at Mike's request. In either case, however, it begged the haunting question - why allow it to happen?

From my jaundiced perspective, she still had a *thing* for him and allowed their mutual attraction to flourish. Although at such a young age, the word *love* seems absurd, my only assumption was, *she may have liked me, but she loved him!* So, despite my short-lived *couple's delusion*, my self-esteem was back in the toilet again! You just can't make this shit up, and If it wasn't so ludicrous, it would almost be funny!

CH - 28
SENIOR YEAR

I was finally a Senior, contemplating which college to attend and what major to choose. Ever since the second semester of my junior year, I found myself gravitating toward the sciences -perhaps something in the medical field. However, I believe this inclination was unduly influenced by a series of haunting flashbacks which began following my father's funeral. Initially, they occurred in short bursts, gradually increasing in frequency and duration.

In reality, memories are merely a series of flashbacks - some humorous, some sad, and some such as these, haunting. Needless to say, these flashbacks played havoc with my young adolescent psyche. In retrospect, however, while attempting to improve my sense of self-awareness, I identified three aspects of my adolescence to possibly explain my sudden mood swings. Namely: Guilt, Vulnerability, and Transitional Instability.

Guilt   When the flashbacks occurred, I would often replay in vivid detail, the events surrounding my father's frightening "Death bed Scene." When reliving my solemn promise and sacred oath, I wrestled with the same haunting, *What If* questions. What If I had done something differently? What if I had called one of my brothers for help, would the outcome have been different? Would he still be alive today?

Pondering the imponderables left me with a sense of interminable Guilt which would inevitably take me to a Dark Place - a pervasive undulating current of darkness producing an unexplainable and unshakable moodiness that I was never able to explain or share with anyone. I feel this perpetual sense of Guilt had a profound influence on my future life choices.

Vulnerability   Even at the age of 13,   having witnessed my father's compromised mentation, I was painfully aware of his potential Vulnerability. The once self-reliant man who loved the challenge of extricating himself from compromising situations was now, ironically challenged by being Compromised. The once fragile man was, once again Fragile, and it was my *mission* to protect him from the ignominy of this frailty. This ingrained fear triggered recurrent dreams or nightmares that would plague me well into my mid-thirties. The basic theme was always the same. I would accidentally come upon my father and recognizing his frailty, I would try to insulate and protect him from former acquaintances or combatants who might take unfair advantage of him.

In fact, during our Easter vacation on Hutchinson Island, when I glanced at the front page of the Stuart News, I noticed the side profile of a man with a striking resemblance to my father and was shocked to see his name, Caesar Cirigliano. As absurd as it sounds, my first impression was, "You're alive! where the hell have you been?" He was my father's first cousin, who was being recognized as a celebrated professional artist with a studio in downtown Stuart. I immediately contacted my cousin and he invited us for a brief visit to his home. While talking with him, I couldn't help, but stare at the striking resemblance. He had the highest regard for my father and his wife recalled babysitting several of my siblings. He took the time to educate me regarding our family tree, and of my grandparent's place of origin in the province of Basilicata, Italy.

The issue of vulnerability, however, related to, not only my father but also to me. With my father's death, our world suddenly changed dramatically. I became aware of an unfamiliar sense of personal vulnerability or insecurity. I was no longer the son of the famous and respected Barrister. No longer protected under the umbrella of his professional stature or charismatic personality. No longer his *Best Friend* and trusted Sidekick.

My world of relative comfort, security, safety, and parity suddenly vanished. I became increasingly sensitive to class and societal distinctions

266

that were commonly associated with wealth and pedigree. Consequently, lacking the wherewithal, I became increasingly uncomfortable when confronted with unfamiliar Social Circles.

It didn't take much to unsettle my fragile state of mind. When confronted with compromising or embarrassing situations, my natural inclination was to quietly withdraw to the safety of my private Dark Room. Unfortunately, this presumed *antisocial* response would play havoc with any future romantic relationship with MM. During these prolonged periods of withdrawal, she would repeatedly ask the same legitimate question, "What's wrong, why are you so quiet?" And I could only reply, "Nothing!" Because, at the time, I didn't know Why, and I couldn't very well explain what I didn't know. Regrettably, however, I failed to add, "Nothing that you've done!"

Transitions During my *abbreviated* period of adolescence, I became aware of three life-changing Transitions. Purely out of necessity, the first was the rapid transition from my father's dream of a family compound to a business. The second was the rapid transition from a happy family environment to one of manual labor, resentment, inner turmoil, and eventual discord. The third was a very rapid transition from early adolescence to responsible adulthood.

Incidentally, regarding the rapid transition to adulthood, in essence, I skipped the normal experience of adolescence. Consequently, having no real frame of reference, I found that I had little or no patience or tolerance with adolescent behavior, which greatly influenced how I dealt with our adolescent children. Needless to say, they would readily agree that I was unduly strict and inflexible. But kiddos, it was the only thing I knew! And, considering the circumstances, I did the best that I could!

Choosing Medicine With regard to my specific interest in medicine. The first and foremost impetus was undoubtedly due to the sequence of events surrounding my father's death, and the associated guilt complex. And it wasn't purely by coincidence that I ultimately developed a love for cardiology. The second person to influence my decision was Dr. Weiser. To me, he was the epitome of a dedicated and caring physician that I would someday hope to be. Ironically, the third influence was the movie, "Not as a Stranger" starring Robert Mitchum, Olivia De Havilland, and Frank Sinatra

Varsity Finale   The varsity swimming season was fast approaching and considering that Nick was Xavier's coach, we again engaged in our familiar banter and faulty exchange of information. Since Caesar was no longer lifeguarding at New Utrecht High School, and I was still under father McGourty's edict, I was left to rely solely on my coaches at the Prep.

As I mentioned, the only occasional spectators at our Tub pool were when members of the Football or basketball teams were taking showers after their practice sessions. I knew that MM's cousins, Dick, and Bill Hegarty both played basketball under the legendary coach, Herb Hess. So, after my workout, I would occasionally walk over and briefly watch their practice session or possibly a game. As a result, I came to know both of them quite well. Bill was one of the best players on the team, his nemesis being his teammate, Buddy Nittle. During his senior year, Bill ran for class president, and I was privileged to be one of his loyal campaign supporters.

NYAC Meet   There was an invitational meet at the NYAC, and John Lupi, Gene Volini, Don Gill, and I were invited to represent St. John's prep. I was slated to swim the 100 yd Butterfly, the 200 yd IM, and both relays. Fortunately, our young assistant coach accompanied us, which was a welcome relief. However, at the last minute, he notified us that Don Gill was unable to make the event. This was a real crusher because it effectively eliminated us from both relays!

Being that the meet hadn't yet started, I remember pleading with the assistant coach to submit his name as a substitute for Gill. Initially, he said, it would look ridiculous, a balding 27-year-old on a High School relay. I felt at least he was considering it, but then he said he was out of shape and didn't have a bathing suit. I said, "Don't worry about the suit, and I've seen you swim in our pool. It's only 50 yds and If need be, just tell them you got left-back a couple of times!".

Recalling the Fordham vs Colgate meet, the plan was to cover his head with a towel and put him in as the anchor. Then, we'd do our best to get a lead, and whether we win, lose, or get disqualified, it would be a blast! I could tell that I had him hooked, and he was actually considering it! However, right before the event, it was a huge let-down when he said, "I can't risk the potential embarrassment to our school!"

Out of the blue, in walks, Joanne Gallagher, and with my back to her, she covers my eyes with her hands. I know, I'm supposed to guess who, but I don't have a clue! I don't recall why she was there, but knowing that she was a swimmer, I jokingly asked if she wanted to swim the anchor? Needless to say, we were forced to scratch both relays.

Thanksgiving Game Thanksgiving was fast approaching, and the entire student body was preparing for the long-awaited annual Football rivalry between St. John's prep and Brooklyn prep. We routinely held the traditional pregame rally in the basketball auditorium, and regardless of the team's seasonal performance, if we lost every game, beat Brooklyn prep, our season was considered a success! One morning, while riding on the subway, I shared the excitement of the event with Vicki and she immediately said, "I would love to see a live football game!" Then I thought "What was a guy to do?" So, at a loss for words, I simply said, "Sure, why not".

At Anita's suggestion, I purchased the traditional Thanksgiving game *corsage.* With the pretty corsage in hand, when I rang Vickie's doorbell, her father was duly impressed, and I was doubly impressed that she was actually waiting for me downstairs. So, off we went, riding the subway to the game. While walking along the front of the bleachers, I suddenly heard my friend, Eddie D'Onofrio yelling for me to join him and his girlfriend, Angel *lips* Salafrio. Talk about embarrassing moments! Although I first met Angela at MM's birthday party, Eddie, and I both attended St. Anselm's and St. John's Prep together. What I didn't know, however, was that MM was also at the game, sitting in the Brooklyn prep bleachers. I don't know with whom, but it probably wouldn't have made any difference since, following Mike's surprise visit to Flatbush, there was a natural lull in our communication.

Even during good times, however, due to the fact that most weekends were spent either studying or working at the Lodge, our weekly communication was limited to a Thursday evening phone call in order to plan for our big Friday night date. Being that money and privacy was always scarce, our dates most often consisted of either going to a movie at the Loew's King's Theatre or Jan's ice cream parlor.

The Kings Theatre   The Kings Theatre was an extremely ornate structure with a tiered ground floor seating area, and a grand center staircase leading to three semicircular tiers resembling a Viennese opera house, with handsome balconies overlooking the ground floor stage. It is presently considered a historic landmark, a fitting testimony to the grandeur of yesteryears. We would, of course, find the most reclusive upper balcony location and *watch* the movie - don't ask me what we saw? Afterward, I would take the bus back to Bay Ridge which required a midway transfer, allowing me to inhale a half-priced slice of pizza while waiting for the transfer bus.

After swimming practice, I would take the train from the Prep to the Cortelyou Rd station in Flatbush and walk to MM's house. Upon arrival, which was fashionably late, despite my bloodshot eyes and wearing my school jacket, without fail, her father would immediately ask, "Where's your tie?" When I said, "But we're only going to the movies!" he barked, "I don't care!" In due time, however, anticipating this, I would purposely stuff my tie in my jacket pocket.

Later on in our *courtship,* if I was very late, I would stop at a local florist close to the train station. It was owned by a Greek named Plato, who was a loyal patron at the Lodge. Being that it was late and knowing my financial situation, he would put together a bouquet of leftover flowers which I would, more often give to MM's mother as a peace offering.

Eighth Encounter SJP vs Xavier In mid-January, we were scheduled for a dual meet against Xavier to be held at Trinity Prep's pool on W 91st St. Manhattan. I was looking forward to another opportunity to kick Mike's ass, this time in a pool. Unlike the Prep's pool, however, this pool had four rows of elevated bleachers. While both teams were on deck warming-up, Mike and I greeted each other cordially by shaking hands. Although I detested it, I felt it was the right thing to do. As I mentioned previously, other than the showering spectators, no one ever attended our swimming meets at the Prep. In fact, as a rule, hardly anyone attended school swimming meets even with bleachers. So, it wasn't unusual to see an entire observation area without any spectators.

The meet was just about to begin when, in walks MM with one of her girlfriends, possibly Joanne! My first reaction was once again, "You can't make this shit up!" My second reaction was, "Hmmm...I wonder who she's here to see?" Given that, in the past, she' never expressed any interest in attending any of my swimming meets, and I hadn't told her about this meet, "It's probably not me!" I was so distracted that I don't even remember my individual events, let alone the outcome of the meet. Perhaps, due to Mary's *selective amnesia*, how or why this surprise appearance came about, I'll never know!

CH - 29
VARSITY CHAMPIONSHIPS

The Varsity Swimming Championships were fast approaching. They were to be held in early March at the Queens campus of St. John's University. I was desperate for additional coaching, and I eventually resorted to Harry Benvenuto, who was coaching at the downtown YMCA. When I met with him, his first question was, "Why are you coming to me when you have your brothers?" - a very legitimate question. I explained that my brothers were committed elsewhere and that, as a young spectator at many NYAC meets, I respected him as a formidable coach. Thankfully, he agreed to help train me, four days a week, for the four weeks before the finals.

I was scheduled to swim the 200 free and 200 IM, as well as both the Free and Medley relays. I only remember one event, however, the 200-yard freestyle. I was slated to swim in the lane next to Tommy Zinkand. At the time, Tommy was swimming for St Francis Prep under their coach, Tom Booras. And whereas I had four weeks to prepare, Tommy was well-tuned for the race.

Being that Nick was Xavier's coach, he was a designated timer for the meet. Just before the race, Nick whispered, "Just stay at his waist and then, take him on the last lap!" I thought, "That's it! That's the long-awaited Pearl - easier said than done!" I should have realized that that was a strategy that worked for the well-conditioned, *Nick the Fish*!

Regardless, putting aside my own inclination to swim *my own race*, I heeded Nick's pearl. I stayed with Tommy for the first six laps, but shortly after the 6th turn, I felt like a guerrilla jumped on my back! On the last turn, unlike my slow agonizing flip, Tommy's was crisp and clean, allowing him to pull away from me. The home stretch was absolute torture. My arms ached like hell and I was barely able to lift the lead weights over the top of the water. My arm speed steadily slowed, and my kick was gone. Unlike in Lake Placid, I wasn't able to close the gap, and Tommy finished a half-body length before me.

When I finished totally exhausted and demoralized, Nick said, "You had him beat, why didn't you stay with him?" If I could have raised my arm, I would have punched him. But instead, my only gasping response was, "You should know, it's all about conditioning!" Unfortunately, I didn't listen to my inner voice. Although the outcome might have been the same, by pacing Tommy, I improved his performance at my expense, and rather than limping into the finish, I would have at least closed stronger!

The swimming season was finally over, and I was seriously considering a Pre-Med curriculum in College. Hoping for a swimming scholarship, When I initially met with Dick Krempecki, St John's University's swimming coach, the first question he asked was," Are you related to Nick Cirigliano?" I guess the Cirigliano name still held some magic- at least in the swimming world.

I was very fortunate to be offered a half swimming scholarship to both St. John's University and Manhattan College. However, Manhattan's scholarship offer was conditional. Rather than Pre Med, I would be required to register as a Phys Ed major - which in hindsight, was very prudent. After careful consideration, I ultimately decided to decline both scholarship offers and registered for the Pre-Med program at St John's University's Brooklyn campus, on Schermerhorn St.

SJP Boat Ride   By early spring things must have improved between MM and me because I invited her to go on the annual St. John's Boat Ride to Rye Beach NY and we decided to make it a foursome with Eddie and Angela. It was a beautiful warm sunny Saturday morning - perfect weather for an exciting Boat Ride! When Eddie and I showed up at the Trum's house. I watched in amazement, as MM made PB&J sandwiches by applying peanut butter on one slice of bread and jelly on the other slice and then quickly, squished the two slices together, hoping that the jelly stayed in between. Meanwhile, Angela had both meatball and eggplant sandwiches and combined, the girls provided enough food for six people, neatly packed into two wicker picnic baskets.

At one point, I remember MM's father turning to Eddie and me asking in his gruff voice, "What did you guys bring?" I quickly turned and looked at Eddie incredulously saying, "Didn't you bring anything?" Then off we went to catch the ferry that was destined to take us on a long-awaited, memorable trip to the famous, Rye Beach amusement Park.

There was a dance floor with a piano and a combo of members from the school's band who preferred mostly jazz music. We had a great time eating and dancing up until the ferry whistle blew, indicating that we were soon approaching the dock for disembarking. Anticipating that our day on shore was about to begin, we gathered our stuff and went on deck to watch with excitement, *the docking*.

As we stood there patiently watching and waiting, however, we noticed that the boat didn't seem to be moving any closer to the dock. After a seemingly interminable wait, we were eventually told that somehow the Ferry became lodged on a sandbar, and that we would have to wait for the rising tide to eventually free the boat! Picture what it was like to be leaning over the side rails watching all the other students, having a great time at the legendary amusement park.

The band stopped playing because the boat started to list to one side making it almost impossible to dance. There was, however, one notable exception, Bob Bryant, our celebrated football cheerleader who was also a great dancer. So, while we did the next best thing, eating more food, Bob entertained everyone dancing up a storm.

At some point, everyone's patience was wearing very thin, and there was the talk of a mutiny of sorts. Some of the football players were threatening to throw the piano overboard. Fortunately, our chemistry teacher, Mr.La

Bassi, caught wind of this and got on the Ferry's loudspeaker warning the students not to jeopardize graduation by doing something so stupid. Eventually, cooler heads prevailed, and the mutiny was averted. By late afternoon it was clear that we would not be experiencing the wonders of Rye Beach. Needless to say, six hours later, when the tide came in and eventually lifted the Ferry off the sandbar, everyone was bummed out, and despite talk of another trip, it never happened.

St Agnes Seminary   While attending High School at St. Agnes Seminary, MM was an active member of the Glee Club for all four years, and whose members also provided the cast for musical plays performed at the Brooklyn Academy of music. I think I attended two performances, the most memorable being, "*The King and I*." In particular the song, "*I Have Dreamed*" always resonated with me! At the conclusion of the play, I remember while waiting for MM in a stairwell, all of a sudden from behind, a pair of hands covered my eyes. Being the second time, it wasn't terribly difficult to figure out that it was, Joanne. After all, how many people did she think approached me the same way? I thoroughly enjoyed her spontaneity and light-hearted sense of humor. And from our first meeting, I felt a kindred spirit and eventually considered her a very close friend.

At some point, I arranged a blind date for her with Frank Giampietro, a St John's quarterback, and I was looking forward to another foursome. Frank was relatively small in frame and although extremely versatile and effective on the field, he apparently lacked a sense of humor commensurate with Joanne's. Consequently, of the foursome, only three of us had a good time, and afterward, Frank didn't talk to me for a very long time.

SJP Prom (June 1962)   It was June and at last, Prom time! Assuming that we were now a couple, I asked Mary to my prom and thankfully, she accepted - the only one in the wings being, Vicki. I rented the traditional white tuxedo jacket, black pants, and matching plaid bowtie and cummerbund. Since we replaced my father's white Turnpike Cruiser with a boring, but economical brown station wagon, Nick either volunteered or was told to drive me to Mary's house in the classy wagon.

When we arrived, I was amazed at how pretty Mary looked in a light blue dress with small violet flowers and thin spaghetti straps! Unaware of the spaghetti straps, fortunately, I took Anita's advice and bought a wrist corsage! Her rationale being that, while dancing, the last thing you want is a corsage to come between the two of you -So true!

When I looked at our photos, I was struck by how much more mature she appeared compared to her date, who looked like a kid who got lucky! Nick drove us to the reception hall which was held at a very large and fancy catering facility in Queens. I remember having a great time dancing and imagining all evening, what would happen if one of those thin spaghetti straps suddenly broke! Then I was terribly disappointed when one finally broke, and nothing happened!

Towards the end of the evening, I remember realizing that, because the Prep drew its student body from such a wide radius, I would probably never see most of my classmates again. With that in mind. I went around to my closest friends, inviting them back to my house for a casual breakfast in Bay Ridge - what was I thinking?

Because it was the thing to do, I have a faint recollection of six or eight of us taking cabs into the city to hit a nightclub that had live entertainment. Afterward, Mary and I took a romantic ferry ride from the 69th St. pier to Staten Island, which cost five cents each way. However, because she was in such a beautiful dress, rather than jumping over the railing, I sprang for the additional five cents - a real Daddy Warbucks!

I splurged again by taking a taxi from 69th St. to 8311. Upon our arrival, however, I was shocked to see a long row of cars lined up along colonial Road. It dawned on me that, unbeknownst to me, apparently word got out that Cirigliano was hosting breakfast at his house! Also, what I also failed to do was, notify my mother that we were having "guests for breakfast!". When I walked into the house, I found 20 of my classmates quietly sitting on the floor in the front Sunroom.

In the meantime, my mother, who was not a happy camper, sent Nick out to buy sufficient eggs, bacon, juice, and rolls for "our guests". As it turned out, everyone was extremely polite and appreciative of the gesture and left shortly after they ate breakfast. I think Nick must have driven Mary back to her house.

Graduation Graduation was to be held in the auditorium of the adjacent Teachers College and just about everyone decided that they would seize a second opportunity to wear their white tuxedo jackets. Naturally, with all the eating and dancing, my white jacket was somewhat soiled. The following morning I was bewildered to find my mother on her hands and knees scrubbing the kitchen floor - no doubt, still smarting from the inconsiderate breakfast debacle. When I tentatively asked her if I could bring my jacket to the dry cleaners, while crying she said, "Where do you think I'm going to get the money to pay for that?"

I felt terribly embarrassed for her, that she should even be on her hands and knees, and ashamed to be asking for something so trivial. Shortly after, my uncle Tony and Aunt Mae paid a surprise visit and sensing some discord asked why my mother was so upset. I explained the situation and, the ever generous, uncle, gave me a dollar and told me to spend it wisely! I cleaned the white jacket, as best as I could and proudly wore it to my graduation.

Admittedly, the rest of the morning is a total blur, but in order to be there for a rehearsal, I took the train to school without even knowing if Nick intended to drive my mother to the ceremony. I don't remember seeing or being congratulated by anyone, and there was certainly no ceremony - after all, everybody graduates from High School!

Incidentally, while discussing this particular event with Mary, she reminded me that I had two tickets, one for my mother and the other for her, But on graduation morning, I called her and said. "It wouldn't be such a good idea for her to come," but failed to disclose why - up until this date.

CH - 30
SUMMER OF '62

It was a fairly uneventful summer season. Unfortunately, Mary failed Geometry and had to go to summer school in Newburg(Deja vu!) Perhaps that's another reason why I was attracted to her. This, however, markedly limited our available time together, especially in the evenings. Knowing of my tormented heart, at just the right moment, Al Florentino would often play a familiar tune on the piano, "If you were the only girl in the world" and looking at me, he would just smile. Ironically, it was also one of my father's favorite tunes. Also, being a romantic at heart, Al would often ask me about my *summer romance,* and when I would lament, he would tease me saying, "Don't worry, it'll all blow over, it's only a summer romance!" - not exactly what I wanted to hear.

At some point, Rocco thought of offering horseback riding for the Hotel guests and asked Mr. Trum or Kip if someone would bring two horses up to the Lodge. He graciously consented, and although Kip initially brought the horses up, I believe it was mostly Mary's younger brother, Dennis, who was available to provide riding lessons. Apparently, due to a lack of interest on the part of the guests, this venture was short-lived.

Donna Unfortunately, Donna's parents separated in April, and instead of staying at the Lodge, Marion and the three girls rented a small bungalow in nearby Lake View Estates. Although she spent some time at the Lodge, Donna more often sought the company of her cousins, Denise, and Ronnie Costarella and, Doug and Nancy Pascarella, all of whom lived at the bottom of Lake View Estates. At some point, I remember stopping to see Marion at her bungalow, and as usual, she would ask," So, how's it going?"- which was her way of asking about my tumultuous love life. When I openly shared some recent setbacks, she summed it up saying, "Pete, she has to decide who she wants, and you have to decide how much you're willing to take!"

Mary's 16th Birthday   The Tums decided to celebrate Mary's 16th birthday by having a private family dinner at the Lodge. We arranged a lovely table setting in the lower screened Patio Room, which provided ample privacy. There were a total of 12 people, including her Grandparents. They were all well dressed for the occasion, and although I was invited to join them and was grateful for their patronage, I was very self-conscious of being in mixed company and of asking someone from our staff to serve me! Having little or no experience with waiting on tables, I felt the next best thing would be to tend the bar and serve their drinks.

About a week before her birthday, I remember going to Charlie Lescher, owner of the Monroe Jewelry store, and proudly telling him that I wanted to buy a *special* piece of jewelry for my girlfriend's 16th birthday. I mentioned who it was for and being that he knew the Trum family quite well, he asked, "How much do you want to spend?" Having pooled my meager tips from the Bar and the chaise lounge concession, when I told him how much I saved, he just sighed, "Hmm.." and I could tell this was going to be a challenge!

Then without rushing me, he patiently looked with me at a myriad of items for at least 20 minutes, until I finally said, "I think this is a good choice!" He readily agreed, but when I turned it over to look at the price, he noticed my shocked expression. After a long pause, he said, "Do you really like it?" When I said, "of course, but" without another word, he began wrapping the beautiful silver heart with a tiny emerald gem in the center - her favorite stone.

Charlie was either extremely generous or just tired of losing other customers by my incessant scrutiny! Even then I demonstrated OCD. In any case, I was ecstatic! Feeling that by now, we were surely a couple, I couldn't wait to give her the gift. When I proudly presented it to her, however, I sensed mixed reviews and raised eyebrows from several family members. Apparently, fearful that a gift of jewelry often signifies a more serious relationship. And especially coming from me at such a young age, it was perceived as both, presumptuous and frightening - But what did I know!

Joanne   In late August, Mary invited Joanne up to her house for several days. But given that most evenings Mary was busy studying for her Geometry final exam, Joanne would occasionally walk up to the Lodge just to hang out. I enjoyed her company, conversation, and sense of humor, but most of all, I considered her a very good friend. Then, on the evening before she was to leave, something very strange happened. We were both sitting on the front steps of the Hotel and all of a sudden, for no apparent reason, she started crying. I didn't have a clue why and said lamely, "Sorry, but I don't have a handkerchief" to which she replied, "Well you should!" and we both started laughing at the absurdity.

The next morning, while driving her to the Short Line bus stop in town, I noticed a distinct difference in her demeanor which was very perplexing. I thought, "What could I have possibly done or what had changed overnight?" Then, with her head on my lap, in my usual suave fashion, I attempted to remove a visibly annoying blackhead on her upper lip. Just as the bus arrived, she asked me to give her "a Goodbye Kiss" - which was very telling.

Given that, by now, her upper lip was painfully swollen, I doubt that I kissed her on the lips! To this day, I don't understand the reason for the sudden change and didn't hear from her for quite a while, which greatly saddened me. I felt that I had suddenly lost one of my closest friends and didn't know why!

Joe Virga   Joe Virga was a frequent guest at the Lodge. He liked hunting and frequently carried his shotgun in the trunk of his car, prompting us to affectionately refer to him as, "Shotgun Joe" He was always very amiable and eventually grew very fond of our waitress, Helen, which meant he became a regular weekender. Their romance progressed rapidly and by summer's end, he proposed to Helen and she readily accepted. We were all excited for both of them, and being that they met at the Hotel, they both felt it was only fitting to plan their wedding at Ciri's Lodge. She loved the rustic ambiance of the large Living Room, and having witnessed Virginia and Caesar's weddings, she likewise envisioned the traditional pictures on the gracious Grand Staircase! So, we were all delighted when they planned their wedding for the following June.

CH - 31
SJU FRESHMAN YEAR

Thank God, Mary passed her Geometry final and she was looking forward to her Junior year at St Agnes Seminary, and I was looking forward to beginning my Freshman year as a Pre-Med student at St John's University. I clearly remember visiting the bursar's office for registration. At the time, the Federal government was offering a 3% matching loan program for full-time students.

Considering that each credit was $35, I signed up for 18 credits, which was the maximum per semester. Since none of us ever derived any direct income from working at the Lodge, I couldn't count on any in the future. However, thanks to Caesar, I secured an evening lifeguard job at New Utrecht High school. Initially, I figured, I should be able to pay for at least half of my first semester's tuition - that was until I saw the "net amount" of my first paycheck!

During the first two years, The Pre-Med and Pharmacy students took essentially the same basic science courses, and then the Pre-Med students switched to the Jamaica campus for the last two years. The Brooklyn campus was also home for the Law School students, and ironically, the Dean of the law school, Dean Volansky, eventually became my student advisor which proved to be very beneficial.

Commuting to the campus by subway was convenient and inexpensive. I happily adjusted to the co-ed environment. However, in order to be readily identified as Freshmen, for the purpose of Fraternity recruitment, during the entire first week, we were supposed to wear red and white beanie caps - which lasted about 4 hrs. for me!

Biosciences I thoroughly enjoyed my science courses, especially Biology, Physiology, and Comparative Anatomy taught by Albert Liberti Ph.D. In particular, I was looking forward to the dissection labs and I remember purchasing my first dissection kit in preparation for the frogs and ultimately, the "big" Cats.

Dr. Liberti was a very animated lecturer, most often delivering his lectures in the front of the class, from an elevated platform. Apparently, he played varsity basketball in college, and during his lectures, for added emphasis, he had a peculiar habit of leaning forward, bending his knees and pigeon toeing his size twelve shoes, as if he was about to take a foul shot.

Also, for some reason, he would occasionally squeeze his big shoes behind two heat pipes, less than 6" from the wall. One day, after successfully wedging his big shoes behind the pipes, when he went to move forward, he couldn't untangle the size twelves in time and fell on the elevated platform! However, Just when I thought I was finished with languages, I learned that I had to take two years of a foreign language and I chose what I thought would be the easiest,

Spanish My Spanish teacher was Mrs. Doyaga, a very attractive and remarkably well-preserved woman, who repeatedly insisted that Castilian Spanish was the only proper form of Spanish. Many years earlier, when Rocco returned from Ohio State during his sophomore year, in order to recuperate from Mycoplasma pneumonia, he often accompanied Anita to St. John's University to presumably audit some classes. Interestingly, however, he only chose those classes that Anita's girlfriends were in! In any event, in order to be close to one particular girl, he ironically chose a Spanish class taught by Mrs. Doyaga!

He would often tell the story of when Mrs. Doyaga asked each student to pronounce a particular sport in the Castilian dialect. Being that he often hid in the back of the classroom, by the time it was his turn, most of the sports were already taken. Consequently, the only thing he could think of was, "la pingo la pongo".

Likewise, since I also sat in the back of the classroom, and being that her routine was exactly the same, I too eventually faced the same dilemma and responded accordingly. Upon hearing this unique response, Mrs. Doyaga just paused and looked towards the ceiling, as if recalling a distant, Deja vu moment. After class, still totally perplexed, she asked me where I came up with my answer, and after refreshing her memory, she just started laughing.

Chemistry   Dr. Curao taught Inorganic Chemistry. I found the Quantitative Analysis labs to be particularly difficult due to the required math calculations. However, the second semester of Qualitative Analysis was much easier. I found the majority of non-science subjects relatively easy, especially Theology, Cosmology, and Philosophy which I thoroughly enjoyed. I found English Literature to be somewhat challenging, mostly due to the professor's thirst for endless Term Papers! Although these courses required a considerable amount of studying, I felt driven towards my ultimate goal and readily accepted the challenge.

Major Renovations   This was another year of dramatic changes. Rocco had plans for major renovations at the Lodge, transforming it to a year-round business, with intentions of living there full time. Meanwhile, between studying, lifeguarding at New Utrecht, and helping at the Lodge on weekends, I was spinning a lot of plates in the air.

As a Junior, Mary's extracurricular time was mostly spent with the Glee Club, practicing for the school play, and modeling A-line dresses in various department stores - ironically, Vickie modeled the same dress styles. Obviously, these commitments put a damper on our precarious courtship. I tried to remain relevant by continuing our Thursday night telephone calls. But even they were periodically interrupted by her Father, silently picking up the receiver and listening to our conversation, which prompted Mary to exclaim, "Please hang up the phone!" In short, presumably due to conflicting commitments, our Friday night "dates" were less predictable.

Painfully Aware   Being that Nick and Mary's brother, Kip, were the best of friends, Nick was readily accepted in the Trum household, but he wasn't dating Kip's sister! By contrast, however, ever since her 16th birthday, I never felt welcomed, which didn't help my low self-esteem. But then again, why should I expect others to like me when even I didn't like me!

In time, I became painfully aware that Mary was receiving considerable pressure from her family to date other guys. It was often *suggested* that perhaps she should consider someone more socially acceptable or with a more suitable pedigree from within their Social Circle. They occasionally arranged dates which, in some cases, she willingly accepted. Such was the case with a long-time family friend, Patrick Mullins, with whom she had a serious crush and with George's good friend, Jimmy Sullivan.

In sharp contrast, however, the members of my family, not only liked but readily embraced Mary, never attempting to undermine our relationship by suggesting or encouraging that I date someone else. These revelations were particularly hurtful and continued to play havoc with our tenuous relationship for the next couple of years.

To be fair, however, while writing this memoir and discussing this particular situation with Mary, although she confirmed this to be true, she offered, "You weren't aware of how often I argued with my family on your behalf!" Despite the apparent disparity between our respective families, however, I came to appreciate that she was somehow different and apart from the rest - choosing to live by a set of values that were often at variance with those of her family. And, notwithstanding personal sacrifice, to her credit, she was somehow able to straddle both worlds.

After reflecting on Marion's advice, It was this unique individuality that was alluring enough to endure the persistent headwinds, making my quiet pursuit even more worthwhile. To complicate matters further, along with my pervasive low self-esteem, I also continued to be plagued by haunting flashbacks. And my sudden periods of withdrawal were interpreted as unjustified moodiness or brooding, for which had no reasonable explanation.

Kenny Powers   One morning, while riding the subway to school, I met Kenny Powers, my former Prep school mate. After some small talk, Kenny began asking me personal questions about Mary's family but seeming to already know a great deal. I thought this was very strange, as though he had already done his homework and wanted confirmation. I found it even more strange when he asked specific questions about the status of our dating relationship. I thought, "Hmm, what did he possibly know that I didn't?"

Then, just before we arrived at my station, he finally showed his hand by bluntly asking, "Would you mind if I asked her out on a date?" I was initially taken aback, and my second reaction was, "What a pair of balls!" However, being aware of her family's sentiment and of Marion's advice, I simply replied, "That's for her to decide!" and thankfully, we parted company.

Incidentally, in keeping with my father's backhanded advice to Caesar, I didn't even want to know if he ever asked her out. Therefore, I never told Mary of my good friend's interest until this date.

I recall these painful memories only to emphasize that they awakened in me the profound realization that my feelings for her were obviously much earlier and much stronger than I was ever willing to admit. In retrospect, I would readily acknowledge that my first real attraction was when I laid eyes on a lovely 15-year-old girl in a blue bathing suit, and to the extent that I even knew what love was, I loved her since she was sweet 16. In fact, I would often sing Perry Como's rendition of, *When you Were Sweet Sixteen* "*When first I saw the lovelight in your eyes, I dreamed the world held not but joy for me, come to me or my dream of love is or, I love you as I loved you when you were sweet sixteen.*" Another song that resonated was Sinatra's rendition of "*Secret Love*"

Torch Songs   Even at a relatively young age, I appreciated the poetic beauty of the lyrics and stylish phrasing of the timeless Love Ballads, especially when rendered by the likes of, Como, Sinatra, Bennett, and

Mathis. I also identified with *Torch Songs* such as Della Reese's, rendition of Puccini's, *Don't You Know....* "I have fallen in love with you. for the rest of my whole life through" and, Dinah Washington's, rendition of, *At Last...* "My love has come along; my lonely days are over, and life is like a song!"

Flatbush Girls   It wasn't unusual for Flatbush girls to come to Bay Ridge and hang out at either Hinche's or Poll's ice cream parlors. In fact, one evening while leaving the 86th St. train station, on my way to a St Michael's dance, I noticed Mary and several of her girlfriends arriving at the same time, but in the opposite direction! Then, like "two ships passing in the night" our eyes briefly met and as we tentatively waved to each other, I thought, "What is she doing in my neighborhood?, I wish she had told me she was coming!".

Joanne   I don't recall why or how, but in the Fall, Joanne paid me a surprise visit in Bay Ridge. I remember that my sister, Maria, was visiting with her two children, John and Kathy and I was across the street in the Park, pushing them on a swing set. All of a sudden, I felt two hands covering my eyes! By now, I was familiar with Joanne's calling card. Unfortunately, however, she didn't pull me back quickly enough and the oncoming swing hit me in the bridge of my big nose!

Aside from the painful bloody nose, I was surprised and truly happy to see her. We eventually took a long walk down by the Narrows and along Shore Rd. I remember being greatly relieved that she seemed more like her old self, and I was conscious of a light airy feeling as we walked and talked. Strangely, it reminded me of a rainy evening when, after leaving Mary's house, we walked up Stratford road imitating Gene Kelly while singing, "Singing in the Rain!"

We hadn't seen each other since our memorable *Casablanca farewell* at the Monroe bus station. I wanted to ask her about the strange crying jag on the Lodge's porch, but I purposely chose to keep the conversation lite and upbeat. Although the rest of the afternoon was somewhat hazy, I thought I sensed a mutual awareness of unique chemistry that seemed more than a kindred spirit. Perhaps it was infatuation or simply my imagination, but for a change, I felt an unfamiliar sensation of being pursued which I enjoyed - uh oh!

In order for her to catch a cab back home, we walked all the way up to Fourth Avenue. I remember while crossing the broad Avenue, she said, "You can at least be a gentleman and hold my hand across this dangerous intersection!" And we both started laughing at the absurdity. As we parted company, I sensed that we were both aware of a reality best left unsaid, choosing to pretend that it never existed.

I honestly didn't know how to handle this delicate situation. Despite all the recent setbacks and revelations, Mary and I were still a couple. And being that Joanne was one of Mary's best friends, the notion of betrayal was abhorrent. I briefly mused, "Perhaps she was aware of the difficulties I was facing with Mary's family and surmised that our courtship was very tenuous." However, none of this was ever mentioned or discussed, and aside from a few innocent letters, I didn't see or hear from Joanne for over a year. I was saddened by her absence, but even more so by the lack of an explanation.

In retrospect, ours was admittedly, a very confusing relationship -one which I never quite understood and never discussed. Ironically, however, despite this confusion, it seemed pleasantly uncomplicated and I welcomed her refreshing carefree presence. This, of course, begged the question, "Was it more than a friendship?" But questions still lingered. Why she suddenly changed on two separate occasions remained a mystery. More importantly, after each occasion, I felt that somehow, I lost a dear friend who allowed me a glimpse of unencumbered frivolity and a brief respite from personal humiliation.

My purpose in writing this memoir was twofold: To highlight the truly wonderful memories of my life while hopefully, bringing closure to unpleasant ones. With this in mind, I recently confided in Mary, explaining how hurtful it was to suddenly lose Joanne's friendship without knowing why! After thinking about it, she said, "I think you should seize an opportunity to privately ask her." Heeding her advice, when I tried to broach the subject, Joanne, simply rebuffed me as though it never happened, which was even more disturbing. Although I still consider her a dear friend, the splendor of our unique friendship seems to have vanished.

Pam   When things were particularly troublesome between Mary and me, her childhood friend, Pam, would occasionally come out to Bay Ridge in order to just talk things through. Although her first allegiance was to Mary, I always found her to try and remain objectively neutral. Weather permitting, during the daytime we would usually take long walks down to Shore Road or, in the evening, sit in Poll's ice cream parlor for hours. I always valued our seemingly endless conversations which I still treasure to this day. She would usually vacillate between, a mostly unbiased diplomatic perspective, to one of brutal frankness, often describing my unpredictable moodiness as intolerable - and that was her gentle delivery! However, I still enjoy her company and, in particular, our animated discussions.

CH - 32
BOLD RENOVATIONS

Rocco's overall plan was to winterize the Lodge by enclosing the front porch and installing jalousie windows in the Dining Room and installing baseboard heat throughout most of the ground floor. The lower screened Patio Room would also be enclosed with jalousie windows and warmed by radiant floor heat. The long rectangular bar would be moved from the upper Bar Room to the back wall of the former, Patio Room.

Then, In order to maximize the space in the Living Room, the original Hotel reception desk would be moved to the right half of the enclosed front porch. Lastly, the beautiful Grand Staircase would be demolished in favor of a simple straight staircase leading from the front reception counter to the front second-floor hallway. This, however, would require the removal of a rather large, second story section of the front of the Hotel. Needless to say, this gutsy renovation agenda would require a lot of money that we didn't have, which would result in a substantial amount of additional debt.

The Family Meeting   As per my father's instructions, a family meeting was called to listen to Rocco's grand vision and citing "Desperate times call for desperate measures!". Virginia was represented by her husband, Lou Harring, and Maria was represented by her husband, Jack Weiser. I don't remember if Anita was present for the meeting, but Bob Hartman was also present. Although not in total agreement with Rocco's gutsy plan, mostly out of a sense of loyalty, Bob and I supported his overall vision. But the shit really hit the fan when it was discovered that Rocco had already made an independent decision to pre-emptively blow a hole in the front of the Hotel, leaving a gaping hole!

This triggered the eruption of a very heated exchange, especially from Lou and Jack citing unauthorized structural renovations and rampant fiscal irresponsibility which was difficult to ignore or defend. Unfortunately, this set the tenor for future discord which was not at all in keeping with my father's original intention or dream. What they didn't know, however, was that, in addition to the gaping hole, he had already moved the reception desk and replaced the Grand Staircase.

Giants Games   Now that Rocco was personally committed to year-round occupancy at the Lodge, when the football season finally arrived, he seized an opportunity to offer televised Giants games. Knowing this, I made a commitment to, at least, spend those weekends at the Lodge. Also, I was now legally able to service the bar, and to cover expenses, we collected $5.00 at the door and sold a hell of a lot of beer! And, having been trained as a "gourmet" short-order cook, we also provided an extensive bar menu, consisting of my specialties, 12" Pizzas, Antipastos, and Italian Heros.

The real challenge, however, was climbing up on the steep roof to *adjust* the old metal antenna in order to hopefully gain reasonable reception. This process required one person on the roof and another on the ground to give precise *adjustments*. Given that Rocco had to *monitor* the TV screen for quality assurance, guess who was chosen to go on the roof!

Marion Visits   Rocco and I visited Donna's house in Oradell NJ twice. Our first visit was on Sunday evening on our way home from the Lodge. In any event, I remember that we were starving, and the only thing Marion had to offer was Waffles. I remember sitting in her kitchen and laughing like hell while inhaling our gourmet Dinner.

The second visit was following her horrific car accident on April 3rd, 1963. After hitting a stone wall, she was ejected from the passenger seat headfirst through the windshield. In addition to pelvic and leg fractures, the most devastating injuries were extensive facial injuries that eventually required multiple plastic surgeries. In addition, she incurred significant trauma to one eye, resulting in permanent visual impairment. This was the ultimate insult to her vanity.

I remember stopping by on our way home from the Lodge. When we arrived, she was in a hospital bed downstairs, and while tentatively peering in from the door frame, she allayed my anxiety saying, "Don't be afraid, come on in!". She had a long slow recovery, and although her features were somewhat marred, she still managed to make herself look beautiful - because she was beautiful!

At some point, Nick decided to become an apprentice in the electrician's union. This required him to change his student status to, part-time, thereby forfeiting the last two years of his swimming scholarship. He mostly attended night classes, and although It took him considerably longer, with perseverance, he eventually achieved a BA degree.

Nick's Wedding   Then, on December 7th, 1962, Nick and Barbara were married by Fr. Neelan in a small church on Long Island followed by a relatively small, but elegant, reception. Despite how close we were, Nick chose Caesar as his best man, and Pat as the maid of honor. Mary was invited to the wedding, and although I drove with Rocco, we had to stop to pick up Mary and then Carol Schalla, who was still getting dressed! Consequently, we arrived at the church disgracefully late. Regrettably, I don't remember any other specifics of the wedding ceremony or the reception.

Candlelight Ball (1962)   On Christmas Eve, Mary and I, along with Angela and Eddie, attended midnight mass in Bay Ridge and then splurged by taking the girls back to Flatbush in a cab. Although I was on a Holiday school break, for some reason, I recall spending more time at the Lodge than with Mary. Then I learned that, during the break, she attended the coveted, Candlelight Charity Ball at the Waldorf Astoria with her early heartthrob, Patrick Mullins! This revelation caused me to wonder, "How many times can you circle the toilet without going down?"

Incidentally, Nick and Babs were invited as guests of the Trums, to the, even more elegant, Emerald Ball, also held in the Grand Ballroom of the Waldorf.

Spanish II   The second semester was a little less difficult than the first, except for Spanish! Fortunately, I sat next to a fairly attractive girl who, by my standards, was fluent in Spanish. During the spot verbal quizzes, unbeknownst to Mrs. Doyaga, she would either bend forward to whisper the answers or quickly write them on a piece of paper. Consequently, I owed her big time and she knew it - at one point suggesting that I take her out for Dinner. She said the slice of pizza was delicious! During the written finals, I wrote voluminously and as illegible as possible, and very grateful for a merciful, C.

I clearly remember that it was during Spanish class that Mrs. Doyaga received a hand-delivered note. After a very long pause, while appearing visibly shaken, she announced that JFK had been assassinated! I still remember the utter shock and turmoil among the students as we gathered in the school cafeteria for the rest of the afternoon.

Dario   In late fall, Rocco hired Dario to prepare an extensive, Italian Menu. I remember first meeting Dario at 8311 when he proudly presented his six-page product, highlighting the personalized Italian descriptors such as, Ziti al Forno Alla Pietro. He was very persuasive, gaining everyone's confidence by claiming that his family was also in the restaurant business and that he had extensive experience as a waiter at some of the finest Manhattan restaurants. Furthermore, he was currently the head bartender at New York's fashionable, La Fonda Del Sol restaurant! He eventually rented a small summer house for his family, located on a side road adjacent to the Lodge which allowed him to work at the Lodge on weekends.

CH - 33
SUMMER OF '63

During the early spring, most of the Hotel renovations were underway. The Grand Staircase and Reception desk were already moved, and most importantly, the gaping hole in the front of the Hotel was almost closed. However, during the winter or early spring, a large section of the pool's patio blocks was vandalized. Many of the cinder blocks were either broken or thrown into the pool. Consequently, in order to remove the blocks, we had to completely drain the pool.

Once I had my senior driver's license, Jack gave me his 1955 green Plymouth sedan, which I affectionately dubbed, *The Green Hornet.* It had a column shift, standard transmission, and proved to be a valuable means of transportation as well as a veritable workhorse. In any event, with Anita's help, I began piling the broken blocks into the trunk and transported them into the woods. At some point, frustrated with how long it was taking, I removed the trunk's hood which made the arduous process much easier.

Then came the monumental job of cleaning the interior of the Gunite pool in order to restore its sparkling white finish. While scrubbing the immense interior with muriatic acid, I remember holding my breath periodically, in order to avoid inhaling the noxious fumes. Then after ordering matching plain and red cinder blocks, we raced against time in order to lay them before the Grand Opening.

Mary's Summer Job I was surprised when Mary decided to take a summer job, working in a local bank in Brooklyn, and staying in Flatbush with her father during the week. Also, at this time, Kip and to a lesser extent,

George, were actively involved with the family business and consequently, they also spent most of the workweek in Brooklyn. So, she would either be driven or take the bus up to Monroe on Friday evenings and then be driven back to Brooklyn by one of her brothers on Sunday evening.

Although I admired her ambitious work initiative, for purely selfish reasons, I was very disappointed by her decision which would further limit our available time together. The stark reality was that, depending on my work schedule, we would only see each other on Friday evening or possibly, on Sunday. However, at least she arranged to take off the last two weeks of the summer - from her birthday until the weekend after Labor Day. Consequently, all summer long, I looked forward to these two precious weeks!

Incidentally, during her two-week vacation, much to the chagrin of her family, she would occasionally surprise me by baking a three-layer chocolate cake and then carry it up to the Lodge in the evening, patiently waiting for me to finish my workout in the pool. And the mere sight of her sitting at the poolside made me swim faster!

With all the changes to the Lodge, we could now seat 250-300 people. And relocating the Main Bar down to the former Patio Room was certainly more conducive for servicing the daytime pool customers. In addition, I also set up a Service Bar in the right front corner of the Dining room which had a convenient side stairway leading to the pool. During the daytime, I tended to the Front Bar, and on weekend evenings, the Service Bar.

The Virga Weeding   When *shotgun* Joe and Helen arrived to finalize plans for their wedding, they were understandably very disappointed to discover that the beautiful Grand Staircase had been removed! Regrettably, I don't recall if their wedding reception was scheduled for late June or September nor any other particulars of their reception.

Donna the Lifeguard   I loved the quiet simplicity of Cottage 10, which I came to regard as my *Sanctuary*! Being a repository of so many memories, both good and bad, I chose to sleep there. Given that Donna's father left home in April, their household changed drastically. So, with assurances from both Rocco and my Mother that she would be well cared for, Donna also stayed at Cottage 10.

Although I continued with the early morning swimming lessons, Donna gladly assumed my position as Lifeguard. She often wore an attractive white bathing suit, and even at the age of 14, I couldn't help but notice that she was quite developed. And being that many of our Hotel guests were young Greek men, they would likewise take note of her. One day, upon noticing one of them *admiring* her, I poked my index finger hard into his chest saying, "Don't be looking at my sister like that!" - and the word quickly got around.

Bartending   Rocco was mostly preoccupied with the Hotel and Restaurant components of the Lodge, and in Caesar's absence, I was essentially in charge of setting up the Bars. This meant that I would regularly meet with the various beer and liquor distributors in order to place the weekly liquor orders. Although on weekends, I was mainly relegated to the Service Bar, I devised a very rudimentary control system for the Front Bar. The plan was before any of the hired bartenders arrived, I would measure the open bottles on the Back Bar in tenths, and stock the Bar with new bottles.

Then, once the bartenders stepped behind the Front Bar, I would have them sign off on the total booze count. During the night, if they needed replenishments, they would have to sign for them and retain all empty bottles for a closing reconciliation. To ensure quick pouring service, I only used *speed pourers* and the *false bottoms* of the shot glasses gave the illusion of a generous full shot. At the end of the night, knowing how many shots were in any given bottle, I could reconcile the total amount of booze used with the cash in the register.

I always assumed that experienced bartenders would attempt to beat the system by 10%, especially by leaving the register open or pouring from smuggled bottles of booze and pocketing the cash. Despite this potential flaw, when we eventually hired several Greek bartenders for the Front Bar, this control system proved to be very useful. In fact, one weekend when I closed out the Bar at the end of the night, I noticed that the empty bottles exceeded the stocked number, indicating that bottles were smuggled in. When I informed Caesar of the discrepancy, he chose the younger of the two bartenders and asked if he would accompany him to the kitchen.

Then he opened the thick door to the large walk-in freezer, and after stepping inside, he pointed to the meat hanging on hooks and said, "You have a choice, you either tell me who brought the extra bottles or freeze with the meat!" The poor guy broke out in a sweat and immediately gave up his partner, who was then fired on the spot, minus the estimated loss in revenue.

The Confrontation   I remember, just before the inaugural 4th of July weekend, I asked to speak with Rocco about some disturbing events that I felt were distracting his attention from the Grand opening. The discussion took place in the Dining room at Cottage 10, in the presence of my Mother. Without being explicit, my intent was to avoid jeopardizing everyone's hard work by ensuring a successful opening.

Predictably, the discussion quickly escalated into a very unpleasant confrontation, with the exchange of many unwarranted hurtful comments. As a fledgling Psychologist, he accused me of, among other things, being Neurotic, after which he stormed out of the room. Then I tried in vain to reason with my mother, but much to my chagrin, she sided with Rocco. I thought, "this was the Mother I had promised to take care of - what to do?"

In retrospect, however, my mother's response was somewhat predictable. It was my impression that, for reasons unknown, my Mother often perceived Rocco as warranting some sort of sympathetic allegiance. Perhaps, it was in response to his jaundiced perspective of being mistreated by my father while attending Ohio State. Admittedly, we had different Fathers under different circumstances. But at least he had the benefit of a loving father during those difficult College years.

Incidentally, In some respects, I believe my Father and I shared parallel family lifestyles, struggling with similar difficulties of raising a large family at roughly the same age. Aside from some extenuating circumstances, at the young age of 46, I'm certain Dad was doing his level best to provide for his family in "every respect". The moral of the story, "Don't judge a man until you've walked the same path wearing the same size shoes!"

With both Caesar and Anita essentially out of the picture, I felt I had to vent to someone and decided to drive to Brooklyn. Before leaving, however, I went over to Dario's house and told him of the bitter exchange and of my plans to, "Get out of town for a while!". Although Mary and I hadn't seen each other in several weeks, purely on a whim, I decided to call her. She apologized saying that she was studying for her chemistry regents exam. Upon hearing the tone of my voice, however, she said, "Meet me at Angela's house!" While riding on the Staten Island ferry. she just listened as I told her of the ugly confrontation. And although unable to offer any meaningful suggestions, her sympathetic ear was comforting.

Later that evening, I called Caesar and he immediately invited me over for dinner. Being newlyweds, they were living in a small upstairs apartment and he asked Pat to buy a Prime Rib to cook for dinner. However, their stove was very old and neither of them knew how long to cook the precious piece of beef. Over the course of the evening, they had to put the precious beef back into the oven at least three times before it was no longer bloody. Consequently, the impromptu Dinner invitation took three hours, which gave Caesar and me plenty of time to talk. Although he was now removed from the day to day operation of the Lodge, as he listened intently, he appeared genuinely disheartened, but remained diplomatically neutral saying, "That's a damn shame, but remain committed for Mom's sake!".

I returned to Cottage 10 later that evening, and the following morning, after finishing my swimming lessons, Dario came to see me at the poolside. He said he was relieved to see me back and told me that he had a long talk with Rocco wherein, he purportedly said that he regretted having the confrontation and couldn't believe what was coming out of his mouth! Considering that Dario was a notorious fabricator and that Rocco neither apologized nor brought up the subject again, I'll never know if their conversation ever took place. In any event, things seemed to smooth over, and as I did my thing and Rocco did his, the season moved forward.

In those days, wine was virtually nonexistent and table *Setups* mostly consisted of a bottle of Scotch, Whiskey, and Gin, along with large bottles of appropriate sodas. The mixed drinks included various Scotch or Whiskey Sours, Gin Tom Collins, and more exotic mixtures such as Brandy Alexander's, Pink Ladies, Daiquiris, Sidecars, Singapore slings. Jamaican Punch etc. On weekends, we could seat about 300 guests and it was common to have table *Setups* for 12-16 people from among Monroe's "crème de la crème".

Dario   Perhaps influenced by working in Manhattan, despite his initial professional guidance, we eventually came to realize that Dario was a pathologic fabricator and a master in the art of illusion- the proverbial shell game. During the early days, we relied on single numbered check pads - that could be purchased anywhere. This meant that one single numbered check would be presented to a table of 10 to 16 people, which would be paid in cash (credit cards being virtually nonexistent).

Unbeknownst to us, however, Dario would occasionally present an inflated check to an unsuspecting patron at one end of a particularly long table. And if questioned about the exorbitant amount, he would deftly whisper in that patron's ear, "The other end of the table were real gluttons!" and vice versa. Then, with cash in hand, he would hand in a different numbered check of a lesser amount and pocket the difference.

When some of the loyal patrons brought these discrepancies to our attention, the embarrassing situation was handled swiftly and after purchasing a *state of the art,* National Cash Register (NCR), we implemented the more sophisticated Dupe system, which provided duplicate numbered NCR checks.

Surprise Visit   During Mary's two-week vacation, it wasn't unusual for me to walk down to her house in the evening hoping to spend some quiet time together. Oftentimes, however, given the late hour, and in order not to disturb anyone, I would usually walk up the driveway and enter their house through the side porch. One evening, after finishing work early, I walked down to her house expecting to surprise her - only to be surprised that she was spending the evening with someone else, George's best friend, Bruce Durland!

Bruce was a frequent house guest - more like a household fixture! I believe that, along with her brothers, Bruce also worked at the family's factory in Brooklyn. In retrospect, whether or not he also frequented their Flatbush home, I'll never know, because fearing the answer, I chose not to ask. With such an unfettered family endorsement, It wasn't a stretch of the imagination to suspect that he had a *thing* for Mary, but I never suspected that it was mutual! But then again, why not? After all, he was a handsome guy who drove an MG convertible sports car and was considered as one of the family!

17th Birthday Surprise   I don't remember being invited to celebrate Mary's 17th Birthday, which I believe occurred on a Friday. After work on the following Sunday, I decided to walk down to her house, in order to give her a belated birthday present. While walking up the driveway, however, I noticed a familiar sports car up ahead, and as I approached from behind, I noticed Bruce with his arm around the love of my life, her head resting gently on his shoulder!

When I approached her side window, Mary was understandably shocked. After Bruce removed his arm, they both straightened up, and staring straight ahead, they sat speechless, which spoke volumes! I lightly tapped her on the cheek and devastated, I simply walked away without saying a word. Sadly, It confirmed my earlier suspicion that he had the *hots* for her, and she had a serious crush on him. Naturally, this was followed by a long period of estrangement, well beyond Labor Day.

Labor Day Weekend On most weekends, Donna and occasionally her cousin, Denice, would assist me at the Service Bar. Donna and I shared more laughs than I can remember. After watching me preparing the various drinks, I eventually allowed her to mix several of them. Although she was a quick study, when she occasionally made a mistake, we would simply store them on a back shelf, hopefully for later use. There were also four waitresses assigned to the service bar for table orders. Two of them were roughly my age, Cheryl Mapes, the former Miss Chester and ditzy, Ronnie, who consistently pronounced, Cutty Sark scotch as, "Cutty Shark".

I distinctly remember the last hurrah of the season, Labor Day weekend. The house was packed, and the table service was in high demand. Donna was helping me mix the drinks as fast as possible. However, feeling constantly overwhelmed, I was growing progressively wearier, to the point of utter exhaustion. Consequently, production suffered, and I was making even more mistakes than usual. However, In order to hide the incriminating evidence, and in an effort to not waste good booze, the only alternative was to drink them! Of course, this led to a vicious cycle! The more I consumed, the more mistakes I made, further adding to the nonstop laughter and inevitable, *mistake conundrum!*

At some point, perhaps due to some complaints, Rocco came back to check on the Service Bar. While momentarily staring at me, he apparently noticed a big grin on my face and simply said, "Oh shit!" and just turned around and walked out.

Cheryl I remember feeling terribly ashamed that I had disappointed my brother, and as the evening mayhem winded down, I went outside to sit on the side steps, desperately trying to sober up and clear my head. After a while, Cheryl came out and sat beside me, presumably to comfort me. I thought she was absolutely gorgeous with full lips and a slight overbite revealing her sparkling front teeth. I guess while admiring her mouth in a stupor, I happened to comment on something about women with false teeth. Then when she asked, "What about Caps?" I immediately thought, "No way!"

Regardless, I always felt she was way out of my league and besides, she had a handsome boyfriend, Richie, who resembled Sal Mineo. The next thing I realized was that she was sitting awfully close and lightly stroking my knee in a very comforting manner - uh oh? From what I remember, she looked into my blurry eyes and asked me about Mary. After some incoherent mumbling, I inquired about Richie. She broke down crying, confiding that she recently discovered he was gay! With that, I almost burst out laughing at the irony - if only I had my wits about me!

Pageant Surprise   After cooling off for a few weeks, and recalling my father's earlier admonition, I decided to give it another shot. Knowing that Mary enjoyed watching the post-Labor Day, Miss America Pageant, I again walked down to her house, and upon entering the side porch door, I was excited to hear that the TV was on in the living room. I expected to surprise her by tapping on the front porch window. However, when I looked through the pane, I was again, the one surprised! She and Bruce were snuggled together on the couch, *watching* the Pageant. In order to avoid a repeat of our prior encounter, I simply walked back to Cottage 10, and never mentioned it until writing this memoir. I remember thinking of Marion's sage advice and decided, I just couldn't stomach the ignominy any further. During another long period of estrangement, she continued to be pursued - and rightly so!

While sharing this portion of my memoir with Mary, I exposed my very heart and soul by describing the pain associated with the preceding events, Mary offered that, on the weekend of her birthday, she and Bruce went to the movies together, and that she had a crush on him. However, she rationalized that it was due to my non-committal nature. That the status of our dating always seemed to be in limbo, somewhere between heaven and hell, because I never expressed my feelings.

This was partly true in that, I assumed that my love for her was self-evident. The danger of such an assumption, however, is the arrogant notion of *possession,* and any perceived transgression might be considered, *betrayal* - especially, as viewed through the distorted lens of an 18 yr. old, in love.

Truthfully, however, I don't recall either of us ever discussing our true feelings for each other. On my part, it was mostly due to a fear of rejection. Or, as with my French companion or the lyrics of, Le Mis' *On My Own,* perhaps our love affair was, "only in my mind!"

Incidentally, just to clarify, I have no issue with teenage crushes which are common and natural. I think many of us enjoy, and even encourage, the thrill of being pursued, oftentimes walking that fine line between the flirtatious pursuer and the pursued, while hopefully avoiding any untoward consequences. Ironically, this subterfuge is often concealed under the guise, "What you don't know won't hurt you!". Although feelings are undeniable, it's what you do with them that's potentially hurtful, and that's what gets you into trouble.

The Blue Screen I just completed the prior 25 pages of my memoir when the *"Blue screen of death" took* over my computer, and all of my efforts to retrieve them were in vain! They dealt with some of the most delicate and hauntingly painful issues during my adolescence. Upon completion, I remember feeling greatly relieved, as though a therapeutic catharsis had removed a heavy yoke from my rounded shoulders.

I also felt that, in some measure, I gained a better understanding of my tattered self-image and low self-esteem, which helped explain my unprovoked periods of sullenness and quiet withdrawal. Perhaps they were the result of a *poor me* resentment for my *unfortunate circumstances.* In retrospect, however, Mary was often the unintended victim and understandably bewildered by my unpredictable mood swings, for which I could offer no plausible explanation.

CH - 34
SOPHOMORE YEAR

Although I began my Sophomore year with renewed enthusiasm, I eventually recognized that my pre-med advisor, Dr. DeMedici, didn't have a clue. He would simply flip through a compendium of medical schools and randomly pick courses that one of the top tier schools might suggest as being *desirable* for admission to that particular school. For example, despite the fact that I failed high school Algebra, he strongly recommended that I take Calculus. So, assuming that he knew what was best for me, I signed up for Calculus 1 - what a mistake!

I struggled through the entire first semester for a lousy C. Then, in the second semester, the wizard strongly recommended that I take Calculus II. However, when I also signed up for Physics, since I already completed Calculus I, they put me in *Advanced* Physics. - go figure!

Consequently, under the Wizard's brilliant oversight, I ended up taking more than 20 credits a semester, which required special permission from Dean Volansky. Unfortunately, In order to accommodate the additional science courses, I made a tactical error by not completing my fourth (final) semester of Spanish - which would eventually come back to haunt me.

Queens Pizza Eddie D'Onofrio had aspirations of becoming a Dentist and eventually joined me in the pre-med curriculum at the downtown campus. Being a year behind me, we rarely shared the same classes. However, we did share something else in common, we both loved Pizza.

The Queens pizzeria was conveniently located one block away and we would often walk up to the window counter for a couple of slices. One morning, for some reason, I went looking for Edie. I searched everywhere, including the bathrooms and nada! Then, purely on a whim, although it was only 11 am, I walked up to Queens and peeked through the closed door. I spotted the back of a person's head, bobbing up and down in a booth. I realized it could only be one person, Eddie!

The Special Bedroom   I finally inherited the privilege of moving into the small *Special Bedroom*. Since I was completing my second semester of Organic Chemistry, which I absolutely loved, the wall facing my small desk was cluttered with all sorts of equations that I committed to memory. I was particularly fond of the professor, Dr. Sarno, and although I was carrying an A average, when it came time for our final exams, I asked him, "What would I have to do to get an, A+?" He responded, "Solve the final bonus equation and, I'll give you an A+!" I felt confident that I had memorized the various equations to such an extent that I could eventually figure out the solution.

When it came to grading my final exam, he pulled me aside and said, "Normally it should have taken only 12 steps to arrive at a solution. However, it took you 23 steps and you probably would've had a *tar residue* at step 12. But, nonetheless, you eventually got there! And I got an A+. Although I wanted to complete the required philosophy and theology courses, in order to appease the Wizard's *Science wish list*, this required me to take additional evening courses for the non-sciences.

Butch the Dog   In Nick's absence, the sole responsibility of caring for Butch the dog fell upon me and my mother. He was not only considered as one of the family, but he actually behaved like one. By now, he was a rambunctious oversized adolescent who, unaware of his size, often behaved like a large bull in a china shop. However, It was uncanny how he would sit on a specific chair in the Sunroom and peer out the window, patiently waiting for me to come home from school. Then he would greet me by nearly knocking me over as he raced through the rooms.

Despite his unusual size, he still chewed on everything, including cotton socks, which he occasionally swallowed. I mention this because, while walking him down 83rd St, it was very embarrassing when the Ft Hamilton high school students would gawk at poor, Butch, as he strained to pass a sock that he had swallowed two days before. I know, more than a need to know!

I clearly remember one fateful evening, while studying in the *special bedroom*, I was shaken by a sudden loud thud, followed by the sound of an animal screeching and squealing. Then I heard, Bob Hartmann, yelling, "you sonofabitch!" I immediately had a sinking feeling and ran downstairs to discover the horrific scene. The squealing was coming from our beloved dog, Butch, lying by the curb across the street and Bob standing in the middle yelling frantically at the driver as he sped away.

Nick was really the one responsible for training Butch to heel and obey verbal commands. If commanded to "stay", Butch would remain seated until released by the command, "come". Bob intended to take Butch for a walk along the front of the Park. Apparently, after giving Butch the command to "come" across the street, a speeding car made a sharp turn from 84th St. onto Colonial Road without braking, and after hitting Butch, simply sped away.

Butch's injuries were extensive, and I vividly remember looking into his pleading eyes. As our eyes locked, our ever valiant protector was desperately trying to raise his head, acknowledging my presence. I also had a distinct impression that he was imploring my help. However, facing an overwhelming sense of abject helplessness, I had nothing to offer my faithful companion.

Out of pure desperation, I ran to our neighbor's house and rang the doorbell pleading with Dr. Hubbard, for his help. He immediately ran outside and upon arriving at the scene he said that nothing could be done. Shortly after, while standing by his side, I watched as Butch's agonizing motion ceased and his breathing gradually slowed until it finally stopped.

The irony of the story, however, is that my brother Caesar's nickname was also Butch, and when we eventually took our puppy to the veterinarian, he looked at his gigantic paws and unwittingly called him, "Butch". Now, this is where the story gets a little dicey.

I had to notify my siblings regarding Butch's tragic death, for he truly was part of the family. Upon hearing of the tragedy, both my sister, Virginia, and her husband, Lou, immediately called my mother inquiring about the condition of the body and what funeral arrangements were being made? My mother said somberly," Virginia, his body is really a mess, and in all likelihood, his remains will be shoveled up by the sanitation department in the morning! My sister was understandably aghast and when she protested, my mother said with resolve, "Virginia, what else can you do?" It just stands to reason!"

However, they were both so taken aback that they immediately drove down to the house with a checkbook in hand, intent on contributing towards the funeral arrangements befitting our Brother. I remember, Virginia sitting with my mother at the kitchen table, trying to console her, and It wasn't until the miscommunication became apparent, when my brother, Caesar, (Butch) walked into the kitchen. Now, this doesn't, in any way, diminish the painful loss of our beloved dog, but, in retrospect, the humorous miscommunication lessened the pain somewhat.

Year-round Restaurant Thanks to Caesar, in addition to New Utrecht high school, I was fortunate to have a second lifeguard job at the St. George Hotel. In the meantime, Rocco attempted a new venture - a year-round restaurant and hired a chef, Eddie, and his wife on weekends. To be supportive, I would often drive my mother up to the Lodge on Friday evenings, and when we arrived, Eddie would make my favorite, delicious manicotti.

The weekend dinner patrons mostly consisted of local *supporters* who wanted to ensure Rocco's success. A list of their last names resembled a venerable "who's who" of the Football season's revered Fraternity - namely:

Degan, Monro, Phillips, Stears, Lucas, Hendriks, Harper, Lang, Buyers, Byce, Maxwell and Sullivan. Plans were also in play for an inaugural Gala New Year's Eve party at the Lodge. *Incidentally, during the same time period, I believe Rocco was also in the process of completing his Master's degree in psychology at St. John's University.*

Candlelight Ball (1963)   Although, I have a very hazy recollection of our courtship during this tumultuous time period, there must've been a reconciliation of sorts because, while writing this portion of my memoir, Mary told me that I was invited to accompany her to the celebrated, Candlelight Ball at the Waldorf Astoria. However, I had absolutely no recollection of the event, and it wasn't until she showed me photographs of her in a lovely print dress and me in a tuxedo, that I finally acknowledged that I must have been there! This triggered the faint recollection of her father offering me $50 to reimburse me for renting a tuxedo, which I believe I reluctantly accepted.

Ironically, however, I also noticed a photo taken the prior year, of Mary and Patrick Mullins attending the same Ball. Then, I was totally baffled when I saw another photo of her and Patrick posing along with her parents, at the very same event that I was presumably at! I immediately thought, "What's wrong with this picture?" And now I know how Waldo feels - where was Peter?

New Year's Eve Party   I guess we had a good time at the Ball because I invited Mary to the Gala New Year's Eve party at the Lodge. We would be staying in separate rooms on the third floor along with Nick and Babs. It was a sold-out event and during the bitterly cold evening, my job was to park the cars.in the vacant lot next to the Lodge. I mostly stayed outside, and in order to stay warm, Bob Hartmann would periodically bring me a shot of scotch.

Needless to say, initially the cars were parked perfectly parallel. As the evening progressed, however, they gradually became more diagonal. In fact, when Dr. Brill arrived in his shiny silver Bentley, he prudently deferred my services and decided instead to park his own car. The scotch and I were a little put off by his arrogance, and while standing in front of his car, I guided him to a vacant spot between two other cars. While I was backing up, he couldn't see the small 3' fur-tree behind me until it was too late. Before he knew it, he and his Bentley drove over the poor tree! I stayed outside until everyone arrived, and when I finally came in, I couldn't feel my face, not knowing if it was a residual from the cold or the 13 shots of scotch!

I remember Mary and me, celebrating the momentous occasion with a kiss, and shortly afterward, we placed a call to Joanne, to wish her Happy New Year. She had graciously volunteered to type my term paper on Edgar Allan Poe, and upon hearing my voice she said, "I hope you're having a nice time while I'm at home typing your damn term paper!" - ups!!.

Incidentally, at the time, I didn't know that, during his senior year at Xavier HS, my father received the Edgar Allan Poe award!- reciting my favorite poem, The Raven.

Mary's Prom   Things must have progressed uneventfully because Mary asked me to her High School Prom which was to be held at the Waldorf Astoria. On the day of her Prom, I was working with Rocco up at the Lodge, repairing the wood trim and caulking around the second- story opening in the front of the Hotel. Somehow, I sprained my right rib cage and couldn't twist or side bend. Rocco decided to tape my rib cage with an old roll of cloth adhesive tape which gave me some temporary relief.

We continued working until the last possible minute, and then we drove down to Brooklyn. Now I was faced with trying to remove the damn cloth tape. When I initially tried, it was like being skinned alive. Then my mother tried mercilessly to peel it off by applying olive oil - until she couldn't tolerate my screams. Now I smelled like a Salad.

Finally, I called Dr. Weiser, who recommended trying to remove it while taking a hot shower. Unfortunately, this caused the tape to shrivel, and combined with the slippery olive oil, I began to imagine myself wearing the wet slippery tape under my tuxedo! Before conceding defeat, however, I decided to give it one last shot and I slowly tore off one strip at a time, leaving large swaths of beefy red skin.

I clearly remember that all the boys were required to attend her High school, St Agnes Seminary, in order to meet privately with one of the nuns prior to leaving for the prom. The frightening specter of my nemesis, Sr. Ermingale, immediately came to mind! The purpose of the meeting was to ostensibly remind each of us to, "Always maintain a gentlemanly demeanor and act with proper decorum" - whatever that was? Then we were politely asked to empty our pockets! - clearly to ensure an evening of chastity!

I don't recall Mary's dress and oddly, we don't have any pictures to refresh my memory. We normally danced well together because we often practiced on her porch in Monroe, especially the Lindy, Rumba, and Cha Cha. However, due to the severe rib cage pain, it was very limited.

Afterward, being that we were in the city, our entire table wanted to go to a *Nightclub*. So, we went to watch Dizzy Gillespie and Miles Davis perform at *The Living Room*. Unfortunately, two of the girls didn't have the required *fake ID*, so none of us at the table were able to order any drinks, which was a real drag, but otherwise, good news for my wallet!

Cars   Over the years, I managed to accumulate a total of six used cars - three of which I purchased and three were donated. Aside from driving the Blue Beetle, my very first car was a 1953 beige Ford convertible, given to me by Bob's mother, Johanna Hartman. It was truly a beauty and an automatic to boot. Although the battery was perpetually dead, jumping was less expensive than buying a new one. Unfortunately, my convertible's life was short-lived.

Somehow, while driving around the first steep turn in front of the Trum's house, I suddenly felt the transmission give out, and I managed to back the car safely into the deep roadside ravine. Then, I tried putting it in reverse, but although it groaned, it didn't budge. The following morning, Nick came down to help, but he said that the linkage was gone - whatever that is. Don Lucas eventually sent a tow truck to pull my beautiful convertible out of the ravine and towed it to the graveyard.

This was followed by a 1955 Green Plymouth (aka, the Green Hornet), a 1958 blue Oldsmobile (aka, the Beast), a 1958 green Opel, a 1960 black Dodge(aka Black Beauty) and a 1960 green Galaxy 500 Ford sedan (aka Limo or Smokey 1). Fortunately, the average price of gas was $ 0.30 a gallon! So, you could fill your tank for $ 5.00

College Interview fiasco   Mary was seriously considering attending the College of St. Elizabeth's in Convent Station, N.J. At first, I chuckled at the combination, St. Agnes *Seminary* and St. Elizabeth's *Convent* station! The Nuns seemed hell-bent on ensuring chastity! For some reason, perhaps as just a cheap date, we decided to drive the Green Hornet out to Huntington NY in order to visit Maria, Jack, and their children.

Mary 's parents were away, leaving her sister, Pat, as a pseudo *babysitter*, in charge of the household. She graciously offered to drive Mary for her college interview in the morning, at 8 am. However, she wasn't particularly happy with our plans, and consequently, gave Mary a stern warning to be home no later than 10:30 pm!.

Other than getting lost, the drive out to Huntington was mostly uneventful, and after a pleasant visit, we headed back to Brooklyn, anticipating our arrival in time for the witching hour. The Green Hornet was notorious for some major rust issues, especially on the floorboards, which provided unpleasant drafts and splashing, and over the headlights which caused them to short out in the rain, But otherwise, it was virtually indestructible!

on the elevated portion of the Gowanus Parkway, and relatively close to her house when I noticed a significant tilt probably indicating a flat tire. Being that the shoulder was very narrow, I pulled over as much as possible, and after turning on my left blinker, when I opened the trunk in order to change the tire, I found a jack, but no lug wrench! Fortunately, we were relatively close to a roadside emergency phone which I used to call for help. We waited in the car for about 40 minutes until the tow truck arrived. Thankfully, the driver was about my age and with only $3.00 in my pocket, after explaining the embarrassing situation, I asked," Could I *Just* borrow your lug wrench?

Being that my blinker was on for such a long time when I went to start the car, the damn battery was dead! Just as the tow truck was about to pull away, I quickly jumped out of the car and began yelling and waving for him to stop. Miraculously, he saw me in his rearview mirror, and when he eventually backed up, I asked," Can you *Just* jump-start us?" After getting started, I thanked him again and generously gave him all my entire wad, $3,00. Incidentally, I accentuated the word *Just* because that was my sister Anita's favorite ploy for a Herculean request. Like "Peter *Just* move those boulders about 100 ft to the right before it rains!"

Feeling confident that we would only be about an hour late, we continued on our journey. However, after roughly 2 miles, once again I noticed that familiar tilt, and I thought, "Impossible, another damn flat - what are those odds!" Now I had no other option, but to take the next exit and continue driving on a flat tire on the cobblestone streets under the elevated Parkway and hopefully exchange cars in Bay Ridge. At some point, the tire had shredded, and we were now hobbling on the metal rim over cobblestones -what a racket!.

Fortunately, by the time we arrived at 8311, I noticed Rocco's white Ford convertible in the driveway. Being that it was now 12:30 am, he was upstairs fast asleep, so I simply borrowed his keys. Noticing that my pants were soiled from changing the tire, before leaving I quickly changed pants, and off we went to Flatbush. Shortly after leaving the house, however, I realized that I left my driver's license in my other pants! So, I purposely avoided the Parkway and drove below on the same cobblestone streets.

At the midway point, a cop car pulls me over because my right front headlight was out! Of course, given the late hour, the cop asks me for my driver's license! Unable to produce it, he says, "Get out of the car and place your hands on the hood!" In utter desperation, I began telling him of the evening's horrific events, after which he said, "No one can make that shit up! Just drive safely and get the light fixed as soon as possible"

Needless to say, I didn't get Mary home until 2 am and Pat was understandably, pissed! The following day, when I asked about Pat's reaction and her Interview she said, "Fortunately, it was too late to explain the litany of reasons for the delay and the drive to, St. Elizabeth, was long and silent

Incidentally, It was only two years ago that we finally told Pat of the whole unbelievable saga. It sounded so incredulous that I doubted if she even believed it!

Trum Parties   Even at a relatively young age, I was aware of the weekend parties at the Trum's Monroe house. I knew that the festivities were often accompanied by alcohol - a household staple that often flowed freely. However, it wasn't until much later in our courtship that I became aware of the same degree of partying in their Flatbush home. In those days, although it seemed that liberal alcohol consumption and occasional inebriation was an accepted norm, I was never conscious of any serious addiction issues.

Addictions   Eventually, I learned that, at some point, in addition to Parkinson's disease, her father became addicted to narcotics. Apparently, he had been suffering from intractable ear pain, presumably due to an acoustic neuroma (inner ear tumor) which often results in partial deafness and loss of balance. However, despite a successful surgical procedure, due to the liberal dispensing of narcotics, he eventually developed an addiction that required appropriate rehabilitation.

In addition, I also became aware of her mother's dependence on alcohol. Virginia was a very intelligent woman who adeptly camouflaged

313

her addiction by always appearing well dressed and carrying her tall slender frame in an elegant fashion. Oftentimes, however, when I would bring Mary home after our dates while standing in the porch breezeway, we would watch as her mother would keep busy by, dusting or vacuuming - apparently providing cover for having several "nightcaps".

Although I was initially oblivious to this routine, Mary was acutely aware of the situation and would become visibly angry and embarrassed. She emphasized how she would cringe at the mere sound of the clinking bottles. Rather than inviting me in to witness the inevitable confrontation with her mother, we would simply say goodnight. After witnessing the same scenario on several occasions, I urged Mary to avoid a worthless midnight confrontation, by simply walking straight upstairs to her bedroom.

I mention these sorted details in order to emphasize how painfully difficult it must have been for her to grow up in a household among liberal drinkers and contend with an alcoholic mother. Consequently, It's no wonder that, while dating, she never chose to drink alcohol. Even during our early married life, as I would make myself a drink, she would cringe at the sound of ice cubes and the clinking bottles. In fact, It's only been during our senior years that she appears comfortable sharing a drink of wine or a light Manhattan with me, and on rare occasions, even a light vodka and tonic!.

To her credit, she constantly reminded our children that they too may have inherited the gene for alcohol intolerance. Thankfully, her mother eventually overcame her addiction by surrendering herself to a successful AA program as did her brother, George.

Mary's Graduation Party   I was invited to Mary's June graduation party, to be held in her home in Flatbush. At the time, I was working at the Lodge and I remember being disappointed to learn that she had decided to work at the same bank during the summer. In any event, although I made plans to drive down to Brooklyn in order to attend the party, I was very self-conscious about my limited wardrobe and extremely nervous attending, what I believed would be, a large well-dressed gathering.

At some point, I found myself driving to Bay Ridge instead of Flatbush. I remember calling her house from 8311, and while waiting for her to come to the phone, I could hear all the loud laughter and envisioning a well-dressed cocktail party. While listening to all the partying, by the time she came to the phone, I had already made a fateful decision and chose the coward's option by simply telling her that, unfortunately, I wasn't able to come down to celebrate her graduation.

Silently, I rationalized that, obviously my presence wasn't important, and it was a matter of personal Survival. Besides," Doesn't everybody graduate from High School!" Her total silence was deafening, and her disappointment was palpable. Without another word, I drove back to my safe zone, Cottage 10. It wasn't until I shared the contents of this Memoir that she heard the shameful truth and I learned of her profound disappointment, for which I am eternally sorry.

CH - 35
SUMMER OF '64

The gradual transition to a predominantly Greek Hotel, featuring classical Greek music and entertainment continued unabated. This, of course, also required hiring additional Greek waiters and bartenders. Rocco arranged for the construction of a small elevated stage in the Main Room, with extensive lighting for various performers, such as a Greek singer, Florrie Papadakanochus, and an array of exotic Greek belly dancers.

Admittedly, these were exciting, but very expensive times. Considering that the weekday clientele consisted of the local Country Club members, and the more lucrative Greek clientele was only on weekends, the net revenue was marginal at best.

Anticipating the additional waiters, I constructed a larger service bar in the back of the Dining Room which provided more room and easy access to the Kitchen and commercial dishwasher. I felt confident that I could serve up to 12 Greek waiters, and In preparation for the hectic weekends, I would premix the Whiskey Sours and Tom Collins drinks.

I particularly liked Barton's Rye, because it was dark in color and packed a punch, giving the impression that it was a very generous shot of booze. More importantly, however, it was relatively inexpensive. Although I stocked some top-shelf labels, they were reserved for shots or "on the rocks" drinkers, and for control purposes, all table *set-ups* were dispensed from the service bar.

Alex the Gorilla   One of our more dedicated Greek patrons came up with the bright idea of wearing a Gorilla costume in town in order to promote more business. Alex was a large burly Greek who was in the Merchant Marines and came up to the Lodge every weekend during the summer. His heart was in the right place, and as crazy as it sounds, he single-handedly took on the initiative by renting the costume and volunteered to walk through Town dressed as a Gorilla.

So, while wearing a heavy gorilla costume, he lumbered through the streets, stores, and supermarkets, dressed as a Gorilla, handing out pamphlets. However, being such a big robust man, while wearing the heavy costume during the height of summer, he failed to consider the effects of dehydration. When he eventually returned to the Lodge totally exhausted and 12 pounds lighter, he claimed that he nearly fainted twice because he couldn't remove the gigantic headpiece in time!

Nick the Waiter   By this time, Nick and Barbara had their first child, Debbie. They frequently spent weekends sharing a small summer bungalow in Monroe with Barbara's parents, Joe and Stacia Brenner. Being that we anticipated hiring more waiters, Nick requested a job. Perhaps influenced by his father-in-law, in addition to splitting the pooled tips, he also expected to be paid a salary. At first blush, this was a stark departure from the family norm of working without expecting any reimbursement. After two weeks, however, I think he found the pace and language barrier more challenging than he anticipated, and his stint as a waiter was short-lived.

Mary's Grandparents   In 1963-64, Mary's paternal Grandparents purchased a beautiful ranch home on Cromwell Hill Rd. The sprawling ranch was one of the finest in the area, situated on 5 acres with a spectacular view overlooking Round Lake. True to form, the expansive manicured lawns and flower beds were always immaculate, and the shrubbery and trees perfectly trimmed. In addition to a part-time Maid, their chauffeur, Dick, also doubled as a cook and butler.

When her grandparents eventually decided to sell the Farm, they very prudently hired someone to walk the entire 100-acre property with a portable Geiger counter-like device searching for oil, gas, and rare minimal deposits. This laborious process took about 2 weeks, during which time, the man stayed at the Lodge. I thought that the mere foresight was ingenious, and I found the process fascinating. I remember while sitting in the Dining room most mornings, asking the man if he discovered anything of interest on his prior day's search.

Jerry Degan was the current CEO of Stuart Dean Inc, a family-owned national enterprise specializing in metal finishing and stone polishing He lived in a modest cape cod on two acres of lawn, directly across the road from the senior Trum's estate. I mention this because, when the Degans eventually moved to southern California, Anita and Bob were delighted to purchase their home - which set the stage for a later chapter.

Mary's 18th Birthday   As with the prior two summers, Mary again chose to work in the same Brooklyn bank which, as in the past, severely limited our courtship. For whatever reason, I wasn't invited to Mary's 18th Birthday celebration, and following the party, emboldened by sufficient alcohol, her father and older brothers decided they were going to come up to the Lodge to *confront* me! Apparently hearing this, Mary came up to the Lodge in a panic, pleading for me to leave work as soon as possible in order to avoid the confrontation. I never learned the whole story, especially the reasons for the confrontation, but in order to save her from further embarrassment, I shamefully did as she asked.

The following morning, Rocco was on my case to explain why I left work early without checking with him. When I explained the situation, he said, "Why didn't you tell me, I would have backed you up" - go figure! I guess it's in keeping with the familiar adage, "I can say something bad about a family member, but don't you dare!" *Incidentally, Mary confirmed that I gave her a jewelry present for her birthday, but honestly, I don't recall what or when I gave it to her.*

George's Rebuke Shortly after this, I remember one evening overhearing George's loud diatribe directed at Mary on their screened porch in Monroe. Obviously imbued with the wisdom of sufficient alcohol, he was chastising her for her "adolescent notion of love" while extolling his more experienced perspective. No doubt this rebuke was directed toward me. I believe a third person was present, perhaps paving the way for Bruce. Following this exchange, however, I wrote Mary a letter, explaining what I overheard and offering my own perspective. I don't recall any further repercussions, but it was clear that, despite *saving his life*, George considered me a persona non grata.

The Appalachian Trail In late August, I decided to take Mary's youngest brother, Dennis, and his friend, Richie DeSchriever, for an overnight hike on the legendary AppalachianTrail. The 2,200-mile trail extends from Maine to Georgia, presumably the longest hiking-only trail in the world. While growing up, I was naively led to believe that the trail was initially forged by North American Indians. However, contrary to this common folklore, the trail was actually conceived in 1921 by a Forester named Benton MacKaye, and eventually completed sixteen years later, in 1937.

In any event, Mary dropped us off at our entry point along Rt 17 with the understanding that she would pick us up at 4 pm the following day. For the sake of my young companions, I purposely shared the Indian legend with them to heighten the wonder and intrigue of our upcoming adventure. Richie was a known gun enthusiast, often shooting his 22 caliber rifle at anything that moved, thereby earning the moniker *Bullets DeSchriever.*

After hiking the forested trails for most of the day, I spotted a towering square granite rock with an unusually flat surface, far in the distance, and I thought, "Serendipity was surely beckoning us! Since we didn't have any tents, I figured, with Richie's rifle for protection, it was a reasonably safe place to camp for the night. It took us a good hour to reach the unusual megalith, which I estimated to be at least 500 ft. High.

Once we scaled the edge of the enormous rock and reached the top, the flat surface provided a panoramic view for several miles, and I felt safe. Of course, sleeping on a hard surface was another matter. After the long rugged climb, we started a fire, and after eating hot dogs and beans, we were all thoroughly exhausted and ready to retire for the night. I remember briefly discussing how each of us should take turns manning the rifle during the night. However, while gazing at the magnificent, crystal clear starlit sky, and listening to the rhythmic hoot of a lowly owl, we all fell fast asleep.

At the crack of dawn, we were relieved to find all of us still alive, and after a simple breakfast, we were ready to move on. Before leaving camp, however, I spotted an illusory object on the side of a distant mountain. It seemed to sparkle in the sunlight like a radiant beacon, beckoning us to visit. Since, from our vantage point, it only appeared to be about a mile away, we decided to venture off in search of the mysterious object. The hike, however, proved to be much farther and the climb, far more difficult than we expected.

When we finally reached our destination, we realized that the illusory object was an enormous smooth granite surface that appeared glued to the side of the distant mountain. After carefully scaling the gradual incline of the smooth surface, we were able to clearly see our original campsite and were truly rewarded with another magnificent view that I still remember to this day.

Admittedly, I was far more enthralled with the journey than either of the boys and having achieved *our goals*, they were eager to return to civilization! While navigating our way back to our drop off location, the boys picked up the pace considerably and I could tell, they had enough of the Appalachian Trail! Thankfully, Mary was waiting at the drop-off location providing a welcoming sight for all of us to behold. Incidentally, after our relatively short, exhausting excursion, neither of the boys ever mentioned hiking again and neither did I!

St Elizabeth (1964)   Mary began her Freshman year at the College of St. Elizabeth (St E's) in Convent Station NJ. The entrance to the college was marked by a quaint train station, requiring students to cross railroad tracks en route to the campus dorms which were within easy walking distance. The main campus was quite beautiful with the interior roads lined by large old trees, appropriately matching the age and grandeur of the original stone buildings. Mary chose Home Economics as her major which primarily consisted of a food and nutritional science curriculum. She described her brief introduction to college as, "I was driven to Convent Station by my father, who simply dropped me off, and without any fanfare, bid me farewell".

The Green Hornet   I believe my first visit to her beautiful campus was on a Friday evening, in order to drive her home to Brooklyn for the weekend. I was accompanied by our friends, Edie, and Angela, and it was their first experience of driving in the notorious, Green Hornet. Being that It had been snowing for quite some time, the roads were quite slushy. Eddie and I sat in the front and Angela sat in the backseat. Due to the absence of the right front floorboard, in order to compensate for the cold draft, I put a piece of cardboard in front of the Hornet's radiator.

Initially, Eddie was unaware of the gap in the floorboard. However, he eventually noticed that his feet were not only ice-cold, but they were also soaking wet! After looking more closely, he said, "Pete, I can see the slushy road under the car!" Fortunately, I brought extra cardboard for the radiator and he placed it under his feet. Also, due to the precipitation, there was the occasional flickering of the headlights due to corrosion, and the radiator cardboard required periodic heat adjustments. The only other minor issue was that the windshield wiper on the passenger side didn't work. So, I had a metal hanger available for Eddie to manually move the wiper blade back and forth. Otherwise, it was smooth sailing!

We eventually arrived safely at Mary's dorm, St. Rita Hall. It had a gracious entrance and large reception area, appropriately adorned with religious statues. All guests, especially males, were required to sign in on a registry, and then instructed to sit in the designated *waiting area* while being closely scrutinized by a nun. This immediately triggered flashbacks of Sister Ermingale!

Eventually, Mary and several of her roommates descended the marble staircase and after introductions and a brief conversation, we headed back to Brooklyn. The girls sat in the back and Edie laughed all the way home, contending with the icy slush intrusion and the right wiper blade. However, he eventually abandoned the slush battle by firmly planting his wet feet on the dashboard. The only other potential issue was that either the battery terminals or the wiring were very fickle, occasionally requiring strategic downhill parking in order to clutch start the Hornet.

Incidentally, Edie found this clutching maneuver fascinating which prompted him to ask me to teach him how to drive a standard car. So, one day, I sat beside him as he attempted to drive parallel to the Park down 83rd St, I was hysterical watching him bouncing up and down as if sitting on a wild bronco, as the poor Hornet bucked up and down the street.

This calls to mind a similar Green Hornet fiasco. One Sunday evening, while driving down from Monroe in the green Hornet, Caesar and I were sitting in the front seat and Pat and Mary were in the back. We were dealing with unusually heavy summer traffic and while navigating a particularly tortuous stretch of the West Side Highway, a sudden thunderstorm erupted with a tremendous downpour. As in similar situations, due to the extensive corrosion over the headlights and despite the black tape, the exposed wiring frequently caused the headlights to periodically short out.

To make matters worse, the right windshield wiper didn't work. Being that this was a chronic problem, I attached a hanger to the wiper arm for just such an emergency. Although quite worn, at least the rubber on the left wiper blade was still intact. So, while stretching his arm out the passenger window to operate the hanger, Caesar did his best to help guide me around the congested sharp turns. Adding to our difficulties was that we both started laughing hysterically at the insane scenario causing me to pee in my pants. Fortunately, the downpour subsided fairly quickly, narrowing averting a near calamity.

Mixers Seton Hall and Drew University were in close proximity to St E's which provided mutual extracurricular activities such as dances and concerts. As in high school, Mary continued singing in the glee club. And although in later years she would often credit me with having a good voice, she has a truly beautiful voice and is able to read sheet music to boot!

Following one of her performances, I remember attending a *mixer* during which they were playing current, Beatles songs. It was during this mixer, that I first met Mary's cousin, Maureen Merner, who also attended St. Elizabeth's. I also met and befriended several of her closest roommates, many of whom we still connect with to this day.

CH - 36
JUNIOR YEAR

Meanwhile, I began my Junior year which was split between both campuses, two days in Brooklyn and three days at the new Jamaica campus. This, of course, required me to drive the somewhat reliable Green Hornet on congested highways. This would also be my first exposure to a large modern campus. I remember exiting the Utopia Parkway and upon entering the campus, I was immediately struck by the tall Administration building. Then, as I drove through the sprawling grounds, I was in awe of, not only the newness but also the rolling hills and spacious lawns separating the individual buildings. My immediate reaction was, "So, this is what a real University Campus looks like!" Fortunately, the relatively small cluster of science buildings was in close proximity to the Athletic building, and in contrast to the Brooklyn campus, parking was very convenient.

Once again, due to the wizardry of my pre-med advisor, Dr. Medici, I signed up for 22 credits which again required Dean Volansky's approval. During the first semester, upon the wizard's recommendation, I took an elective course, Biochemistry, which I absolutely loved.

I remember sitting in the main lecture amphitheater when the professor came in accompanied by three graduate associates. He was a tall distinguished Ph.D., currently on a research grant dealing with plant physiology. At some point, I was thrilled when he invited me to visit his laboratory, and I was so fascinated by the nature and scope of his experiments, that I ultimately decided to take a second semester.

Although quite challenging, Embryology turned out to be one of my favorite Biology courses. I remember a particular project requiring progressive chemical denaturation of a small piglet, suspended in a clear jar. I explained the elaborate process to my mother, and being that it required partial sunlight, I placed the clear jar on top of the dining room liquor cabinet -making it plainly visible.

At specific intervals, each morning before leaving for school, I would add specific chemicals intended to first, denature the skin, then the fat, followed by muscles, ultimately leaving only the skeleton. I didn't realize how hideous it looked until my mother said, "How long do I have to look at that ugly thing?"

Although I loved the sciences, in order to comply with my academic curriculum, I ended up taking additional evening courses at the Brooklyn campus. In particular, I recall Moral Theology, taught by a crusty Jesuit Priest. Interestingly, there were also several Nuns in the class, and Fr.Hamlin seemed to take great delight in quizzing or challenging them. At one point he posed the following question, "Sister if you were held at knifepoint next to an open window by a male intruder who gave you the option of submitting to being raped or committing suicide, which would you choose?"

Several courses in Philosophy and Cosmology were taught by an affable middle-aged bald professor, who still retained a few long wisps of hair on the top. When he initially introduced himself by writing his name on the chalkboard, Mr. Curley waited for the snickering to die down before he turned around with a big smile on his face! - I thought his timing was impeccable. He was very engaging, and we often had extended conversations after class. By contrast, a young handsome Ph.D. professor taught Sociology, and, of course, all the girls sat in the first two rows swooning as he sat on the edge of his desk communing exclusively with them.

Then there was a Capuchin Friar who I thought was well-read and delivered very practical theological insight. However, he had a strange attachment or reverence for Rudyard Kipling's, lengthy poem, "The Female of the Species". Consequently, after charging everyone to memorize the poem, the first portion of the lecture was on, Theology, and the remainder was reciting the poem. In fact, the final exam entailed reciting the poem by calling on each student to pick up where the prior student left off, and no one failed the course!

Flashbacks   Being that I was much closer to my ultimate goal of attending Medical School, the Flashbacks returned with a vengeance. The same haunting dreams of recognizing my father in a familiar setting and immediately perceiving the same altered mentation that I observed as a 13-year-old. Although I wasn't plagued with the Death Scene, the basic scenario was always the same. Sometimes he appeared somewhat younger, but offering no consoling message, I interpreted his silence as a sign of compromised vulnerability, requiring my protection. This was invariably followed by the same sense of Guilt, the same Promise, and the same horrible outcome. The only variation being the different measures that I would take to ensure his protection - which I hoped, would only be apparent to me.

Wishing   My father would often say in a very convincing manner, "Listen and I'll tell you the secret!". He seemed to always be teaching a lesson and willing to share his *secrets* on a myriad of subjects to anyone who would listen. And yet, while looking at me peacefully, he never uttered a word! Was I misinterpreting the Flashbacks? Did I mistake his silence as a sign of weakness? At such a young age, the notion of *quality time* might seem irrelevant, but I would often exclaim, "What I would give for just one more day - 24 waking hours, with my father!" A unique opportunity to take heed of his counsel and hopefully learn his Secrets. To this day, when I think of my father, the poignant lyrics of Phantom's "Wishing you were here again" resonates within me.

"You were once my one companion; You were all that mattered
You were once a friend and father, Then my world was shattered
Wishing you were somehow here again, Wishing you were somehow near
Sometimes it seemed, if I just dreamed, somehow you would be here
Wishing I could hear your voice again, Knowing that I never would
Dreaming of you won't help me to do, All that you dreamed I could"

Maria   Mary and I weren't seeing much of each other lately, and now it would be even less. At some point during my first semester, I was swimming breaststroke in the campus pool and with each turn in the shallow end, I noticed a lovely pair of legs just standing against the wall. After six laps, I decided to *take a rest,* pausing long enough to take in a full view - after all, maybe she was in distress! Then she looked at me and said, "Could you help me with my Breaststroke?"

As my eyes slowly drifted upwards, I simply smiled and said, "Sure, why not" and then started to laugh. At that point, she caught the double entendre and with feigned embarrassment, she also started laughing. We briefly introduced ourselves and upon learning that her name was Maria, I immediately associated her with West Side Story - only makes sense!

Incidentally, for the second time, I thought of the familiar refrain, "I took one look at you, that's all I meant to do, and then my heart stood still".

Truth be told, however, as with my imaginary French companion, although my attraction to Maria was greatly exaggerated, I was, nonetheless, emotionally torn. I felt I could no longer weather the constant headwinds of the Trum's resistance which only added to my low self-esteem. I wanted to once again experience a relationship that was carefree and devoid of social parity. Perhaps, In some respects, I used Maria as a legitimate excuse to break-up -allowing for some much-needed distance.

In any event, I wrote Mary a long letter explaining that I had met someone with whom I wanted to spend some time. However, in keeping with the motto, "He who lives by the sword dies by the sword" I also felt the unmistakable slice from the double-edged sword of *Betrayal* which awakened in me, a profound sense of Guilt.

Although my short-lived infatuation allowed for, at least a brief respite from the constant stream of resentment. After a couple of months, however, I realized that, despite the many setbacks, my love for Mary was undeniable, and as such, I was willing to endure even more of the difficulties yet to come. In short, I don't remember how, but we apparently had a reconciliation of sorts.

Separation Anxiety   Ironically, this brief period of separation would eventually result in another disturbing recurrent dream. I would suddenly awaken startled, aware that I hadn't heard from Mary for several months - followed by the crushing realization that, while I wasn't paying attention, she had finally acquiesced to her family's wishes and quietly moved on - losing her forever! Just what I needed - another recurrent nightmare!

Sale of 8311 (1964)   Eventually, we had to face the inevitable painful reality that we had to sell our beloved, 8311 Colonial Rd. I remember there was a sense of urgency, and of not having the luxury of time in order to negotiate a fair selling price. In essence, we had to accept an offer of $34,000. I vaguely remember my mother, Mary, and I in the basement, and for whatever reason, my mother was rummaging through and discarding old photographs and memorabilia. Fortunately, however, unbeknownst to her, some of the items were subsequently retrieved, but the majority were lost forever. Consequently, as I write this memoir, I realize how helpful they would have been in order to refresh my memory.

Mrs. Moffat's Apartment (1964)   My mother's dear friend, Peggy Moffitt, owned a two-family house on 83rd St. She lived alone in the upper apartment and, knowing that we had to sell 8311, offered for us to rent her lower apartment. I don't remember much about the move, but in the Fall of 1964, we occupied the small, 2 BR 1 Bath apartment. The simple floor plan consisted of a small enclosed front sun porch, small living and dining rooms, a tiny kitchen, and a bathroom. Mom's bedroom was small and mine was even smaller! Talk about downsizing, compared to 8311, it was claustrophobic, requiring a radical spatial adjustment! But, as they say, "Beggars can't be choosy!"

However, we no sooner moved in when Rocco decided to make some structural "improvements" in our "rented" apartment. Although I don't question the nature of the improvements, true to form, he didn't have the owner's permission. The unauthorized renovations initially came to light when Mrs. Moffat's daughter came to pay a welcoming visit and was understandably aghast at the site of demolition in progress!

Al Florentino   At some point, Al Florentino and Lee came for Dinner in the "refurbished" apartment. At the time, Al was driving an awesome supercharged Oldsmobile 442 equipped with a console-mounted Hurst gear shift and Hollywood mufflers. It was an absolute Beast that accelerated like a rocket! They lived in a trendy section of Greenwich Village and when they arrived, they parked curbside two houses from our Apartment. Bob and Anita also came to join us, and we all enjoyed a wonderful dinner with lively conversation and laughing fueled by a generous supply of wine.

The hours seemed to fly, and when it was time to leave, we bid them farewell. Shortly after they left, however, we heard the doorbell ring - it was our guests! Al appeared totally bewildered, exclaiming, "I can't find my car!". At first, we thought, with all the wine, surely he must have forgotten where he parked the car. After a thorough search, however, we reluctantly accepted the impossible, that his car *might* have been stolen! - after all, this is Bay Ridge!

Being an attorney, Bob accompanied Al to the local police precinct in order to file a stolen vehicle report. However, when Al described his car to the police, they assured him that it was probably taken for a joyride and that, in due time, they would probably find the car, but most likely, not in one piece! A month later, the police finally located the car with considerable damage.

Rocco and Carol's Wedding (May 1965)   Rocco and Carol were married in May of 1965 in a private civil ceremony, witnessed by his best man, Bob Hartman, and Anita, as a bridesmaid. At a later date, a relatively small reception party was held for the immediate family at the Midtown Hotel in Manhattan where Rocco was hired as the manager in their catering facility.

Nancy with the Laughing Face   After we moved into Mrs. Moffitt's downstairs Apartment, I would occasionally take a break from studying by sitting on the front stoop, either reading or just daydreaming. It was on such an occasion that I first noticed a young college girl, Nancy Gilbride, who lived two houses away. I soon learned that she was the oldest sibling of a large family and that her father was a prominent law professor. I remember seeing her several more times, but we never spoke.

Incidentally, my childhood friend, Chris Gruening, lived next to the Gilbrides and knew the entire family quite well, and I was taken aback when, several months later, he mentioned that Nancy was inquiring about me. I was stunned, however, when he said, he offered to arrange a "Double-blind date" with Nancy and his new girlfriend, Mandy! Although I experienced a prior disastrous "blind date" that I swore I would never repeat, I reluctantly agreed - what the hell was I thinking?

In mid-August of 1965, Anita and Bob were away in California and I was in the middle of painting their house on Cromwell Hill Rd. On a bright sunny morning, while in the midst of painting, I received a call from Chris saying that we were on for the "Double-blind date!". After quickly washing, I borrowed Bob's brown, Ford convertible, and with great trepidation, I raced down to meet Chris and Mandy and the three of us drove to Mary Mount College to pick up Nancy. From there Chris suggested that we head for Hyde Park.

While driving I was perplexed why I was having such difficulty seeing until Nancy commented that my dark sunglasses were heavily speckled with white paint - quite debonair! Although she was sitting in the front seat, being that we were driving with the top down, it made it very difficult to have any meaningful conversation with either of the "blind dates".

While touring FDR's homestead, Chris was his usual crazy self, and although Nancy put on a fixed, Mona Lisa, smile, I sensed that she wasn't having a very good time. At some point, to hopefully lighten her mood, I affectionately referred to her as," Nancy with the laughing face" (A beautiful Sinatra Ballard). However, judging by her bewildered expression, I realized that the unwitting phrase would require a very long explanation!

After touring FDR's homestead, we drove to a small Italian restaurant for an inexpensive dinner, which allowed for polite conversation and introducing her to Manicotti. Then after dropping Chris and Mandy off, I drove Nancy back to College. After a brief tour of the campus, she suggested that we stroll down to a quiet secluded pond and I thought "Ah, alone at last!"

The pond was very picturesque, with pretty flowering water lilies covering much of the pond's perimeter, and with the full moon reflecting off the placid water, I thought, "This is perfect!" Then, while sitting comfortably on the pond's stone wall perimeter, l began to notice periodic whiffs of a particularly foul odor. Fearing that perhaps it was due to her lactose intolerance, I initially chose to ignore the awful smell. In time, however, it became progressively more pronounced causing me to almost choke. While swimming in Walton Lake, I was certainly familiar with water lilies, but I'd never known them to stink to high heaven.

Although I'm sure she must have smelled the same horrific odor, lacking a plausible explanation, we both pretended not to notice. The smell eventually became so overpowering that I almost gagged and couldn't concentrate on formulating appropriate answers to her questions. I finally surrendered by saying, "I have a long drive home!" With that, we parted company and never saw each other again. Following this near catastrophic event, upon further inquiry, someone offered that perhaps the smell was from a variety of the dreaded, Skunk Cabbage plant.

Summer of 65   For a change, Mary accepted a summer job working for A&S. So, naturally, our time together was once again very limited. The gradual Greek transition accelerated, requiring additional Greek-speaking employees. I seem to remember that the summer season was relatively uneventful. Carol became increasingly more involved with the weekend operations at the Lodge, strategically positioning herself at the doorway as food trays exited the kitchen and reconciling the duplicate checks. Donna and her cousin, Denice, mostly spent the weekdays at Bulls concession stand, only coming up to the Lodge on occasional weekends.

Donna's Wedding (Aug. 1970)   One summer afternoon, I was briefly introduced to Donna's boyfriend, Frank Schaffield, at the Lodge. Being that he was 6'7" and she was only 5'2" I thought, "What an incongruous pair - more like *The Odd Couple!*". Then, I didn't hear anything further until July of 1970, when I was notified that she and Frank intended to get married in August. Although I was very happy for her, I was also hurt that, despite our long history together, I didn't receive an invitation to their wedding. Given their current financial situation, I would have readily accepted not being invited to the reception, but not even to the church? In any event, although I never received the courtesy of an explanation, we remain the closest of friends and I love both of them dearly.

CH - 37
SENIOR YEAR

There was finally light at the end of the tunnel, but the anticipation of the Medical school application process was now a looming reality. I remember studying in my small apartment bedroom, preparing for the dreaded, MCAT exam! I took the lengthy exam in a huge auditorium in the Grand Army Plaza in Brooklyn N.Y.. In the past, I never fared very well with multiple-choice exams, and I had no reason to believe that this would be any different.

Our apartment was next to a dentist, Dr. Brancaccio, the father of my neighborhood friends, Mike, and Lyn. Knowing of my ambitions, he would occasionally ask me how I was doing, always reassuring me that I would surely be accepted to Medical School. Regrettably, I never discussed my fears and concerns about the application process. In hindsight, in addition to Dr. Weiser, I could have asked for advice or letters of recommendation from several neighborhood physicians, including Eddie's father, Dr. D'Onofrio, or my former neighbor, Dr. Hubbard. Naively, I never considered this important and the wizard, Dr. Medici, never even mentioned it.

Once again, I sought Dean Volansky's cooperation by authorizing me to take more than 20 credits, and with the Wizard's strong recommendation, I took another elective, Physical Chemistry. However, due to my stellar math background, it relied heavily on Calculus - what a bear! I struggled the entire semester and somehow, squeaked by with a C+.

Med School Applications Unfortunately, I didn't start the application process until mid-April which, by any standard, was extremely late. The average number of credits necessary for graduation was roughly 128 and to date, I had already accumulated over 145 credits. In addition to the mounting debt, rather than getting A and B+ grades, I ranged between C+ and A+. The moral of the story - it would have been far better to have taken fewer credits with the probability of achieving higher grades!

Also, in addition to the accumulation of impressive courses, and without regard to my overall GPA and MCAT scores, the Wizard had me applying to the finest medical schools in the country! In short, his only meaningful advice was, "Be prepared to explain why you want to be a Doctor and how you plan to pay for Medical School!

In early June, anticipating that a passport photo would be required to accompany my applications, I had a picture taken of me standing against the white exterior clapboard of Mary's summer house. However, being that it was partially shaded by a nearby tree, and I already had a dark suntan, it produced a very dark photograph. Furthermore, I sabotaged myself further by volunteering that, my father was deceased, and I was the youngest of 7 children.

Needless to say, I began receiving my *acceptance* letters with the salutation, "We regret to inform you!" With each subsequent letter, my heart sunk, and a sense of despair took hold. Although I was "waitlisted" at the University of Cincinnati School of Medicine, by mid-July, I began applying to B and C schools. Also, knowing that Mary's mother was very intelligent and highly educated, I sought her assistance in reviewing my Applications.

She quickly pointed out that, when asked about my Nationality, I indicated, Italian and regarding my mother's occupation, I stated that she was, Domestic. So, in addition to my marginal grades and MCAT scores, I became ruefully aware that, from all appearances, I was a poor black Italian from a large family with a deceased father and a widowed mother whose lowly occupation was as a Domestic. Had I applied to Howard University; I surely would have qualified as a minority candidate!

Feeling totally dejected, I reached out to our Monroe neighbor, Jerry Kowell MD, who reassured me that I would eventually be accepted to a Medical school. I had no idea what he was basing this on and thought, "Maybe he's clairvoyant!". He was so sure that he even gave me a huge steamer trunk in order to ship my clothes, books, etc. to the lucky school of my choice.

In retrospect, my world view was terribly myopic in that, I never even considered applying to European medical schools such as Italy or Mexico - especially considering my mastery of Spanish. Likewise, the Wizard never mentioned foreign schools, whether in Europe or elsewhere, such as Grenada or St Thomas. Furthermore, being that I'd never even flown in an airplane, the very thought of traveling across the Atlantic ocean seemed incomprehensibly far from home and loved ones.

Incidentally, during my training at St Barnabas Medical Center, I forged lifelong friendships with four American Residents, all of whom attended various Medical schools in Italy.- and they loved it!

Osteopathy   Then, in the depths of despair, I ran into a fellow classmate, Harvey Green, at the Jamaica campus. He was very excited exclaiming, "I'm as happy as a Lark! I've been accepted to COMS (College of Osteopathic Medicine and Surgery) in Des Moines Iowa. I had absolutely no idea what Osteopathy was, let alone, any Osteopathic physicians!

After briefly researching the mysterious profession, and feeling that I had nothing to lose, I requested applications from both the Des Moines and Philadelphia Osteopathic colleges. The application process required letters of recommendation from three Osteopathic Physicians, one of whom would be assigned to provide an initial oral interview. I was surprised when my Aunt Mae informed me that we had an elderly *cousin*, Joe Pelletiere DO, who was an Osteopath in Sheepshead Bay, .

I immediately made an appointment to see our *cousin* and I was very impressed with his gracious encouragement. After giving me a brief overview of the origin, and Holistic *philosophy* of Osteopathy, he supplied me with several articles and books. They explained in more detail the differences and advantages of Osteopathy(DO) compared to Allopathathy(MD)- which I committed to memory.

At the time, there were only five Osteopathic Medical schools, and after reviewing the material in great detail, I considered Osteopathy in a much different light - providing an opportunity of *choice*, rather than a last resort. Then I sought Dr. Weiser's input, and after reviewing the four year curriculum, when I asked for his opinion, he said humorously, "Why? I have no intention of switching!" Then, however, he offered that he knew of an Osteopathic general surgeon, Jerry Rosenblatt DO, currently an Attending at Leroy hospital in Manhattan, and he very kindly arranged for an interview.

During our brief meeting, I learned that Dr. Rosenblatt was the Chief of Surgery at Leroy and coincidentally, also a graduate of Des Moines College. At the time, Leroy was considered a prestigious Osteopathic hospital, frequently treating such notables as Nelson Rockefeller and Jackie Onassis -thereby dispelling any preconceived notion of voodoo medicine.

The third Osteopath was located on 79th St. and Fourth Avenue. He was a former graduate of the Kirksville College and coincidentally, a designated Interviewing Physician. Apparently, I must have impressed him with my recent interest and knowledge of Osteopathic Medicine, because shortly afterward, I received an invitation for an interview at the Des Moines College.

COMS Interview (June 1966) It would be my first time flying and being that there were no direct flights nor jet service to Des Moines, it would require changing planes in Chicago, to a DC-3 prop aircraft to Des Moines. I remember borrowing Bob Hartman's suit for the interview, and my uncle Bass driving my mother, Anita, and me to JFK airport for the grand send-off.

Prior to departure, however, we noticed a ground attendant surveying the aircraft and kicking the tires, at which point uncle Bass said, "Oh, that's a bad sign, the left one looks a little flat!" - just what I wanted to hear! While walking up the gangway, I was so nervous, I don't even remember saying goodbye to anyone. During the flight from Chicago to Des Moines, we experienced tremendous turbulence. Fortunately, there were very few passengers in the small cabin, and for safety reasons, we were all moved forward to the "First-class" section - which required stepping over a small hump in the center aisle!

After arriving safely, I experienced another first -staying overnight in a small Motel, which was two blocks from the College. Bob cautioned me to hang the suit neatly overnight and ask for a wake-up call in order to ensure that I arrived on time for the interview. After a fitful night's sleep, while getting dressed in the morning, I noticed the suit was a little *snug*, especially in the crotch area, which immediately triggered a flashback of the Vickie fiasco.

Dressed in my borrowed suit, I walked briskly down to the College, which was an unimpressive five-story white building. I remember waiting nervously in the anteroom alone, mentally rehearsing "The history and scope of Osteopathy". Then the moment of truth finally arrived. After being introduced to the committee members, I was instructed to sit across from them at a large oval conference table. As I cautiously sat down, I noticed a familiar *tug* in the crotch area followed by a discernible *give* in the seam. This caused me to break out in a cold sweat, anticipating the even more ominous, audible "tear"!

The interview panel consisted of the Dean of Academic Affairs, Michael Barry, a Psychologist, several faculty physicians, and the revered anatomist, Dr. Marianas Ph.D., whose claim to fame was inventing a wintergreen scented formaldehyde solution for preserving the cadavers. The senior faculty members fondly remembered Dr. Rosenblatt and commented on his glowing letter of recommendation. They were equally impressed that I *knew him personally!* - a notion I wasn't about to dispel.

Among the many non-pertinent questions, the psychologist asked, "How many children would you like to have?" Somewhat flustered, I said, "Although I hadn't given it much thought, coming from a large happy family, I would be blessed to have five children". Hearing that, he immediately countered with, "How do you reconcile that with the global crisis overpopulation?" Thankfully, before I had a chance to manufacture a response, Mr. Barry, chimed in by saying, "I think there are far more pressing issues in the world than speculating about his procreation!"

Then, with a very thick accent, Dr. Marianas asked, "What's your favorite poem?" Being fond of poetry and surmising that he was Greek, somehow I pulled an answer out of my back pocket (ass) saying, "Bryant's, Thanatopsis - meaning a meditation on death", and he appeared both surprised and delighted. Following the interview, I was given a brief tour of the College, especially the gross anatomy lab, which was my first exposure to a cadaver! Dr. Marianas took great pride in pointing out the obvious pungent wintergreen aroma of his anatomy lab. Following the tour, I was emotionally drained and anxious to return home without further delay,

I caught the next flight out of Des Moines, and I was thankfully spared a repeat of the hair raising turbulence on the outbound flight. I remember that I hadn't eaten while in Des Moines, and having fallen fast asleep, I missed the food service. On my bus ride back to Brooklyn, I remember feeling proud that I had accomplished this "daring journey" halfway across the continent!

Fr. Trainor   Another potential hurdle was that most of the Medical schools expected that you would have attained at least a bachelor's degree, prior to admission. With this in mind, I went to see the Dean of the University, Fr. Trainor, who also taught Thomistic Theology, which I thoroughly enjoyed. Considering that we would often spar in class, followed by extended discussions afterward, I felt confident that, by now, he knew me well. After reviewing my academic transcripts he said, "Although it's very commendable that you will have accumulated 156 credits in four years, you failed to complete your last semester of Spanish!"

Despite explaining that I followed my pre-med advisor's advice and the importance of a Bachelor's degree for admission to Medical school, he remained steadfast, refusing to waive the second semester of Spanish! My profound disappointment must have been very apparent because he reluctantly made what he considered to be a very generous concession. That he would accept completing the second semester at another University, provided I received a C or better.

For expediency, this would require summer school, and considering that I hadn't taken Spanish in two years, I knew this option was very unlikely. Besides, my college tuition debt had ballooned to over $20,000 - admittedly, a mere pittance by today's standards. As a result, I reconciled that, after accumulating 156 credits with majors in Biology and Chemistry and a minor in Philosophy, I still didn't have a Bachelor's degree and wouldn't be graduating with my class. But what the hell, it's only a piece of paper!

With this major setback, I went to see Dean Volansky and pleaded my case. After a long sigh, while shaking his and shrugging his shoulders, he explained that, although he was the Dean of the Law School, Fr. Trainor was the Dean of the University's Downtown Campus, and as such, he was *the boss.* Obviously disappointed, I shared my disheartened soul with my mentor.

I explained how I was always torn between Medicine and Law. And, although I greatly admired my father as a well-respected Attorney, for personal reasons, I also felt committed to hopefully become a Physician. However, in light of the current situation, perhaps it was a sign for me to reconsider my professional options. After a very long pause, he said, "Since you were a freshman, I've admired your perseverance!" Then, I was blown away when he offered to admit me to the Law school in the Fall - in effect, waiving the LSAT exam!

Then, in the midst of my darkest despair, a small ray of hope arrived in the mail with the shocking salutation, "Greetings, I'm pleased to inform you that you have been accepted for the fall class at the Des Moines, College of Osteopathic Medicine and Surgery (COMS). Now I was faced with two dilemmas, and time being of the essence, I had to make two difficult decisions. Considering that I was still on the waiting list for a *Real* Medical School in Cincinnati, do I accept the proverbial bird in hand, or do I gamble?. Do I base my future on the nontraditional and relatively unknown College of Osteopathy, or do I take a position in a well-known and respected school of Law?

Considering that, if I chose, Des Moines, it would mean a prolonged period of separation from everyone I loved, I felt I had to share this conundrum with Mary. I clearly remember the two of us sitting in the Green Hornet parked along Shore Road. We talked for a couple of hours, carefully weighing the pros and cons. When all was said and done, however, knowing of my paternal *reverence*, Mary summarized her perspective very succinctly. While looking into my eyes she said, "If you choose Law school, you will forever chase the ghost of your father, never achieving the desired outcome. Instead, trust that by charting your own future course, you'll find happiness and satisfaction" With that said, I felt my path was clear!

For me, the most distressing issue was the prospect of abject loneliness, being separated from her for such an extended period of time. I think subconsciously, I was fearful that the distance would more likely materialize my terrifying dreams. That I would suddenly realize that, in my absence, she had acquiesced to her family's wishes, and simply *moved on!*

PCOM Interview Shortly afterward, I received a letter from the Philadelphia College of Osteopathy (PCOM) inviting me for an interview - the allure being the close proximity of Philadelphia. Once again I borrowed Bob's suit and he offered to drive me down to Philadelphia for a 9 am interview.

Being that we left in his Ford Fairlane convertible fashionably late, it prompted him to declare, "Now let's see what this baby can do!". We raced down the NJ Turnpike at 90 mph and while negotiating a sharp exit at high speed, Bob managed to hit the curb with his tire, bending the left front A-frame, causing the tire to bend inwardly. Pressed for time, however, we continued driving through the city streets of Philadelphia on the bent frame. Despite power steering, Bob's face turned red while trying to negotiate the street corners. As we drove on a constant tilt, the smoke and noxious fumes of rubber burning trailed close behind. The constant grinding of the outer margin of the tire continued until the rim was fully exposed - you can't make this shit up!.

Needless to say, despite a valiant effort, we arrived on a bare metal rim 40 minutes late - not a good first impression! There was only one other candidate waiting to be interviewed which allowed for a brief conversation. He offered that, because his initial attempts to gain admission were unsuccessful, he persevered by ultimately attaining a Master's degree in Virology! I thought, "Thanks to Fr. Trainor, I didn't even have a Bachelor's degree!" Being that I was the last applicant to be interviewed, I was emotionally drained, and the panel appeared tired as well. So, I didn't even bother to explain why I was late. Besides, they wouldn't have believed it anyway!

Consequently, the interview was relatively brief and thankfully, no tours were offered. Not surprisingly, I only received a *waitlist* status. So, with Des Moines's acceptance deadline looming, and the only other prospects being two *waitlists*, the handwriting was on the wall, and I decided to accept Des Moines offer.

The Next Hurdle The next hurdle was to beg for personal loans from family members, starting with the ones I felt could most easily afford it. My mother immediately thought of her sister, Lee's husband, Tom Antonice. Uncle Tom had a very successful real estate title search company. He always drove the latest model Cadillac, and they lived in a beautiful upscale home in a very desirable section of Bridgeport Ct. According to my mother, he could well afford it and I thought, "If I could borrow the entire amount from one person, it would make life so much easier"

Uncle Tom   So, my mother and I anxiously drove to Bridgeport to visit, Uncle Tom. After a brief visit, he said, "You wanted to see me, young man? Let's go into my Study". While we both sat in his plush Study, I seized the opportunity by briefly mentioning my aspirations and current financial dilemma. After listening to how fortunate he's been as a result of his hard work, he asked me what I wanted to talk to him about. I was initially taken aback thinking, "Surely, the purpose of my visit was either implied or self-evident!". Regardless, I proceeded to rc- explain that I was asking for a "loan". Then he muttered, "How much do you need?" When I told him, $1200 for the first year's tuition, his mouth just remained open for a long time.

Realizing his apparent shock, I quickly said, "But I promise to start repaying the loan after I graduate! After another long pause, he eventually closed his mouth, coughed several times, and said, "Young man, I'm not in a position to loan such a large amount on a dream!". I thought, "Talk about a dream. There goes the notion of a single benefactor!" Then when I said, "If you can loan me $300, I'll ask three other people for the balance," I was shocked when he declined saying, "If you get the other $900, come back to see me and we'll talk again" I didn't want to embarrass my mother, so I waited until we were in the car. After telling her of his response, It was a long quiet drive home, and my heart acked witnessing her devastating embarrassment.

Uncle Tony   Next on the list was my aunt Mae's husband, Uncle Tony Agolia. He was a successful banker who owned a modest two-family brownstone, living in the upper apartment while renting the lower apartment. They never had children and lived a very comfortable life. He always managed to have a few crisp singles in his pocket and would ingratiate himself by occasionally slipping me one with the familiar admonition, "Now, spend it wisely!" In my case, it was the same single at age 18 as it was at 10! Aunt Mae was my father's only living sibling, and this time I chose to see both uncle Tony and Aunt Mae alone.

After I arrived, I thanked her for her encouragement and referred me to our mutual *cousin*, Dr. Pellittieri.DO. Then uncle Tony asked to talk with me alone - maybe Uncle Tom called to warn him! After some small talk, I explained that I would like to "loan" $300, which I promised to repay shortly after graduation. Again, I was shocked when he said that he couldn't afford such a large amount, and never even offered a lesser amount - at least he didn't pull out "the single!"

Caesar With two strikeouts, I had to resort to my siblings. Although this was uncharted waters, I was pleasantly surprised at how painless each of them made this humiliating ordeal. At the time, I felt that Rocco was in no position to loan money, so I turned to Caesar. Although he was only a fledgling lawyer, without hesitation he immediately wrote out a check for $300.

However, this wasn't the first time that he bailed me out. Once, while driving the Green Hornet home on the Gowanus Expressway, I was involved in a minor fender bender with a doctor's shiny black Cadillac. When we each got out of our cars to assess the damages, he was understandably very upset when he noticed a small scape and a minor dent on his Cadillac. I immediately countered by pointing to the extensive damage his car must have inflicted on my precious vehicle.

By now, the minor collision was tying up traffic, and being tired and totally exasperated, he threw up his hands, suggesting that we exchange any pertinent information. Then, before leaving he said, "I'll call you with a repair estimate". Since the Hornet wasn't worth the price of a policy. I didn't carry collision insurance which I naively considered, a reprieve. After a couple of days, however, I was surprised when the doctor called with a repair estimate of $150.

When I called Caesar for legal advice and described the particulars of the accident, he said, "It's very simple, you have to pay it!". Although, he wasn't very happy when I told him that I didn't have the money, the following day he came over to 8311 and wrote out the check, sparing me a well-deserved lecture about responsibility".

Nick and Lou Harring   Next, I drove out to Nick's apartment in Douglaston Long Island and explained my situation. I felt awful asking him because he had two children and was struggling as an apprentice in the electrician's union. Maybe I caught him after he smoked some pot, because without interrogation, he said he would send me a check for $300 within the week.

Now I was on a roll. So, next, I went to see Virginia's husband, Lou Harring. He was financially stable, and as a brilliant electrical engineer, he had a fond appreciation for all forms of scholastic endeavors. Besides, I figured if he was willing to pay for Butch the Dog's burial, what's $300! He immediately wrote out a check for $300. At the time, I felt that my other siblings were financially strapped and therefore, I was at a loss for a fourth benefactor.

Papa Datre   Out of desperation, I went to see my mother's stepfather, Papa Datre. He was a Truant officer by profession, and I came to know him, because he would frequently stop by around noon to visit my mother. While walking home for lunch, I would occasionally notice his black car parked in front of the house. Upon entering the kitchen, he would always greet me, "Peter boy, I'm here on official business to make sure that you went to school!"

By this time, my Grandmother had passed away and he lived alone in their small Brooklyn apartment. He greeted me warmly with his familiar salutation, "Peter Boy, come on in!". I felt he was probably living on a fixed income and financially, the least able to help me. But being desperate, I would've been grateful for any contribution. However when I explained my ultimate goal, I was taken aback by his generous offer, writing out a check for the remaining $300. I had calculated that $1200 would hopefully cover my early living expenses and anticipated that the tuition would be covered by accruing additional federal student loans.

I promised each of my generous benefactors that I would repay the loans as soon as possible after graduating from Medical School.

Accordingly, during my internship, I began the slow process of repaying each of them in $300 lump sums. Ironically, however, Papa Datre was the only one who absolutely refused the repayment saying, "It was a gift!"

Solicitation At some point, Rocco invited me to his and Carol's apartment in Queens, in order to "discuss" the upcoming summer season at the Lodge. I listened intently as he proposed a bold plan to hire (steel) the top Greek entertainers away from the Monte Carlo. In essence, he was "doubling-down" on his commitment to draw the Greeks away from the famous Hotel. For the first time, I had the distinct impression that my singular allegiance was being solicited.

In many respects, I was flattered that he was sharing this ambitious plan with his youngest brother! I suspect that my pride wouldn't acknowledge that, I was perhaps the only one who would agree to such a gamble. He laid out his bold plan that entailed hiring the George Stratus Orchestra, as well as the famous, Trio Bel Canto! He rationalized that, although the total weekend entertainment expenses were estimated to be, $7,000, we should more than cover that with the enhanced revenue.

In any event, his plan came to fruition and now the task was to hire the appropriate amount of staff, the great majority of which were Greek. We hired a total of 15 waiters and 3 front bartenders - all Greek-speaking. I felt confident that, while he managed the Hotel, Kitchen and Entertainment, I could handle the Service bar and manage the Front bar by ensuring strict adherence to my *liquor monitoring system*. Also, since switching to the more professional Dupe system, we would have far better control of the nightly receipts.

Summer of 66 Carol continued to be very involved in the business, especially on weekends, ensuring the collection of all cash receipts. At some point, her brother, Jack, also came to visit on weekends. I knew Jack from when we were kids in Monroe, and I was aware that he had considerable business experience, managing a successful ski shop on Long Island. Although I was initially open to his suggestions, in time it became apparent that he had no experience with the Bar business. I also sensed that, from a management perspective, I was gradually being displaced! Not physically, but more importantly, regarding my experience and lifelong dedication.

Although I readily acquiesced to my brother's control of the finances, I felt that, with his tacit approval, even the Bar operations, which were always my sole domain, were being encroached upon. It seemed as though my experience, loyalty and opinions were no longer relevant -relegated to a mere employee. By mid-season, I shared my personal humiliation with Anita, but sadly, she had nothing to offer.

Towards the end of the summer, I became increasingly aware that we were constantly hounded by creditors, and ultimately relegated to COD status. I couldn't fathom how, with such a seemingly robust business, we were perpetually without sufficient funds. Perplexed, at some point, I asked Rocco to see *The books*. At first, he blew me off by saying, "You wouldn't know what you were looking at!" Readily acknowledging this, I asked, "Then, maybe you could explain them to me?". When I asked a second time, he finally got the books, and without offering to help, threw them on the table in front of me saying, "Here's the books, have fun!" While spending hours trying to make sense of them, sadly he remained conspicuously absent.

The dreadful season finally ended with Rocco saying to my mother and me, "Pay whoever screams the loudest!" and drove off into the Maine sunset, avoiding the onslaught of creditors and bringing his eight-year tenure to an abrupt end. While memorializing these events served as a sort of therapeutic catharsis, and although they were very painful, I carry no malice whatsoever, for I love them dearly to this day.

1958 Olds (The Beast)   As the summer drew to a close, anticipating that I would eventually drive out to Des Moines, I purchased a 1958 Oldsmobile for $150 from my tips. Before the purchase, however, I brought the car to Don Lucas' service station in town. After looking under the hood he said, "Although you have a four-barrel carburetor, the engine was originally designed to accommodate a second four-barrel!" He installed a second four-barrel carburetor at no charge which made the car a potential, gas-guzzling *Beast,* especially when opening the second carburetor by flooring it!

I remember test driving the Beast on the long straightaway between Monroe and Greenwood Lake, well known for drag racing. Just to test it, when I suddenly floored it, while the rear tires screeched releasing the pungent odor of burning rubber, the Beast vibrated violently, but didn't budge! And when simulating a passing situation, the result was much the same. Apparently, given the condition of the bald *snow tires,* the sudden power of the engine didn't allow for sufficient traction. So, I decided to mostly limit the Beast to a single carburetor.

The Umanskys My childhood friends, Howard, and Philip Umansky were both Black Belts in Karate. For some reason, I asked them to give me a *crash course* in the essentials of Karate. First and foremost, they emphasized that Karate was intended solely for self-defense! They gave me daily lessons and drills for two weeks, and before leaving for Iowa, as a parting gift they gave me a pictured textbook demonstrating all the maneuvers, training exercises and drills - for which I am eternally grateful.

CH - 38
COMS FRESHMAN YEAR

Now that the Labor Day weekend was over and the dreadful summer of 66 was history, it was time for me to leave for Des Moines and begin a new chapter of many unknowns - an unfamiliar midwestern city, school, and profession. I had pre-arranged to room and board in the Phi Sigma Gamma (PSG) Fraternity house at 3200 Grand Ave. I had packed as much as I could in Jerry Kowal's trunk and had it delivered to the house in advance of my arrival. Fraternity

The thought of prolonged separation from all the people I loved was depressing and unnerving, to say the least. I felt terrible abandoning my Mother in such a state of financial turmoil. I delayed my departure until the last possible moment and ironically, I don't remember how or when I said goodbye to my Mother or Mary. Nor do I remember the flight to Des Moines. When I asked Mary about this unusual lapse of memory, she told me that she accompanied Bob and Anita to the JFK airport to see me off. Strangely, however, even upon hearing this, it didn't jog my memory and still doesn't now!

Incidentally, earlier in June, I applied to a Medical College in Kingston, Jamaica. This was in part due to Anita and Bob's recent vacation trip to the beautiful island of Jamaica. They were accompanied by two very dear friends and loyal patrons, Bill, and Betty Munroe. Apparently, they all had an absolute blast and their description of the Caribbean Island was very alluring, and only 3 hrs. away! Much to my surprise, I was placed on their waiting list. Periodically, I would inquire about the status of my application, even after I arrived in Des Moines.

PSG   My next recollection was of arriving at the large Fraternity House and discovering that my trunk hadn't arrived yet!. Fortunately, I brought one large suitcase in which I had the bare essentials for at least a week. I was readily welcomed by the upperclassmen. However, being the last student to arrive, I was shown to the only available room on the third floor of the brick Mansion. I would be sharing the large room with two other freshmen, Carlos Corrales, an immigrant from Cuba and Jim Eustis, a pharmacist who was the only black student in the school. I thought, "Being of Italian descent, it was like the League of Nations!"

I must admit, although just about every other student had either a private or double room, ours seemed spacious enough and overlooked, St Joseph's Academy (SJA), a private Girls High School, directly across the street, on an absolutely beautiful gated Campus. Iowa had basically two seasons, summer, and winter, and both were brutal. Being that it was now September and my trunk containing my bed linens, towels, and a blanket, were in the trunk, I slept on a bare mattress without covers until it finally arrived 10 days later.

In due time I was introduced to four other third floor students. Another pharmacist, Sig Kulessa, and his roommate, Dick McGrath shared an adjacent room, while both Don Gross and Joe Esposito had small private rooms down the hall. Initially, Carlos, Sig, and Joe comprised my inner nucleus of close friends with both Carlos and Sig remaining very close even to this day. Two other students, Chuck Ressinger and Bob Krause, both of whom were privileged to have large private rooms on the second floor, eventually became part of the outer nucleus.

3200 Grand Ave.   3200 Grand Ave was "Home" to 18 Freshman and 12 upperclassmen, most of whom had single rooms. There was a large Living room which also served as a Meeting room. The large Dining room was arranged with rows of long tables and chairs and It didn't take long before everyone settled into *their chairs*. The large commercial Kitchen was staffed by Francis (Fran), the cook - a loveable black woman who was only responsible for preparing dinners and treated all of us as *Family*. However, being that I had no prior exposure to Fraternity or Boarding house living, this was totally foreign to me.

After retrieving a tray, a drink, and utensils, Fran would dish out food *cafeteria-style,* through a large opening to theDining room. When finished, we'd clean the tables and carry our trays into the kitchen, rotating regularly for KP duty. Breakfast was *continental style,* consisting of coffee, juice, bagels, and donuts and then, out the door, carpooling to school. Strangely, I don't remember if, or where we ate lunch at school. The Basement was an expansive solid structure that housed a full-length bar easily accommodating crowded parties as well as PSG meetings - of course, followed by a party! It was also the designated safety area upon hearing the tornado sirens - of course, followed by a party!

Both the second and third floors had a single Bathroom and shower at the end of their respective hallways, which were cleaned weekly on a rotating basis. Although each floor had a pay Phone, it was standard courtesy to limit calls to 10 minutes, And due to time constraints, there were rarely any incoming calls. My phone calls to my mother were always disguised as, "A collect call from Peter", indicating that I had arrived safely. But other than a call from Mary every three weeks, I don't remember receiving any other calls from home or my siblings.

I still tease my wife regarding her *scented* letters, which were initially three or four pages long. Over time, however, the size of her script gradually increased while the number of pages and frequency, steadily decreased, but I still longed to receive them! Likewise, although the frequency of Mary's calls hadn't changed much, since she had similar constraints at St Elizabeth, I assume the brevity and lack of privacy was equally frustrating.

Despite living in the midst of all these students, most of the time I felt alone and lonely. I was so homesick, that when my trunk finally arrived, I didn't totally unpack it for at least a month - still hoping against hope for a favorable response from the beautiful island of Jamaica !

Dahls Shortly after arrival, we were told that the first order of business was to establish local credit. We were directed to go to Dahls Supermarket, located a few blocks away, which provided free check cashing services for COMS students. This was initially confusing, because the locals referred to our school by its former name, Still College of Osteopathy. Dahls also had an old fashion counter service which Sig and I would often frequent on Sunday mornings.

My usual Sunday morning routine would be to walk to the local Catholic church, which was four blocks away, and then meet Sig at Dahls for breakfast. Our waitress of choice, and possibly the only waitress, was Nan. We both enjoyed her friendly mid-western cordiality, and in due time she came to appreciate our warped sense of humor. Consequently, she always took care of us, by offering us portions much larger than we paid for!

Orientation The first week of orientation was a stark reality check, portending the rigors that lay ahead. I still remember the initial *sticker shock* in the college bookstore when I wrote my first check for over $300 ! Of course, many of the professors insisted that we purchase *their* required textbooks, which I suspect were priced according to weight. Just carrying Gray's Anatomy was ample exercise! Unfortunately, as with my OCD compulsion to underline in red and highlight in yellow, rendered my textbooks non-resalable.

During the first week, we were issued our spiffy White Jackets which, along with casual dress pants and a shirt and tie, were required at all times. We quickly acclimated to our course curriculum which, including labs, I estimated to be the equivalent of 32 credits per semester - and I thought 22 credits was a lot! The major freshman courses included a full year of Gross Anatomy, Biochemistry, Pharmacology, Neuroanatomy, Physical Medicine and Rehabilitation (PM&R), Microbiology, Physical Diagnosis and Osteopathic Manipulative Therapy (OMT).

Culture Shock   Eventually, I ventured "Downtown" and experienced my second shock. Coming from Brooklyn, Des Moines was definitely a *culture shock,* to say the least. Granted, I was now in the Midwest, but I guess I expected more from a Capital city. There were no hot dog stands or Pizza counters. For that matter, Pizza was nowhere to be found, and it wasn't until junior year that a Pizza Hut opened in Des Moines.

The supermarkets didn't carry mozzarella, Ricotta cheese or spaghetti sauce. After complaining several times, my mother eventually sent me two jars of Ragu sauce which, unfortunately, turned out to be a disaster for me as well as the poor postman! - discussed in detail elsewhere. The sprawling Drake University campus was within walking distance and Mercy hospital was only a short drive away.

Hazing   COMS had two competing Fraternities, composed of students with different religious persuasions. Phi Sigma Gamma was primarily Christian and Sigma Sigma Phi, primarily Jewish. In addition to an overall competitive atmosphere, the rivalry between the two fraternities was intense. In mid-October, the recruitment and subsequent hazing process for each fraternity began in earnest. Ironically, our fraternity house had an unusual mixture of both Christians and Jews. Consequently, the efforts of both fraternities to solicit members provided for an interesting interplay of personalities and religious allegiances, but eventually, the lines of demarcation became well defined.

I still remember *most* of the stag party hosted by PSG, in the Mansion's Basement. The invitation was open to all freshmen, regardless of religious persuasion and it turned out to be an absolute bash! Towards the end of the evening, I remember Sig pushing me up the backstairs to the third floor. When we finally reached the third-floor corridor, I heard Sig say, "OH shit, Jim put a padlock on the door!" Infuriated, I wobbled away from the door, turned around and delivered a perfectly executed karate kick at the lock, causing the door to fling open. The rest of the evening remains blank until dealing with the agony of the following morning. Incidentally, Jim Eustis never said a word!

During the hazing period it was impossible to avoid the ongoing pressure to join the PSG Fraternity. It was no surprise that virtually all of the Christians in the Mansion joined PSG, while most of the non-Christians joined Sigma Sigma Phi (SSP). Before the induction ceremony, I remember being lined and blindfolded before descending to the Basement. Following a series of nonsensical questions and tasks, we all took the Fraternal oath - followed, of course, by a party! This inevitable shakeout caused a further competitive atmosphere within the Mansion. prompting many of the SSP members to eventually leave during the following Christmas break. Incidentally, many of the students also seized the break as an opportunity to get married.

Freshman Class Our freshman class began with 110 students of which, only 73 graduated. Approximately 15% of the students were prior pharmacists and 30% were either married or became married by sophomore year. There were only two female students who weren't necessarily attractive. considering the options, however, by Senior year they didn't look quite so bad!

During the fall, I was asked to send home some pictures of our Medical School. Being somewhat embarrassed by the 5 story white cement building, I took pictures from my third-floor window of the beautiful Campus grounds surrounding St. Joseph Academy. Ironically, however, It must've had a premonition because in 1972, two years after our graduation, our school acquired the girls Academy and the sprawling, 22-acre campus for their New Medical School.

25th Class Reunion (1995) In early spring of 1995 I was solicited to become involved with the Alumni Association's appeal for a 25th class reunion to be held at the *New Medical School,* renamed Des Moines University Osteopathic Medical Center, located on the former SJA campus. Consequently, during the summer, I personally called as many of my classmates as possible and, I'm proud to say, I was told that we had the best alumni turnout to date.

When Mary and I arrived at the designated meeting room, we were warmly greeted by classmates that I hadn't seen or heard from since graduation. Aside from Sig and Dianne, of course, it was great to see Carlos and Maria once again and most especially, Joe Esposito. I took great delight in introducing Mary to this bevy of aged, phantom classmates. Aside from all the reverie, laughter, and storytelling, I realized that approximately half of the formerly married couples were now, either separated or divorced. Considering that, in most cases, the spouse was the breadwinner, I seriously questioned if their marriages were based primarily on matters of convenience and economics rather than love.

In any event, after several hours of reminiscing, it seemed as though everyone was just content to linger. It was as though, no one wanted to leave, perhaps knowing it would likely be the *last goodbye!* As the final moments slowly ticked away, there was a sudden rush to update everyone's phone and email information. It was consoling to hear universal agreement that the reunion was well worthwhile, and we all promised to repeat it again in 2020. While walking in downtown Des Moines, Mary wondered why there were no pedestrians on the sidewalks only to discover that, because of the fierce winters, the streets were now interconnected with elevated crosswalks.

After touring the modern classrooms and *state of the art* laboratories of the new Medical Campus, it was disheartening to find that nothing of my past still existed. My former School, our Fraternity house and my Apartment complex were all gone! Although, writing one's memoirs momentarily turns back the hands of time, when I scan the obituary column in the D.O. Journal, and see the names of my former classmates, I'm saddened and painfully reminded of how truly fleeting those hands of time are!

Subjects   Despite having taken a full year of Biochemistry in college, the course as given by the Celanders seemed totally foreign. Dr. Celander Ph.D. and his wife, who had a Master's degree in biochemistry, were both involved with research. He, being legally blind, relied on his wife, both in class and in the laboratory. In my opinion, the content of his class material had absolutely no relevance to clinical medicine, and I found his weekly, multiple-choice exams, to be impossibly difficult. In short, June couldn't come soon enough!

Likewise, Bacteriology and Parasitology were taught by another husband-and-wife team, Dr. Harvey Newcomb, Ph.D., and his wife, who had a Master's degree in microbiology. Initially, I had difficulty with their exams because, even though it was a four-hour course, the tests were limited to two hours of multiple-choice questions. I suspect, ever since childhood, I suffered from some form of Dyslexia. So, when reading, I would repeatedly scan sentences from right to left. Fortunately, however, my ability to memorize was well preserved. Consequently, given my slow reading skills and OCD, I was only able to finish 75% of the questions.

Unsatisfied with a grade of 75%, I went to see Dr. Newcomb about allowing me additional time to complete future exams. At first, he bristled at the notion, but after reviewing my test score, he realized that I had a very high percentage of correct answers for the questions answered. Consequently, he decided to allow additional time to complete the exam for any student who required it.

I thoroughly enjoyed Neuroanatomy and Gross Anatomy, especially the dissection lab. There were approximately 12 tables in the lab with six students assigned to each cadaver. Somehow by default, I became the designated dissectionist. Being that our table had one of the two female cadavers, we frequently had other student visitors which made for a very crowded table. We had two seniors as student assistants, Ted Knight, and Neil Varner. Both were brilliant but Neil was exceptional. He was a former chiropractor who also taught Neuroanatomy.

Since the dissections were by specific regions, only that section of the wintergreen scented muslin would be unwrapped. I have to confess that Dr.Marianas' formula was far better than plain formaldehyde. However, since I was the dissectionist, by the end of the lab session, the oily wintergreen solution still permeated my white lab coat and clothing. And trust me, by June the aroma was very pungent!

Although my lab coat was always wrinkled and soiled, Carlos's always appeared absolutely clean and freshly pressed. That's because he refused to even touch the cadaver. Instead, he would use his pen to point to a particular structure and, with a thick Cuban accent, would ask. "Pete, what the hell is that thing called?" Each table was also issued a large wooden box containing skeletal bones which we were allowed to take home in order to review. In addition, it was strongly recommended that everyone purchase a human skull for the same purpose - which I still have.

Interestingly, over time I came to fully appreciate and embrace the philosophy and intrinsic benefits of Osteopathic Manipulative Therapy (OMT). Historically, emphasis on the musculoskeletal system's homeostatic relationship with the circulatory and neuroendocrine systems was surely a forerunner of today's preventive medicine approach to Integrative or Complementary Medicine. In addition, the current techniques of Manual Medicine facilitated the lost art of a *Hands-On* approach to patient care and well-being.

The course was taught by an OMT guru, Dr. Byron Laycock DO who had truly gifted hands. He was always available in his office for students who might require periodic *adjustments*. I was always amazed at how precise and painless his delivery of, high velocity- low amplitude manipulative techniques were. Unlike a common *shotgun technique,* he focused more on the patient feeling relief rather than hearing popping sounds. However, it was also common knowledge that, failing his course was often the deciding factor of whether you stayed in school or went home!

In sharp contrast, the director of Physical Medicine and Rehabilitation (PM&R), Dr.Bob Conair DO, utilized a more painful, shotgun technique. He seemed somewhat immature, always eager to mix socially with the students. He had a glass eye, and while lecturing, for pure shock appeal, he would periodically remove it in order to ostensibly clean it!

He was also the faculty advisor for PSG, often conducting the meetings at the Mansion and of course, always attending the parties. He also transported and supervised the sophomore students to the County Jail for the purpose of rendering medical care to the inmates. However, he was very adamant about punctuality, stressing the need to arrive before 8 AM in order to get hot coffee and donuts before seeing any patients.

Hutchinson ISL   I'm very fortunate to be writing this portion of my memoir while spending the Easter holidays at our 5th-floor oceanfront condominium on Hutchinson Island, a beautiful barrier island on Florida's Treasure Coast. Just gazing out at the beautiful blue-green ocean and the rhythmic swells of frothy white caps, are both relaxing and inspirational. And when I'm able to steal some quiet time, I have to laugh when my loving wife bids me farewell saying, "See you later Earnest!"

While in Florida I had an unexpected visit from my brother, Caesar, his wife, Pat and my nephew, Charles, a Benedictine priest in the order of the Divine Will. During their stay, we were all blessed to witness Charles celebrating a private mass while overlooking the beautiful ocean from a 5th-floor vantage. - truly cleansing of mind, body, and spirit.

Also, my brother, Rocco, and his wife, Carol, made prior arrangements to spend several weeks in Maria and Jack's 4th floor Condo in the same complex. I was looking forward to spending some quality time with my brother. However, he appeared to be physically and or emotionally hampered by some lingering side effects following a successful course of treatment for prostate cancer. I also had the feeling that he wanted some space, and I was dismayed by an all too familiar sense of reclusiveness. Regrettably, this seemed to markedly limit our interaction which, for me, was a missed opportunity - a *Mulligan moment!*

My Inner Core   This caused me to, once again, reflect on my Inner Core. In addition to witnessing Rocco's obvious physical limitations, I was further disheartened when a picture of my brother Nick was forwarded to me. Despite a gastric feeding tube, it still depicted his state of progressive debilitation.

Anita recently suffered a traumatic fall, severely injuring her right shoulder. Sadly, I've become   increasingly aware of her mental and physical fragility. While frequently speaking to each other on the phone, I emphasized the medical and psychological benefits of physical therapy and of staying purposeful by remaining actively engaged. I was delighted when she eventually told me that she had recently started active physical therapy with considerable success - which bolstered her spirits and self-confidence.

Despite her many infirmities, my sister Virginia seems to have nine lives. Unfortunately,   the need for continuous care required a painful family decision. With considerable reluctance, she was admitted to an assisted living facility in Northport L.I. Meanwhile, perhaps due to the beautiful California weather and lifestyle, her twin, Maria, seems to be in relatively stable health.

And my brother, Caesar, who claims that, during his coronary bypass operation, the surgeon physically removed his heart from his chest, and while holding it in his hand, repaired the damage and then placed it back in his chest! Despite numerous attempts to correct his gross distortion of the events, his rendition always remains the same. Although he recently underwent a procedure to remove plaque from his femoral arteries, he has already resumed his daily exercise ritual, and at age 79 he remains a Toro testa dura! (thick-headed Bull)!

Oftentimes, I'm disheartened that the outer protective petals, now long gone, have allowed the natural wilting process of the inner colorful soft petals. In the past, I found it somewhat disturbing to view this process from afar. That is until I recently gazed in the mirror of Truth. The stark realization that I'm not far behind is ample motivation to complete this memoir - time being of the essence!

Carlos' Birthday Reunion   While in Florida, Mary and I were invited to attend Carlos Corrales' 70th surprise Birthday Party. We were both very honored to be invited for the small family gathering, and even more so to see how excited he was to see us. We hadn't seen each other in over 10 years. I was asked by his wife, Maria, to describe what it was like rooming together on the third floor of the fraternity mansion. I described him as being brilliant, but with strange, annoying study habits, which I took great delight explaining in great detail.

"After dinner, he would routinely shower, get dressed in his pajamas and by 7:30 pm, start studying by sitting in a comfortable soft armchair with a flat board across the armrests. Shortly after placing a book on the board, he would light a cigarette, crack open a can of beer and start thumbing through the pages, scanning the contents. Then, in lieu of congas, he would periodically start tapping his fingers on the surface of the board, simulating a conga skin.

Meanwhile, I'm trying to read, underline, highlight and memorize while envisioning Desi Arnaz singing "Babalu". The faster he drummed, the faster he turned the pages, while deftly taking a swig of beer, followed by a long drag on his cigarette. Incredibly, he would turn off his light by 9:30 pm - while I continued studying until at least 12:30 am."

When it came time to post the grades on *The Wall,* a frenzy would ensue with everyone elbowing for position to see everyone else's grades - like they were going to change in the next 15 minutes! However, I took the time to observe Carlos patiently waiting for the frenzy to subside, and after everyone's competitive curiosity was satisfied, he would merely take a passing glance at his grade and then simply move on, knowing that he scored in the high 90s!

Incidentally, I don't remember our roommate, Jim Eustis, ever studying in our room, and not surprisingly, after the first marking period he was placed on academic probation.

Also, due to the fierce competition for class ranking, during our sophomore year, they switched the postings from numerical values to alphabetical grades, and by Senior year, to pass or fail!

Although Mary and I sat somewhat removed from his immediate family members, following my lengthy description, I was pleasantly surprised when Carlos came and sat with us. After ordering another bottle of wine, he seemed eager to reminisce about our first year at the College and of the fraternity house. Other than Paul Wolfson, who was gifted with a photographic memory, Carlos was always a close second. Obviously, having had too much wine, when I again remarked to Mary about his brilliance, Carlos became irate shouting, "You're full of shit!, you were the brilliant one, always studying. You saved my ass in Anatomy!"

That single comment triggered an immediate flashback of him asking, "Pete, what the f....k is that thing called?" Following his gratuitous compliment, however, as a highly respected Board Certified Pulmonologist, he offered a backhanded compliment, loudly exclaiming, "You were so f...kin smart, you could have been somebody!" After a brief pause to reflect, I quipped, "I thought I was somebody!

Mini-Reunion   Shortly after celebrating Carlos's birthday, I received a surprise phone call from Sig Kulessa, informing me that he and his wife, Dianne, would be attending a seminar on Hutchinson Island. I immediately called Carlos in order to arrange for a *Mini-Reunion* of the six of us at a Cuban restaurant in West Palm Beach. We shared lots of wine which prompted endless stories and laughter. It was interesting how our recollections may have differed somewhat, but the essential takeaway was the same - we all made it and did pretty well to boot!

Incidentally, while writing this memoir, I recall being greatly saddened to witness that my, once brilliant friend, was now somewhat compromised by a recent stroke, and as a result of degenerative arthritis and severe spinal stenosis, he was now walking with a tentative shuffling gait.

Likewise, the former baseball catcher was now suffering from advanced macular degeneration and severe osteoarthritis with spinal stenosis, causing him to walk hunched forward. But most of all, his profound sadness following the sudden death of his beloved wife, two weeks before celebrating their 50th wedding anniversary! And yet, perhaps to fill the void, he retains his sense of humor and a willingness to reminisce about the humorous good times!

Admittedly, everything is relative, and although, I reluctantly accept the untoward side effects of the inevitable aging process, for some reason I was particularly struck by their apparent suddenness! Thank you Lord, for sparing my loving wife, who still appears remarkably radiant before my eyes.

As I mentioned previously, Sig shared an adjacent room with, Dick McGrath, and they had a completely different study schedule. They would study until 9:30 pm, sleep for several hours and then resume studying until 2 to 3 am. For big exams, they might pull an *All-Nighter* until 6 am. The problem was that my desk and bed were on the opposite side of the paper-thin wall between our rooms. Sig and Jeff had an annoying routine of reviewing out loud. And when studying alone, Sig had a peculiar habit of reading to himself out loud. Being a light sleeper, even when he read with a whisper, it was not only too loud, it was worse, because then I strained to hear what he was whispering!

A Drake Break   On Friday evenings, as a respite from the sheer boredom of studying, Sig and I would occasionally walk over to one of the female dorms at Drake University, to see if any girls were available for casual company. Considering the late hour, however, you can imagine who might still be available! While waiting patiently in the reception area, as the damsels descended the staircase, judging purely by the size of their calves, Sig would make an immediate decision whether or not to stay.

On more than one occasion, I would no sooner hear him say, "OH boy! "and before I knew it, he was out the door, leaving me standing there to fend for myself. Embarrassed and unable to offer any plausible explanation for my friend's abrupt departure, I would quickly decide to either sit and talk for a while or offer some lame excuse to get the hell out of there! Meanwhile, Sig would be waiting outside in the dark, laughing his ass off.

The Consortium   At some point I received an update from home regarding the dreadful situation with the Lodge. However, I wasn't privy to any of the details. Apparently, realizing how the abrupt turn of events ultimately affected my mother, Caesar and Nick put together a consortium of four investors which included two of Caesar's professional colleagues, John Leone, and Bill Gallagher - both of whom were also his partners, managing the St. George Hotel's pool.

The most pressing issue was satisfying the outstanding debts, and then carrying the Lodge through the winter in preparation for the next summer season. It wasn't until I returned home for Christmas that I had a chance to review some of the legal documents involving this management transition, which was ostensibly, intended to salvage something for my Mother.

Thanksgiving Blues   It was strange spending Thanksgiving so far away from the festivities of home. Carlos was eager to fly home to Miami to see his girlfriend, Maria Elena, and many of the local guys made plans to drive home for the holiday. But at least Sig was stuck here and as they say, "Misery loves company!"

I remember while having Thanksgiving dinner with several other students, Sig handed me a sealed envelope containing a card. When I excitedly opened the colorful card and began reading the lovely poem, I noticed a strange-looking face wearing dark sunglasses and a green pea cap inserted in a round cutout. When I recognized Sig's signature hat, I realized it was just a cruel example of his bizarre sense of humor! In the midst of my depression, I was determined to somehow get home for Christmas!

Christmas 12 - 21 club.   Fortunately, Des Moines eventually emerged from the dark ages and the airlines began providing nonstop jet service from Des Moines to various cities on the East coast. They also launched a special promotion called, the *12 - 21 club*. Basically, anyone between the ages of 12 and 21 could fly for half price provided you were a member of the Club and produced proper identification indicating your age. Somehow, I was able to satisfy both conditions, and following final exams, Carlos flew to Miami and Sig and I flew to LaGuardia for the Christmas holidays.

Ironically, Mary's brother George was due to arrive from Chicago at roughly the same time. I remember Mary meeting both of us at the airport, which certainly dampened our long awaited reunion! She eventually drove me to my mother's apartment in Bay Ridge. At first, it seemed strange being in the apartment, but after a while, I became re-acclimated to the small confines. I believe we celebrated Christmas dinner at Anita and Bob's new home on Cromwell Hill Road.

I remember my mother and I visiting Maria and Jack's family on Long Island and being pleasantly surprised that Dr. and Mrs. Weiser were also there. At some point, Dr. Weiser commented about my apparent weight gain, and commented that It wasn't healthy! I don't recall if Mary and I went to midnight mass together or, for that matter, much of anything else.

CH - 39
THE BEAST GOES WEST

In late December, I offered to drive Sig and two upperclassmen back to Des Moines in *The Beast,* sharing the travel expenses along the way. It had been snowing lightly and when I arrived at Sig's house in N.J, after meeting his father for the first time, he immediately asked, "Do you have snow tires?" After proudly saying yes, just to be sure, he went outside to check them. After his inspection, he just shook his head and we both acknowledged that they were indeed, *former* snow tires - now quite bald!

We said our goodbyes and off went, the four of us battling the snow across six states on bald snow tires, intent on driving straight through to Des Moines. It was a long terribly monotonous drive, the most difficult stretch being through the seemingly endless tunnels through the Pennsylvania mountains. At some point, I remember taking a power nap in the back seat, and after six hours, I suddenly popped my head up asking, "What state are we in?" They all started laughing, "We're still in *beautiful* Pennsylvania!" Sixteen hours later, we arrived safely in *beautiful* Des Moines.

When we arrived back at school, we learned of some unfortunate news. Jim Eustis had flunked out, and over the holiday, Dick McGrath became engaged and underwent an appendectomy with serious complications. Apparently, the combination of a lengthy post-operative recovery and his fiancée obligations were significant distractions from which he couldn't recover. As a result, before the end of the first semester, he accepted an option to repeat freshman year - which left Sig with a private room. Unfortunately, the same was true of another fraternity brother, Frank DiBenedetto who, following the final exams, was also given the option of repeating the first year, which he also accepted.

Also, during the Christmas break, I learned that Carlos and Maria were married, and she would be accompanying him back to *beautiful* Des Moines. At the time, Carlos was quite portly and when I finally met the new Mrs. Corrales, she was his equal in size and shape. They drove a new gray Dodge Dart and Maria either stayed briefly in a motel or perhaps in their intended apartment, because I remember her chauffeuring him to school in the mornings.

In fact, being that it was a very blustery winter, after wiping all the snow off the car, she patiently waited until the car was toasty warm before beeping the horn for Carlos to emerge warmly dressed, including a fur hat and matching gloves - what a woman! They eventually moved into a furnished apartment, leaving me with the entire front bedroom. The tide had finally turned, and I was now the envy of everyone in the fraternity house - Patience really is a virtuous luxury.

Des Moines Winters During the long brutal winters, although the streets and highways were readily plowed, being that it never melted, the snowbanks just kept rising, obstructing the view from the car's side windows. During the first semester, each morning we would carpool to school with those fortunate enough to have a car. We passed the time by listening to the absurd, five-minute episodes of "The Adventures *of Chicken Man.*" For some reason, each riveting episode always ended with, *Well-Know!-* signifying either dismay or some form of titillating delight! In any event, Sig and I would often use this silly phrase to imply the same nebulous context.

I was proud that the Beast was now part of the carpool caravan. However, given the perpetual snow and frigid weather, getting the big engine to turn over was always a challenge. Of course, the notion of investing in a new battery was out of the question, so I purchased a set of jumper cables instead. Each morning was a crapshoot if the Beast would turn over, so one of the other cars would patiently wait to see if I needed a jump start. Fortunately, driving home was never a problem.

YMCA   At some point, heeding Dr. Weiser's advice, I went on a strict diet and gradually shed about 30 pounds, ultimately reaching a weight that I was finally satisfied with.

I also managed to get a student discount at the local YMCA, which was within walking distance from the fraternity house. Initially, I started with free weights and boxing, using both speed and heavy bags. I also hooked up with a Junior student, Dave Kramer, who had a black belt in karate and occasionally joined me at the Y. When time permitted, we practiced various practice and defensive drills depicted in Umansky's textbook, and we'd go through some basic maneuvers and kicks against the heavy bag or the padded walls.

By Sophomore year, however, I learned the hard way to properly wrap my hands before working out on the heavy bag. I eventually developed considerable pain and swelling across all my knuckles (capsulitis). And when I conferred with Wade, a respiratory therapist at Des Moines Gen Hosp (DGH), who was a former, light heavyweight Golden Gloves champion, he just started laughing. He instructed me in the proper method of wrapping my hands, especially prior to using the heavy bag. Then, when I also described my shoulder pains, he again laughed, advising me to elevate my hands above my shoulders when practicing on the speed bag.

Chuck Ressinger   In time, I developed a close friendship with Chuck Ressinger, a fraternity brother on the second floor. I discovered that we shared something in common. He also had a serious, long-distance relationship with the girl named, Charlene, back home in Ohio. Towards the end of the semester, he started talking about both of us driving down to Florida right after final exams. The plan was to drive the Beast to his home in Ohio, and after switching to his 1960 red Ford Galaxie convertible, we would leave for sunny Florida, picking fresh oranges along the way - sounded fantastic!

As the winter snow gradually receded and the summer heat rolled in, we both agreed that the initial plan sounded better than it was practical.

Besides, I think we both realized that we didn't want to delay returning home to our loved ones. So, instead, I extended an invitation for him and Charlene to drive to New York during the summer for an extended stay at the Lodge.

Beastly Death   I don't remember the circumstances, but at some point, I allowed the designated class Hippies, Howie Greenspan, and Mike Quicker, to drive the Beast to Chicago over the weekend. Then on Sunday evening, I received an urgent phone call from Howie saying, "Pete, I think the transmission went on the Olds!" When I asked their location he said, "Someplace on route 80 between Chicago and Des Moines" and I thought, "Great, that narrows it down!" Although my heart sank, I felt my hands were tied. So, I told them to take the plates off and just leave the car on the side of the road, and I assume they either hitchhiked or took a bus back to Des Moines.

58 Opel   Uncle Tom's son in law, Al Harlow, was a lawyer and a true Virginia gentleman. Apparently, aware of my recent car situation, he offered to give me his 1958 green Opel, which I eventually drove to Des Moines. Towards the end of the second semester, most of the freshmen were making future plans to live elsewhere, making room for the incoming Freshmen. In the midst of studying for final exams, as if besieged by some overhanging dark cloud or ominous omen, the Opel's engine blew!

Knowing that I would have to move all my belongings out of the fraternity house, I desperately needed a car to temporarily transport all my *Stuff* back home. So, I scrounged $250 to have the Opel's engine rebuilt. Apparently, either my car or the job wasn't considered a priority because a week went by and nothing had been done on the car. After explaining the urgency and hounding the mechanic to finish the job, I received a call that the Opel's engine was finally ready for the long drive back to NY. However, I was warned not to exceed 50 mph for the first 1000 miles!

Marathon Drive   Coincidentally, during the second semester, Joe Esposito, had driven his classic 1948 woody station wagon out to Des

Moines, which he now intended to drive back home to N.J. Unfortunately, it suffered from a chronic overheating problem which required placing a 5' long 2x4 under the front hood and tied down by a thick marine rope. Consequently, this would limit his traveling speed to under 45 mph! In addition, I agreed to drive another roommate, Bob Krause, and all his *Stuff* back to Brooklyn. However, Bob didn't know how to drive a standard transmission! - you can't make this shit up!

So, right after finals our ridiculous caravan took off for the long journey home, traveling at warp speed, averaging 45 mph! Adding to the endless agony, during "pit stops and refueling, Joe and I were both afraid to turn off our engines for fear that they wouldn't start again. All toll, this made for a nonstop journey of 27 hrs. staying awake was the real challenge. While I was popping Ritalin tablets like they were tic tacs, I was relying on my copilot, Bob Krouse, to hopefully keep me awake and on the road.

When we finally arrived at Bob's house in Brooklyn, he offered me some money, and when I refused, he said, "Pete, you'll never be rich!" Without turning the engine off, after unloading his *Stuff*. I drove directly upstate to Anita's house on Cromwell Hill Rd. When I arrived, Mary greeted me, but I was so wired from the Ritalin that, even though I was in the living room, I couldn't stand to hear the sound of utensils all the way in the kitchen!

Summer of '67 My mother had already moved from Mrs. Moffat's apartment to Anita and Bob's home in Monroe. Their upstairs Cape Cod was tastefully renovated into a private apartment in order to accommodate my Mother. This was very generous and a necessary undertaking on the part of Anita and Bob.

By this time, Bob and Anita had adopted three children, and although it was a decent-sized apartment, I think living upstairs in someone else's home was a difficult adjustment for my mother. My sister loved outdoor gardening, so my mother made herself useful by cooking most of the meals and helping with the general household chores. Initially, it seemed to work with only minor tensions.

The Consortium Meanwhile, Caesar's consortium was actively preparing to open the Lodge for the upcoming summer season. Considering that both Caesar and Nick had been long removed from the routine preparations of opening and operating the Lodge and that Caesar's partners had absolutely no experience, it was obvious that they would need help.

Their initial plan was for each of them to oversee the Lodge's daily operation for three consecutive weeks. Since they had no experience with catering or running a Hotel, nor any intention of pursuing the Greek clientele, they focused on the Bar business and the Country Club memberships. However, they didn't have a clue about how to open or maintain the Pool!

Faced with these obstacles, Caesar offered me a summer job doing, among other things, bartending, lifeguarding, and pool maintenance for, $300. I say, "among other things" because each of them desperately needed advice. Every three weeks, it was truly a challenge dealing with a new face and temperament, advising, and orienting each of them in succession.

In any event, It was during Caesar's rotation when Chuck and Charlene accepted my invitation to visit the Lodge by driving nonstop from Toledo OH. I remember the four of us sitting at the bar and Caesar graciously offering my guests, "Drinks on the house!" with the admonition," Now take good care of my brother!" to which Chuck replied, "Are you kidding, he takes care of me!" We had a wonderful time as a foursome, especially water skiing on Greenwood lake - which was a first for Mary and me. Before leaving, Chuck suggested that we rent a place together for the upcoming sophomore semester which I readily agreed to and left the selection to him.

Cottage 10 At the time, Rocco and Carol were occupying Cottage 10 during the summer and I would occasionally walk over to pay them a visit. However, for the very first time, I felt strange in my *safe place*, as though I was intruding on their privacy. I also had the sense that they were, not only occupying but had taken possession of the Cottage. It wasn't until much later when I learned that, in fact, that was the case.

Apparently, at some point, Rocco offered to purchase the Cottage from my mother for, what I believe was a nominal fee of $13,000, with a very creative payment plan. In hindsight, however, I doubt that my mother offered the same opportunity to any of my other siblings, and therein lies the rub. In time, it became apparent that he didn't buy the Cottage for nostalgic reasons!

On several occasions, I asked Rocco if he would like to come with me to the Lodge and meet either John Leone or Bill Gallagher. But each time he declined saying, I just can't do it!"- which I understood and readily accepted. I felt that perhaps during his doctorate program in Psychology, Rocco went through a long period of introspection and self-analysis which, from my limited perspective, resulted in a strange metamorphosis.

He seemed somehow different or estranged, as though we weren't cut from the same cloth and no longer shared the same values, which was very disheartening. During several discussions, he expressed a strong resentment of my father's perceived overbearance which was in sharp contrast to my Mother's more nurturing nature which I believe, forged their close mutual bond.

Admittedly, we had different parents, and I viewed his jaundiced perspective of my father as the antithesis of my obvious overzealous, reverence. As he seemingly became more introverted, he appeared to lose, not only his voice but also his marvelous sense of humor, allowing it to only resurface on rare occasions. I truly loved and missed my hero which compelled me to share with him my analogous perspective saying, "It seemed as though you entered a long dark tunnel as a Cadillac and emerged as a Chevy"- not that there's anything wrong with a Chevy!

Bar Melee   I resumed my familiar routine of placing the weekly liquor orders and since there was no need for a service bar, I only tended the main front Bar. Although the bar remained active on weekends, given the change in patronage, at times the bar scene tended to become unruly. I remember one particular evening when it was so busy that I needed Caesar's help behind the front Bar. Sure enough, an altercation erupted among several of the larger patrons, and although we usually kept a blackjack, a sealed roll of quarters or a small baseball bat behind the bar for just such occasions, things appeared to be getting out of hand very quickly and Caesar decided to intervene.

Before I knew it, he leaped over the bar by swinging his legs smoothly over the countertop in one fluid movement - resembling a gymnast dismounting from a pommel horse. Then I watched as he squared off, face-to-face, with the largest of the patrons in the melee. Fearing for his safety, I decided I would replicate his agile move and attempted to clear the bar in the same graceful manner.

Unfortunately, while attempting to swing my legs over the top of the counter, I managed to knock over everyone's drink and inadvertently caught my right foot between the padded armrest and the edge of the countertop. Now I was dangling helplessly upside down until one of the patrons sitting at the bar mercifully released my foot. Then I deftly limped over to help my brother who, by this time, had the situation well under control - Talk about embarrassing moments! I'm just thankful cell phones didn't exist in those days!

Later that evening, while cleaning the back bar, Caesar handed me a handful of singles saying, "You forgot to collect your tips!" This was truly a first for me, for two reasons; It wasn't customary nor was it expected to tip an owner, and as a service bartender, I never received nor shared in the pooled tips.

Black Beauty The Opel never completely recovered from the marathon trip and towards the end of the summer, I knew I had to get rid of her and purchase another beauty. I was considering a 1960 black Dodge (aka Black Beauty) driven by members of the Country Club, Mr., and Mrs. Shea. They were each roughly 300 lbs. and I noticed that the car had a moderate tilt on the left side. I brought the car to Don Lucas and he said it was the torsion bar adding, "you would also tilt if you had to carry 600 lbs.!" Trusting their honesty, I asked Mr. Shea if he thought the car would make it to Iowa and he said, "Just don't *push* the car and you should be fine" At first, I shuddered at the term, *Push*, but I decided to buy Black Beauty from my tips, for $200.

Brooklyn VA   Needless to say, I was kept pretty busy throughout the entire summer and since Mary was now working as an extern dietitian at the Brooklyn VA, we occasionally saw each other on weekends. The Brooklyn VA was an impressively tall building in Bay Ridge, overlooking the Narrows waterway. At some point, Mary unwittingly mentioned that she was being pursued by a foreign Neurology resident. Ignoring the possibility that perhaps she might be flattered by his attention, I naively assumed that he was annoying her and therefore, decided to pay her a visit.

I remember talking with her in front of the tall building when, as if on cue, guess who just happened to walk by! She introduced me while casually saying that I was in Medical school, inferring that we had something in common, but failing to mention that I was also her boyfriend!

He was tall and slender with a light tan complexion and spoke with a mild accent, presumably from Iran. As we cordially shook hands, while crushing his knuckles, I took my time glaring into his eyes sending a telepathic message, "I know we have more than medicine in common!". Thereafter, she never mentioned him again, and in keeping with the motto, "what you don't know won't hurt you", I chose not to ask any questions!

Painful Departure   It was late Monday afternoon, and I waited until the last possible moment to broach the embarrassing subject. With Black Beauty fully packed, I finally drove up to the Lodge to say goodbye to Caesar and collect my summer's salary of, $ 300.

When I arrived I found Caesar sitting at a round table in the Bar area, playing poker with his two partners. They had obviously been drinking a lot, and when I walked in and said, "I came to say goodbye" Caesar asked, "How are you getting to school?" When I told him, he said, "Ok kid, goodbye, and have a safe trip!" But no mention of the money! He didn't get up to give me a hug or even a handshake! He just kept playing cards and drinking with his friends. When I finally gained enough courage to remind him about the money, he got pissed and said, "Jesus Christ, can't you see I'm losing money here!"

I was so taken aback that I just walked out and sat in my car, well camouflaged behind a row of tall lilac bushes, and not since my father's funeral, I just started crying. I knew it was the booze, but I felt ashamed and devastated, not so much by the money, but more importantly, this was the first time my hero had disappointed and embarrassed me!

I finally gained my composure and I had no choice, but to go back inside. Upon seeing me he said, "Christ, I thought you left!" Then, when I told him that I needed the money for school, he got up, stormed over to the cash register and took whatever cash was in the till (approximately $300) saying, "Here, take it all!"- which ironically reminded me of my father's retort to my mother's plea for $20! I was made to feel that, rather than having earned it, I was stealing it! Following that humiliating exchange, I just left with a heavy heart without saying another word.

I drove Black Beauty for 18 hrs., straight through to Des Moines, and arrived safely the following evening. By mutual agreement, Chuck had pre-arranged for us to rent the downstairs floor of a small two-family house for the first semester. We had a small kitchen and a decent-sized living room with a small T.V. which I hardly ever watched. He drove out in his mint condition bright red classic 1960 Ford Galaxie 500 convertible, and being that he arrived before me, he occupied the larger of the two bedrooms, directly off the living room.

I planned on going to the bursar's office before classes began, in order to make a partial tuition payment which had increased from $1200 to $1500. Once again, I felt I had just enough money for the first semester's living expenses and anticipated that the balance of my tuition would hopefully be covered by the federal student loan program.

The Scholarship   The following morning, when I went to the bursar's office, I was absolutely stunned when the Dean of Academic Affairs, Michael Barry, pulled me aside and told me that I was being granted a half academic scholarship, provided that I remained in the upper 10th percentile - that meant, $375. Per semester.

Shortly after basking in my reverie, however, I began to question, why me? After all, I knew I did fairly well, but in my opinion, not well enough to warrant a scholarship! I began to speculate; did I have an anonymous benefactor? - possibly Dr. Weiser? At some point, I asked Jack if either he or his father had anything to do with my good fortune and he said, "Not that I'm aware of". Truthfully, however, I didn't want to investigate too thoroughly for fear of discovering the truth. Besides, this was an additional motivation to do my very best in order to maintain my *unwarranted scholarship*.

Upon his return to Des Moines, Sig took up residence in a small apartment above a local Funeral parlor, which he shared with another fraternity brother, Harry Brink. The rent, if any, was nominal since he was also responsible for assisting with the transportation of the deceased *Residents* to the parlor. Harry was a thin Iowan farm boy, who accompanied his guitar with an amazing talent for vocal harmonizing. In the near future, however, their tiny apartment would prove to be my refuge of last resort.

Diane   Due to our separate living arrangements, my conversations with Sig were very limited. I don't remember the particulars, but during the summer break, Sig apparently met a girl named, Diane, at a Polish dance who was ironically, also a Day Hop at St Elizabeth's. I don't recall meeting her, and to my knowledge, she and Mary only had a passing acquaintance. Although Sig was obviously smitten with her, she remained somewhat mysterious, only offering that she was a good Polish dancer. However, I eventually learned that, as a young girl, she and her family emigrated from Poland via Argentina and ultimately arrived in the US with no money or worldly possessions. She was eventually granted an academic Hardship scholarship to the college of St Elizabeth.

CH - 40
SOPHOMORE YEAR

*M*icroscope Dilemma   Prior to leaving for Des Moines, I was aware that during our sophomore year, Histology, Pathology, and Microbiology would require all students to purchase a microscope. Several brands were "strongly recommended - all of which were binocular scopes with triple lenses and a movable stage with a pointer, costing between $450-$500! Even used models were way out of reach. In utter desperation, I reached out to Dr. Weiser, and he graciously offered to lend me the microscope that he used as a medical student in Vienna.

By comparison, it was certainly ancient-looking - early 1900 all brass scope housed in a simple narrow wooden box with a thin rope handle. The scope was monocular with only two lenses and, instead of a movable stage, it had two metal clips to hold the slide in place. Although it resembled an original Van Leeuwenhoek special, considering its source, I knew it had to be of high quality.

The microscopes would be used individually by each student and collectively during periodic slide exams. During these exams, all of the individual scopes would be set up on tables in the laboratory and the students would move every two minutes from one microscope to the next, hopefully identifying whatever was under the pointer.

My old nemesis, Dr. Harvey Newcomb, also taught Microbiology and Parasitology and was in charge of inspecting each student's microscope for *quality control*. Just how he looked at the wooden box, I knew I was in trouble! Then, quickly glancing at my Scope, without even looking through the lens, he immediately said it was unacceptable!

I explained that this put me in an untenable situation since I wasn't able to afford even a used model of the recommended brands. I pointed out that, despite its appearance, it was a superbly crafted, Leitz Wetzlar, German scope. I begged him to at least set up a slide and look through the lens. As with our prior encounter, he finally relented, and after looking through the scope he was astounded by, not only the craftsmanship but also the superb resolution of the lenses. He graciously accepted that, although it didn't have a movable stage or a pointer, he would use it for a fixed or stationary slide and, if need be, use a toothpick as a pointer!

In addition to Microbiology, the microscope was essential for Pathology and Histology, taught by Dr.Donald Bunce Ph.D. He was very intelligent and his claim to fame was inventing the *Bunce double hemostat*, of which he was extremely proud. I'm not convinced it had any clinical application, but he used his single clamp to slice segments of vessels for pathologic review. He also had a particular penchant for well-trimmed fingernails, well-groomed hair, and the correct pronunciation of *Ophthalmoscope*.

Likewise, when he initially looked at my Van Leeuwenhoek special, he had the same knee jerk response as did Dr. Newcomb. However, when I offered that his esteemed colleague thought it was a marvelous instrument, he thankfully passed on it.

I think we were very fortunate to have two young progressive D.O.s at the academic helm, Sam Williams, and Tom Vigorito. Dr. Williams was the Director of Clinical Medicine who also taught the Fundamentals of Physical Diagnosis. He exited from private practice after only two years when a young patient tragically died in his office following a shot of penicillin.

Dr. Vigorito was the Dean of the College who also lectured occasionally on specific topics of Physical Diagnosis. In particular, he lectured on the correct examination of the abdomen and chest. He also gave a lecture on vector cardiology which, at the time, was a relatively new science and heightened my early interest in the specialty. I will never forget his admonition, "You're not a seasoned physician until after you've been in practice for at least 10 years" - which I always kept in mind.

Clinical Courses   At least the course material during my Sophomore year had some clinical relevance which was far more interesting. I'd have to say, I enjoyed all of my subjects with the exception of Biostatistics taught by Dr. Orcutt Ph.D., who also taught Pharmacology. It was rumored that he was somehow involved with *The Manhattan Project*. Regardless, to this day, Sig swears he was on Pot! We both had difficulty with the course, but I managed to get a C+.

Among the more clinically relevant courses was Neurology, taught by Dr.Nelson D.O. who was absolutely brilliant, having completed his Residency at the prestigious Mayo Clinic which was exceptional for a D.O. For some reason, on Saturday mornings, Sig and I would also go to the Neurologic Institute to make rounds with their Medical Director who was not only brilliant but also an awesome teacher. After every session, we would come away with a pearl or two.

I also loved Dermatology taught by Harry Elmets D.O, who also taught Toxicology. I particularly enjoyed Earl Fitz D.O. He was a very eccentric, unorthodox Psychiatrist who, despite his advanced age, still played semi-professional ice hockey. Endocrinology was taught by Keith Simpson D.O, who was primarily a Diabetologist and also the Medical Director for the Alcohol Detox center in the adjacent, Old College Hospital.

Papa Joe McNerney D.O. was a venerated elder Internist who was truly a living legend at Des Moines General Hospital (DMGH) for his swift clinical diagnosis and practical treatment solutions. Following every one of his lectures, I came away with a clinical pearl based on his vast experience. I was also privileged to shadow him at DMGH for one month, making hospital rounds along with his preceptee, Eli Rose. Incidentally, Eli's brother, Norman, was a young *hotshot* surgeon who constantly competed with the more seasoned surgeons for worthy recognition.

Roger Senty D.O, taught, "The Fundamentals of Surgery". He recently returned from a six month sabbatical in Sweden, learning and sharing some of the latest surgical techniques. One of our laboratory assignments was to perform surgery on one of the stray dogs housed on the fourth-floor kennels. Although the dogs were said to be strays from downtown Des Moines, I often wondered how hard they actually searched for the rightful owners. I can just imagine some of the downtown neighbors asking, "have you seen sparky lately?"

Freddy the Dog   We were assigned in teams of four, and of course, Sig and I were on the same team. We had a choice of procedures to perform and we arbitrarily chose to do a splenectomy - who knows why? Dr. Senty was present for the initial incision and exploration of the abdominal cavity, and after identifying the major vessels that would require ligation, he left the room assuming that we knew what the hell we were doing. Since I did most of the cadaver dissection, I had a rough idea of the anatomy and was therefore delegated to be the *Surgeon*. Somehow, we managed to tie off the correct vessels and after careful dissection, I was surprised to remove the spleen intact.

Now, the next hurdle was closing the abdomen by matching the respective muscle layers. Unlike the cadavers, however, with a bloody field, it was pure guesswork on everyone's part. While completing the closure with *Catgut* sutures, I briefly wondered if Freddy would be upset with using a feline substance. More importantly, when we finally finished the closure, I noticed that one side of the margin was at least 1/4" higher than the other side - oops! Hopefully, they'll find each other!

In addition, after completing the closure, we realized we weren't operating under sterile conditions. So, we decided that poor Freddy should receive a shot of Terramycin. Being that Sig was a pharmacist, we relied on him to calculate the appropriate *dog dose* based on a rough estimate of the dog's weight. After calculating the *appropriate* dosage, Sig injected the dog in the right thigh. Of course, we all knew to avoid the Sciatic nerve in humans, but none of us thought to ask, "where's the sciatic nerve in a dog?" - Google didn't exist then!

At some point, we decided to personalize the dog by giving him the name, Freddy. The next day we were anxious to visit Freddy and were delighted and pleasantly surprised to see that Freddy was still alive! After a week of close observation, when we notified Dr. Senty that we felt Freddy was ready to be released from his cage, he said, "Good, I'd like to be present for the celebration!"

However, when Freddy was removed from the cage, we all noticed that he was dragging his right hind leg. Perplexed, Dr. Senty asked, "You did a splenectomy, right?" Of course, when we answered yes, he asked "Then why is he dragging his right leg?" At a loss, someone offered, "Maybe he had a stroke!" But none of us ever mentioned the injection!

The Apartment   Initially, Chuck and I seemed to be getting along reasonably well in the small apartment. Although Drake University's close proximity provided ample opportunity for occasional social relief, on most weekends, while I was studying, Chuck enjoyed drinking beers while watching football games in the living room. Honestly, I don't know which was worse, the noise of the TV or my jealousy, but either way, it was an annoying distraction.

Beauty Crunch   One evening, while we were eating dinner, we heard the sound of screeching tires followed by a sudden loud crash. We both ran outside to discover that someone crashed into the rear of Black Beauty, bending the rear bumper, and crushing her trunk. When the well-dressed driver exited his car, he immediately produced a business card indicating that he was, of all things, an executive with the Allstate insurance company.

While talking with him, however, I noticed that he was a little unsteady on his feet and smelled of alcohol. When the police finally arrived, he and the officer had a lengthy conversation, and when I privately mentioned to the officer that, I suspected he was under the influence of alcohol, the officer merely shrugged saying, "I didn't smell anything!".

In any event, after exchanging information, I was surprised when an insurance adjuster showed up the following day, essentially totaling my precious car and offering me a check for the estimated book value, which far exceeded what I originally paid for Beauty. Considering my poultry finances, this was truly a Godsend. Although the rear bumper and trunk were crunched, despite its appearance, she was still operational. The only inconvenience was that the trunk no longer closed and had to be fastened down with a wire hanger.

The Pizza Connection   The designated class Hippies, Howard Greenspan, and Mike Quicker, took over the operation of a small pizza parlor close to Drake University. It was a perfect location and size, with a small counter and three small booths. At some point, Howard told me that several members of Drake's football team would periodically visit their pizza Parlor on Friday evenings for the express purpose of instigating trouble. Then he hesitantly asked Dave Kramer and me if we would be willing to come over next Friday around 8 pm just to lend some *moral support*.

Shortly after we arrived, all the Drake patrons seemed to be having a quiet, peaceful time. While walking through the parlor, however, I surmised why the Drake jocks were intent on crashing the place. Instead of sprinkling Oregano on their Pizzas, my classmates were sprinkling a different *spice* that looked similar but smelled very different. Then, as predicted, we saw three gigantic goons walking shoulder to shoulder toward the parlor - very intimidating to say the least.

I noticed Howie's imposing, 5'8" 140 lb. frame emerging from behind the counter in order to confront the monsters. He must have mentioned something about Dave and me because all of a sudden, all the Goons turned in unison, and while glaring and sneering, they started to slowly walk towards us. Upon seeing this, I heard Dave say, "Oh shit, remember, defensive stance, back to back and circle slowly!" I think that was the last thing I heard because, being the smaller of the two of us, one of the goons came directly at me. I delivered what I thought was a perfect kick to his groin, but after momentarily wincing, he proceeded to pummel me. I suspect he came prepared by wearing his cup!

When I briefly looked up to see where my black belt companion was, I noticed him on the ground valiantly fending off the other two goons. Meanwhile, Howard and Mike were cowering behind the counter, but when they saw what was happening, they reluctantly jumped into the Frey, to either overpower or exhaust, the two goons on Dave - leaving me the last one to be helped. That fateful night taught me two very *painful* lessons - Don't volunteer for confrontation and Don't rely on something you're not proficient at!

Incidentally, the pizza parlor was eventually raided by the police, because, the next time I saw Howie and Mike, they were sitting in class dressed in brand new suits, presumably awaiting a court appearance later in the day.

Flashbacks   Although I enjoyed most of my clinical subjects, for obvious reasons, I had a particular preference for Cardiology. It seemed, the closer I came to the reality of becoming a physician, I noticed an increased incidence of the, all too familiar, flashbacks. Although essentially unchanged in content, now they were accompanied by recurrent severe headaches. Thinking that perhaps they were secondary to eyestrain, I had my eyes examined by our faculty specialist, Dr. Calan DO and finding no apparent need for glasses, I also consulted with our neurologist Dr. Nelson, who felt they were most likely due to suboccipital muscular and cervical strain due to reading *slowly* with my head down. He recommended OMT and physical therapy, which seemed to help, at least temporarily.

Mary's Senior Prom   By Thanksgiving, Chuck and I decided that the luxury of an apartment was needlessly expensive and that we wouldn't extend our lease for the second semester. In the meantime, I was anxiously making plans to drive Black Beauty home for Christmas in order to take Mary to her Senior Prom. Of course, it was to be a formal event held at the elegant, Pierre Hotel in Manhattan.

Honestly, I don't remember much of the evening other than, it was raining, and I must have borrowed someone's car because I certainly wouldn't allow a parking attendant to casually handle Black Beauty! One of my favorite photographs is of Mary and me posing in our formal attire. Being tall and slender, she looked absolutely elegant in a long dark pink gown, and thankfully, I appeared slightly taller than her, in my rented tuxedo. I presume we went to some local nightclub, but I don't remember where or with whom.

Love and Marriage   At some point, I was taken aback to learn that, during the Christmas break, Sig had flown home in order to propose to the Polish mystery girl, Diane. But truthfully, I was taken aback in more ways than one. It seemed as though, with each passing year, at least one of Mary's lifelong girlfriends were getting married. First, Angela, then, Joanne followed by, Eleanor and lastly, Pam. Likewise, Mary volunteered that several of her College roommates planned to get married right after graduation - not exactly music to my deaf ears!

And when Sig told me that he and Diane intended to be married in September, I realized, one of my closest friends was making the fateful commitment that I had successfully dodged for a long time. Also, I knew that quite a few of my classmates, who got married primarily for convenience or financial necessity, were now on shaky ground. Although I knew the ultimate decision was looming, I wasn't about to make such an important commitment under similar circumstances.

I remember the long drive back to Des Moines as being very painful. I don't remember how or where Mary and I said goodbye, but the thought that it could be two full years before I would be able to return home again was very depressing. To further complicate matters, upon my arrival in Des Moines, Chuck told me that he rented a room in an Apartment complex within walking distance to the College. When I visited his single room ground floor apartment, I was taken aback at how small it was compared to our former Diggs. As a consolation, however, he said it was considerably larger than the ones on the second floor, and as I was leaving, he said he would let me know of any vacancies.

Deadly Companions   Being that I desperately needed a temporary place to stay, I asked Sig if I could bunk with him and Harry for a couple of months in their crowded apartment above the funeral home. Our deceased *companions* resided in an adjacent room, each lying comfortably on metal tables lining both sides of the room, their tagged feet pointing towards a center aisle. Naturally, this configuration only allowed for a narrow passageway to access a separate small embalming room in the far rear.

In the evenings, purely out of curiosity, we would occasionally view the embalming procedure while reviewing any pertinent anatomy or interesting pathology. One evening, following an embalming, when the mortician left to go home, Sig and I followed suit, leaving Harry alone in the room. The only light switch controlling both rooms was at the entrance of our Bedroom. Upon exiting the room we purposely turned off the switch and locked the door to our Bedroom. After a few seconds, we heard Harry's muffled voice yelling from the inner sanctum," Turn on the lights!".

Needless to say, we were laughing hysterically behind the locked door, listening as he was trying to make his way down the narrow corridor, screeching as he inadvertently touched the cold toes of our deceased companions. With each horrifying touch he would let out a scream and his voice changed from asking to demanding, "Hey you guys, turn on the goddamn lights!" When he finally made his way to the door and found it locked he became even more hysterical, feverishly pounding on the door. I thought for sure he'd awaken the dead! - what an awful thing for Sig to do to his roommate!

Barber College   In order to save a few dollars, Sig and I went on a hunt for the least expensive barbershop in town, and we finally hit the jackpot! - the Barber College in downtown Des Moines. When we walked in, we noticed a long mirrored wall extending the entire length of the building, in front of which were approximately 25 barber chairs. The *would-be barbers* appeared to be supervised by three *barber professors*.

As we sat there listening to the professors commenting on their student's mistakes, we were trying to judge which one was worth the $ 2 gamble. Unfortunately, we didn't have the luxury of choosing who our *scalper* would be. But we figured, for another three dollars, we could always buy a hat. In retrospect, this selection quandary reminded me of trying to avoid Caesar, the barber *butcher, when I was* a kid!

Since Sig had considerably less hair, I figured, "How much damage could they do?". So, I let him go first. I soon realized, however, that for a *would-be barber*, less is not necessarily better, and I watched as the professor tried in vain to rectify the damage. Perhaps this explains why thereafter Sig resorted to wearing a green Pea cap!

The Apartment Complex After six weeks, Chuck told me of a vacancy on the second floor of his Apartment complex. When I went to see it, the stark contrast from Chuck's apartment was depressing, to say the least. But it was affordable and conveniently located within walking distance to the College.

It was truly a one-room *efficiency* apartment with a Murphy bed, a combination stove -refrigerator unit, a tiny bathroom, and just enough room for the small desk - Ah, home sweet home! It took a little time to emotionally acclimate to the tiny confines, but in many respects, the location was perfect, and the adjacent dirt parking lot was ideal for protecting Black Beauty's mangled frame.

Cooking was manageable on the two-burner stove and the tiny refrigerator below, large enough for my limited menu. Breakfast was a Carnation instant breakfast, and the rotating dinner menu consisted of Spaghetti with butter and cheese two nights a week, hot dogs two nights a week, homemade pizza two nights a week, and potatoes and eggs on Sundays. What more could you ask for!

One evening, while cooking pizza in the tiny oven, someone apparently noticed smoke billowing out my window and called the fire department. Despite turning off the gas, by the time they arrived, there were flames coming out of the oven. When they were just about to use the fire extinguisher, I stood in front of the stove begging them not to ruin my pizza. Upon opening the oven door, one of the firemen took pity, reaching in to retrieve my burnt pizza and then, extinguished the hell out of my oven. During my Junior year, I purchased a small used TV for $15. However, despite adjusting the telescopic rabbit ears and improvising with metal hangers, they only garnered two grainy channels.

During Christmas break, when I complained to my mother about the lack of commercial spaghetti sauce, she decided to send me two large jars of Ragu sauce wrapped with newspapers in a small carton box. To this day I can still picture the poor mailman standing at my door, juggling a totally deformed and utterly saturated cardboard box dripping with red spaghetti sauce.

Despite the newspaper packaging, the jars had obviously cracked and although I tried in vain to strain the sauce through paper towels, they also gave way. Although It killed me to flush the precious sauce down the toilet, I told my mother it was delicious and tried to tactfully suggest that, in the future try using a few more newspapers!

Detox Center   Directly across the street from the Medical College was the former College Hospital which now functioned as an Alcohol Detoxification Center. During the second semester, in addition to his Endocrinology lectures, we also had the option of doing a one-month rotation in the Detox Center, under the direction of Dr. Simpson. The Center provided a 10-day compulsory program in a locked facility. Once the patient signed himself in, he was required to stay for the full 10 days.

As students, we had a written protocol for treating the full spectrum of acute alcohol withdrawal, including delirium tremors which usually lasted for several days. The initial medicinal armamentarium was fairly limited. During the acute phase, seizures were controlled with phenobarbital and Dilantin, Compazine for vomiting, and Valium for severe agitation. In addition, on admission, they were routinely given high doses of injectable

B vitamins. After the acute phase subsided they were required to attend informative classes, explaining the root cause of their addiction, hoping to achieve long-lasting results - which was rare.

During this second phase, I found that it wasn't unusual for patients to suddenly demand an injection to control their severe "agitation". After facing this dilemma several times, I quickly learned a valuable *suggestive* technique. I would first tell the patient, "Now, I'm going to give you an injection that will probably make you very drowsy, so you must lie down right after the injection"! Then I would inject 2 ccs of sterile water in his butt which, unlike saline, hurts like Hell, further reinforcing its *potency!* Invariably, they would go out like a light bulb!

After their mandatory stay, the patients would be given an adequate supply of Antabuse, which produces severe nausea if one also ingested alcohol. However, this wasn't necessarily an effective deterrent, because patients quickly learned to just stop taking the Antabuse. During the cold winter months, patients would occasionally attempt to gain readmission to the Center by complaining of severe nausea from the Antabuse when they'd already stopped it. Clearly, the intent was to gain shelter from the cold, with a warm bed and three hot meals - who could blame them, the winters were brutally long!.

Outpatient Clinics Attached to the College was also a wing that provided several Student Outpatient Clinics, mostly supervised by third and fourth-year students under the direction of the various faculty specialists.

Orthopedics Dr. McClain D.O taught Office Orthopedics and had oversight over the Orthopedic Clinic. I was seeing a follow-up patient in the clinic who required a *Cast change*. Since this would be my first exposure to the procedure, I was nervous about using the vibrating *buzz saw*. At the time, I didn't realize that the circular device didn't actually cut, but merely vibrated. So, after gingerly removing the outer cast, I was amazed that there were no cuts on the patient's skin, and I thought, "So far, so good!" Then after applying a thin layer of wadding, I proceeded to apply a generous amount of plaster, ensuring a solid cast.

Proud of my unsupervised achievement, I scheduled a revisit in two weeks or sooner if the cast felt too tight. However, much to my dismay, the patient returned two days later, complaining of intense burning for which he was referred to, Dr. McClain. There were several of us in attendance as Dr. McClain carefully removed the cast. Everyone was aghast to see the patient's skin - it was bright red, resembling a severe sunburn! Dr. McClain yelled, "Who the hell applied this cast?". When I sheepishly raised my hand, it dawned on me that I had forgotten to apply the protective cloth sleeve - exposing the patient's skin to the chemical heat generated by the plaster cast.

OMT Clinic   Another mandatory rotation was the student OMT Clinic. This was actually pretty good, providing an early opportunity for direct *hands-on* patient contact. Each small treatment room had a simple padded manipulation table and a small wall mirror. I mention the mirror because, while giving *soft tissue* massage to a patient's back, in order to compensate for periods of sheer boredom, I would entertain myself by making grotesque faces in the mirror - I know, very weird! At some point, however, I mused, "Why would they have a small mirror in each room?" And I immediately became alarmed that perhaps, it provided remote observation!

House Calls   In addition to affordable direct patient care, the student College Clinic also provided an opportunity to make some extra money by performing House Calls for the immediate indigent population. It was based on a voluntary rotating schedule whereby, each student would sign out the unusually large black, House Call Bag, with a list of needy patients. Upon return, the student would submit an attendance receipt signed by the patient and In return, we would be paid two dollars for each house call. Of course, given the designated neighborhoods, we never carried oral or injectable narcotics.

I remember being totally exhausted after carrying that humongous black bag up four flights in a multi-story tenement building, just to check someone's sore throat. Although we were authorized to dispense simple analgesics and oral antibiotics, much like the current Visiting Nurse

Services, it was mostly intended for patient evaluations- taking vital signs and, if need be, referral to the College Clinic for immediate treatment or follow up.

National Boards Part I   The second semester seemed to fly by and before I knew it, I was studying for final exams and, Part One of the National Boards! Surprisingly, I managed to do fairly well in both, which meant I was about to traverse a major threshold - I would now be an *upperclassman.*

As Juniors, our white jackets would now be accompanied by classic, white pants and white shoes. As was the custom, we were courted by Eli Lilly, and given the basic accouterments of a real doctor. The hallmark being, the doctor's *Black Bag,* containing a shiny Stethoscope, tuning fork, reflex hammer, tape measure, flashlight, and a small black loose-leaf binder for essential notes. However, we ultimately had to purchase the more expensive items such as a blood pressure cuff and Welch Allyn Oto-Ophthalmoscope.

Bloomingdales   Meanwhile given her background in home economics, shortly after graduation, Mary was hired as a managing Dietitian for the Bloomingdale restaurant in Manhattan. I think I only visited her once or twice at this particular location, but I was struck by how attractive she looked in her crisp white uniform while supervising food preparations in the large commercial kitchen. And given her sparkling personality, it was evident that she was well respected and admired by those that she supervised.

I believe she supervised the Manhattan restaurant for about a year and a half. Then in late 1969, when her family moved from Flatbush to fashionable Upper Saddle River, she transferred to the Bloomingdales in Paramus N.J. She proved to be far more industrious and productive than me, saving enough money to eventually buy a sporty bright yellow, Chevy Nova, for $1700. In the future, both her Bloomingdales employment and her Chevy Nova would prove to be true Godsends.

CH - 41
JUNIOR YEAR

During the next two years, in addition to academic lectures in the morning, we were also assigned to both mandatory and elective clinical rotations. Along with 12 of my classmates, my first mandatory three-month rotation was at Des Moines General Hospital (DMGH). Although we anticipated and prepared for this day for a long time, we were finally turned *loose* in a real teaching hospital.

DMGH Naturally, our first assignment was to perform admission History and Physicals (H&Ps). We memorized and rehearsed the extensive questioning required of this initial patient encounter - an essential prelude to the all-important, *thorough* physical exam. And, lest we forget some vital piece of information, we each carried a Cheat sheet! However, I never remember young Dr. Kildare resorting to a Cheat sheet, but then again, Dr. Kildare, I was not!

Each of us would pull a random chart and then march into the patient's room to begin our Mayo Clinic query. There were usually two beds in each room, designated as A and B, and separated by a retractable curtain. In any event, I chose a woman in room 323, bed A. Thankfully, when I entered the room, I took note that my patient was considerably younger than the patient in bed B, who was easily in her 90s and on nasal oxygen. Unbeknownst to me, shortly after I chose my chart, Sig immediately chose the chart of the woman in bed B.

After introducing myself and drawing the curtain between the two beds, I began my laborious questioning of my patient's past medical history.

In the midst of my questioning, however, I heard thunderous footsteps entering the room and then a deep dramatic voice, as proudly proclaimed, "Good morning, Mrs. Schwartz, I'm Dr. Kulessa!" I thought, "Of course, who else would it be!" However Just to be certain I knew it was him, he purposely positioned himself next to the curtain in order to display his big shoes protruding from under the curtain.

Then, presuming the woman was deaf, in a loud baritone voice, he began his robust questioning, "Well, Mrs. Schwartz, at what age did you begin menstruating?" Hearing no response, he continued, "When was your last menstrual period?" Still, hearing no response, with increased vigor he asked, "Did you ever have measles or chickenpox? How about Gonorrhea?" With that, I absolutely lost it and had to immediately excuse myself, running out of the room before I peed in my pants.

Rib Raising   Regrettably, we also paired up to perform a common OMT technique known as *Rib Raising*. If done correctly, it's very effective for promoting lymphatic drainage and lessening recumbent atelectasis, thereby preventing pneumonia. The technique is most effective when performed by two assistants, one on each side of the supine patient. Then using both hands and fingertips, the goal is to *synchronously* raise the patient's rib cage. To be effective, however, the operative word is synchronicity - and therein lies the problem.

Sig would often volunteer to be my partner and then, while facing each other, he would purposely do just the opposite. when I was raising, he wasn't and vice versa. Consequently, rather than the patient's chest moving rhythmically up and down, it caused the patient to rock from side to side. Subliminally, this reminded me of when my brothers would prod me to rock my head violently back and forth.

OB/GYN   The two D.O.s responsible for teaching Ob/Gyn were Carl Waterbury, who was pretty good, and Elizabeth *Betty* Burrows, who was a witch. While doing a surgical rotation, Sig and I were scheduled to assist Betty in the OR to perform a routine hysterectomy. Although I enjoyed surgery, I couldn't stand Betty's fanaticism. Fortunately, I was the second assistant, leaving Sig as the first assistant. Throughout the entire operation, Betty was reprimanding Sig yelling, "Anticipate my moves, Doctor!" and each time, I would just shake my head, as though, in full agreement with the good Doctor.

At one point, in order to effectively anticipate Betty's moves, Sig decided to gain better visibility by extending his head into the operative field, inadvertently blocking Betty's view and she went absolutely ballistic! Again, I just shook my head in total agreement. Another time anticipating her moves, when Sig went to cut one of the sutures, she whacked the top of his hand with a pair of long forceps. And again, I just shook my head!

Up until then, as the second assist, my boring job was to hold the retractors in order to ensure good visibility. However, after Sig's latest blunder, he was told to, "Just hold the damn retractors!" and I was assigned to cut the sutures. Ah, finally, my big moment! I followed Betty's directions to the tee. If she said, "cut long", I dutifully left a healthy tail, and conversely, if she said, "cut short", I complied with perfection. Now, I was considered the *golden boy* - and rightly so! That is until I cut one a little too short - right on the knot, thereby releasing the suture and my stardom was short-lived!

E R   As part of our surgical rotation, Sig and I were assigned as observers in the Emergency room. At DMGH, aside from the attendings, we only had two interns and one surgical resident to handle surgical emergencies. When one would arrive, we would be paged to come to the emergency room stat!

One evening, a man was wheeled into the emergency room on a stretcher. Apparently, he fell off a horse, injuring his right ankle. Although his ankle was still wrapped with a bloody towel, he was otherwise, in no apparent distress, sitting upright on the stretcher explaining how the injury occurred. As the resident was gently unwrapping the bloody towel, I was assisting him on the opposite side of the stretcher and Sig was standing behind me on a step stool, observing everything over my right shoulder.

When the towel was finally removed, however, it revealed a compound fracture with the bone protruding from an open wound. Upon seeing this gruesome sight, Sig let out with a loud gasp exclaiming, "Oh my God!" Upon hearing this, the patient suddenly became pale and diaphoretic, prompting the resident to quickly lower his head of the stretcher while telling Sig, "Get him the hell out of the room!"

SIG & Diane's Wedding   In August Mary and I were invited to Sig and Diane's wedding and Sig asked me to be in his wedding party. The wedding was scheduled for early September in N.J. and although I was flattered by the unexpected honor of being included in the wedding party, this also meant the unexpected expense of a tuxedo and a flight back home for a very brief visit. All I remember of the celebration was being paired with a bridesmaid who was taller than me. This meant that I was separated from Mary for a good portion of the time which was very uncomfortable. Following the wedding, Sig and Diane drove their packed car back to Des Moines and eventually found a very nice apartment together.

Satellite Clinics   Following my Hospital rotation, I was assigned to one of the Community Satellite Clinics for three months. Initially, I mostly shadowed senior students who were, in turn, supervised by a faculty physician. In due time, however, depending on the particular senior, I eventually assumed the role of the primary healthcare provider. As with the College Clinic, the fee for service was based on a sliding scale which gave me a true taste of practicing rural medicine, which I found to be very rewarding.

Public Health   The next requirement was a one-month rotation in Public Health. This consisted of unannounced site visits to various restaurants and food distribution centers as well as community Pools and Shelters. In addition to assisting with immunization clinics, we were also tasked with designing and distributing various surveys from which we would hopefully generate some meaningful outcome data.

Thanksgiving in Chicago   I was excited to learn that Mary decided to fly out to Des Moines for Thanksgiving, and I remember excitedly crossing off the days on my calendar anticipating her arrival. Of course, when the big day arrived, the weather was very nasty with dense fog and high winds. With a fresh shave followed by an ample amount of Old Spice and my hair neatly combed, I waited nervously at the small airport for the arrival of flight 3740. After pacing back and forth for forty minutes, I noticed the arrival monitor flashing- Flight 3740 Delayed!

Two hours later, I noticed that her flight was re-routed to Omaha Nebraska! I thought to myself, "you can't make this shit up!". At first, I thought, perhaps it was just for refueling. However, I learned that the passengers were to be transported by bus from Omaha to Des Moines. After another two hours, with my Old Spice now completely evaporated, she finally arrived on a bus, looking absolutely drained.

Given my limited accommodations, Sig and Diane graciously invited her to crash in their apartment. The following evening we both seized the opportunity to have dinner in their comfortable home and Mary planned to make Lasagna, only to discover that they didn't sell Ricotta cheese in Des Moines. So, she improvised with cottage cheese and our Polish hosts never noticed the difference! The evening provided an opportunity for both of us to get to know Diane better, and as a foursome, we enjoyed a lot of laughs during the shortened weekend.

Then we drove Black Beauty to Mary's sister's home in Peoria Illinois, for Thanksgiving. Aside from the lack of privacy, we spent two pleasant days together, and before I knew it, it was time to say goodbye again. With a huge pain in my chest, I drove slowly to Chicago's O'hare airport for Mary's flight back home. The drive back to Des Moines was painfully long, and the quiet solitude of my apartment was both deafening and depressing.

Communication   During my entire stay in Des Moines, other than two packages of broken Ragu sauce, I don't recall receiving any letters or phone calls from my mother or siblings. I'm not complaining - I guess it's just the way it was in those days, or perhaps just in my family. There was never any doubt that they cared - it just wasn't communicated. I guess, akin to our lack of showing or expressing love, it was just assumed or taken for granted. In addition to the phone restrictions at the Fraternity house, when Chuck and I roomed together, I don't remember if we even had a phone in the apartment. So, I assume that calls between Mary and me must have been far less frequent.

Even more disconcerting was that her letters continued to diminish in size, content, and frequency and, no doubt, mine was even less. Consequently, the thought of spending Christmas alone in Des Moines was unbearable. Of course, there was never any mention of sending some traveling money from home - that would require a letter!

I'll Be Home For Xmas 1968   Shortly before Christmas, Sig, Diane, and I started thinking of an inexpensive way to fly back home for the holidays. At the time, United Airlines was again promoting the *12/21 program*, featuring 50% fares for *Standby* status. Obviously, this was targeting the high school and college students who had the luxury of waiting in an airport for hours. Considering this option would, of course, require that we each obtained the necessary fraudulent documents, stipulating that we were still under the age of 21.

Once we had all the necessary documents, we each purchased some used Drake sweatshirts as a disguise, and Sig would wear his green pee cap to cover his balding scalp. Purely by chance, the night before we planned to leave, I noticed that my electric alarm clock had the wrong time - indicating that we must have had a power outage.

Figuring that this would apply to a host of other travelers, at 4 am I called Sig, letting him know of our good fortune - a golden Standby opportunity! After quickly getting dressed in our disguises, we all rendezvoused at the airport two hours before flight time. Thankfully, the waiting area was relatively empty, indicating that the power outage had obviously affected a majority of eligible passengers. So, with Sig in his green pee cap and Diane sporting conspicuous pigtails, we nervously waited for the call for Standby passengers!

The full fair passengers boarded the plane first, followed by the Standby passengers. We anxiously counted as each passenger was called up. Finally, with four seats left we were called up one at a time. Then we each held our breath as we were about to face the second hurdle - passing identification scrutiny at the gate. We each attempted to look as nerdy and as adolescent as possible, with Sig and Diane posing as brother and sister. Finally, with a great sigh of relief, despite our scattered seat assignments, we all boarded the big bird for LaGuardia airport.

When we arrived at the airport, I remember being so joyful we all made it home that, as we exited the gate area, we started singing, *"I'll be home for Christmas!"* When the passengers waiting in the boarding area began clapping, Sig removed his pea cap soliciting monetary contributions. To this day, it's still one of my favorite holiday songs and I still get goosebumps just listening and remembering the thrill of it all!

Other than visiting Mary at Bloomingdales, I believe much of our time together was spent in Monroe. In retrospect, however, although I must have spent a good portion of the Holiday at Anita's house, I don't remember any particulars. Time seemed to slip away and before I knew it, I was wrestling again with the depressing notion that it would likely be a year before I would return home again.

Satellite Clinics II   After arriving back in Des Moines, I settled back into my small apartment, only to learn that the entire Apartment complex had been condemned and was scheduled for demolition in the near future. Also, I was scheduled for another two-month rotation at one of the satellite clinics. In the morning, when I went to start Black Beauty, the battery was dead. But I had jumper cables in the trunk for just such an eventuality. After begging for someone to jump-start Beauty, when I backed out of my parking space, I noticed a large pool of motor oil in the dirt.

Fortunately, I had two quarts of motor oil in the trunk, but when I finally arrived at the Clinic three hours late, I didn't receive a very warm reception. Already, the familiar dark cloud hovered over me!. Slowly, I managed to dig myself out of the deep hole, and by the second month, I became the lead provider. I was fortunate to have a very seasoned, elderly physician as my Clinic advisor. Although he trusted me to do just about anything, he was always available for guidance and sound advice, and It proved to be another golden opportunity to practice Rural Medicine.

Mental Health   Following the Clinic rotation, I was scheduled for a two-month rotation at a large State Mental Health Facility in Missouri. I carpooled with several of my classmates for the long 2-hour journey. Not surprisingly, everyone agreed that Black Beauty was not even a consideration. The State Mental facility consisted of several enormous brick buildings surrounded by an expansive array of flower gardens and manicured lawns. We were each assigned to one of several full-time staff physicians, and I was fortunate to have a very sharp elderly, General Practitioner. Each morning we would make rounds and then meet with a staff Psychiatrist to discuss patient care. After the first week of observation, we were assigned to provide new patient intake interviews and physicals. In time, I became very familiar with the appropriate questioning for assessing cognitive perception and awareness.

In those days there was a very limited variety of medications and electroshock therapy was commonplace. In time, we were permitted to make supervised medication adjustments. Although the facility's Medical Director was a prominent Psychiatrist in his own right, he invited Dr. Earl Fitz to come and demonstrate a dynamic therapeutic encounter with a very difficult patient. I will never forget the setting and quiet atmosphere.

The patient encounter took place in the silence of a small semi-circular amphitheater and I watched in awe as Dr. Fitz slowly walked the patient through a difficult area of resistance. This was followed by an unmistakable expression of enlightenment and emotional relief on the patient's face- an everlasting memory.

Incidentally, an ancillary benefit of working at the facility was that the Medical director's pretty daughter worked in the front office. This made for ample reasons to frequently sharpen my pencils.

In any event, we discovered that, in the basement of one of the buildings, there was a four-lane bowling alley. During a lunch break, several of us would periodically walk over and sneak into the basement to play a couple of games. Then one day, upon hearing the loud noise, a janitor walked in and exclaimed, "It's only intended for staff use!" When I responded, "But we are the staff!" he looked befuddled. When I explained that we found the door open, I could tell by his facial expression that he must have mistakenly left it unlocked, which provided some wiggle room for negotiation. After some gentle persuasion, he agreed that, in the future, he would let us in, provided we asked for his permission first!. - however, he was often difficult to find.

National Boards Part II & Final Exams   Part II of the National Board exams were fast approaching. There was really no way to adequately prepare for them, so it was just a matter of winging it. I don't remember them as being particularly difficult and I guess I did fairly well. Shortly after the Boards, I began preparing for our Final exams. Since they consisted of mostly relevant clinical subjects, they were likewise, uneventful. With these two hurdles behind me, I was excited to be in the home stretch, and barring some unforeseen catastrophe, come December, I was looking forward to completing my last two rotations in New Jersey.

CH - 42
SENIOR YEAR

Since my apartment complex was scheduled for demolition in July, I made arrangements to move in with two classmates, Steve Papish, and Lou Resnick - my Jewish brothers. They rented a spacious upstairs apartment in a two-family house that had a large Living - Dining room area and four bedrooms. We agreed upon a monthly rental through to December 1. The living arrangement was ideal because the fourth bedroom was occasionally occupied by other classmates who were doing brief rotations.

At some point, Steve was diagnosed with acute appendicitis and ultimately underwent a successful appendectomy at DMGH. Fortunately for us, his mother flew out and stayed in the apartment for 10 days, in order to take care of poor Stevie and the rest of us! She was an absolute Godsend! She went food shopping every day, and being a fabulous cook, she prepared delicious Dinners every evening, prompting us to actually eat on the Dining room table.

At the time I was an avid Chicago Bears fan, and I remember watching the Sunday afternoon football games, followed by a delicious prime rib dinner. Truthfully, we were all saddened to see Steve recovering so swiftly, but it would be a stretch to say, we hoped for a relapse! She tended to all of us as though we were her sons and we came to affectionately call her, Mom. Needless to say, it was a sad day when she left us hungry. As infants, who are separated from their mother, temporarily forget how to suckle, we forgot how to cook.

Vietnam (July 1969)   In those days there wasn't universal acceptance of D.Os as being equal to Real Doctors (MDs) In fact, I believe it wasn't until 1966, during the onset of the Vietnam War, that Osteopaths (DOs) were recruited to serve in the Armed Services, on an equal basis as Allopaths (MDs). Then in 1967, there was another breakthrough with the creation and endorsement of a 6th Osteopathic medical school - The University of Michigan, School of Osteopathic Medicine. Following this event, a further statement of parity was when both, the US Public Health Service and Indian Health Services offered Internship and Residency programs to both, DOs, and MDs alike.

Many of my classmates and I shared something in common - we hadn't been accepted to an Allopathic medical school. As Osteopaths, we would rationalize that, in addition to the same academic curriculum, and passing the equivalent National Board exams, we had the advantage of also being trained in the Art and Practice of present day, Manual Medicine (OMT). I firmly believe that the inherent benefit of a direct *Hands-On* approach to patient care, gave us a unique edge over the Allopaths. However, despite this self-reassurance, there was still a sense of lingering doubt or idle curiosity. I must admit that I would readily seize every opportunity to be in the company of the MDs - in many respects, out of pure curiosity. Were they really better trained or more intelligent?

More importantly, as future physicians, how do we overcome the erroneous sentiment that Osteopathy entails *Vudu Medicine*. Ironically, having found no appreciable difference, it prompted me to work and study harder in order to overcome this perceived stigma. This was especially true during my Internship when I would become the first *token* Osteopath.

Internship Road Trips   It was time to give serious consideration to our choice of available Osteopathic Internships. At the time, they were virtually all Rotating Internships, and It was customary for hospitals to recruit candidates for their respective programs by offering to host and entertain interested candidates for an entire weekend. They provided simple sleeping arrangements and delicious food and alcohol - what more could you ask for!

I remember taking periodic weekend car trips with several of my classmates, to the Osteopathic friendly states of Michigan and Ohio. Based on their accommodations, we would plan to hit two or three Osteopathic hospitals per weekend. I found each excursion to be both informative and, of course, very entertaining - often plying us with an abundance of food, booze, and an occasional, pre-arranged, mixer dance.

Then, at some point, the hospital administrator would press each of us for a frank assessment of their Internship Program and our level of interest. It was almost comical because, the greater our perceived level of interest, the more they wined and dined us. Likewise, the stipends being offered by the various Hospitals were very competitive, often fluctuating on their current needs and an assessment of our anticipated contribution. Needless to say, there was a sufficient amount of bullshit on both sides of the discussion.

However, even though the individual Hospital Programs and Stipends were very attractive, the bottom line was, "Would I even consider an internship in the Midwest?" Further adding to the uncertainty was the fact that COMS' charter had a stipulation enabling the Board of Directors to grant either a DO or MD diploma. At the time, our Dean, Tom Vigorito, was in favor of offering either degree subject to the student's preference. In fact, it wasn't until shortly before our Graduation ceremony that we learned, the Board voted to continue issuing D.O. Diplomas.

Laura   Living in the apartment with the guys went smoothly and was very affordable. At some point, one of the guys befriended a nurse at nearby Mercy Hospital. This led to occasional impromptu visits by several of her nursing friends, none of whom I found particularly attractive. Initially, the visits amounted to brief *hanging out* sessions, which I paid little attention to. However, the number of visitors gradually increased, which became annoying until one particular nurse named, Laura, caught my attention. She was far prettier than the others and quietly set herself apart from the rest, which I found to be somewhat alluring.

401

At some point, Chuck said that Charlene came out for a visit, and that they planned to go to a local dance club and asked if I wanted to join them. The only companion I could think of was, Laura. Although I hadn't seen her in a couple of weeks, when I called her, I was pleasantly surprised when she accepted the invitation.

The next obstacle, however, was how to get there. By now, Black Beauty was leaking oil like a sieve - approximately 2 quarts of oil on a daily basis. Each morning when I left the Apartment, I left a pool of oil. In fact, I would routinely buy a case of motor oil and keep it in my dismantled trunk in order to constantly replenish Beauty's insatiable thirst.

When I mentioned to Laura that I was having *car trouble* she offered to pick me up in her car - what more could you ask for! Being that several weeks had passed, I didn't have a clear recollection of what she looked like. Since I was a little late trying to find something to wear, she came upstairs to the apartment. I took note of how smartly she dressed and how attractive she appeared, and I wasn't disappointed. Although It was nice to see Charlene again, it was understandably, awkward. Despite this, however, I think Laura had a good time.

Interestingly, the notion of betrayal never entered my mind. From my perspective, she was purely a companion and I considered our relationship purely platonic. Besides, while at St Elizabeth, I was aware that Mary attended Mixer dances and had Concert dates with students from Seton Hall and Drew University.

Laura lived with her parents and at some point, either she or they invited me to have Thanksgiving dinner at their house. Although I was self-conscious about leaving a pool of oil on their driveway, I thought it would have been even worse to have her chauffeur me to and from her house. So, I decided to drive Black Beauty and parked discreetly, two houses away. Her parents were very cordial offering pre-dinner drinks and appetizers followed by a delicious three-course dinner.

Following dinner, Laura casually mentioned to her father about my *car problems*. I was embarrassed when he insisted on putting Beauty up on ramps in their garage in order to check for a leaking gasket which he thought could probably be fixed. However, after I pulled Beauty into the garage he politely said, "A leaking gasket is the least of your problems!" Thirty minutes later, he came into the house and said, "Virtually all of your gaskets are leaking!"

While having dessert, I had the distinct impression that they were pulling out all the stops! This triggered my internal alarm button - uh oh! was this more than just a nice dinner or was I *meeting the Fakers!* This alarm was further heightened when, upon visiting me at the apartment, she said her parents loved having me for dinner and welcomed me back anytime!

Then she asked me to take a ride up to Lookout Point. Thankfully, knowing that Beauty's engine smoked like a chimney, she offered to use her car. After parking at the peaceful summit and taking in the gorgeous vista, I was suddenly taken aback when she seized the moment to tell me that she loved me - double uh oh! It was clearly evident that we had different degrees of attraction. I was content with simply enjoying her company. After a long awkward pause, I told her that I would soon be driving back home, and without missing a beat, she asked if it would be okay if she visited me in New York!

Obviously at a loss for words other than several *um and ahs*, being very intuitive, she asked, "Do you have a girl back home?" After reluctantly confessing that I did, I felt awful as I lamely explained that I didn't mean to lead her on. Thankfully, she graciously accepted the reality of the situation, which greatly relieved my anxiety of possibly being surprised by an impromptu arrival at one of the New York airports. In retrospect, however, I truly regret any of my actions that may have unwittingly hurt such a lovely girl.

Pediatrics My last monthly rotation at DMGH was Pediatrics, which I thoroughly enjoyed, but which was also fraught with a near disaster!, While making rounds in the nursery we were instructed to always have at least one hand on any infant, especially when lowering the side rails. I was preparing to take an infant's rectal temperature, and as I reached for the thermometer, I momentarily lifted my other hand. In that brief moment, the infant suddenly rolled onto the floor! I immediately picked the infant up and did a brief assessment. Although there didn't appear to be any visible injuries, our faculty pediatrician, Dr. Nelson, was immediately summoned to the nursery. Of course, I imagined the worst - expecting that this was the end of my career in medicine, let alone pediatrics.

After Dr. Nelson's initial rebuke, he reassured me that he didn't detect any obvious injuries. However, he instructed me to monitor the infant every two hours for the next 12 hours. Our clinical medical director, Dr. Williams, was also notified and he was far more reassuring, that it was premature to consider changing my profession to plumbing. It was a truly horrifying lesson, one that I vowed I would never make again. Thankfully, the remainder of my rotation was uneventful.

Black Beauty's Demise At some point, I was asked by one of my classmates, Frank Rotella, if I would be willing to drive his car back to his home in New Jersey. Considering the choice of cars, it was a no-brainer. By comparison, aside from the cost of oil, his late-model Dodge drove like a Rolls-Royce. Then, on the last day of my rotation, I was paged to report to the hospital administrator's office as soon as possible. Totally bewildered, I immediately thought of the infant casualty. When I arrived at his office, however, I was informed that, while exiting the hospital parking lot, the Chief of Staff's wife accidentally backed into my precious, Black Beauty.

He explained that she was so upset that he arranged for her to meet with me. When I met with the elegantly dressed elderly woman in the parking lot, I noticed that she was driving a brand new, Cadillac sedan. Although her car only suffered a minor scratch on the left rear bumper, she was confused by the extensive damage to the rear of my vintage car. Noting the concave fender and crushed trunk she apologized profusely for causing such damage! Shamefully, I seized the opportunity by appearing equally astounded by the extensive damage and politely asked, "How fast were you going?"

The lovely lady offered to have her insurance company appraise the damages in order to make prompt restitution. When I explained that I was due to leave for New York the following morning, she offered me $ 150 cash to settle the issue - music to my ears! With cash in hand, I drove Black Beauty to the nearest salvage yard, removed the license plates and bid her good riddance. After packing Frank's car with all my worldly possessions, I said adios to my roommates, and started the long journey back home.

Galaxie 500 Limo   The following morning, Mary followed me in her new yellow Chevy Nova as I reluctantly returned Frank's luxurious car to his home in N.J. Considering that I would need a car for my next two rotations, I knew I had to buy another *reliable* car. This time I upped the ante by purchasing a green 1960 Ford Galaxie 500! for $300. Although she was a gas guzzler, In its day, she was synonymous with success - a real, status symbol! By comparison, I felt she was luxurious, with clean comfortable upholstery and spacious backseat with extra leg room - surely befitting her moniker, *the Limo!* *B*ut then again, who would be sitting in the back seat?.

Preceptorship Bayonne NJ (Jan- Mar 1970)   My next clinical rotation entailed spending the next 3 months in Bayonne N.J, shadowing my Preceptor, Joe Mastromonaco DO. Joe's father was a prominent MD, who was professionally and politically very influential in Bayonne. His large stature was intimidating, but in reality, he was a very gentle and compassionate man. He was very proud to have been trained at the enormous, Jersey City Medical Center - in its day, one of the largest and most prestigious Medical Centers on the east coast.

He drove what appeared to be an extended, Fleetwood Cadillac, that I often referred to as, The Limousine. Joe's parents lived in a large, elegant brick corner home. The household was maintained by a very dedicated full-time caretaker named, Francis, who was treated like one of the family. Two of Joe's brothers were also DO's, a radiologist, and an Orthopedist, currently serving in Vietnam. I remember this because he would frequently ask his father for advice and to send surgical textbooks.

Joe lived next door to his father, in a smaller, but quite substantial, brick house and they both shared office space in a single-family wood-framed house, directly behind Joe senior's house. Joe's third brother, Vito, ran the family's liquor store and managed the family's Jersey City landmark restaurant, The Villa Capri - a place where all the *important* people meet, and all the *deals* were made.

Shortly after I began my rotation, knowing of my lengthy commute from Monroe, Joe's father had a bedroom prepared for me above their offices. Ironically, this reminded me of sleeping above the Funeral parlor and therefore, I only stayed there a few times. In addition, being that my sister, Virginia, lived in Wyckoff, N.J. and the Trums had recently moved to Upper Saddle River N.J. this provided for two alternate sleeping arrangements. As it turned out, I would routinely drive down from Monroe on Monday mornings and return on Friday evenings.

Virginia's House   During the week, I mostly stayed at Virginia's house with her husband, Lou, and their two children, Maria, and Louis. My sister was very gracious by providing me with delicious dinners and a private bedroom downstairs in their attractive bilevel. The only potential disaster was that, although the bed was a decent sized cot, it folded in the middle, propelled by a very powerful spring that was held in place by a small metal latch.

Each morning, the kids would come down to wake me and say goodbye before leaving for school. One morning, however, almost immediately after they said goodbye, the damn latch mysteriously came undone and the bed sprang closed with such violent force that I was squished in the middle. I suspected something nefarious because, as they exited the room, they were giggling.

After struggling for a while and feeling embarrassed, I began calling for them to come down and help me, but there was no response. Since I could hear them upstairs, I put shame aside and began yelling from downstairs - still no response. When I heard them leaving for school and closing the door, I began screaming until my sister finally came down. While looking at my dire predicament, she just stood there hysterically laughing. By this time, I was having difficulty expanding my lungs and was fast approaching *panic mode*. Then, while she pulled down on one end of the bed, and I was pushed up from within, I was finally able to wiggle out from the suffocating jaws of death!

Each morning, when I would arrive at the *Godfather's* house, I would usually find Joe conferring with Francis regarding the daily *house call* list. Then, after conferring with his father, we would all leave to make rounds at Bayonne General Hospital. Joe Senior, arranged for me to make rounds on their patients and to even write orders which, of course, required a countersignature. He was a seasoned diagnostician from the old school, who still relied on the five basic tenets of a thorough examination: Inspection, Observation, Palpation, Percussion, and Auscultation. Having unlimited privileges, including surgery, he arranged for me to assist him in the operating room for minor surgical procedures.

Following hospital rounds, Joe and I would make house calls in Bayonne and Jersey City. One day, while crossing over the Bayonne Bridge, Joe pointed across the bay and proudly said "That's Bayonne, the eighth wonder of the world!" Unlike the College Clinic house calls, these were truly learning experiences that I vowed I would try to emulate when in private practice. After finishing the house calls, we'd routinely drive to his house for a quick sandwich prepared by his lovely wife, Jerry, and then walk to the office to see patients.

Joe and his father shared adjacent offices on the ground floor of the small wood frame house. Consequently, twice a week, I had the benefit of two preceptors, spending time with each of them and nothing was considered off-limits. The small house was merely a temporary office arrangement pending the construction of a large brick professional building intended to eventually accommodate his two brothers.

Joe had completed one year of an internal medicine residency and demonstrated a good grasp of Cardiology. By this time I had memorized the text, Practical Cardiology, by H. Marriott MD, Courtesy of Eli Lilly. I compiled detailed notes in my small black loose-leaf binder, which I carried with me at all times. Perhaps, as a means of refreshing his own memory, Joe would often ask me to quiz him on any subject matter, but especially Cardiology - which was something we shared in common.

In the office, I would routinely take 12 lead EKGs on patients, after which he'd ask, "Well, what do you think?" As my preceptor, his academic retention was both amazing and inspiring. The three month Preceptorship seemed to fly by, and when I told him that my next rotation was, an Externship at Cherry Hill Medical Center, he said, "That's where I did my Internship". I was sorry to see the preceptorship end, and as a fitting tribute he insisted on taking Mary and me out to dinner as a foursome, to any restaurant of my choosing, Of course, I chose, the Villa Capri.

CHMC Externship (April-June 1970)   My next 3-month rotation was as an Extern at Cherry Hill Medical Center (CHMC) in Cherry Hill N.J. The commute would be almost twice as long as to Bayonne, driving all the way down to exit 4 on the New Jersey Turnpike. So, far, other than excessive gas consumption, the Galaxy 500 Limo was holding up as well as could be expected. I often slept in the hospital *on-call room* which lessened the commute considerably.

However, I began to notice that the Limo's muffler was sounding a little louder than usual. In time, this was followed by a faint whiff of exhaust fumes, and I found myself breathing a little easier if I drove with a window cracked open a snitch. As the gentle purr of the muffler became a gentle vibration, I noticed that I coughed less if I drove with all the windows lowered at least halfway. During cold or rainy weather, this was a chilling reminder of the Green Hornet!.

The Medical Center was much larger than I expected and having a mixed DO and MD staff surprised me. Similar to DMGH, it was a Rotating externship requiring a two to three-week rotation in each of the specialties. Early on, I latched on to three Interns, but one in particular,

Sal Cerniglia, became my mentor and close friend. Considering that he knew Joe Mastromonaco, and had a reputation as a *hot-headed* Sicilian, we quickly forged a close bond of friendship. In fact, because we were often seen walking the halls together, everyone assumed that I must also be a feared Sicilian. Consequently, we were dubbed, the *Sicilian Duo* or *Connection*- I know, Silly.

Surgery   In any event, I loved every one of my rotation, but most especially, Surgery. There was a first-year Orthopedic resident, Carl Mogel, a gentle Bear of a man who, for whatever reason, took me under his wing. He had already completed two years of General surgery and therefore, was often called upon to assist with both Orthopedic and General surgical cases. Consequently, he often scheduled me as the second assist which was in sharp contrast to my agonizing experiences with Betty *the Bitch*!

There were two eminently pompous, General surgeons known collectively as Silverman and Bonnier. For reasons unknown to me, while we were both assisting Fred Silverman DO, he was taking great delight in harassing and making disparaging remarks about my giant mentor. Apparently, Dr. Silverman must have recognized my distaste for his unwarranted ridicule saying, "You don't like that do you?" I simply responded, "Nobody deserves that!" Then Silverman said to the giant, "Carl, I don't know why I treat you that way" to which I said, "Then don't!" and Silverman retorted, "If you don't like it, you can leave." - which I did.

Dr.Ablaza   Cherry Hill successfully launched heart and lung bypass procedures by recruiting a Filipino cardiothoracic surgeon, Dr.Ablaza, and his Japanese assistant, from New Jersey's Deborah Heart & Lung Hospital. Since Dr. Ablaza's procedures were always very long, no one ever volunteered to assist him. I seized upon this golden opportunity and I was richly rewarded when, after a thoracotomy (Chest operation), he allowed me to close the muscle and skin layers. His assistant was a very short man who required a step stool in order to see the operative field, and, towards the end of the procedure, when Ablaza gave the signal, his assistant stepped down and I was thrilled to take over.

Over the course of time, I would volunteer to scrub on any of his cases, mostly because he was always willing to teach and I was anxious to learn. One afternoon, while eating alone in the cafeteria, I was shocked and honored when he and his assistant asked to join me at my table. After some small talk, his message was simple, "continue to seize every opportunity to learn!"

Obstetrics   I also enjoyed Obstetrics and knowing this, Sal Cerniglia would call me to observe whenever he was called to assist one of the attending Obstetricians. In like manner, he identified those attendings who he felt were *teachers* and then would personally introduce me to them. In turn, they would also call me to observe and eventually allow me to assist in the deliveries. By this time Sal was a pro, and when he was confident in my ability, he allowed me to perform the deliveries while closely observing me. Eventually, I graduated to episiotomy repairs and the application of outlet forceps - and I felt a sense of accomplishment.

E R   Sal also guided me through my rotation in the very busy Emergency room. I enjoyed learning to suture, especially facial wounds that required fine detail. By May, Interns and Residents were either tired or bored doing the same routine procedures and therefore, they readily delegated them to those who demonstrated a willingness to learn and a reasonable level of competence.

Medicine   When it came to my final Internal Medicine rotation, having had Joe Mastromonaco as my preceptor, I felt very confident to handle most medical emergencies, especially cardiology. This connection was also advantageous because many of the residents and attendings still spoke highly of Joe's aptitude. I can honestly say that I thoroughly enjoyed all phases of this particular rotation and of the Medical Center in general.

In retrospect,   In my opinion, the first year of medical school was pure academics with no clinical relevance. The second year was still primarily academic with only marginal clinical relevance. Ironically, however, being that the third and fourth years were mostly clinical, as a neophyte clinician, this

410

often required me to review the academic basis for my clinical assumptions. I found this to be an ongoing process until the clinical presentations become more routine or second nature. Sadly, however, in light of my failing memory, rather than reviewing the academic basis for my clinical "Impressions", I find myself more often relying on pure clinical, "Intuition".

Having spent the past 6 months in New Jersey afforded me a rare opportunity to explore possible Osteopathic Internships within the tristate area. Foremost, of course, was Cherry Hill Medical Center.- they knew me, and I knew them. The next consideration was Union Hospital, a relatively small Osteopathic Hospital in Union, New Jersey. I applied and was accepted by both New Jersey hospitals.

Also, since I knew that Sig was accepted by Lancaster Osteopathic Hospital, in Lancaster, PA, I decided to check it out. It was a relatively small hospital in the middle of the Amish country. Although I knew we would have a lot of laughs, given our past history at DMGH, I suspected that we were more likely to get kicked out of the program.

SBMC Interview (June 1970)   Mary's father had been suffering from progressive Parkinson's disease and underwent an amazingly successful operation performed by two neurosurgeons, Cooper, and Star, who were affiliated with St. Barnabas Medical Center (SBMC) in Livingston, New Jersey. Purely on a whim, despite knowing that it was an Allopathic Hospital, I decided to submit an application anyway. Much to my surprise, I was invited for an interview.

I remember getting lost while driving the Limo, now dubbed, *Smokey,* through some very affluent areas of Short Hills and Livingston N.J. When I eventually reached my destination and approached the enormous five-story structure, I was in absolute awe. I remember ascending the wide semicircular granite stairway leading to a second-story outdoor balcony. When I opened the highly polished brass entry doors and entered the two-story marble interior, I just stood there with my mouth open! The main floor was flanked by a bank of elevators, all with highly polished brass doors.

411

I had a 2 pm appointment to meet with the Director of Medical Education, Dr.Islami MD, on the third floor. When I walked into his large suite, I was greeted warmly by each of his two secretaries, one of whom was quite shapely and fairly good looking. After a brief wait, I was escorted into Dr.Islami's personal office. I didn't know it at the time, but he was a very well respected surgeon and in charge of St. Barnabas' ECFMG education and certification program for foreign medical graduates.

Acknowledging that I was a DO, he complimented me for having the courage to apply for an Allopathic rotating internship. At first, I was taken aback by his last statement until he said, "Being a teaching hospital, each year we recruit approximately 40 interns, and if accepted, you would be the first (and only) D.O!"

When the interview was over, we shook hands warmly and he asked the prettier of the two secretaries to take me on a walking tour of the entire 800-bed hospital - which took almost an hour. She emphasized St. Barnabas' self-adulation of always being the *First in N J* - such as the First renal transplant, the First to have a Hyperbaric chamber and hyperbaric beds. It was also hailed as the area's only level 1 Burn Unit with Hubbard tanks and an emergency Heliport on the roof. They were very fortunate to have Dr. Hutchins, as the Unit's Medical Director since he trained at the renowned Brooks Army Medical Center in Texas.

Then she offered that the Heliport was also used to shuttle *Celebrities*, such as Jackie Onassis, and Col. Sanders, to the Hospital's VIP Suites on the 6th floor. For privacy and security, the *Special floor* was only accessed by a private elevator. Upon hearing this I mused, "considering the affluent area, Barnabas was sounding more like a high end, Country Club Hospital!

Incidentally, at the ripe old age of 84, Col. Sanders, was a frequent visitor to the Hyperbaric Chamber and hyperbaric beds for Rejuvenation! And as a lowly intern, I *was* rarely *privileged* to do H&Ps on the *Special* patients.

I left the tour feeling exhilarated but acknowledged a potential dilemma. By accepting an internship in an Allopathic hospital, I could conceivably be perceived by the Osteopathic hierarchy, as a *Traitor*. It wasn't until much later that I discovered that, Howie Greenspan, made a last-minute commitment to satisfy his military and Osteopathic internship obligations by serving two years in the US Public Health Services. And I thought, "He was always smarter than me!" At the time, I believe this was the only known exception sanctioned by the American Osteopathic Association(AOA).

Missouri Licensure   Having finished my final rotations and after several days of rest, I made plans to drive out to Missouri in order to take a lengthy written exam for a Missouri license. Passing this exam was considered a valuable means of attaining future state licenses by reciprocity. In any event, Mary offered to let me drive her new spiffy Chevy Nova out to Missouri and then on to Des Moines in preparation for Graduation, which was scheduled for June 4th!

The plan was for Mary to fly out to Des Moines a couple of days before graduation and then, we would drive back home together, stopping overnight at Pat's house in Sycamore, Illinois. I accepted the fact that none of my siblings expressed any interest in attending my graduation. Truthfully, however, I didn't necessarily encourage anyone to come because I was somewhat ashamed of my school. Coming from St. John's University's new sprawling campus, I recall how I was initially disappointed with the size and location of our school. This is what prompted me to send home pictures of the St Joseph Girls Academy.

Regrets   However, one of the many regrets in life was not being more proactive by pre-arranging for my mother to fly out with Mary. Considering that my mother had never flown before, I willingly presumed that she shared the same sentiment as my siblings, and as in the past, I simply rationalized - what's the big deal!. However, the sense of guilt became overwhelming, and on very short notice, I hoped to redeem myself by offering to fly her out with Mary, but she declined. My heart ached for her apparent disappointment and I felt awful that perhaps with a little more effort, I could have convinced her to fly out, but would she be willing to fly home alone? Unfortunately, I'll never know.

After packing Mary's car with enough clothes, I set out for Missouri. Driving a new car was like a dream come true, and I ended up driving straight through the night. I don't recall the precise location, but I remember walking into a large semicircular amphitheater-like room and seeing 8 or 10 of my classmates. I don't remember the exam as being particularly difficult or perhaps, after the prior 6 months, I was well prepared. True to form, however, I was one of the last ones to leave the room but feeling unusually confident about the outcome. I felt even better when, despite the razzing, I saw my classmates waiting for me outside. Having completed the first step toward achieving state licensure, we all decided to celebrate with a few *reunion beers*. After a lot of laughs while comparing our horrid rotation stories, we formed a mini caravan and headed back to Des Moines.

CH - 43
GRADUATION

I arrived back in Des Moines for three days of partying before the big event. I was fortunate to stay in the same apartment with my former roommates. Knowing that I was a former bartender, Carlos loved how I made Bloody Marys. For some reason, he decided that, during the next few days, we should resume our prior Bloody Mary recipe - the more vodka, black pepper, and Tabasco sauce the better! It didn't take long before we mounted the familiar bar stools at our favorite joint, O'Grady's.

He insisted that I go behind the bar to instruct the bartender on how we wanted our Bloody Marys. In fact, he recently reminded me that, for posterity, we carved our initials in the wood paneling under the padded armrest. Our time alone was precious, because Mary was expected to arrive the following day and would be staying with them.

In the meantime, I made an appointment to meet with our Dean, Tom Vigorito DO in order to discuss my Internship options - namely, regarding St Barnabas Medical Center. Being that he was relatively young with a progressive mindset, I valued his unbiased opinion. I explained how impressed I was with St. Barnabas, and although I wanted to remain loyal to the Osteopathic profession, I realized that, at least academically, there was no comparison with what St. Barnabas had to offer.

After listening intently, without hesitation, he surprised me and put my mind at ease by saying, "Go wherever you feel you can get the best possible education!". That simple sentence eased my conscience, making the basis of my difficult decision much easier. little did I know, however, that this decision would present a monumental hurdle in order to eventually sit for the Osteopathic Family Practice Board exams!

When Mary arrived, we only had two days to celebrate - and celebrate we did! That evening we attended a semi-formal dinner-dance hosted by the College in a Hotel banquet room for all the Graduates. Following the dance, Tom and his wife joined Carlos, Maria, and us in an adjoining lounge for a *Nightcap*- which Tom graciously paid for. He seemed very relaxed, and at one point he became very emotional saying, "After tomorrow, you'll change from students to colleagues, and sadly our paths will part". On that note, we all raised our glasses and I said, "Then, here's to tonight!"

The following day, we went for a picnic at Gray's Lake, wading in the water and enjoying the sunny afternoon together. Following dinner that evening, Carlos invited several other classmates over to his apartment for Bloody Marys! Somehow, Tom Vigorito showed up alone and I remember spiking his drink with extra Vodka and Tabasco sauce. Surprisingly, he asked for a second, followed by a third. Then, around one in the morning, after most of the others left, Tom called his wife to come and pick him up. But before she arrived, with glasses raised we toasted, "Here's to tomorrow!" With that said, Tom just nodded his head and mumbled. "Hasta Manana".

The big day finally arrived! With great difficulty, and after sufficient coffee and Tylenol, at 11am,we joined our fellow classmates assembled in front of the stately, Veteran's Auditorium. We donned our caps and gowns and *quietly* prepared for the long-awaited procession. For a brief moment, I felt my father's presence, and although I was thrilled that Mary was here, my joy was dampened by a mixture of sadness and guilt for not doing more to insure my mother's presence! This prevailing sentiment would continue to haunt me for many years to come. Perhaps it was the *Alice Curse*, "Mark my words, you're not gonna have a good time!"

The interior of the auditorium was more like a church with pews and a marble interior. After being seated and enduring the endless speeches by several Board members and assorted dignitaries, we were ready to receive our diplomas from Dean, Tom Vigorito. Strangely, however, while standing on an elevated marble platform, I noticed that Tom was wearing dark sunglasses!

We were to process singularly up the center aisle, and after being congratulated, we would be handed our diplomas by the venerable Dean of the College. Interestingly, it seemed as though the entire process was proceeding in slow motion. When I finally approached Tom to shake hands, I smiled and whispered, "What's with the dark glasses?" After slowly lowering them halfway to reveal his puffy, bloodshot eyes, he said, "I can't get my eyeballs back in their sockets!" Sadly, those were the last unforgettable words we exchanged.

Following the ceremony, while still adorned in our colorful caps and gowns, a brief flurry of picture taking in front of the Auditorium was quickly followed by warm goodbyes. While Sig and Dianne and Carlos and Maria lingered a while longer, before I knew it, the seemingly endless journey and long-anticipated celebration came to a sudden anticlimactic conclusion, followed by the rapid dispersion of all the active participants.

Ironically, the joy of accomplishment was paradoxically tempered by a profound sense of sadness. These same colleagues with whom I had lived, partied, and competed for the past four years, suddenly vanished, more than likely, never to be seen again. Furthermore, the daunting realization that having finally cleared a significant hurdle, I would soon have to compete again - albeit, in a different arena!

After saying goodbye to Carlos and Maria, Mary and I left for Sycamore, Illinois. After spending an overnight at Pat's house, in the morning we drove nonstop to New York. When we finally arrived at Anita's house, I was thrilled to open a letter of acceptance from St. Barnabas. The letter stipulated a starting date of July 1st and a stipend of $1000 a month! Furthermore, It was suggested that I come down as soon as possible in order to arrange for *convenient housing* - whatever that meant?.

Nick's Lodge (June 1970)   Meanwhile, I was surprised to learn that an agreement was reached among the members of the Lodge's consortium whereby Nick would become the sole proprietor of the Lodge. Strangely, from my limited perspective, during the transition, he seemed to play it very close to the vest. I was never privy to the terms of the agreement, or if my mother or other siblings were made aware of the particulars. In fact, It wasn't until after returning home from Iowa that Nick reached out to me, asking for my help to prepare the Lodge for the next season.

Before starting my internship, I spent two weeks at the Lodge, cleaning and opening the pool, mowing the lawns, and preparing the snack bar for the 1970 season. Despite working together on weekends, Nick never divulged why or how he came to assume control which remains a mystery to this day. However, considering that, without a question, he loaned me $300, I felt it was the least I could do for him- likewise, without question,

SBMC Apartments   Following three weeks at the Lodge, I drove down to St. Barnabas in order to secure my housing. All the *convenient* housing was in a large Apartment complex directly across the street from the Hospital - very convenient indeed! However, when I met with Dr. Islami's secretaries, they informed me that, at this late date, the only housing still available was a small Apartment on Northfield Avenue, approximately 3 miles from the Hospital!

When I expressed my disappointment, as a consolation they both offered to show me the Apartment. When they walked in, they were visibly embarrassed by the location and the condition of the small Apartment. They apologized and suggested that I move in for a month, and in the meantime, they would try to secure one of the *convenient* Apartments. When I was issued my white uniform and shoes, I was notified that my first rotation would be, Ob-Gyn. Being that I would be mostly in scrubs, I figured I would need very little in order to move into the *inconvenient* Apartment for the month.

CH - 44
SBMC INTERNSHIP

On June 30th Smokey and I moved into my temporary housing on Northfield Ave. The following morning I showed up at 7am for Orientation which was held in a large amphitheater on the ground floor of the Hospital. It was used primarily for the ECFMG courses, as well as for the monthly, surgical morbidity and mortality conferences.

All of the respective Department Heads and new interns and residents were present. Harvey Nussbaum MD stood up and introduced himself as the Chief of Staff and Chairman of the Department of Medicine. I'll never forget his opening statement, "You will see virtually every medical condition or illness at least once in this Hospital!" Then he offered that, the admitting diagnosis of every patient was available for your perusal - take advantage of every learning opportunity.

Then the Chief of Cardiology, Dr. Leff, gave a scintillating lecture on the use of a relatively new drug called lidocaine, expressing the importance of its early utilization in order to prevent fatal arrhythmias. This was followed by brief introductions and comments by each of the other distinguished Department Heads - the big three being, Drs James Breen(OB-GYN), James Hogan (Medicine-Hematology) and Louis DelGuercio (Surgery).

Ob-Gyn Dr. Breen   Following the orientation, I reported to the Ob-Gyn department on the third floor and met with the Residents, all of whom were very cordial and seemed willing to teach even a DO. One in particular, Phil Massimino MD, was a first-year Resident who quickly took me under his wing.

The routine in every specialty was that each morning the first-year resident and assigned Intern would make rounds together. This wasn't always the best teaching arrangement, especially on your first rotation. Being that the resident was also a beginner, the intern was mostly relegated to either, *scutt work*, an observer, or even worse, a *goffer!* However, to his credit, Phil recognized early on that we were almost equals, and for the most part, he treated me as such. In fact, it wasn't unusual for him to eventually ask me to cover for him.

As bad luck would have it, on the very first weekend, I was scheduled for, *On Call* duty! The weekday shifts were every 12 hours and the *On Call* schedule was every third night and every second weekend. The weekends were absolutely brutal - an 84-hour marathon beginning at 7am on Friday morning, thru to 7pm on Monday evening. - naturally requiring you to sleep in the Hospital's *On Call* room. This was followed by the normal 12 hr. weekday schedule, 36 hours every third day etc. I mostly celebrated the alternating weekends, by getting the hell out of Dodge!

In any event, on the initial Friday evening, I was faced with the onslaught of H&Ps which were mostly for weekend surgical admissions. I remember feeling so overwhelmed that the covering resident finally took pity on me. After scanning my work he said, "Christ, there only presurgical H&Ps.You don't have to do Mayo Clinic physical!" Then, by 9 pm, seeing how many more I still had to do, he lightened my load by quickly handling several charts. When I saw how brief and concise his entries were, I finally got the hang of it. However, feeling dejected and totally exhausted, later that night I remember calling Mary at her home just to unload and hoping for some sympathy!.

Bed Delivery   During my first week on the floor, one of the Attending physicians grew impatient with a young woman's progression of labor and started her on a slow Pitocin drip. I was surprised, however, when he left to make rounds, leaving me to monitor her progress. Ironically, shortly after he left, her contractions increased in frequency and intensity and I suggested that the charge nurse should notify the Attending physician. Unable to reach either the Attending or the Resident ,however, she called on me to evaluate the patient's progress - uh oh!.

When I walked into her room, I was shocked to see the protrusion of black hair! - she was obviously *Crowning!* I immediately told the nurse to stop the Pitocin drip, and after putting on sterile gloves, with my hands folded, I started to pray! Then I asked again for the Nurse to page both the Attending and Phil Massimino *Stat!*

While she was gone, I gently placed my gloved hand on the baby's head. Failing to reach either of the Doctors, when she came back into the room she asked, "Dr, what are you doing?" When I said, "I'm waiting for the Doctor to arrive" she snapped, "You are the Doctor!" By this time, I could see the baby's eyes, and with her moral support, I delivered my first and only *Bed Delivery* at St. Barnabas - where you will see everything at least once!

Two third year Residents, Eli Rose MD, and Jeff Franklin MD were more than willing to supervise me doing just about anything. In fact, Jeff assisted while I did my first C-section. Since I volunteered to observe and assist with every delivery, the attendings eventually came to know me. Eventually, they allowed me to handle the deliveries and episiotomy repairs with one notable exception, Dr. Papas.

Dr. Papas Dr Papas was a short Greek who prided himself on his seamless episiotomy closures, using subcuticular stitching - definitely overkill. Besides, who's going to ask, "Can I see your episiotomy scar?" He wouldn't allow anyone else to do his cosmetic closures because it was never good enough! Consequently, none of the other Interns or Residents wanted to assist him. Despite this, after persistently observing and studying his technique, he allowed me to close one. Afterwards, the nurse came to me and said, "Apparently, you're the only one he trusts!". I considered this a personal victory, and for the first time, I felt a sense of professional vindication.

In stark contrast to Dr. Papas, there was a large Polish General Practitioner, Dr Wojakowski, who had a different perspective. He had unlimited privileges in both OB and General Surgery. His crude philosophy was, "When her legs are down, who's gonna know the difference!" Consequently his episiotomy repairs consisted of four or five through and through catgut sutures without any regard to cosmetics.

Apartment Complex   In the meantime, after 4 tough weeks, my life became a little brighter when Dr. Islami's secretary told me that she managed to move me into the *convenient* Apartment complex. Comparatively speaking, the apartments were not only larger and much nicer, but more importantly, they were conveniently located across the street from the Hospital. The brick Apartment Complex consisted of 8, neatly spaced rows, each row with 4 attached Apartments. Most contained two bedrooms and two baths. However my ground floor Apartment consisted of a single bedroom and bathroom, a Living- Dining room area and a small kitchen.

It was my good fortune to assist and befriend two spectacular Attendings, Sydney Lefkowitz MD and Sam Fortunato MD. Originally, they were both seasoned General Practitioners who now specialized in Ob-Gyn. Given their background, they possessed a wealth of knowledge and experience which they were readily willing to share. Although they had different styles and techniques, their level of expertise was the same. At the time, vaginal Hysterectomies were relatively new surgical procedures, and as such, were the craze. Consequently, they allowed me to observe and eventually assist, on many occasions.

St Barnabas was also at the forefront for providing Epidural anesthesia. One particular Anesthesiologist was a big Bear of a man with a surprisingly gentle touch. For whatever reason, he took a liking to me, eventually teaching me how to perform Epidurals. Both of these factors would prove to be very valuable attributes in the future.

Cocktail Party   In any event, he invited me and another intern, Tomtonovich MD (Dr. Tom) to his house for a Cocktail - Dinner Party.

Tom was a tall handsome fellow with an appealing, Ukrainian accent. When we arrived, we were both shocked by the size of the elaborate party and were certainly underdressed for the occasion.

Then, after a few drinks, our host introduced us to the Hall of Fame Yankee catcher, Yogi Berra. The retired legend was now actively promoting a new soft drink,Yoohoo. I still remember a split moment that I will always regret. Being mildly intoxicated, and flustered by his image, while shaking hands with the legend, all I could think of slurring was, something stupid about the damn soft drink!

Then, when Tom and I were introduced to our host's two daughters, a dim light bulb went on. Comparing the two, one of the daughters was far prettier than the other, and guess which one I was ultimately paired with. Following the shameful evening, I was surprised that our host continued to favor my presence.

Incidentally, he would eventually perform the epidurals on most of our children, all of whom were delivered at St Barnabas. Likewise, Sam Fortunato MD, who ultimately became my mentor as well as a dear friend, delivered all of our children, except for our daughter, Christy, who was delivered on Christmas day by my former Chief Resident, Eli Rose MD.

Dr. Breen   James Breen MD was a renowned Gynecologic surgeon known for performing extensive laparoscopic procedures as well as total abdominal exenteration for advanced ovarian and uterine malignancies. Whenever possible, I seized every opportunity to scrub as a second assist with either him or his associate, Dr. Caterina Gregori. In any event, before completing my 3-month rotation, I was shocked when Dr. Breen called me down to his office and offered me a position as a first-year Resident starting in July 1971. I was absolutely blown away by the offer and just the thought of training under his tutelage was reason enough to accept the position on the spot.

Dr. Fortunato   During uncomplicated deliveries, Sam would often stand in the doorway observing me in the delivery room, and would only come to my aid if, either he or I, felt the need for his advice or assistance. During difficult deliveries, he often expressed his concern with the rising rate of C-sections, which he attributed to the ever-increasing dependence on fetal monitoring. He felt this trend was becoming a vicious cycle governed mostly by fear and expediency, especially those who lack sound clinical judgement which only comes from experience.

I remember one night, while he was delivering prima-para twins, openly lamenting, "If the Residents don't even show up for these more complicated deliveries, they will invariably resort to a C-section. They'll never learn how to safely deliver a prima- para ((First Pregnancy) Breach or how to safely use mid forceps!"

Dr. Diamond   Another prominent name was Dr. Diamond, who was famous for performing laparoscopic infertility reversal procedures on blocked or severed fallopian tubes. I guess lacking the blood and glory appeal of major surgery, no one seemed interested in scrubbing with him. Consequently, by volunteering, I was a first assist and he took an interest by allowing me to peer through the laparoscope, eventually doing minor procedures.

Medicine Dr.Hogan   My next rotation was Internal Medicine, under James Hogan MD. He came from St Michael's Medical Center in Newark N.J and his subspecialty was Hematology and Oncology for which he was very highly regarded. He was known as a real taskmaster, keeping a very tight rein on his Residents.

Eventually I became very well acquainted with three of the Medical Residents, all of whom, despite growing up in N.J, attended different Medical schools in Italy. Mario Criscito MD attended the University of Padua, Ronnie Viscuso MD, attended the University of Roma and, Kenny DeFusco MD, the University of Bologna. However, rather than the usual starting date in July, they all started in January. From a teaching perspective, this was very beneficial because, being only six months ahead of me, they were willing to allow me to readily do procedures which they

424

were all accustomed to doing. Also, from a personal perspective, this fostered a more collegial relationship that blossomed into a close and lasting friendship, which still exists to this day.

Before my arrival, they were known as, "The Three Musketeers" - which soon became, "The Four Musketeers". From the start, Mario knew that he wanted to be a Cardiologist, and this was music to my ears. Due to his magnetic personality, I followed him everywhere, and he not only taught me, but he also allowed me to do procedures normally reserved for Residents. In fact, by mid-December, as they prepared to transition to second-year Residents, I was asked to fill a temporary On-Call gap for those first-year residents who started in July.

Cardiology St Barnabas was well known for its commitment to interventional cardiology with Dr. Higgins MD, performing Angioplasties on a regular basis. They were also one of the forerunners in Cardiac Telemetry, dedicating an entire wing on the 5th floor with a very impressive semicircular bank of telemetry screens. CCU occupied a separate wing on the 6th floor, serviced by its own elevator. There was a Filipino Cardiology Fellow permanently assigned to the unit, and while sticking to him like glue, we became good friends and he always left me with a daily pearl.

I remember one morning, however, while Dr. Nussbaum was making-rounds in the unit, he asked the Fellow an academic cardiac question for which he had no answer. I felt terribly embarrassed for my friend, especially when Dr Nussbaum pointed to me saying, "Ask him, he probably knows the answer!". Nobody deserves that degree of humiliation and with that single comment, Dr. Nussbaum's stature shrunk several inches. I practically lived on those two floors and loved every minute. Whenever I heard the loudspeaker announcing *Code Blue* I would race to be the first one to respond- at times, second only to Mario!

Mario's idol was Dr. Higgins, and he assisted him with angioplasties on every possible occasion. Mario would eventually become an interventional Cardiologist, eventually forming one of the largest and well respected interventional cardiology groups in N.J. Meanwhile, Ronnie gravitated to Nephrology, under his chief, Martin Jacobs MD, eventually becoming the Director of the Dialysis unit. And Kenny became a Pulmonologist under his chief, Fred Jacobs MD.

If I wasn't in CCU or the Telemetry unit. I was making- rounds on the 3rd floor Medical wing. The charge nurse was Anita Drelich, and I would routinely stand at the counter directly in front of her while ordering the patient's daily coumadin dosages. However, I would occasionally notice her just staring at me. Being that she was basically a very lovely person, I would playfully pretend to gaze at her adoringly. Truthfully, however, although I thought that her younger sister, who was also a nurse, was prettier, she wasn't as much fun. Anyway, after one of these seemingly innocent flirtations she said, "yeah, but I mean it!" - Uh Oh. This simple response pierced my conscience and thereafter I tried to treat her as purely, a good friend.

Towards the end of my rotation, Dr. Hogan called me down to his office and, without much fanfare, made my day by offering me a position as a first-year Resident in July. Although I was truly flattered by Dr. Breen's residency offer, I came to appreciate how much I loved Cardiology. I didn't feel I had to deliberate, and therefore I accepted his offer. However, now I had to make an appointment with Dr. Breen, in order to explain that I had decided to pursue a residency in Internal Medicine. My utter embarrassment was assuaged somewhat by his gratuitous compliment, "You'll be a valued asset to any specialty you choose!"

Pediatrics   My next one month rotation was Pediatrics. I was fortunate to be under the wing of Dr. Parthasarathy, (Dr P) a very well trained, female Pediatric Fellow. She appreciated the fact that, unlike many of the other Interns, I actually liked Pediatrics and expressed an eagerness to learn. She always exuded confidence and had a very simple approach to Pediatrics, which was often at variance with many of the Attendings. As a matter of fact, the only Attending that I was impressed with was, Dr. Marano. Consequently, he would be the only Pediatrician for all of our children while in Barnabas' newborn nursery.

The atmosphere on the floor was very congenial, especially among the nursing staff and station clerks. At times this became a little sticky because, sometimes they misinterpreted friendliness as *Attraction*. One clerk, in particular, was a lovely girl from Georgia, who casually mentioned that she would be happy to make me a traditional Georgian desert pronounced, *Apple -pan-dowdy.*

The following morning she brought in a large pie for the floor. After tasting it, however, I obviously made more of a fuss than perhaps I should have, which led to a seemingly endless supply of the same delicious pie. Each morning, while hovering over me, she would make sure that I took a healthy portion, and I gained about 10 lbs. in 4 weeks! This continued until finally, one of the older clerks pulled me aside saying, "Don't you know that she's crazy about you!" -Uh Oh! I didn't realize that it was apparently *a labor of love,* and I felt awful that I had unwittingly led her astray, forcing me to gracefully extricate myself from this embarrassing situation.

Louis Periodically, I kept in touch with Dr. Hogan, especially considering that he was the consulting hematologist for several of our Pediatric cancer patients. I clearly remember a seven yr. old boy named Louis, who was suffering from acute myelogenous leukemia. It was shortly before Christmas and being that I was scheduled to be off for the weekend, I was looking forward to going home for the Christmas holiday. However, on this particular evening, it was snowing like hell and Louis's blood counts indicated that he desperately needed a transfusion of packed red blood cells.

The treacherous weather made it extremely difficult to navigate the roads, so I decided to spend the night in the On-call room. Louis had a relatively rare, A negative blood type, and whether due to the weather or the late hour, I wasn't able to locate a satisfactory donor match. When I informed Dr. Hogan, he said he would also try to locate a source. I had never given blood before and didn't even know my blood type. So, I figured I might as well go down to the lab and have it checked out. As fate would have it, I had the same blood type which proved to be compatible.

Over the course of the night, I don't remember if I ended up giving one or two units, but considering that they paid $25 per unit, I probably gave two! The next morning while making rounds, I told Louis that I had given him my blood. After a long pause, he looked at me and asked, "Does that mean that I'll grow a mustache like you?" I laughed and said, "Louis, Ya never know, but I want you to check for it every morning in the mirror!"

He remained stable for the next couple of days, and when I left for the weekend, I continued to remain hopeful. Upon my return, however, I was immensely saddened to learn that he had died. But I was somewhat consoled that, at least, it was on Christmas Day. I signed over the blood donor check to the grieving parents and received a beautiful letter from them, thanking me. But, more importantly, they told me that their son never stopped looking in the mirror!

Holiday Party   I don't remember the details, but the word got out that there was to be a Friday night, pre-holiday bash, at someone's very spacious apartment. One of the nurse's aides always wore a very provocative Hillbilly type outfit, similar to those worn on Petticoat *Junction,* with front straps accentuating her enormous breasts. Then she really caught my attention by suggesting that, if I showed up at the party, she would spray me with whip cream anywhere I wanted -Oh boy! Truthfully, however, her unabashed forwardness reminded me of Barbara the lizard, which literally scared the hell out of me! Party news spreads through the floors like wildfire, and when asked about it, I told Anita that I had plans of driving home for the weekend but intended to make a brief appearance.

When I arrived at the party, before I knew it, *Chesty* was right beside me with a can of whip cream in her hand. I thought, "uh oh, she's for real!" I tried dodging her for most of the evening until I finally caught Anita's attention and she swiftly came over to rescue me. Then, right in front of *Chesty,* she surprised me by planting a big kiss on my lips and whispered in my ear, "That should take care of her!". Following that, upon hearing a lot of "oohs and aahs," I guess everyone assumed that Anita and I were an item.

In hindsight, however, after four long years of competing and scraping by, I finally had some money in my pocket, and I was finally having Fun! I explained to Anita that I intended to make a quick quiet exit, and no one would question it if she and I left together. With that said, despite a few more "oohs", we quietly excited the raucous room and she walked me to my car. After thanking her for coming to my rescue she smiled and said, "The pleasure was all mine".

Porcelain Statue   The Pediatric rotation seemed to fly and as a parting gesture, the staff decided to present me with a token of appreciation. They all gathered around as I opened a smartly wrapped 10" box. For some reason, Dr. Hogan was standing behind me and as I gently unfolded the interior tissue paper, I uncovered the front of a long slender white porcelain statue, depicting the outline of a *Robed Monk*. I said, "The statue is beautiful and, having a religious connotation, is personally very meaningful".

Then, after a few giggles, they suggested that I take it out of the pretty box to fully appreciate its beauty. So, I carefully removed it from the pretty box and while holding it firmly in one hand, when I slowly turned it over I realized that I was holding an emasculating, porcelain penis! Dr. Hogan, who was even more embarrassed than I, said, "I'm not quite sure how to interpret this!"- and I figured, there goes my Residency slot!

Incidentally, in the future, I proudly displayed the "Monk" on a shelf in my Goshen office, facing forward!

E R Dr. Abbott   My next, one-month rotation was in the Emergency Room. My resident of record was my good friend, Kenny DeFusco, who had absolutely no interest in the compulsory Emergency Room rotation. What I remember most about our interaction was lunchtime and sharing chicken parm heros made by his wife. Then, after lunch he would say, "Call me if you need help with a medical case!" Other than lunchtime, I never saw him again for the rest of the day!

On the other hand, Chuck Abbott, MD, was well trained in Cardiovascular Surgeon from the prestigious, Charity Hospital in New Orleans. I first met Chuck shortly after he arrived from New Orleans. He was the son of a very prominent General Surgeon, who arranged for Chuck's entry by covering shifts in the ER. I loved working with him and listening to his *war stories* while at Charity Hospital.

Compared to Newark's Martland Hospital, St. Barnabas was truly like a *Country Club*. I remember one evening being excited by the arrival of a rare injury - my first and only, gunshot wound. Rather than an ambulance transport, the patient arrived in a very large black sedan, accompanied by two *Associates*. Fortunately, Chuck was on duty and certainly well-equipped to handle any surgical trauma case. After he asked the associates to wait outside, we both assessed the wound and determined it was non-life threatening. When I asked, "Don't we have to notify the police?" Chuck just looked at me and smiled saying, "In New Orleans, yes. But in Short Hills, he goes quietly to the private suits on the sixth floor!"

Surgery Dr. Del Guercio   My last 3-month rotation was, General Surgery. Louis Del Guercio MD was the head of the department and his illustrious reputation preceded his arrival from the Albert Einstein School of Medicine, where he was a full professor, His mere presence attracted a bevy of surgical Residents as well as very qualified Surgeons, who wished to witness his floorless, methodical surgical technique.

Many of the Interns were doing either straight medical or straight surgical Internships. And, in particular, those were the ones vying for a position in the great man's Residency program. Being that I was doing a traditional, Rotating Internship, although I loved surgery, I naturally viewed myself as inferior to those who were obviously more committed by taking the straight Surgical track.

Then shortly after our initial orientation, I felt that my suspicion was validated when Dr. Del Guercio asked for a show of hands of those Interns who were doing a straight surgical internship. I was embarrassed to be among only three Interns who didn't raise their hands. Then he said, "To be a good Surgeon, you also have to know Medicine!" and that he prefers his Residents to have at least one year of Medicine before a Surgical residency - and I felt, at least, partially relieved.

I remember when, Dr. Del Guercio, was scheduled to do a delicate operative procedure, a partial adrenalectomy. Hearing this, Frank Dispaltro MD seized the opportunity to be the first assist for his former mentor, and somehow, I was scheduled to be his second assist. Frank was a 6' 4" first-year plastic surgical resident who completed a four year General Surgical residency at NYU. I quickly noticed that *the great man* didn't necessarily have fast hand speed, but this was offset by the fact that he had no wasted moves. Afterward, Frank acknowledged my observation adding, "And there was minimal blood loss. It's his operative judgment, technique, and finesse that makes him a great surgeon!"

On another occasion, Dr.DelGuercio, asked, "Do you want to assist me with a procedure in the Xray department?" I knew that he had a special interest in liver disease, and in particular, the intrahepatic portal system, but I couldn't imagine what type of procedure would require my assistance. With the patient supine and under intravenous conscious sedation, he performed a *mini-laparotomy* in the right upper abdominal quadrant right on the X Ray table. Then he took the time to explain what he was about to do. After cannulating various intrahepatic ducts, he took pressure measurements and calculated pressure gradients in the process.

After the procedure, he again took the time to sketch a diagram of his findings on a piece of paper right on the X-Ray table. I realized that my assistance was minimal, and that it was more about an opportunity to teach someone willing to learn - which reminded me of my previous experiences with, Dr. Ablaza, at Cherry Hill

Carlo Corazon MD As with my Ob Gyn rotation, Surgical rounds consisted of accompanying the first-year surgical Resident each morning on the third floor, surgical wing. This entailed mostly wound assessments and dressing changes. I was again, very fortunate to have my assigned Resident, and being that this was my last major rotation, he was eager to allow me to take on more responsibility. In fact, after a brief period of orientation, I was more often making rounds by myself.

My resident was a Filipino named, Carlo Corazon MD, and while standing at the nurse's station, he would crack me up by loudly exclaiming in a thick accent, "The doctors are here, would somebody please Help the Doctors!" Not seeing or hearing any response, he would pretend to patiently stand there with a puzzled expression and repeat the same refrain, only much louder and accentuating the word Please! While maintaining his deadpan expression of utter dismay, I had all to do to contain myself.

Incidentally, It's uncanny how or why I remember such a silly experience. However, I mention it because, in the future, while making rounds in Arden Hill Hospital, it was recalling his self-effacing sense of humor that I would often find myself trying to emulate.

The Battle of Heads   Angel Prado MD was a Puerto Rican, Surgical Resident who completed 4 years of a General Surgical Residency at Martland Hospital - a level one trauma center in Newark NJ. The hectic pace within its Emergency Department was a sight to behold. Angel was an experienced and gifted Surgeon who, unfortunately, had a fatal flaw - he didn't take his surgical talents seriously.

One morning Angel and I were scheduled to assist Dr. Simmons, the hospital's pre-eminent colon-rectal surgeon, on a hemicolectomy. Angel hated assisting Dr. Simmons because, being only 5'6" tall, in order for the eminent surgeon to see the entire operative field, he had to lean over the patient with the aid of a step stool. And, as in the past, they would repeatedly bump heads while trying to peer into the same field.

While we were scrubbing, I heard Angel muttering under his breath, "I'll be damned if he's gonna win the battle!" At the time, I had no idea what he meant, and when I asked, he simply said, "Just watch what happens!" As the operation proceeded, I watched intently as each of them initially alternated for the optimal view of the operative field. Then I noticed Angel's forehead slowly approaching Dr. Simon's forehead. Eventually, their foreheads were not only touching, but they appeared to be glued together. Meanwhile, while I'm busy holding various retractors, it appeared that Simmons was totally unaware that the ensuing *Battle of the heads* was underway.

Neither of them appeared willing to yield, and with their foreheads firmly pressed together, they were now pushing their heads back and forth, resembling two Billy Goats battling with locked horns. Meanwhile, while holding the retractors, I'm watching the entire comedy unfold. I was inwardly laughing so hard, I couldn't stop my hands from shaking - to such a degree that Simmons yelled, we can't see the field if you don't hold the retractors steady!" Then when Angel shouted,"Yeah Dr, hold them steady!"- I lost it and almost peed in my pants!

Dr. Peer   Another Barnabas giant was, Dr. Peer MD, a world-renowned plastic surgeon who specialized in reconstructions of severe cleft lips and palates, and his Peer Group, drew patients from around the world. At the time, he was in his early 80's and still operating on a daily basis, and his reputation attracted Residents from all over the country. There was an entire wing dedicated to children and adults waiting for his team to perform *Miracles*. Robby Myer MD was one of the junior partners and having achieved a sterling reputation in his own right, he was now considered the heir apparent of the Group. was and earned

They usually performed elective surgeries after 1 pm, occupying 4 or 5 suites at a time. Much like Dr. Debakey, after finishing his own procedure, Dr. Peer would often go from room to room supervising his Residents. This was relatively easy considering that other than wearing a mask and gloves, you didn't have to necessarily gown-up. I would occasionally go up after 2 pm and wander from room to room, just watching the residents and asking questions. I was struck by the quiet relaxed atmosphere in the operative suite, often accompanied by soft classical music and polite conversation, and I thought to myself, "This wouldn't be tough to take!"

After a while, I came to know the residents on a first-name basis. As a matter of fact, the Apartment directly above mine was occupied by a married couple from Taiwan, both of whom were Plastic surgical residents. One evening they invited Mary and me up to their apartment for a traditional Taiwanese dinner.

Peer's Garden   As you entered the main entrance to the hospital on the right, it led to a large semi-circular roadway and exiting on the left, with a large dedicated parking lot in the center. To the right of the exit roadway was a large Garden - affectionately referred to as Dr. *Peer's Garden*. Perhaps due to his advanced age or his prominent stature, the elderly pioneer was regularly driven to the hospital in a simple black limousine. And upon leaving the hospital at 7 pm, I would notice Dr. Peer's limousine waiting by the roadside while he walked through *his garden*. I still have a clear image of the elegant surgeon dressed in his tailored suit while carrying a hand trowel, I would pause to watch him bending over to pick the weeds, as well as fresh produce. Ironically, that scene would trigger a sudden flashback, reminding me of my Father.

Dr. Sabety   I remember one evening checking the OR schedule and discovering that, in the morning, I would be scrubbing on a chest case with both Chuck Abbott MD, and Dr. Sabety, an arrogant French Cardiothoracic surgeon. I always had suture material in my apartment, and I remember being so ecstatic that I immediately started practicing my one-handed ties, using my bedpost as an anchor.

It was a delicate cardiothoracic case and I quickly surmised that, along with his arrogance, Dr Sabety, was extremely territorial. Despite Chuck's extensive training, Sabety let it be known who was in charge. I remember being embarrassed for Chuck when Sabety actually hit him on the knuckles with a pair of long forceps, indicating that he should remove his hands from the field - essentially demoting him from the first assistant to a mere observer. Following this disappointing fiasco, Chuck swore that he would never assist "the arrogant SOB again!"

Dr. Filippone   One of my favorite Surgical Attendings was Dennis Filippone MD. He was a graduate of the University of Virginia College of Medicine and had the most peculiar method of performing a one-handed suture tie -for which he was lovingly ridiculed. He loved working with both the Surgical and Medical Residents, and we, in turn, universally loved him.

I remember one time responding to a *Code Blue* on one of his patients in surgical ICU. When I arrived, he was fiddling with an intracardiac needle, and I could tell, he was clearly out of his element. Seeing this, I gently ushered him to the side and took over the code. Thereafter, he would frequently embellish the story by saying, "He just came in and pushed me aside yelling, get out of the way!"- not true. But I took comic delight in not refuting it. Long after I left St Barnabas, he would remain my *go-to*, surgical consultant.

Dr. Del Guercio   After the second month of my surgical rotation, Dr. DelGuercio called me to his office. Of course, I immediately thought uh oh, what did I do wrong?" After some small talk, he finally broached the reason for our meeting by offering me a slot as a first-year Resident in General Surgery. My first thought was, "I guess the Department heads don't confer with each other!" Remembering his prior comments about preferring residents with a firm grasp of Medicine, I said," But I've only had 4 months of Internal Medicine". With a faint smile, he responded, "Your reputation precedes you and I'm willing to take the gamble!"

Knowing, however, that I was already committed to Dr. Hogan, I asked if I could think about it for a few days. I noticed that he was taken aback by my response and I guess, assuming that I was destined to be a surgeon, he asked, "Have you decided to take a position elsewhere?" I figured this could be considered a question of semantics, so I said, "I just need some time to consider my options." He graciously accepted my request, but added, "Don't take too long deciding!"

For obvious reasons, I knew that I had a predilection for Cardiology, and felt that I had attained a decent grasp of the specialty. Over the next several days, however, I weighed the pros and cons of Internal Medicine and Cardiology vs. the genuine excitement that I experienced with Surgery, especially Cardiovascular surgery. I further reasoned that, as a Cardiovascular surgeon, at least in some measure, I could combine my love for both specialties. With this in mind, I now had to go back to Dr. Hogan and sheepishly explain that, although I was very grateful for his offer, I decided to pursue a Surgical Residency under Dr. DelGuercio. He was initially very disappointed, but then said, "You have to follow the path where your heart and talents lead you".

Draft Notice I resumed the last month of my surgical rotation with renewed enthusiasm. I felt I had a clear mission, and although it would be a long haul, I was looking forward to the challenge. Then my world of dreams suddenly faded when I received a certified letter with the ominous salutation, "Greetings" - a formal notice that I was being drafted into the US Army, and no doubt, headed for Vietnam!

I immediately went to see Dr. Islami, who took me straight to the hospital administrator John Phillips. I explained that earlier in December, I applied to the US Army Reserves and that I met with my army recruiter, Sgt, Kazin, at the Newark Armory. And although I filled out endless forms, thus far, I hadn't heard anything. The administrator became very upset saying," Why didn't you come to me sooner?" - how should I know? After he finally settled down, he said, "let me look into it"

Dr. Lotman I occasionally scrubbed with Dr. Lotman, an elderly Chest Surgeon, who wore a hideous toupee. He often complained that none of the residents wanted to assist him. Initially, I thought it was probably because he mostly performed minor elective procedures such as implanting cardiac pacemakers, etc. However, after assisting him several times, I realized the reason. All I did was retract and cut sutures. In any event, hearing of my Residency dilemma, he urged me to get my N.J. License as soon as possible and offered me an interim job at his, Newark Dispensary -an Industrial Medical Clinic at the Newark Airport.

Two weeks before the end of my internship, the hospital pulled out all the stops by hosting a pre-graduation Dinner at the posh, Chantecler restaurant, in Short Hills, N.J. Mary and I attended the gala event and I had an opportunity to introduce her to each of the Department heads. Since my military commitment was still in limbo, it was somewhat embarrassing when each of them would ask me about my future plans.

Despite that minor glitch, however, we both had a great time. Given the unfortunate circumstances, despite having forfeited my Internal Medicine Residency, Dr. Hogan graciously offered that, should my military dilemma be favorably resolved, he would still be willing to accept me in his program, even at a later date.

CH - 45
GRADUATION CEREMONY

S oon afterward, the official Graduation and Awards Ceremony was conducted where it all began, in the Hospital's large Amphitheater. Once again, Mary was my sole companion and we both sat in the theater, watching as each Intern was called up on a stage. After Dr. Islami presented each of them with a certificate of completion, he acknowledged those who were pursuing a Residency and specifying their chosen Hospital and Specialty.

However, when my name was called he merely said, "We don't know where he's going!" Then, I was shocked when he presented me with the coveted, *Intern of the year award* and presented me with a complete collection of the Netter Series of anatomical sketches. I treasured not only the beauty but also the sentiment attached to the collection. In the future, whether in my office or at home, I proudly displayed the collection in my bookcases. Eventually, I would come to part with the series when I passed them on to my son, Vito, who also became an Osteopathic Physician.

Following the ceremony, despite spending the last year together, I experienced a sense of Deja vu as the crowd quickly dispersed without any fanfare, good wishes, or sad goodbyes. I thought of how similar this was to what I experienced following my High School and Medical School graduation ceremonies. Much like at the end of a dance, when the music suddenly dies and all the couples quietly leave the floor, never to return. With the ominous specter of Vietnam still looming and no definite future goal or job, I suddenly felt like a purposeless Nobody!

Although it was late in the evening, I remember Mary and I quietly strolling through the silent polished halls of the Great Hospital. While sadly bidding farewell to my former home, I experienced an eerie sensation of recalling all the fond memories with mere whispers. Then serendipitously, a lone figure emerged from a quiet side hallway and congratulated me. I immediately recognized him and introduced him to Mary as last year's recipient of the same coveted award, and now a new second-year Surgical Resident.

The Newark Dispensary (1971-72) Heeding Dr. Lotman's advice. I applied for my New Jersey medical license and by mid-July, I began working at the Newark Dispensary, practicing something totally foreign, Industrial Medicine. During the week, I relied on Smokey, to shuttle me to either the Trums house in Upper Saddle River or, Virginia's house in Wyckoff N.J. And on weekends, to Anita's house in Monroe.

When I arrived at the clinic, I was greeted warmly by two unlicensed Cuban physicians, Dr. Alvarez, and Dr.Picone. I worked five days a week, from 8 AM to 5 PM, earning $500, which was a windfall! At the end of each week, I would ask the clinic manager, Ed, to cash my paycheck, requesting five crisp $100 bills, just so I could hold them in my hand. I never dreamed I would be making so much money so soon!

It was a very busy Clinic with an abundance of pre-employment physicals and a variety of traumatic injuries. However, given that Dr.Lotman only visited the Clinic once a week, I realized that, on a daily basis, I was the only licensed physician. Also, despite the fact that the majority of the physicals and injuries were work-related, and therefore, fraught with potential litigation, Dr. Lotman always made light of potential malpractice exposure. In addition, despite the fact that he was a surgeon, he wouldn't order or supply sterile gloves, even for suturing.

Finally, I decided to bring in my own sterile gloves, which I willingly shared with my two unlicensed colleagues, and In return, they occasionally brought me a sampling of authentic Cuban food, which was absolutely delicious. They often shared stories of practicing Medicine in the rural areas of Cuba, sharing treasured techniques which I found fascinating.

The Money Cycle   During my internship, I was netting roughly $500 a month, and while visiting my mother at Anita's house, I would periodically contribute to the household expenses by giving her whatever I could afford at the time. But now, I was able to visit on weekends more frequently and it gave me great pleasure to be able to give her substantially more. When I would slip her the money, she would often say, "Peter, that's way too much!" But I knew that it also gave her great pleasure to pass it on to Anita. Frankly, it made her feel self-sufficient and benevolent, which she rightly deserved. I was well aware of this clandestine *money cycle* which, although quite comical, added to the pleasure of giving.

I noticed that my mother would often watch her soap operas, sitting as close as possible to a tiny 12" black and white TV screen. So, I thought I would surprise her by buying a large Magnavox TV with remote controls - what a disaster! Although well intended, she couldn't figure out how to use the remote. So, I ended up bringing it back to the store.

The Lodge (June 1971)   In late June, I began helping Nick at the Lodge on the weekends, mostly cutting lawns, and preparing the pool for the 1971 season. Nick was always uncomfortable managing the bar business and therefore, he asked me if I wanted to run it for the summer season. I discussed this with Mary, and although not her favorite thing, we decided to open the **P&M lounge** only on weekends.

At the time, Nick had a large group of friends who would frequently come up on weekends, most often occupying the rooms in the rear Cottage. I never knew if they were paying guests, and being that their recreational substance of choice was, marijuana, they weren't Bar drinkers and mostly stayed by themselves at the Cottage. In any event, I hired a local bartender, hoping to attract the country club members, and even arranged for a weekend band, ironically hiring Joanne's brother, JT.

From one Joint to another   I remember one evening, Nick and I were sitting alone at the bar, and while I was sipping a Manhattan, he was smoking a joint. We both knew that he couldn't handle booze, and for whatever reason, he was determined to try and get me high. So, after rolling a joint, he explained how I should inhale deeply, and after holding it, slowly exhale the smoke. After each Toot, he would look at me and ask, "well?" And I'd reply, "well, what?" Frustrated, he rolled another joint, and after repeating the same process, he asked the same dumb question, and after I followed with the same response he'd say, "Impossible! This went on for a good hour, and after several joints, I finally felt an unusual *Buzz* - and he was in his glory.

Then he drew my attention to a large black carpenter ant crawling on the countertop. Amazingly, for the next 20 minutes, we were both fixated on the *enormous* black ant, following its search for sugar. Now that we were clearly in sync, my older brother decided that we should revisit our youth by reminiscing on the Idle Hour Dock. So, being in command, he drove us down to Walton Lake, and while lying on the old dock, I was amazed at the vividness of our recollections- as if in real-time! In particular, we both saw my mother with her hair up in a short kerchief, wearing a white terrycloth robe and carrying a brown paper bag filled with delicious sandwiches.

This revelry, however, was abruptly interrupted by the flashlights of two State Troopers. As they slowly walked towards us, Nick had the presence of mind to stash the pot below on the rocks supporting the dock. When asked what we were doing, Nick went on needlessly explaining that his younger brother, just returned from Medical School in Iowa, and we were reminiscing about our youth, etc., etc. Even though I realized this was far more than they needed to know, he was on a roll! By the time he finished, they couldn't wait to get the hell out of there saying, "Have a nice evening and just be careful."

Of course, by this time, we both had the *Munchies*. So, Nick decided we should drive down to the town of Monroe to get something to eat. Since we were only driving 15 mph, it took us 30 minutes before we finally arrived in front of a Chicken Wings joint. While contemplating what to order, I expressed some concern about being able to speak intelligibly. My guru brother, however, seized the opportunity to demonstrate how he could masterfully *Control* me, bringing me back down at will. So, I dutifully followed my experienced brother inside.

As we both stood in front of the counter trying to decipher the selections, the young girl behind the counter asked, "What would you guys like?" Almost immediately, he heard me start to snicker which caused him to start laughing, and within seconds, we were both standing there like two idiots, laughing hysterically. Instinctively, we both made a dash for the door, leaving the lovely young girl just standing there understandably, bewildered.

Now we were both sitting in the car watching the young girl staring at the two idiots in the front seat rocking the car back and forth still laughing hysterically. Nick eventually resorted to his masterful *Control* technique and we both reentered the joint, intending to respectfully place our order. Our composure, however, lasted about 30 seconds, causing us to, once again bolt for the door, never to return. We drove back to the Lodge defeated and hungry and I thought, "So much for his "mind control!"

Another evening, Nick, Babs, Mary, and I were sitting in front of the Lodge's beautiful fieldstone fireplace, enjoying the glow of a warm fire. Nick had already had a few joints and was professing how harmless pot was compared to alcohol. I was growing tired of his proselytizing and decided to switch *mind controllers.* He was obviously stoned, and I noticed very slight drooping of his right eyelid - presumably, a precursor to nodding off. After simply commenting about this he asked me, " What could it signify?"

Purely in jest, I shamefully offered, "it could be Horner's syndrome or possibly a Brain tumor." Apparently, those words were the last and only thing he heard. When we saw each other in the morning, I commented that he looked exhausted. Then Babs explained that he was terrified and obsessed about his eye all night, for which I sincerely apologized, but added, "I guess it's not so harmless!"

European Health Spas My former Medical Schoolmate, Howie Greenspan, was completing a two-year commitment as a commissioned officer at the USPHS Hospital on Staten Island. He and one of his hospital colleagues, Barry Adelman, were in the process of negotiating an enterprising arrangement with Jerry Jerome, the owner of several

European Health Spas in northern N.J. They arranged to provide new spa members with a comprehensive, Executive Physical, including an EKG and an extensive laboratory panel.

Because of their hospital commitments, however, they were unable to provide the service themselves. So, at some point, they asked if I would be willing to perform these medical evaluations in the evenings at one of the Spas. Although the details of compensation or a future partnership were sketchy, trusting Howie, I agreed to do them. In time, however, this arrangement was short-lived. Despite going two or three evenings a week, after several months I hadn't received any payment. I held no malice toward Howie, feeling that the culprit was his associate. Incidentally, although Barry was very successful, buying a very large home in Tiburon Ca, he ended up committing suicide.

Howie's scorcher   As I may have mentioned, Howie was known to frequently procure marijuana for personal use. At some point, Nick asked if I could buy some high-grade pot, and I immediately thought of Howie. I met him at his Staten Island apartment, and before I could even make the purchase, a fire erupted in his kitchen stove. Seeing smoke billowing out his kitchen window, someone apparently called the Fire Department.

Upon hearing the approaching sirens, Howie immediately covered his head with his canvas jacket, and as he made his way toward the cabinet above the stove, he told me to keep dousing his jacket with water. Having no time to ask questions, I did as I was told. It wasn't until he removed a 4x6" metal container from the cabinet that I realized what was so important – his treasured stash of MJ. As the firemen entered the apartment, he quickly tucked the container under his scorched jacket and ran outside. Fortunately, they quickly put out the fire and left the premises none the wiser.

Howie Greenspan In Memoriam   My fondness for Howie is somewhat of an enigma. As I previously mentioned, in Medical School, he and his close friend, Mike Quicker, were considered the class Hippies. In dress attire and mindset, they were emblematic of the anti- Vietnam peace movement. Typical of the period, they often wore colorful wrist beads, headbands, and old army jackets adorned with peace symbols.

They were truly comfortable in their own skin and really didn't care what anybody else thought about them. Although he and I represented the opposite ends of a spectrum, I liked and admired his guts and tenacity, and would readily accept criticism for unabashedly calling him my friend. Despite the European Health Spa fiasco, I held him in high regard, and I was honored when he accepted a last-minute invitation to my bachelor party at the Officer's Club in the Brooklyn Naval shipyards. Being that he came directly from the Hospital, as a commissioned officer, he was decidedly overdressed, which was in stark contrast to his traditional garb.

At the time I was the Medical Director of the N J Industrial Medical Clinics, and he was completing an MPH program at Harvard. He was married to a young lady who gave riding lessons on their sprawling horse farm in Mendham N.J. Somehow, after a long hiatus, our lives reconnected, and we decided to meet each other at a diner in New Jersey. As if the hands of time stood still, our mutual recognition was instantaneous, and we greeted each other with a long warm embrace. Although slightly older, he was still the same Howie, wearing a colorful turquoise necklace and wristlets. We briefly exchanged family updates, and having married a much younger woman, he was now the father of a precious child of his own.

Being a Jewish boy who grew up in Brooklyn, he was very familiar with the Catskill Region of N.Y. and was looking forward to our families getting together at Wolf Lake in Sullivan County. When it was time to leave, we again hugged each other, knowing it was a genuine expression of mutual love. And before departing he said, "Remember, just call my wife with the date and time and we'll be there!" I remember excitedly telling my daughter, Christy, of our meeting and how anxious I was for her to meet my long lost friend - someone I considered the *epitome of Cool*

Several weeks later, when I called Howie's wife, she sadly informed me that he was undergoing some medical tests at Harvard's Mass General Hospital for an undisclosed illness. I followed up with a call to him and he was more forthcoming - he was being evaluated for a suspicious lesion on a recent chest X-ray. Trying to project optimism, I said, "You couldn't be in a better place!". Several weeks later, Howie called me from his home in Mendham, informing me that he was diagnosed with lung cancer, and would be starting Chemo in N.J, with re-evaluations in Boston as needed. I was speechless when he apologized for delaying our family reunion, vowing to do so as soon as he was feeling better.

After several weeks I called his home again and his wife handed him the phone. He sounded very weak with labored breathing. I asked if I could come to visit him at home and he said "Sure, but before coming just check with my wife" I ended our final conversation by saying, "Hey, Pally, if anyone can beat this, it's you!" The next call was from his wife, and without saying a word, I knew my dear friend had passed to the other side. Although only 5'9" in stature, his unmistakable image remains permanently etched in my mind's eye. Our fateful reunion was bitter-sweet - the gratefulness of reconnecting only heightened my profound sadness of his loss.

Pot Conclusion   My initial foray with marijuana was short-lived. No doubt there are undeniable differences between alcohol and marijuana. However, from a purely personal perspective, I was uncomfortable with the notion of *Mind Control*. I also recognized that, upon entering the *exclusive* mind-altering enclave among pot users, the non-users are relegated to disconnected *Observers* - always on the outside looking in at what would ostensibly be, unintelligible gibberish. Given her family history, Mary was understandably not fond of alcohol, let alone pot. So, this wasn't a recipe for a marital accord or mutual respect.

Incidentally, in addition to Nick's repeated exposure to herbicide sprays, I often wondered if his prolonged marijuana use had a synergistic effect contributing to the Lewy's component of his Parkinsonian dementia.

CH - 46
THE PROPOSAL

By this time I knew that Mary was surely expecting a marriage commitment, and rightly so. After all, any reasonable person would expect that, after a ten-year courtship, a proposal would be imminent! Well, ever the procrastinator, I managed to negotiate an additional two week grace period to *think it over*. So, while working with Nick at the Lodge, I was hoping to sort things out or pray for a miraculous epiphany. Interestingly, however, I don't remember ever discussing the pressing issue with Nick.

Truthfully, It wasn't a question of love. I loved her since she was 15 years old, and I couldn't even imagine my life without her. Considering that, for the past eight years I was a reclusive bookworm, perhaps It was the overwhelming sense of Freedom! Perhaps due to low self-esteem, I eventually became a competitive overachiever with obsessive-compulsive tendencies. Always studying more and working harder than the truly smart guys. Now, at long last, I experienced a profound sense of Relief. I felt I was able to breathe again, even if short-lived.

Two weeks later, on the Saturday evening of August 21 St. Nick answered the fateful call, and turning to me with a big grin said, "It's for you!". When I answered the phone, Mary simply said, "Well?" Although I was tempted, I didn't dare say, "Well what?" Instead, I said, "I'll drive down later this evening." During the *long* drive down to her parent's home, I found myself constantly ruminating, "What to do, What to do?" I sensed that I'd reached the end of my proverbial rope, and I presumed and feared that she had also. So, I was mentally prepared to pull the trigger!

Incidentally, Mary later confirmed that my assumption was correct - It was "Do or Die"- Adios Amigo! Of course, my Narcissism found that hard to believe, but I wasn't about to gamble!

In any event, While driving, I must have been daydreaming, because I didn't see the cop before I went sailing through the red traffic light in Ramsey. After being pulled over, I started to explain my dreadful situation. That, if I didn't get to her house by a certain time, I would miss my *Golden Opportunity*! He just stood there shaking his head - either in sympathy or disbelief. Then, he asked for her address, which I fortunately remembered, and said, "You better be telling the truth, because I'm going to follow you!". I thought, "Oh Great, now I have a police escort!" When we arrived at 33 cottontail Trail, he patiently waited at the top of the driveway and watched as I slowly entered the house, and, once inside he took off - thankfully without issuing a ticket!

The Trum's had moved from Brooklyn to a beautiful sprawling Cape Cod-style house on a large well-maintained corner property in Upper Saddle River - a very desirable section of Bergen County, N.J. The property included an Ivar Martin, Gunite pool with attractive underwater lighting for night swimming. By the time I arrived, Mary looked very sexy in a bright pink *Hot Pant & Top* outfit that I had given her as a present. She and the outfit were generously sprinkled with her signature perfume, Chanel no. 5 - which I could never afford.

After greeting her parents, since dusk was descending, Mary quickly ushered me outside to the pool where she conveniently arranged two poolside chaise lounges overlooking the tranquil oval pool. After a brief exchange of small talk, without mentioning it, her eyes told me that she not only expected but deserved an answer. She looked absolutely gorgeous and the smell of her perfume was intoxicating. Then, before I could even utter a word, the pool lights magically went on! Now the setting and the mood were complete. As she would later admit, "My mother didn't raise a dummy!"

When she finally posed the delicate question at hand, being the ever smooth talker, I muttered, "As my classmate, Joe Esposito, would say, You might as well try everything at least once'!" I guess that was good enough because she burst out with joy, kissed me, and immediately grabbed my hand to drag me inside to tell her parents the good news!

I remember her mother, Virginia (Ginny), was in the kitchen, and after a little prodding when I announced that I had asked for her daughter's hand in marriage, she was both ecstatic and relieved!. Then, without pause, she said that I also had to tell Mary's father the good news! When I looked around the room, however, I was relieved that he was nowhere in sight, and I thought, "Ah, a temporary, reprieve!" Just as quickly, however, Ginny said, "Oh, he's in the Bedroom!"

So, I slowly approached the open doorway to their bedroom, and seeing no sign of Walter, I was greatly relieved. However, when I went to walk out of the room, Ginny was blocking my escape by standing on the threshold with her arms crossed. Then she pointed her long finger to the only other doorway, the Bathroom. Respectful of his privacy, I said, "Oh, I'll wait!". But Ginny stood her ground, still pointing to the Bathroom.

Then, while calling his name, I slowly approached the open doorway to the Bathroom until I finally heard his deep gruff monotone voice," What the hell do you want?" Having no other option, when I tiptoed into the bathroom, I was shocked to find him sitting on the toilet! I think I was more embarrassed than he was, and after saying, "Excuse me," he blurted, "Well, what the hell's so damn important?" I thought, "Ah, just the opening I needed!" So, I quickly mumbled, "I've just asked Mary to marry me!"

However, rather than offering *Congratulations*, he responded, "Well, it's about time!" Then when he asked, "when?" and I said, "Possibly in mid-November," he immediately said, "That's too soon!" I thought, "I can't win, and it's just the beginning!" When he eventually came out of the bathroom, he joined us in the kitchen for an open bottle of chilled champagne and delivered a well-deserved toast. Apparently, there were subsequent discussions regarding the actual wedding date, and January 8th was ultimately decided upon -a date that will live in infamy!

My mother   At the time, my mother was visiting Maria and Jack at their summer house on Huntington bay L.I. So, the following morning Mary and I drove out to tell her the good news. She was likewise very excited and happy, especially since August 22nd was also my Father's birthday. Considering the size of her family, Maria's household was very busy, so there was far less fanfare. After driving my mother back to Anita's house, the subsequent events and plans are hazy. Then again, maybe I was still in shock!.

I remember deliberating, which one of my brothers I would ask to be my *Best Man*. As I mentioned previously, my sibling relationships expanded and contracted according to our respective life circumstances. At the time, Nick and I enjoyed a very close relationship, and considering that he hadn't yet been asked, the choice seemed self-evident and he graciously accepted.

Rocco   Purely out of respect, I went to visit Rocco at Cottage 10, informing him of my marriage proposal and that I had asked Nick to be my Best Man. Then I offered that I intended to ask Caesar and Mary's brother, Dennis, to be groomsmen and that I hoped he would also be in my wedding party. Naturally, expecting a positive response, I was taken aback when he declined saying, "I can't accept a lesser position!"- meaning anything less than Best Man. I was truly devastated, and although I was initially at a loss for words, I finally said, "It's not always about you. This is my special day and I had hoped you would be happy to join in the celebration!" With that, he said that he'd be there, but only as a spectator.

I reflected on how much of my adolescent and teenage years were spent with him. Being the last two siblings living together at 8311 and 83rd street, traveling subways together, sacrificing precious weekends while dutifully working together at the Lodge. Perhaps he had forgotten that I stood by him for years, and yet, he couldn't stand by me for one hour!

Incidentally, when it came to selecting one's "Best Man", Caesar chose Rocco, Nick chose Caesar and Ironically, despite how close he and Caesar were or how close I thought he and I were, Rocco, chose Bob Hartman as his Best Man. Come to think of it, the only one who hadn't been chosen was, Poor Me. In any event, I subsequently asked my former roommate and dear friend Sig, if he would take his place and he graciously accepted.

At some point, apparently, Mary had a lengthy discussion with my mother in order to determine the *optimum* date for our wedding - presumably, to ensure a smooth honeymoon. Ironically, this advice was coming from a woman who had 9 unplanned pregnancies! Thus between Mary, my mother, and the Almanac, the optimal date was set for January 8th. Needless to say, "The best-laid plans of mice and men often go awry!"

Wedding Plans   The wedding plans got underway fairly quickly, and for the most part, I was left out of the loop, which was fine with me! Mary's parents decided to have the reception at the Apple Ridge Country Club, in Upper Saddle River. Although, quite beautiful and conveniently located only a couple of miles from their home, it had limited seating capacity. Consequently, coming from two large families, the guest list went from a *wish list* to a *reality list* which was never really an issue. I believe Mary and I had a combined guest list of around 20-30 close friends, and the total number of guests was approximately 160.

Her parents were extremely generous, graciously posing few conditions or restrictions. I expressed a preference for a Buffet style Dinner which was initially considered, *nontraditional*. However, considering that it was considerably less expensive, her parents eventually relented. The wedding ceremony was to be held in the brand new, Church of The Presentation.

Military Status   By mid-September, my military status was still in limbo, and I hoped against hope that, barring a military escalation, I might possibly remain stateside. However, the infamous black cloud of doom loomed overhead. My world was suddenly thrust upside down when I received an official notice to report for active duty, and

I had every expectation that I was headed for Vietnam! Mary was understandably very distraught, and at one point, even suggested that we get married prior to my deployment. However, knowing that her cousin, Rick Merner, facing a similar dilemma, chose to get married prior to deployment, and was tragically killed in Vietnam, I didn't want to expose Mary to a similar fate.

Two weeks later, however, I received a certified letter from the USAR, informing me that I was being assigned to the 322nd General Hospital, and ordered to report to the Newark Armory. I was initially ecstatic but naturally perplexed by the conflicting orders. Apparently, each of the respective letters crisscrossed in the mail, and when I conferred with, Sgt. Kazin, he told me to honor the earlier of the two order dates, which was, fortunately, for the Reserves.

USAR (October 1971-79)   At the time, my cousin, Sal Datre, was in the Army assigned to Ft. Hamilton in Brooklyn NY. I remember him taking me to the base in order to pick up my summer and winter uniforms, shoes, socks, combat boots, Poncho, winter overcoat, and gas mask. I have to admit, all of the clothing was first-grade quality, and I still treasure them to this day. I was eventually commissioned as a Second Lieutenant on October 31, 1971, and honorably discharged with the rank of Major on Oct 31, 1979.

MEPS   t's been nine months since I began writing this Memoir, and I'm, once again, very fortunate to continue writing while overlooking the quiet serenity of Wolf Lake. To date, I've only covered the first 24 years of my life with a long way to go. But hopefully, by describing less of the boring details, it will ensure an accelerated pace. Currently, I'm commuting two days a week to the Military Entrance Processing Station (MEPS) in Albany N.Y. Officially, I practice Accession Medicine - a fancy term for the initial processing interview and physical examination of military recruits for all five branches of service. Although I detest early rising, this commitment requires me to awaken at the dreadful hour of 4:50 am and drive two hours to the Leo O'Brien Federal Building in Albany N.Y.

Sunrise The only positive aspect of these weary mornings is that, while overlooking the placid vista of the lake, I'm privileged to witness the gradual unfolding of a magnificent sunrise. It's truly stunning when the dawn's early light provides a faint silhouette of the dark mountains lining the opposite shore, and seemingly within seconds, a radiant orange glow slowly reveals the outline of the distant treetops. Then the sun gradually peaks over the mountain top exposing its large orange crest which, within minutes, manifests its full radiant glory. I expect, however, that the impending bleak darkness of Fall will soon rob me of this simple joy!

I was initially lured to apply for the coveted position after receiving an interesting letter with the opening salutation, "Greetings Doctor, pardon my intrusion....." The last time I received a letter beginning with Greetings, I was ordered to report to Schermerhorn St, in Brooklyn, for a pre-enlistment physical exam for the Selective Service System. I think everyone remembers their enlistment Physical exam!

The body of the letter was a heartfelt appeal for physicians willing to serve their country by providing Accession Physicals on our military recruits. This resonated within me, striking a sentimental *soft spot*. The application process, however, was a very lengthy five-month credentialing and security clearance process. At one point, I even quipped, "I could probably qualify for the CIA quicker!".

The Battle of Newark Being that it was during the height of the Vietnam offensive, recruitment efforts for fresh recruits were at a feverish pace. Consequently, as a General Hospital, we would perform, on-site, *Accession* Physicals in the Armory. Unlike the lengthy process today if you could hear, see, and walk, you were in! The main meeting room in the Armory was the size of the basketball court. The prospective young recruits would be lined up in two rows, 30 in each row. Then, while facing the recruits, one Doc would slowly go down the row listening to their hearts while another Doc would go down on the opposite side listening to their lungs. Truthfully, with all the noise in the Armory, It was difficult to hear.

Then, In like manner, one doc would walk down the line, quickly checking their eyes, ears, throat, teeth, and presence of hernias. When finished, the Doc on the opposite side would have them bend forward and spread their cheeks - some actually spread the wrong cheeks! Lastly, when the exam was finished, they were told to give a urine specimen. We used a visual eye chart, and the hearing was tested by the recruit acknowledging the sound of a ticking watch or by rubbing two fingertips together 5 inches from each ear. I don't remember any audiograms or more sophisticated visual testing. Ultimately, we were the decision-makers and disqualification rates being extremely low, I never heard anything about *Waivers*.

The Armory vs MEPS The early 70s assembly line process was in stark contrast to what we currently provide at the Alban Military Entry Processing Station (MEPS). Each *Applicant* receives a thorough initial History and Physical examination in a private room, and their suitability for accession is governed by a detailed 4" thick compendium of *Accession Guidelines* known as the DoDI (Dept. of Defence Instructions). In my experience, the combined rate of initial disqualifying conditions or PDQ's (Permanent Disqualifications) seems more like 20%, all of which go directly to a Waiver Board for consideration. In my experience, this self-perpetuating *revolving door* invariably grants a waiver for virtually all of the potentially disqualifying conditions with the rare exception of overt Psychiatric disorders, such as self-mutilation.

M16 Rifle As a General Hospital, we were constantly reminded that we could be called up at a minute's notice!. Despite these threats, however, we were perhaps the most irreverent group of professionals in the Army. In the interest of preparedness, we were expected to disassemble and reassemble the M16 rifle in 60 seconds. So, they set up rows of tables in the main Armory room and placed a rifle before each of us,

Then, with a stopwatch in hand, they gave us the signal to begin dismantling the rifle - that's when the comedy unfolded. We looked at each other with blank expressions, trying to figure out how to dismantle the damn thing. Utterly exasperated, the Sergeant eventually demonstrated the proper method of dismantling the rifle. Then, after placing all the parts in front of us he said, "You now have 30 seconds to reassemble it!". The problem was, they dismantled it so quickly that none of us could remember how to reassemble it. Consequently, when 30 seconds were up virtually everyone had various rifle parts strewn on the table in front of them. Needless to say, in total frustration, they finally decided to abandon the exercise.

Ft Dix Officer Training   In early November we were told to report to Ft Dix NJ for a three week, Officer Orientation course. We were told to bring our gas masks with us because we were required to experience the pleasure of the Gas Chamber. They positioned one *real soldier* with a roster clipboard at the entry door and another just outside of the exit door. The procedure was, we were to enter the chamber with our gas mask on and when instructed, to quickly remove it and, while inhaling the noxious fumes, recite our name, rank, and serial number.

Gas Chamber   I remember lining up and after watching the first few Docs exiting the door coughing their brains out, I thought to myself, "This is nuts!" It didn't take long for many of us to figure out a more suitable alternative. Those of us who had prescription pads provided medical excuses for some to avoid the *torture chamber,* while others merely snuck around the back of the chamber, and with the gas mask in hand, pretended to be coughing violently enough to satisfy the exiting clipboard bearer.

Firing Range   Another memorable exercise was when we were marched out to the Firing Range in order to demonstrate our prowess with the M16. There was a long deep trench, and on each end, there was a tall tower with a *real soldier* giving the firing orders and observing our performance. Also, positioned strategically behind the trenches were *military advisors* in order to ensure proper procedure and safety. The targets were approximately 400 feet away and hung on thin cable wires enabling one to pull the target in for review.

After lining up in the trench, we took our positions and sighted our targets, patiently waiting for the command "Commence Firing". We all expressed great anticipation of firing real bullets, and when the command finally came, we fired like hell. All I remember was a furious barrage of deafening thunder accompanied by the eruption of enough dirt to simulate a dust storm. The targets, however, didn't appear to budge, and when they pulled them in for inspection, they didn't have a mark on them!

The tower masters decided to give it another try, pulling the targets in, 200 feet closer. Shortly after hearing the order, "Commence Firing" one of the Docs stood up and turned towards one of the military advisors claiming that his gun was jammed. Suddenly there was screaming coming from both tower microphones, "Ceasefire, Ceasefire!!"

45 Side Arm   Thereafter, our CO decided to abandon our command of the M16, and instead, we were relegated to a *45 sidearm* (pistol). However, that was even worse. One winter evening, while in the Armory Hall, our CO caught some of us twirling the pistol on our index fingers, hoping that the tip of the barrel would find its way back into the holster. But the shit really hit the fan when he walked in during a reenactment of a typical *Gunsmoke* gun duel. While facing each other with our dark green uniform jackets pulled aside exposing our pistols, we suddenly drew our guns on each other. I know, absolutely juvenile and unbefitting responsible military officers. Thereafter, we were never allowed to carry real bullets.

I still remember with fondness the cast of characters. Rocco Tutela and I often hung out together at summer camp. He was a plastic surgical resident at St. Michael's and coincidentally, also a recipient of the *intern of the year award*. Tony Caputo was an ophthalmologist who later joined me at West Point and now specializes in pediatric retinal disorders. Joe Asta was an older Pediatrician who ended up treating our children while we still lived in New Jersey. And Hank Salzman, was an OB/Gyn who ironically, ended up practicing in Goshen N.Y.

240Z   Smokey and I continued commuting to the Newark Clinic, earning $500 for a 40 hr. work week. Also, as a Second lieutenant, I received a small monthly stipend, and from my perspective, I was now rolling in dough! So, being that Newark was a major port of entry for the foreign car imports, each day I would gawk at the shiny new cars lined up on the docks, and one in particular caught my eye, the 240 Z.

So, in mid-November I bought my first new car, the inaugural edition of a silver, Datsun 240Z. Nick came with me to pick up my new sports car, and as I drove my sleek car off the dealer's lot, Nick said, "Let's see what this baby can do!" When I floored it, however, the gas pedal got stuck causing the engine to "redline!" So, after manually releasing the gas pedal, we ended up limping back to the dealership for maintenance. Once again, the *black cloud* loomed overhead and I thought, "you can't make this shit up!"

Wedding Plans   As the wedding date approached, I eventually spent fewer evenings at Virginia's house and more at the Trum's house. This was both a matter of convenience and also an opportunity to adjust to a different family dynamic. I always felt that the Trums loved Nick and merely tolerated me. After all, he wasn't marrying into their family. Also, it didn't help that I was still wrestling with my familiar flashbacks accompanied by long periods of unexplained moodiness. Being that alcohol was a household staple, I foolishly thought that, perhaps this would pave the way for social acceptance.

The wedding plans seemed to be going smoothly and Mary and I started apartment hunting. I knew that it was expected that, along with the rest of the family, we would live close enough to attend Sunday dinner at Cottontail Trail. During these early years, I often bristled with pressures of expectant conformity, and the thought of being obligated to attend Sunday dinners *anywhere* was objectionable. However, with age and maturity, came the art of subtle diplomacy, and at the risk of appearing aloof, I felt it was far better to establish our independence early, rather than resorting to bogus excuses later on.

Haledon NJ   In early December we eventually zeroed in on a nice one bedroom upstairs apartment at 23 Lupton Lane in Haledon N.J. It had a nice view overlooking the local High School football field and track and was about a 25-minute drive from the Trum's house and 50 minutes from the Newark Dispensary Clinic. The only drawback was that I had to drive through the least desirable section of Paterson N.J. which prompted me to carry a high powered pellet gun in my car, which resembled a 357 Magnum.

At some point, while visiting Anita's house, I noticed an old wooden refrigerator standing upright in the tall grass outside the Barnsider, a restaurant in the hamlet of Sugar Loaf N.Y. I was pleasantly surprised when the owner accepted my generous offer of $10 - I think they were just happy to get rid of the eye saw. I envisioned converting it to an upright bar, and with the Trum's permission, I eventually transported it to their garage. I removed the interior metal lining of the upper icebox and lower refrigerator compartments. After some modifications, I stripped, sanded, and stained the exterior, and it remains a treasured bar in our home to this day.

Furniture Shopping   Next we went furniture shopping, which was another exposure to, *Sticker Shock!* We had already accumulated some basic kitchen and living room furniture, including a very solid and extremely heavy, 72" maple hutch, affectionately dubbed the (expletive) "beep- beep Hutch!" which we still possess. Then we selected the big-ticket items such as a Mediterranean style Bedroom set, a sturdy kitchenette table with a single leaf and six chairs, and a black La-Z-Boy recliner - both items still float around in our children's apartments. Then In early December, we went to the Liberty travel agency, to make arrangements for our honeymoon in Montego Bay, Jamaica.

The Wedding Day   During the wedding Rehearsal, Fr.Jack offered us a unique opportunity to compose and recite our own vows, provided they contained the "essential elements" of the traditional version. However In the unlikely event that we suddenly developed "brain freeze", he wisely offered the option of merely repeating the traditional wedding vows after him. A simple Rehearsal dinner was graciously hosted by Virginia and Lou at their home in Wyckoff. Although, I don't remember much of the details, I believe my sister arranged for various trays of cold cuts and pastries and Lou provided plenty of Henkel champagne!

At last, the moment of truth had arrived, Saturday, January 8th, 1972. I remember awakening to a bright clear blue sky, and the absence of wind made the dry crisp cold air truly invigorating - a perfect day for a wedding! While Mary was getting dressed at her parent's house, Nick was getting dressed at her brother Kip's house, and I was still undressed at Virginia's house.

At some point, Nick called to check on me saying, "Why don't you come over to Kip's to get dressed!" which sounded like a good idea. Shortly after I arrived, however, Nick offered me a stiff Bloody Mary to *settle my nerves*, and I suspected that he'd already had a *Joint* or two to settle his nerves. Then, not completely satisfied, while I was struggling to get dressed, he offered me another stiff Bloody Mary, spiked with extra Gin, which, on an empty stomach, quickly took effect!

Incidentally, over the preceding two years, I constantly struggled with fluctuating weight gain and slowly losing the battle. During my Internship, while relying on mostly cafeteria food and without the benefit of exercise, my weight steadily increased. Also, being that, for several months prior to the wedding, I often stayed at the Trum's house, I readily adopted the pre-dinner cocktail ritual, ensuring my considerable girth. Consequently, when I attempted to squeeze into my Morning Suit (Tails), the pants were so tight, I had visions of a potential, Vickie disaster. I could barely button the jacket and if I took in a deep breath, I feared the buttons would pop. I literally felt and looked like the Pillsbury Doughboy!

The Church of the Presentation was beautifully decorated, and I guess for spiritual insurance, there were a total of four Jesuits on the altar. Fathers Charlie Dolan and Jack Leonard officiating the ceremony, and Barney McIlroy and Bill Farricker as witnesses. Plus, we also received a Papal blessing from Pius XII. With all those prayers, it's no wonder the marriage lasted so long! Music was provided by my Weiser nieces and nephews along with Julie Haring singing a selection of contemporary folk songs and hymns of our own choosing - quite a departure from the traditional music.

While nervously waiting for the Limo to arrive, I clearly remember being in the sacristy with Sig and Nick, and despite the two Bloody Marys, I was pacing back and forth trying to memorize our creative vows written on the little index card. Seeing this, Sig was laughing his ass off saying, "Pete, relax, it's not a test!". Then, when Nick and I were alone, he astonished me saying, "If you don't want to go ahead with this, I'll just go out on the altar and say, "There's been a change of plans!" I thought for sure this must be the pot talking. Besides, the last thing I needed was my old nemesis, Indecision!. However, the longer we waited for the Limo to arrive, the last-minute option was starting to look a lot better!

Then a little after 11:30 am, we received word that the Limo had just arrived with Mary and her parents. As they congregated in the vestibule, Nick peered out from the sacristy and said, "Pete, she's radiant, absolutely beautiful! I quickly peeked out and witnessed the same vision. It was as though time had suddenly regressed, and once again, I saw the young girl I fell in love with so long ago, and all my apprehension vanished in a heartbeat.

Then, seemingly within minutes of assuming our position at the foot of the altar, I heard my nieces and nephews singing in three-part harmony, *Let there be Peace on earth*. Mary was absolutely glowing as she and her father slowly processed up the center aisle. To this day, I still get chills when I hear that hymn. In fact, it seemed as though the entire ceremony was accompanied by *upbeat singing!*

Mary inscribed my ring, "*My friend and love*" and I inscribed her's, "*My life is yours*". Surprisingly, we both managed to say our vows without a hitch, and with the exchange of rings, it was official. During the offertory procession of the gifts, once again, our chosen Choir began singing my all-time favorite song, *IF - "If a picture paints a thousand words, then why can't*

I paint you? The words will never show the you I've come to know"..... During communion, they sang the *Peace Prayer of St.Francis "Make me a channel of your peace, where there is hatred let me bring your love"*.....*followed by* "*Joy is Like the Rain!*"

The recessional song was, *I'll never find another you* - "There is always someone, for each of us they say, And you'll be my someone, forever and a day. I could search the whole world over until my life is through, But I know I'll never find another you!"

Fr. Charley had a very commanding deep baritone voice, which he used to his advantage while delivering numerous lectures and radio broadcasts. I think he surprised both of us by delivering a very heartfelt speech wherein he complimented us on our, "perseverance despite many obstacles and adversities". I wasn't even aware that he was cognizant of our long arduous journey. He was truly in his element when he described our long courtship as an *Enduring love story*- which, not only resonated with me but pretty much summed it up.

In my *biased* opinion, our wedding ceremony was truly unique and unlike any that I've attended since. The hallmark was the lively nontraditional harmonized singing accompanied solely by guitars and tambourines, which would probably never be permitted today. Unfortunately, although we thought we had arranged for the entire ceremony to be recorded and videotaped, apparently there was a failure in communication, leaving us with only traditional photos and beautiful memories. After the ceremony, I took Fr. Jack aside and asked, "Considering that I recited my vows under the influence of alcohol, is it possible to have a 2yr commitment, with an option to renew?" After a long blank stare, he acknowledged my warped sense of humor.

We had a *traditional* receiving line outside of the beautiful church, and surprisingly, despite the frigid temperature, we didn't seem to mind the cold. I believe we went directly over to the Apple Ridge Country Club for formal pictures. However, we both felt it was imperative to attend the entire cocktail hour. The reception room and guest tables were elegantly decorated and the entire far wall of the reception room was windowed, allowing for an expansive view of the adjacent golf course.

The cocktail hour lasted about one and a half hours, which allowed us ample opportunity to spend time with many old friends that we hadn't seen in a long time. I was especially happy to see my former Barnabas colleagues, Ronnie, Kenny, and Mario. I treasure a picture of my groomsmen, Dennis, Sig, Caesar, and Nick, toasting a drink. But truthfully, it would have completed my day to have had my brother, Rocco in the picture.

We were anxious to celebrate and mingle with our families and friends and didn't necessarily want to spend time with lengthy traditional wedding party introductions. However, a very dear friend of the Trum's, Pat Marone, who owned a large catering facility in Brooklyn, voiced an opposing opinion, and wanted to personally act as the MC for the *Traditional introductions*!

So, when it was our turn to enter the reception room, upon hearing, "And now, for the very first time as husband and wife" while walking towards the camera, everyone gasped as I pretended to trip and stumble forward towards the wedding cake. Likewise, neither of us necessarily wanted the *traditional Cake cutting ceremony,* but Mr. Marrone had other plans. So, when it came time for Mary to offer me a slice of wedding cake, with the photographer poised to capture the special moment for posterity, I opened my mouth wide while holding my big nose!

A live band was very important to both of us, so we searched and scouted for just the right group. The most important caveat was that they had to provide continuous music. Understandably, the expense of a live band, especially playing continuously, was initially a serious bone of contention for the Trums, until we offered to pay for it. Mary was always very fond of the Carpenters. So, for our first dance as husband and wife, it was a toss-up between two of their songs, *We've Only Just Begun* - "We've only just begun to live, white lace and promises, a kiss for luck and we're on our way…….."

Tough choice but eventually, Mary decided on their beautiful rendition of *For All We Know* - "Love, look at the two of us, strangers in many ways. Let's take a lifetime to say, I knew you well, For only time will tell us so, and love may grow, For all we know"

Incidentally, although there's no doubt that the first song we danced to was, It had to be you, when I think of "Our wedding song" it's twofold, Como's rendition of, IF and Karen Carpenter's rendition of For all we Know. However, when I recently listened to Barbra Streisand and Johnny Mathis sing, One hand, One heart from West Side Story, it says it all! In any event, I think everyone had a great time, but I have to admit, following the cocktail hour, the details of much of the reception remain somewhat hazy.

After the reception, we went to change at the Trum's house, which was quite crowded with friends of the family. Then, before leaving for the Intercontinental hotel at JFK airport, we stopped by Virginia's house to say goodbye to my mother. Pam and her husband, Al Booth, offered to drive us to the Hotel, and after bringing the luggage up to our room, we went down to the lobby to say goodbye. However, unbeknownst to us, Nick and Babs thought it would be hysterical to *surprise us* in the hotel's lounge for a "nightcap!" Just what I needed, more booze. This wasn't exactly how I expected to spend the first night of our honeymoon!

The Honeymoon   We boarded an 8 am jet to beautiful Montego Bay, Jamaica, but given that I was nursing a gigantic hangover, the 3 hr. flight seemed interminable. A taxi dropped us off directly in front of our cozy Hotel, nestled quietly behind a high walled gated courtyard. Upon check-in, however, due to rampant drug solicitation, we were strongly advised to remain within the confines of the courtyard during the evenings!

The small Hotel was truly lovely, offering an American meal plan which included a bottle of wine during dinner. Each evening, the sommelier would come to our table offering a sampling of his recommended wine pairings. Unfortunately, however, Mary didn't particularly care for wine, and certainly not more than a glass. So, considering that the wine was prepaid, I felt compelled to finish the bottle. This resulted in many early evenings and just as many late mornings!

After several quiet evenings, we decided to put aside their stern warnings and venture over to a much larger Hotel which was within easy walking distance. Much to our delight, we met another honeymoon couple from N.J. During our conversation, we learned that Sue and Al had also been advised to stay within the confines of their Hotel. However, putting this aside and bored with the local calypso bands, one evening the four of us decided to take a taxi to a highly recommended local, *Night Club*. When we arrived at the *Club*, we noticed that only two other tables were occupied. The Band was *performing* on an elevated stage, and it didn't take long to recognize that they were all *stoned and* staring at our wives!

Unsettled by the scene, when we were just about to ask for a taxi, someone sauntered over to take our drink order. In an effort not to offend the establishment, we ordered drinks and decided to wait and see if any other patrons would arrive. While the band played on, however, one by one, the other two tables quietly left, leaving us as the lone survivors. After enduring the constant stares, I decided to ask one of the female employees to please call us a taxi. The next thing I knew, a rather large Jamaican man was in my face questioning, "Hey man, where you going, don't you like the music?" Fortunately, the female employee came over to our table and whispered that she called for the taxi. So, while patiently waiting for our Taxi to arrive. we all sat at the table pretending to really dig the music!

Upon the arrival of the taxi, when we all stood up to leave, several members of the band stopped playing and just glared at us repeating, "Hey man, don't you like the music?" Being that Al was a tall thin fellow, I suggested that he lead the girls out while I walked out backward towards the door. This triggered a flashback of getting my ass kicked protecting Howie Greenspan's Pizza Shop. Once the others were safely outside, I raced for the door and the waiting Taxi. Once inside, however, the driver asked, "Hey man, you enjoy the band?" and I said, "ya man, dynamite!"

In those days flights were relatively inexpensive and it was easy to book a last-minute flight. In any event, I don't remember if this was spontaneous or pre-arranged, but after five days in Jamaica, we flew to Puerto Rico and stayed at the Caribe Hilton. Compared to our small Montego Bay Hotel, the Hilton was a tall, elegant building in the heart of San Juan which made for easy sightseeing. It was also my first exposure to a real gambling casino.

After watching a croupier at one of the blackjack tables for a while, and feeling that we had mastered the game, we decided to give it a whirl. Being that Mary could count and add numbers faster than me, she sat at the table while I stood behind her, ready to give sage advice - How was I to know that wasn't allowed! After the first infraction, the dealer just stared at me. However, the second time he said, "You're not allowed to whisper to another player". When I protested saying, "But she's my wife," he said, "That's even worse!" So, rather than whispering, I devised a plan of tapping her shoulder. However, he was watching me like a hawk and eventually said, "If you keep it up, you're gonna be barred from the casino! After losing ten straight hands, I decided to take up another profession, and after four days of sightseeing, we were on a jet plane back to JFK.

ABOUT THE AUTHOR

In his Autobiography, Dr. Cirigliano describes the life and times of growing up in a large Italian family in Bay Ridge, Brooklyn and the Catskill Mountains of Monroe, NY. Truly the best of both worlds during a bygone era seemingly frozen in time.

He's a graduate of the College of Osteopathic Medicine and Surgery in Des Moines, Iowa and earned Board Certifications in Family Practice and Occupational Medicine. Throughout his manuscript, Dr. Cirigliano shares many humorous vignettes while overcoming numerous adversities.

As a practicing physician for over fifty years, Dr Cirigliano (aka Dr C.) demonstrated unwavering compassion in the private sector and an entrepreneurial spirit in the corporate- medical sector.

He and his adorable wife of fifty years are the proud parents of seven loving children and so far, fourteen grandchildren. They continue to live happily in Orange County, NY.

DEDICATION:

I wish to dedicate my manuscript to my adorable wife
and my darling sister, Maria.

GRATEFUL ACKNOWLEDGEMENTS:

To My Nephew Lewis Haring,
for his diligent supply of treasured Family Photographs

To Heather Larsen,
for tirelessly cropping and inserting the numerous photographs.

To All my Children,
for providing invaluable computer support while patiently
enduring my endless Memoirs!

Made in the USA
Middletown, DE
01 March 2021